'In *Co-production and Japanese Healthcare,* Victor Pestoff provides a compelling new vision for healthcare in the post-COVID-19 era, based on a rich analysis of the co-production by patients, staff and volunteers in Japanese health co-operatives and public hospitals, in a country so far neglected in the co-production literature. This is a must read for policymakers, practitioners and academics interested in health innovation and participatory governance'.

Dr. Elke Loeffler, *Director of Knowledge Exchange (Work, Employment and Organisation), Strathclyde Business School and Director of Governance International, U.K.*

Co-production and Japanese Healthcare

Healthcare in most developed countries faces a complex and partly contradictory mix of financial, social and political challenges. Fiscal strains combined with the New Public Management agenda have caused severe cutbacks and calls for greater efficiency in public healthcare, resulting in a growing concern about service quality. *Co-production and Japanese Healthcare* explores a possibility to address these issues from a new perspective that emphasizes greater collaboration between the staff and patients. Here professionals and patients/clients act as 'partners to co-produce healthcare through their mutual contributions'.

Japan has a unique system of two user-owned healthcare providers with nearly 200 hospitals, 500 clinics and 50,000 beds. However, they differ from one another and from public hospitals, in terms of their work environment, service quality, governance models and social values. This volume compares cooperative and public healthcare providers at ten hospitals across Japan with survey data from the staff, as well as from the patients and volunteers at four hospitals.

This study will be of interest to researchers, academics, and students in the fields of healthcare management, public and nonprofit management, human resource management.

Victor A. Pestoff is Professor Emeritus in Political Science at Ersta Sköndal Bräcke University College in Stockholm, Sweden and a former Guest Professor at the Faculty of Human Sciences, Osaka University, Japan.

Routledge Studies in Health Management
Edited by Ewan Ferlie

The health care sector is now of major significance, economically, scientifically and societally. In many countries, health care organizations are experiencing major pressures to change and restructure, while cost containment efforts have been accentuated by global economic crisis. Users are demanding higher service quality, and health care professions are experiencing significant reorganization whilst operating under increased demands from an ageing population.

Critically analytic, politically informed, discursive and theoretically grounded, rather than narrowly technical or positivistic, the series seeks to analyse current health care organizations. Reflecting the intense focus of policy and academic interest, it moves beyond the day to day debate to consider the broader implications of international organizational and management research and different theoretical framings.

4. Healthcare Entrepreneurship
Ralf Wilden, Massimo Garbuio, Federica Angeli and Daniele Mascia

5. Medical Professionals
Conflicts and Quandaries in Medical Practice
Edited by Kathleen Montgomery and Wendy Lipworth

6. The Management of Wicked Problems in Health and Social Care
Edited by Will Thomas, Anneli Hujala, Sanna Laulainen and Robert McMurray

7. Making Sense of Organizational Change and Innovation in Health Care
An Everyday Ethnography
Anne Reff Pedersen

8. Innovating Healthcare
The Role of Political, Managerial and Clinical Leadership
John Storey and Richard Holti

9. Co-production and Japanese Healthcare
Work Environment, Governance, Service Quality and Social Values
Victor A. Pestoff

Co-production and Japanese Healthcare

Work Environment, Governance, Service Quality and Social Values

Victor A. Pestoff

Routledge
Taylor & Francis Group
NEW YORK AND LONDON

First published 2021
by Routledge
605 Third Avenue, New York, NY 10017

and by Routledge
2 Park Square, Milton Park, Abingdon, Oxon, OX14 4RN

Routledge is an imprint of the Taylor & Francis Group, an informa business

Library of Congress Cataloging-in-Publication Data
A catalog record for this title has been requested

ISBN: 978-0-367-56737-8 (hbk)
ISBN: 978-0-367-56740-8 (pbk)

Typeset in Sabon
by MPS Limited, Dehradun

To the women and men at *Koseiren* and the health co-ops: thank you for allowing us to study your inspiring models for providing healthcare

and

To Generation Z: may you succeed in bringing about the transformative changes, based on justice and equality, that we so desperately need.

Contents

Tables

Figures

Foreword to *Co-production and Japanese Healthcare*

Akira Kurimoto

Victor Pestoff is well known for his *welfare triangle*, locating the third sector as an intermediary of the public, for-profit and community sectors since the 1990s. He has also applied the idea of 'co-production' to childcare, comparing co-operative, nonprofit and municipal providers in Sweden, afterward in Europe. During a five-month sabbatical in Kanazawa in 1998, he made a preliminary field study of healthcare providers including health co-operatives, *Koseiren* and nonprofit hospitals. In 2013, he initiated a joint study of the Japanese healthcare co-operatives, together with Prof. Yayoi Saito of Osaka University. I was involved in this study as a co-operative specialist in institutional matters. He visited Japan every year to interview healthcare providers and to undertake a questionnaire survey of three main stakeholders, i.e. the staff, patients and volunteers of co-operative and municipal hospitals. This study encompasses issues related to enriching the work environment and increasing the staff's work satisfaction; institutionalizing democratic, inclusive governance models; facilitating a multi-stakeholder dialog; encouraging greater patient participation and influence; highlighting community-oriented social values; and promoting affordable and acceptable service quality. This volume presents the findings from the interviews and questionnaires as well as the theoretical analysis.

The Japanese healthcare system is characterized by universal health insurance coverage based on the Bismarckian model and weakly coordinated service provision mainly by non-public hospitals/clinics. The former was accomplished in 1961 by involving the third of the nation who were not already covered by employee health insurance schemes. The latter combined with consumers' free access resulted in imbalanced healthcare provision in terms of locality/specialty and severe congestion in large hospitals. Among the service providers, medical corporations are set up as nonprofits with the permission of the government, and they occupy a dominant position (e.g. 68% of hospitals and 42% of clinics). However, their nonprofit status is compromised since the nondistribution constraint is not evenly enforced. The publicly run hospitals set up to serve the specific needs of public interest have decreased in number and share due to a persistent deficit. Health co-ops as consumer co-ops and *Koseiren* as welfare federations of agricultural co-ops have a unique position. Both are classified as user-owned co-operatives rather than provider-owned in the UN Survey on *Co-operative Enterprise in the Health and Social Care Sectors* in 1997. The former are authorized by the government under the Consumer Co-operative Act, and they can accommodate healthcare workers as members, thus enabling multi-stakeholder governance. This facilitates member participation both in health promotion and governance. The latter are authorized by the government under the Agricultural Co-operative Act and provide services to rural areas where access to healthcare is limited. They were designated as public-interest medical institutions by the Ministry of Health and Welfare in 1951.

In recent years, the author developed his co-production theory by positioning it in relation to four public administration regimes: traditional public administration, New Public Management, New Public Governance and Communitarian regime. He also distinguishes between individual and collective co-production, as well as aspirational and transformative co-production. I think readers can learn from the arguments in the concluding chapter. One thing I wish to make note of is his remarks on the Community-Based Integrated Care (CIC) proposed by the Japanese Ministry of Health, Welfare and Labour. Engaging proactively with organizations that promote transformative co-production and wholeheartedly support CIC provides the government with a unique opportunity to explore the costs and benefits of collective co-production in a more systematic and focused fashion. Without mutual collaboration between the government and organizations that are willing and able to promote collective co-production, it is highly unlikely that they will thrive and survive. This would be a lost opportunity for promoting CIC and instituting collective co-production, together with a well-established and highly motivated group of health and eldercare providers. I agree with this comment since health co-op's engagements in CIC have not been fully recognized.

How does co-production theory relate to Julian Le Grand's four models concerning the provision of public goods: trusting professionals, command and control, voice and choice? Out of these four, he argues a quasi-market model, based on 'choice and competition', is the best way to ensure the optimal provision of quality public services. At this point, we are interested in the voice model, but Le Grand placed some conditions on collective action to amplify users' voices. Perhaps, the NHS foundation trust would be one example where all residents are entitled to vote in hospital decision-making, but we do not know how effective it is in governing these institutions. Participation by the members of health co-ops potentially provides a much more effective way of achieving sustainable collective action, but perhaps this requires another round of investigation and another research project.

This volume gives us plenty of food for thought on the future of healthcare. Now that all medical institutions are struggling with the COVID-19 crisis, they are threatened by the risk of contagion and financial sustainability. Healthcare systems are collapsing in some parts of the world. In such a crucial time, there is a crying need for effective healthcare systems that allow for user participation and co-production. I hope readers will greatly benefit from lessons drawn in this study.

Preface

This book presents the results of a research project on Co-production, Work Environment, Service Quality, Governance and Social Values in Japanese Healthcare. It started as a dream in 1998, during a sabbatical semester at the Faculty of Economics, Kanazawa University, with a grant from the Japanese Society for the Promotion of Science (JSPS). After finishing the manuscript for a new book, *Beyond the Market and State* (1998), I began traveling the country to interview leaders of nonprofit providers of healthcare. Years later, this research took a step closer to realization when my colleague, Professor Yayoi Saito from Osaka University spent a sabbatical year at Stockholm University in 2011. She became interested in my discussions about alternative healthcare providers in Japan. It took another step the following year, when I was invited as the keynote speaker for a conference in Tokyo to celebrate the Year of Cooperatives. Mr. Kohei Hara of the Norinchukin Research Institute also became interested in the topic during our visit to the *Koseiren* Hospital in Nagano, where we spent the most part of a day learning about their activities. The following year, Prof. Saito received a grant from the JSPS to start the fieldwork at nine cooperative hospitals in various parts of Japan. The project group spent an intensive month visiting all of them, interviewing their CEO and board and observing some of their unique activities in 2013. The following year, the project received a three-year grant from the Mitsubishi Foundation for planning and undertaking a survey study of the staff at eight of these hospitals, plus a smaller study of the patients and volunteers at four of them. I was also nominated as a Guest Professor at the Faculty of Human Sciences, Osaka University for a three-year period, 2014–2017. I resided at the International Guest House at Osaka University once or twice a year during that period and had the opportunity to teach a Master's course on co-production. During my final stay, Prof. Saito arranged for two public hospitals to join our project.

The results of Prof. Saito's efforts to promote systematic knowledge about cooperative healthcare cannot be measured by a simple metric. Yes, we succeeded in collecting 6,859 staff questionnaires from ten

Japanese hospitals, 631 patient questionnaires from four of the cooperative hospitals and 236 volunteer questionnaires from the same four cooperative hospitals. However, we learned so much more. We met so many interesting, engaged people wherever we went and heard moving stories about the origin of their hospital and their heroic efforts to serve the interests of their members and promote good quality healthcare. It would be impossible to put on paper all that we learned, saw and experienced during the past six, seven years of this research project. I will never forget the 99-year old woman living in a cooperative eldercare facility in the Minami section of Nagoya. She had two daughters and an apartment of her own in town but felt safer living together with 15 other residents and compassionate staff. I remember her telling us that each morning, the seniors decided together what they wanted to have for dinner they went shopping for and gave it to the staff - who prepared dinner for them. That is an excellent example of involving clients.

One thing is certain, none of the many enriching experiences nor the unique data on co-production and healthcare in Japan would have been possible without the effort and contribution by numerous dedicated women and men at each and every one of the hospitals included in our study. I am deeply indebted to all of you for everything you have done for us and this project. Therefore, it is a great pleasure to be able to share some of the results with you. Nonetheless, there is so much more that can be learned from you and your unique experiments in humanizing and democratizing the provision of healthcare. I genuinely hope that this report can inspire other scholars to look more closely at ways to involve citizens more actively in the provision of the services they depend on in their daily lives both as service users and service providers.

Currently, the COVID-19 pandemic illustrates the heroic efforts of first responders in protecting citizens from new, unknown and potentially deadly diseases. However, it also underlines the importance of the behavior of ordinary citizens in meeting such challenges. Wearing a mask, keeping a safe physical distance and washing your hands often are not things that someone else can do for you. Everyone must do their part if we are going to succeed. On the other hand, the importance of a coherent and consistent message from public health authorities encouraging citizens to do the right thing is also clearly evident, especially for someone witnessing it from shelter-in-place isolation.

Acknowledgments

The data collection for this project on Co-production and Japanese Healthcare was financed by the Japanese Society for the Promotion of Science (JSPS, #15K03913), the Mitsubishi Foundation and the International Joint Research Program of Osaka University. It was supervised by Prof. Yayoi Saito, Osaka University. The project was conducted within the framework of established cooperation between senior researchers at Ersta Sköndal Bräcke University College in Stockholm (Prof. V. Pestoff and doc. J. Vamstad) and the Faculty of Human Sciences, Osaka University (Prof. Y. Saito). This interdisciplinary group of Swedish and Japanese researchers was facilitated by a reference group of the relevant cooperative healthcare providers in Japan, *Koseiren* and the Japanese Health and Welfare Co-operative Federation HeW CO-OP JAPAN.

A number of people have encouraged and contributed to my continued interest in co-production and Japanese healthcare, through their writings, discussion and interactions with me over the years. Unfortunately, I can only mention a few of them here. Ever since I first shared my idea about a research project on Co-production and Japanese healthcare with Prof. Yayoi Saito, she has provided the framework that made it possible. Prof. Saito succeeding in obtaining grants in 2013 for the initial fieldwork allowing interviews with the CEOs and board members of nine cooperative healthcare providers in Japan. The following year, she received a grant for developing the empirical tools to carry out a large empirical study with the staff of eight of these hospitals and the patients and volunteers at four of them, as well as two public hospitals in Osaka, making our results more relevant and comparative.

Mr. Sven Åke Böök was the head of the Cooperative Research Institute in Stockholm, Sweden in the 1970s and 1980s, Chair of the Swedish Society of Cooperative Studies and author of the report, *Making Membership Meaningful*, that was eagerly discussed at the 1992 World Congress of the International Cooperative Alliance in Tokyo, Japan. He provided the encouragement to continue a quest for knowledge about cooperatives, how they work and could work even better to serve their members. This volume and my earlier books on Swedish cooperatives would not have been possible without his support and encouragement.

Mr. Haruyoshi Yanagida was the International Officer at the Japanese Consumer Cooperative Union, Tokyo, and he attended the 1988 World Congress of the International Cooperative Alliance in Stockholm. He provided my first insights into the Japanese cooperative movement and the unique treasures it held. Starting with my first visit to Japan in 1996, we continued to meet well into retirement. It was always a pleasure to share a meal, a beer and a hearty discussion about the future of cooperatives. You left us way too early, but I am sure that you would enjoy this new book on *Co-production and Japanese Healthcare*, and take pride in knowing the indirect role you played in encouraging it. You are truly missed.

During a JSPS financed sabbatical at Kanazawa University in 1998, I met Professor Akira Kurimoto, as the newly appointed Head of Research at the Consumer Cooperative Institute of Japan (CCIJ), Tokyo. We shared an interest in cooperative development and cooperative healthcare for more than 20 years. Later, he became the Professor of the Cooperative Program, Institute of Solidarity-Based Society, Hosei University, Tokyo. Thank you for your support and encouragement.

In 2011, in connection with the Japanese celebration of the International Year of Cooperatives, I met Mr. Kohei Hara, the Head of Research at the Norinchukin Research Institute Co., Ltd., Tokyo. I was slated as a Keynote Speaker, but following the Tohoku earthquake, tsunami and Fukushima nuclear disaster, it was rescheduled for 2012. Afterward, Mr. Hara graciously arranged for visits and meetings at the Nagano *Koseiren* and *Koseiren* Hospital and showed us some special and lovely parts of Japan along the way. It was an interesting and productive trip, and we received valuable insights and a wealth of materials for our future project and both benefited greatly from our time together. Your interest in cooperative healthcare helped facilitate this research. Thank you very much.

Finally, I was assisted in the editorial preparation of the chapters of this volume, as with earlier books, by my wonderful wife, Kathleen. Without your help and support it would never have reached fruition. I want to thank you, especially for your love and support.

More recently, Dr. Caitlin McMullen, a Postdoctoral Research Fellow, Concordia University, Canada, provided useful assistance with some challenging SPSS data runs. I look forward to our continued collaboration.

I also want to acknowledge the right to reuse some of my own copyrighted materials that have recently been lightly revised in preparing this volume. The following chapters have been adapted from:

Ch. 2. Pestoff, V., 1992; Third Sector and Cooperative Services – an Alternative to Privatization; *Journal of Consumer Policy*; 15: 25–40. It is reproduced by permission of Springer Nature BV and Taylor & Francis Group, LLC, a division of informa, plc.

Ch. 3. Pestoff, V., 2008; Democratizing Medical and Healthcare – the Japanese Example; Ch. 7 in *A Democratic Architecture for the Welfare State*; Reproduced by permission of Taylor & Francis Group, LLC, a division of informa, plc.

Figure 6.1 is from my book *Beyond the Market and State*, (Ashgate, 1998). It is reproduced by permission of Taylor & Francis Group, LLC, a division of informa, plc.

Figure 8.1 is from my book *Co-production and Public Service Management* (Routledge, 2018). It is reproduced by permission of Taylor & Francis Group, LLC, a division of informa, plc.

Figure 10.1 is from my book *Between the Market and State. Co-operatives in Sweden* (Campus Verlag, 1991). It is reproduced by permission of Taylor & Francis Group, LLC, a division of informa, plc.

Figure 11.1 is from my book *Co-production and Public Service Management* (Routledge, 2018). It is reproduced by permission of Taylor & Francis Group, LLC, a division of informa, plc.

1 Introduction

Co-production and Japanese Healthcare

This chapter introduces the concepts, theoretical considerations and model building necessary for successfully undertaking a project on Co-production and Japanese Healthcare. Key theoretical concepts include work environment and toxic workplaces, co-production, governance models, multi-stakeholder dialog, social values, public administration regimes and organizational logics. It discusses the steps and phases of this project. The methodological considerations result in an analytical model of work environment and service quality in Japanese healthcare.

A Contemporary Healthcare Challenges

Healthcare in Europe and most other developed countries is now facing a complex and partly contradictory mix of challenges. Fiscal strains combined with a New Public Management (NPM) agenda have resulted in cutbacks and calls for improved efficiency in public-funded health and eldercare. This development is a significant contributor to the growing concern about service quality in healthcare, while other developments such as increased demand due to an aging population and an increased level of individualization of services also add to the mix. The proposed solutions to these challenges in European healthcare help to illustrate the severity of the problems. One solution suggested by market proponents is to further increase efficiency so that the existing resources can cover more care with better quality. The problem with this solution is that many European countries already have some of the most streamlined healthcare sectors in the world, and there is probably a limit to how 'efficient' one can make healthcare services while maintaining acceptable levels of service quality. Another possible solution would be to increase public funding, but most European countries already have the highest taxes in the world. Thus, given these alternatives, a key issue for the future of healthcare in Europe is to find a way to provide high-quality services to a greater number of patients at an acceptable cost.

A different kind of solution is reflected in the growing interest in and practice of public participation in healthcare. A decade ago, the World Health Organization (WHO) maintained that there were basically three ways or mechanisms to channel public participation in healthcare governance: 'choice', 'voice' and 'representation'. 'Choice' mostly applies to individual decisions in selecting insurance providers and/or services. 'Voice' tends to be exercised at the group or collective level for expressing public or group views. 'Representation' implies a formal, regulated and often obligatory role in the process of healthcare governance (2005). Co-production can combine all three: choice, voice and representation, by actively engaging citizens in the provision of public services, including healthcare (Pestoff, 2008, 2009). Ten years later, the WHO broadened its perspective by adopting a 'Global Strategy on People-Centered and Integrated Health Services'. It recommends five closely connected steps: 1) Engaging and empowering people; 2) Strengthening healthcare governance and accountability; 3) Reorienting healthcare through models that prioritize primary and community care services and the co-production of health; 4) Coordinating services and 5) Creating an enabling environment (World Health Organization, 2016). Calls for greater public participation in the National Health Service (NHS) were recently reiterated in the United Kingdom. Hudson argued that public and patient engagement in healthcare is 'an idea whose time has come' (2014), while the Office of Public Management states that 'co-production is the new paradigm for effective health and social care' (Alakeson et al., 2013).

The purpose of this project is to explore the possibility to address the challenges facing healthcare in OECD countries from the perspective of greater staff autonomy and more user participation. The idea that the patients can play a more active role in the provision of their own healthcare services is grounded on an expectation that it may result in high-quality services without adding to the costs for the public sector, or perhaps even reduce these costs. Healthcare is a highly professionalized service sector, and most healthcare services are provided by medical professionals without much involvement by patients or their relatives. The hypothesis to be tested by this project is that a significant part of healthcare services can be provided by professionals and patients acting as 'partners in a continuing process of inquiry' Fotaki (2009, 2011), where the two parties co-produce the service by mutual contributions of information and treatment. This partnership can take many forms and should naturally fit the individual patient's needs and abilities. However, information asymmetry between the professionals and patients, as well as patient uncertainty, will decrease through their communication and joint efforts to improve the health of patients. This is done in equal measure by professionals teaching patients about health issues and patients providing detailed and operable data on their conditions in order to reach an informed opinion of what ought to be done about it. The ideal outcome of this interaction is better, more individualized care, active and more satisfied patients and better use of existing or additional resources in terms of patient input. Patient inputs can vary in form and be can limited to providing information or be extended to taking responsibility for simple self-tests and keeping a journal. This partnership between professionals and patients can also take collective forms.

Vamstad (2014) argues that there are two potential paths to high quality individual social services at an acceptable societal cost: quasi-markets and co-production. Innumerable volumes have been written about the advantages and disadvantages of quasi-markets, as well as their costs and benefits. In contrast, co-production is a less well-known and understood alternative for achieving similar important social goals. In England, the NHS has recently promoted several pilot projects related to the co-production of health and social care (Alakeson et al., 2013). These projects seek to unite the 'lived experience of individuals with the learned expertise of professionals to improve health and well-being' (ibid.). The NHS focuses on encouraging greater public participation at the individual level, where individuals and professionals work together to reach decisions and achieve improved outcomes. However, co-production also takes place at the group or collective level (Hudson, 2012). Individual co-production often promotes customized and personalized services, while collective co-production emphasizes collaboration and collective participation in healthcare.

Moreover, this project is premised on the assumption that service quality and work environment are closely interrelated or linked to each other. An employee who has tossed and turned all night worrying about work related problems, who feels tired and exhausted when they wake in the morning, who displays typical stress symptoms, who dreads the idea of going to work because they have little or no control or influence on the what, when, why, where and how of their daily routines, who has little chance to learn new things or advance at work – such an employee will not provide as good quality service as one who has the opposite experience and feels good about their work. Likewise, a client who experiences an unhappy, stressed or disgruntled service professional will not experience as good service quality as one being served by an employee with the opposite feelings. This project hopes to shed more light on the importance of such mechanisms for the relations between the staff and their clients and on how this is reflected in service quality in healthcare.

B Cooperative Healthcare in Japan

A plan to study co-production in healthcare should preferably include a theoretical sample of user-owned healthcare providers; however, there are few such providers in Europe. By contrast, Japan has a unique healthcare system with not just one, but two different user owned healthcare providers, according to the United Nation's global survey (1997). In addition, healthcare is financed by mandatory insurance in Japan; whereas, it is financed by taxes in most European countries. The user-owned healthcare providers in Japan include the Agricultural Co-ops or *Koseiren* in rural areas and the consumer or health co-ops in major urban areas. Both the agricultural co-ops (Japan Agriculture, JA) and the health co-ops provide services that include hospitals, primary care clinics, eldercare facilities, dental clinics, etc. These two cooperative healthcare providers employ nearly 95,000 staff – including 7,000 doctors – and together they have 180 hospitals with a total of about 45,000 beds, which exceeds the total number of hospital beds in Sweden and Denmark combined. However, cooperative hospitals are nevertheless a marginal phenomenon in Japan and little is, therefore, known or documented about their impact on work environment, patient involvement and service quality.

Kurimoto (2010, 2015) provides the historical and societal context of the cooperative healthcare sector in Japan. Cooperative hospitals in Japan have developed and prospered as an alternative to public and private nonprofit provision with universal coverage in a public-funded healthcare system for the following reasons. First, through a nearly 70-year public private partnership (PPP) between the agricultural co-ops (JA) and state, *Koseiren* provides healthcare services in rural areas where no public healthcare providers were or are available. Second, the Medical Co-ops can offer higher quality services and the added value of patient insight and influence in the major urban areas (Kurimoto, 2004: 136–137). Thus, cooperative healthcare and cooperative hospitals are not seen as a low-cost alternative, but rather they provide a unique type of healthcare with a heavy emphasis on accessibility and/or patient participation and preventive medicine. They have managed to survive, grow and thrive in a healthcare system that otherwise is not all that different from the public-funded, universal healthcare system in Scandinavia and elsewhere in Europe.

These two user-owned healthcare facilities will be compared with each other and with public providers of healthcare in Japan, hence allowing us to identify and isolate the factors that facilitate greater staff control of their work environment and active patient participation in their own healthcare. Thus, this project aims to collect empirical survey data from patients, volunteers and medical professionals at a total of eight co-operative hospitals across Japan and then compare this with similar data from two public hospitals.

However, for the sake of clarity, it should be pointed out that this volume employs the terms *Koseiren* when referring to the healthcare services provided by the agricultural co-ops and Medical Co-ops for the services provided by the consumer or health co-ops. It also refers to the medical services and facilities where they are provided as hospitals, but, in fact, that also includes some primary clinics and eldercare facilities, in addition to hospitals. Therefore, when a text refers to the staff at Medical Co-ops, *Koseiren* and public hospitals, that also includes staff at these other facilities, if they were included in the sampling procedures. Chapter 5 discusses the data and sampling procedures for this study.

C Some Key Concepts: Work Environment, Co-production, Governance, etc.

Below, we will introduce four key concepts: work environment, co-production, governance and multi-stakeholder dialog that play a central role in the design of this project.

1 *Work Environment and Toxic Workplaces*

Human resource guru – Pfeffer's latest book on work life and management – laments the fact that management practices can literally sicken and kill employees, yet they fail to improve organizational profitability or performance (2018). He notes that ill health from workplace stress adversely affects productivity and drives up voluntary staff turnover that costs employers and society more than half a trillion dollars per year in the U.S. (ibid., 3). He notes that the physical work environment is closely regulated and inspected in most countries, but the psychosocial work environment usually is not. Therefore, he argues the costs of toxic workplaces result in social pollution that is passed on to the public health and welfare systems – not to mention, individual employees in the form of ill health. His list of the ten most hazardous work life stressors includes some that also feature in this project – like high work demands, the lack of control at work and inadequate social support at work (ibid., 39).

Nearly three decades earlier, Karasek and Theorell (1990) noted that work life stress is related both to physical illness and lower productivity. They developed a two-dimensional demand/control model to understand, analyze and explain work environment and its physical and psychosocial impacts on workers and organizations. Combining these two dimensions results in a fourfold classification of jobs: low strain, active, passive and high strain. This is illustrated by Figure 6.1 in Chapter 6 of this volume. They expanded their model by adding a third dimension, 'social support'. Social support at work refers to overall levels of helpful social interaction available on the job from both co-workers and supervisors.

Furthermore, Karasek and Theorell argue that additional factors are important for understanding work life and deserve closer study. Among others, they note the significance of interaction between the staff and their clients – particularly in social services that can result in positive benefits for both parties. Their demand/control model was expanded to include a new dimension based on the degree of interaction with service users (Pestoff, 1998). This will be discussed in greater detail in Chapter 7 of this volume.

2 *Co-production*

Nobel Laureate Elinor Ostrom and her colleagues analyzed the role of citizens in the provision of public services in terms of co-production (Parks et al., 1981). The concept of co-production was originally developed by Ostrom and the Workshop in Political Theory and Policy Analysis at Indiana University during the 1970s to describe and delimit the involvement of ordinary citizens in the provision of public services (Ostrom, 1996). They struggled with the dominant theories of urban governance – whose underlying policies recommended massive centralization of public services – but they found no support for claims of the benefits of large bureaucracies. Moreover, they also realized that the production of services, in contrast to goods, was difficult without the active participation of those persons receiving the service (ibid.). Co-production is, therefore, noted by "the mix of activities that both public service agents and citizens contribute to the provision of public services. The former are involved as professionals or 'regular producers', while 'citizen production' is based on voluntary efforts of individuals or groups to enhance the quality and/or quantity of services they receive". (Parks et al., 1981).

Co-production can achieve better quality services and/or result in the provision of more services – often at a lower price – than what is possible without citizen participation. Recently, there has been a renewed interest in the study of co-production, as seen in the notable increase of academic conferences that include or focus on co-production, and in the number of books recently published on this topic (Pestoff and Brandsen, 2006; Alford, 2009; OECD, 2011; Pestoff et al., 2012; Pestoff, 2018), as well as several hundred journal articles recently devoted to co-production in major journals on public administration and management (Vorberg et al., 2015). This research shows that co-production can take place in a variety of different fields and contexts – ranging from local safety and police activities (Parks et al., 1981; Freise, 2012; Meijer, 2012); childcare (Pestoff, 1998, 2006, 2008; Prentice, 2006; Vamstad, 2007; Vancoppenolle and Verschuere, 2012); basic education (Davis and Ostrom, 1991; Porter, 2012); housing (Brandsen and Helderman, 2012); urban regeneration (Osborne and McLaughlin, 2004; Schlappa, 2012), etc.

In healthcare, citizen engagement in service provision takes different names – like patient-centeredness, patient experience, patient empowerment and sometimes co-production. The focus can range from patient compliance and adherence to professional advice on one hand and to reforming entire health systems on the other (Coulter and Ellins, 2007; Dunston et al., 2009; Fotaki, 2009; Anderson and Funnell, 2012; Batalden et al., 2015; Meijer, 2016). Ostrom states that all public goods and services are potentially produced by the regular producer and those who are frequently referred to as clients. However, she argues that client is a passive term – indicating that they are acted upon – or passive recipients of services. Co-production, by contrast, 'implies that citizens can play an active role in producing public goods and services of consequence to them' (Ostrom, 1996: 347). The role of patients as healthcare co-producers is explored in Chapter 7 of this volume.

However, it is necessary to distinguish between individual and collective co-production. Individual co-production is the collaboration between individual citizens and public servants to provide public services individually, while collective co-production involves the participation of groups of citizens and public servants to do the same. Individual co-production is usually a necessary but not sufficient condition for achieving collective co-production. The latter involves citizens engaging in collective action in addition to their individual acts of collaboration with public servants. Nonetheless, co-production can also involve a mix of both individual and collective participation by citizens. Taking primary education as an example, individual parents perform several tasks necessary for their son's and daughter's educational performance. They feed them, wash their clothes, help them with their homework and instill the habits necessary for getting to bed in the evening and getting up in the morning, so they arrive at school rested and on time. In addition to this, some parents contribute their time and effort through a parent-teacher association on campus during and after school hours. In this study of co-production and healthcare, we will consider both forms of co-production but with an emphasis on collective co-production.

3 Governance Models

Governance of third sector organizations (TSOs) refers to systems and processes concerned with ensuring the overall direction, supervision and accountability of an organization (Cornforth, 2004). Major perspectives on governance include agency theory, stewardship theory, democratic theory, stakeholder theory, resource dependency theory and managerial hegemony theory (Spears et al., 2014). Both control and collaboration are essential elements of these theories. Accordingly, control helps to overcome human limitations through vigilance and discipline, while collaboration taps individuals' aspirations via cooperation and empowerment. Notwithstanding, there is always a need to balance them (ibid.).

The three most relevant governance models for studying healthcare in Japan are the 'command and control' model, the stewardship model and the democratic model. The command and control model was inspired by Max Weber and served as a norm for modern public administration for more than a hundred years (Ostrom and Ostrom, 1971). The stewardship model assumes that managers want to do a good job and will act as effective stewards of an organization's resources, in collaboration with the main stakeholders. As a result, senior management and the stakeholders or members of an organization are often seen as partners. The role of the board is primarily strategic: to add value to important decisions and improve organizational performance. In this way, board members are selected on the basis of their professional expertise, skills and contacts, and they should receive proper training. By contrast, the democratic model includes key ideas of open elections on the basis of one member one vote, pluralism, representation of different interests and accountability to its members. In this manner, the board is often recruited from lay members and its main function is to represent the diverse interests of the organization's members. (Cornforth, 2004).

From a business administration perspective, governance models usually focus on the relationship between the board and top management of a TSO or social enterprise. However, employing a more holistic or encompassing approach based on different academic perspectives – like political science, social work or sociology – would call for broadening the focus considerably. The CEO and board do not provide the whole picture, so we intend to include other major stakeholders in our purview. However, the CEO and board provide a natural starting point, and they were interviewed with a semi-structured interview schedule in May, 2013. Interviews with the eight co-op healthcare providers comprise the Organizational Study of this project. Preliminary results suggest that agricultural co-ops and the *Koseiren* comprise a stewardship model of governance, while the consumer and Medical Co-ops embody a democratic model. Finally, public healthcare providers represent the classical 'command and control' governance model. However, it is worth noting that these concepts are initially considered heuristic tools and it remains an empirical question how they actually differ in terms of the governance of the hospital groups and healthcare organizations as well as the role attributed to various stakeholders, like the staff, patients and volunteers. Issues related to the governance of Japanese healthcare are explored in Chapter 9 of this volume.

4 Multi-Stakeholder Dialog

The main stakeholders in this study of Co-production, Work Environment, Governance and Service Quality in Japanese Healthcare are the staff, patients and volunteers. Results from the Staff Study are discussed in Chapter 6, results from the Patient Study are found in Chapter 7 and results from the Volunteer Study are presented in Chapter 8 of this volume. Multi-stakeholder governance implies a system of formal representation that provides both a voice and vote to all major stakeholders, while a multi-stakeholder dialog insures informal representation and a voice, but not necessarily a vote to all major stakeholders (Vidal, 2013). The existence of institutions that can promote a multi-stakeholder dialog or governance should also have an impact on the efficiency of an organization and its quality of service. Vidal explores how multi-stakeholder techniques can promote co-operation between key stakeholders providing public services – in particular, between the professional providers and users of public services (ibid.). The concept of multi-stakeholder governance assumes that an organization's decision-making bodies include different stakeholders. Therefore, they engage in a dialog with one another and reach a compromise on complex or important issues. Such organizations do not promote the interest and values of a single stakeholder, but rather promote the interests and values of various stakeholders (ibid.). This is particularly important in the provision of social services – since users or clients are locked-in to such services – often for the life of the service from the user's perspective (Pestoff, 2018).

Vidal noted that both these techniques can also help to avoid some of the negative consequences of asymmetric information and power relations between providers and users of social services. Asymmetric information stifles communication between users and producers of services which results in greater user frustration and greater inefficiencies. One classic way to reduce such inefficiencies would be for clients to use their exit option (Vidal, 2013). However, exit is often not feasible in social services, so voice becomes more viable or at least the 'second best' option. Moreover, it is more advantageous if the main stakeholders involved in service provision enter into a continuous and systematic dialog about important issues that can help alleviate the asymmetric information and power relations between them. (ibid.). For example, in most parent co-op preschools in Sweden, the teachers attend the board meetings; they have a say but not a vote on important issues. Parents do, of course, listen closely to them and weigh their arguments carefully before deciding (Pestoff, 1998).

Vamstad shows that parent cooperative preschool services in Sweden promote a dialog between the parents and teachers that leads to higher quality services than those provided by the public sector (2007, 2012). Parents in parent co-ops felt much more informed about the activities and operation of their preschool than parents in municipal services, and they also claim higher levels of influence than parents in municipal services (ibid.). Similar differences apply for the staff at these two types of preschool services. Thus, the high level of communications that characterize parent co-ops facilitates reaching a mutual understanding of diverse problems – ranging from service quality to work environment – and allows for such problems being addressed swiftly and in close collaboration between the parents and staff (ibid.).

D Additional Research Issues

In recent decades, growing attention has been given to the impact of far-reaching changes in the institutional structure of society – for example, the introduction of NPM. It has the power to change the focus of and to set constraints for the delivery of most public services, including healthcare. Some scholars view such broad changes in terms of contrasting institutional logics, while others focus on competing public administration regimes (PARs). Below, we intend to briefly introduce two different perspectives and discuss the methodological implications for this study of Co-production and Japanese Healthcare. This begins with a brief discussion of PARs followed by considering the organizational and professional logics of complex organizations like hospitals and the groups or stakeholders within them. This concludes by presenting the analytical model that informs and guides this project.

1 Social Values and Public Administration Regimes

Efficiency is an important societal goal, but far from the only one necessary to consider. An organization's social value orientation can be defined as its preference on how to allocate its resources, both financial and human, between or among its goals. In other words, it is the weight that an organization attaches to the promotion of its goals and the achievement of their outcomes. Resource husbandry is important for realizing goals, both in times of scarcity and surplus. Nonetheless, making a financial surplus is a means to achieve a variety of organizational goals and is not an end in itself. Sound financial management and prudent goal fulfillment can help sustain an organization in the long run. However, no single goal or value should be allowed to dominate an organization for too long, lest it atrophies and transforms itself into a different kind of organization. Hospitals need, therefore, to balance a variety of goals – cultural, financial, political and social. The social values of Japanese hospitals are explored in Chapter 10 of this volume.

From a historical perspective, most of the 20th Century was dominated by traditional public administration and public services were delivered by public agents. However, starting in the 1980s, this was challenged by a new paradigm or perspective called NPM that was combined with the introduction of market principles and competition in the delivery of public services. The public sector continues to finance services but it 'contracts-out' the delivery to private actors. Nevertheless, NPM also experienced some flaws, and its detractors began developing a new paradigm – called New Public Governance (NPG) – at the turn of the century. NPG has a more inclusive perspective. It relies on network governance and collaboration between a variety of actors – like public, private for-profit and nonprofit or TSOs. However, given the semi-permanent austerity ushered in by the Great Recession in 2008, we note the contours of an emerging paradigm that puts much greater emphasis on community and civil society as providers of what were traditionally delivered as public services during most of the 20th Century. These different perspectives or paradigms are referred to as PARs. They are compared in Chapter 11 of this volume in terms of their values and concepts, as well as their implications for the key actors in co-production.

2 *Organizational Logics in Healthcare*

Institutional logics are defined as 'the belief systems and associated practices that predominate an organizational field' (Scott et al., 2000). They affect decision-making by steering the attention of decision-makers to certain issues, values and practices consistent with a given logic and deflect their attention from other issues (Vickers et al., 2017). The academic discussion of institutional logics primarily focuses on the macro-level (e.g. institutions like the market, state civil society, etc.) (McMullin, 2020). However, some authors suggest that it is also manifests at the micro-level in organizations like hospitals (Cucciniello and Nasi, 2014; Van de Broek et al., 2014). The rigidities of professional boundaries and hierarchical cultures within the public sector have tended to prioritize the views of senior clinicians and healthcare managers without allowing an active role for service users and citizens (Vickers et al., 2017: 11). However, the rapid diffusion of NPM throughout OECD countries in the 1990s contributed significantly to the spread of market mechanisms in many areas of public services, and healthcare was no exception.

Two European studies explored the adoption and implementation of innovations in healthcare where multiple logics were at play. The first was in Holland (Van de Broek et al., 2014), and the second in Italy and Spain (Cucciniello and Nasi, 2014). Both studies argued that the decision-makers are board members – the director and senior managers – and they often adhere to a business-like logic. The users, according to this approach, are primarily nurses who practice a professional or caring logic. Therefore, in highly complex organizations like hospitals, it is important to recognize that their logics may come into conflict. However, there is some ambivalence about whether the focus should be on institutional, professional or organizational logics. Chapter 11 of this volume explores the impact of organizational and professional logics on the social values of managers and non-managers as well as the main professional groups at these ten hospitals.

3 *Methodological Implications*

Both of these studies employed a multi-actor and multi-methods approach to generate a more complete picture of the processes under investigation. This implies adopting a combination of quantitative and qualitative methods based on a multidimensional and multi-method approach to the subject matter of co-production and healthcare. This includes collecting public and private documents, semi-structured in-depth interviews with the leaders of these hospitals, questionnaires for the staff, patients and volunteers, focus group discussions, among others. This will facilitate triangulation between data sources, and it will also help us to better capture and assess the diverse interests of various stakeholders who may promote different organizational and professional logics inside the highly complex organizations under study. The purpose of choosing to employ this multidimensional, multi-method framework is primarily to explore the tensions and ambiguities that exist in hybrid organizations that promote more than one goal. They do not simply pursue a management perspective that focuses on maximizing their financial surplus, rather, they attempt to achieve other political, social and cultural goals in addition to guaranteeing financial survival.

E The Analytical Model

We have discussed several key concepts that are central to this research project. They include work environment, co-production, governance models, multi-stakeholder dialog, social values and organizational and professional logics and a multi-actor, multidimensional and multi-method approach. It is time to pause and ask how we intend to bring them together in a coherent fashion. What kind of data can shed light on these ideas and concepts? In order to study the role of work environment in Japanese healthcare, we will use a large survey of the staff employed at ten Japanese hospitals situated in different parts of Japan. In order to study co-production and the participation of patients and volunteers, we will conduct two smaller survey studies – one of patients and another of volunteers at four of the ten hospitals that participated in this project. In order to study governance, we will use the staff, patient and volunteer data – in combination with information from the initial Organizational Study. In order to study a multi-stakeholder dialog, we will we will use the staff, patient and volunteer data. Finally, in order to study social values and organizational and professional logics, we will employ empirical data from all three surveys in this project – the Staff Study, the Patient Study and the Volunteer Study.

These considerations suggest the following analytical model. It is comprised of three main pillars: 1) The hospitals' organizational setting; 2) The intervening work environment variables from the Staff Study and 3) The output and outcome variables – in particular, service quality. Considered together, the institutional and environmental conditions, a hospital's organizational setting and the intervening variables are expected to determine a hospital's outputs and outcomes. However, we will primarily focus on social aspects and the quality of its support services as observed in the three surveys, rather than examining economic and financial aspects of hospital performance in order to better understand its outcomes.

The institutional and environmental conditions or setting for each hospital are basic to understanding their institutional logic or frame of reference. The hospital's organizational setting (A), found on the left hand side of the diagram, captures the organizational conditions and organizational complexity of each hospital, its governance model as

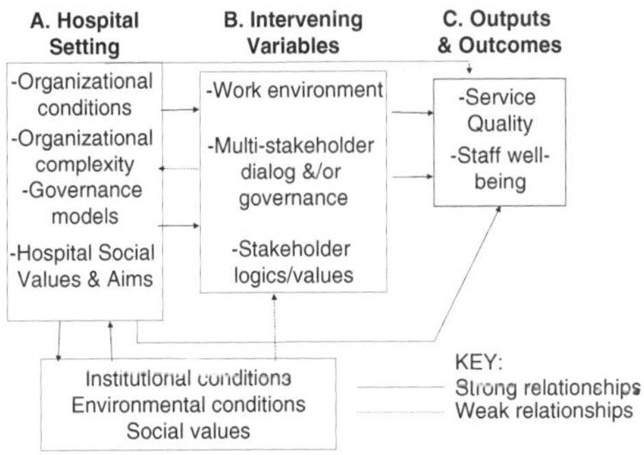

Figure 1.1 Analytical Model of Work Environment and Service Quality in Japanese Healthcare.

well as its aims and organizational and professional logics. The intervening variables (B) in the middle of the diagram include the staff's work environment, institutions for promoting a multi-stakeholder dialog and the stakeholder logics and values and the staff's perception of the quality of support services to the hospital's patients. Variables found under A and B are expected to influence a hospital's outputs and outcomes (C) – in particular, the quality of its healthcare services. Using this, we will rely on and compare staff, patient and volunteer evaluations of service quality in order to determine the overall quality of a hospital's services.

We expect the three hospital groups to differ from one another and be distinct in several important ways. Their social values will be reflected in an organization's governance model, its relations with the staff and the relations between the staff, patients and volunteers. We should also expect that some of these relations will be strong while others will be weak, as indicated by the lines in the analytical model.

The main study will produce an extensive and rich material describing how the healthcare providers in Japan organize their care according to the principle of co-production, but also in which kind of organizational setting this is possible. This is important for understanding what aspects of the collaborative healthcare model are unique for Japan and which ones could realistically be utilized in other settings such as those found in Europe.

F Brief Summary of this Book

The following section provides a brief overview of the chapters included in this book. They are divided into two parts. The first part includes two chapters related to the theoretical background of this project that were published previously along with a new, conceptually oriented chapter on co-production in public services and healthcare. Next, the project's main results are presented in six chapters. Finally, a summary and conclusion about Co-production, Work Environment, Governance and Service Quality in Japanese Healthcare is presented. A brief summary of each chapter is provided below.

2 *Third Sector and Cooperative Services – An Alternative to Privatization*

The third sector could make a significant contribution to renewing the public sector and enriching the welfare state, if given proper attention. The potential contribution of third sector alternatives includes the empowerment of service users, the renewal and enrichment of work life and the enhancement of public sector goal fulfillment. Taking Swedish childcare or preschool services as an example, this chapter argues that parent co-ops, worker co-ops and voluntary organizations can each make a direct contribution to achieving one or more of these goals while simultaneously promoting the other two indirectly. The disadvantages or trade-offs associated with each alternative are also considered.

3 *Democratizing Medical and Healthcare – the Japanese Example*

Nobel Laureate Kenneth Arrow contended that the predominance of nonprofit providers in the U.S. healthcare market was largely an attempt to overcome the lack of optimality and the imperfect nature of medical information. This chapter reports a 1998 survey of five alternative healthcare providers in Japan. It includes written materials from relevant organizations and semi-structured interviews with representatives of alternative healthcare providers in several Japanese cities. It reveals that Arrow's assumptions about the healthcare industry in the U.S.A. in the 1960s also appeared to hold true in Japan at the beginning of the 21st Century. However, it shows that society could either act to fill this gap on the initiative of the government and public authorities or through citizen initiatives by directly engaging civil society in healthcare provision.

4 *Co-production of Public Service Delivery and Healthcare*

This chapter introduces the idea of greater citizen participation in the provision of public services and three schools of study with different approaches to co-production. It continues with a discussion of co-production in healthcare – noting that there is not one single perception of the role of patients and professionals in healthcare, but rather several different ones. It is, therefore, important for researchers to make clear their own understanding of this phenomenon from the beginning for the sake of clarity and to avoid misunderstandings.

5 Research on Japanese Healthcare – Background, Data and Methods

This chapter provides an overview of the data collection for this project. It begins with a brief background of cooperative healthcare in Japan. Next, it discusses the project plan, the data sources and questionnaires, followed by the sampling procedures for each of the three main studies – the Staff Study, the Patient Study and the Volunteer Study. It then continues by discussing the data presentation and explains the preference for using correlations rather than regression analysis, and finally, it notes some of the project's limitations.

6 Work Environment and Service Quality in Japanese Healthcare

This chapter explores the relation between work environment and service quality at ten healthcare providers in Japan. It contrasts the ideal typical model suggested by the 'demand control' model with the patterns found in the three hospital groups included in this study; public, agricultural co-op and consumer co-op hospitals. Staff with greater autonomy was clearly more satisfied than those with less autonomy, as seen in several of the tables presented herein. This, in turn, had a positive impact on perceived service quality.

7 Two Patterns of Patient Participation in Japanese Healthcare – Aspirational and Transformative Co-production

This chapter explores key issues related to patients and co-production in Japanese healthcare. How can hospitals develop institutions that facilitate, foster and institutionalize patient participation? What role do patients' needs and hospitals' social values play in determining the type of co-production that develops? It asks if there is more than one type of co-production. Data presented herein suggests that being a patient in a Medical Co-op probably does not mean the same thing as being a patient at a *Koseiren* hospital. This leads to the conclusion that there are two different kinds of co-production – an aspirational type and a more activity oriented kind of co-production. The latter has the potential to transform traditional relationships of power, control and expertise in healthcare.

8 Volunteering and Co-production in Japanese Healthcare

This chapter explores the role of volunteers in Japanese healthcare. It recognizes volunteers as essential actors in co-production of healthcare, under certain conditions. This chapter also reports findings from the Volunteer Study concerning how long and how much they volunteer, why they volunteer as well as the tasks they perform. It also considers their relations with the hospital staff and other stakeholders – how they feel about volunteering, the perceived benefits from volunteering and their perspective on the hospital's service quality.

9 Participatory Governance and Japanese Healthcare

This chapter explores the contribution of participatory governance to the external efficiency of Japanese healthcare. Three differentiated models are considered for governing the provision of healthcare: a democratic, multi-stakeholder model; a stewardship model and a more traditional 'command and control' model. An inclusive governance model not only allows the staff more autonomy, but it also promotes a multi-stakeholder dialog and greater patient participation in their own healthcare that contributes to external efficiency. The participatory democracy found in social enterprises can serve as a 'best practice' for other public and private healthcare providers that want to promote a better work environment and more co-production in Japan and elsewhere.

10 The Social Values and Mission of Cooperative and Public Hospitals in Japan – Comparing the Perspective of the Staff, Patients and Volunteers

An organization's social values reflect its preference on how to allocate its resources – both financial and human – between or among its goals. It is the weight that an organization attaches to the promotion of its goals and the achievement of their outcomes. Nevertheless, hospitals need to balance a variety of goals – cultural, financial, political and social. This chapter provides unique insights into the social values of Japanese healthcare. Each hospital group has a distinct mission based on a different set of social values. Moreover, the staff, patients and volunteers provide a similar and coherent view about what is most important and what is less important for each hospital group.

11 Co-production at the Crossroads and Organizational Logics in Japanese Healthcare

Co-production has been called a 'partnership between citizens and service providers', yet the nature of this partnership is determined by the Public Administration Regime (PAR) in which it operates. Various PARs are found in different countries and operate in different service sectors of a given country. This chapter contrasts the idea that co-production is constrained by PARs with the concept of organizational and professional logics. It finds scant evidence of conflicting logics either between managers and non-managers or among key hospital occupations. However, it notes the assent of Community-Based Integrated Care in Japanese hospitals as an example of a sector-wide Communitarian PAR.

12 Lessons Learned and Implications for Research on Co-production and Healthcare

The final chapter provides a summary of the main findings, considers the implications for further research on co-production and healthcare. This volume compares and contrasts two widely different approaches to co-production, i.e., aspirational and transformative co-production. Finally, it asks if the COVID-19 pandemic has changed the course of development for co-production and healthcare. Will the importance of citizens/users and front-line staff receive equal recognition compared to the economic models of control in future research on healthcare management?

References

Alakeson, V., Bunnin, A., Miller, C., 2013. *Coproduction of Health and Wellbeing Outcomes. The New Paradigm for Effective Health and Social Care*. Office of Public Management, London.

Alford, J., 2009. *Engaging Public Sector Clients. From Service Delivery to Co-Production*. Palgrave Macmillan, Houndmills, Hamps., UK & New York, NY.

Anderson, R.M., Funnell, M.M., 2012. Patient empowerment: myths and misconceptions. *Patient Educ. Counseling 79/2*, 277–282.

Batalden, M., Batalden, P., Margolis, P., Seid, M., Armstrong, G., Opipari-Arrigan, L., Hartung, H., 2015; Coproduction of healthcare service. *British Medical Journal: Quality & Safety*, 10.1136/bmjqs-2015-004315.

Brandsen, T., Helderman, J.K., 2012. A Case Study of German The Conditions for Successful Co-Production in Housing Cooperatives. Ch. 9 In: Pestoff, V., Brandsen, T., Verschuere, B. (Eds.), *New Public Governance, the Third Sector and Co-Production*. Routledge, London & New York.

Cornforth, C., 2004. The governance of co-operatives and mutual associations: A paradox perspective. *Ann. Public. Co-op. Econ. 75/1*, 11–32.

Coulter, A., Ellins, J., 2007, 2011. Effectiveness of strategies for informing, educating and involving patients. *Br. Med. J. 335/7609*, 24–27.

Cucciniello, M., Nasi, G., 2014. Evaluation of the impacts of innovation in the healthcare sector. A comparative analysis. *Public. Manag. Rev. 16/1*, 90–116.

Davis, G., Ostrom, E., 1991. A public economy approach to education: Choice & co-production. *Int. Political Sci. Rev. 12/4*, 313–335.

Dunston, R., Lee, A., Boud, D., Brodie, P., Chiarella, M., 2009. Co-production and health systems reform - from re-imaging to re-making. *Australian J. Public. Adm. 68/1*, 39–52.

Fotaki, M., 2009. Patient choice in healthcare in the UK & Sweden: From quasi-markets and back to markets? A comparative analysis of the failure of un-learning. *Public. Adm. 84/4*, 1059–1075.

Fotaki, M., 2011. Towards developing new partnerships in public services: Users as consumers, citizens and/or co-producers driving improvements in health and social care in the UK and Sweden. *Public. Adm. 89/3*, 933–995.

Freise, M., 2012. Co-Producing Safety or Participative Window Dressing? Regulative Partnerships in German Local Governance Arrangements. Ch. 14 In: Pestoff, V., Brandsen, T., Verschuere, B. (Eds.), *New Public Governance, the Third Sector and Co-Production.* Routledge, London & New York.

Hudson, B., 2012. Competition or co-production? Which way for governance in health and wellbeing? In: Loeffler, E., Taylor-Godby, D., Bovaird, T., Hine-Hughes, F., Wilkes, L. (Eds.), *Making Health and Social Care Personal and Local. Moving from Mass Production to Co-Production.* London Governance International & Local Government Information Unit: London.

Hudson, B., 2014. Public and patient engagement in commissioning in the English NHS. An idea whose time has come? *Public. Manag. Rev. 17/1*, 1–16.

Karasek, R., Theorell, T., 1990. *Healthy Work: Stress, Productivity, and the Reconstruction of Working Life.* Basic Books, New York.

Kurimoto, A., 2004. What Can Co-operative Health and Social Care Offer? Ch. 19 In: Tsuzuki, C., Hijikata, N., Kurimoto, A. (Eds.), *The Emergence of Global Citizenship: Utopian Ideas, Co-operative Movements and the Third Sector.* Robert Owen association of Japan, Tokyo.

Kurimoto, A., 2010. Medical Co-ops: Evolution and Challenges. Ch. 7 In: CCIJ (Ed.), *Toward Contemporary Co-operative Studies: Perspectives from Japan's Consumer Co-ops.* Consumer Co-op Institute of Japan, Tokyo.

Kurimoto, A., 2015. *Social Enterprise Models Providing Health and Social Services in Japan.* ICSEM Working Paper, Liege, pp. 2005–2007.

McMullin, C., 2020. Co-production of Public Services: Institutional Barriers to the Involvement of Citizens in Policy Implementation. In: Sullivan, H., Dickinson, H., Henderson, H. (Eds.), *The Palgrave Handbook of the Public Servant.* Palgrave Macmillan, Cham.

Meijer, A., 2012. Co-Production in an Information Age. Ch. 10 In: Pestoff, V., Brandsen, T., Verschuere, B. (Eds.), *New Public Governance, the Third Sector and Co-Production.* London & New York: Routledge.

Meijer, A., 2016. Coproduction as a structural transformation of the public sector. *Int. J. Public. Sect. Manag. 29/6*, 596–611.

OECD, 2011. *Together for Better Public Service. Partnering With Citizens and Civil Society.* OECD, Paris.

Osborne, S.P., McLaughlin, K., 2004. The cross-cutting review of the voluntary sector. What next for local government voluntary sector relationships. *Regional Stud. 38/5*, 573–582.

Ostrom, E., 1996 [1999]; Crossing the Great Divide: Co-production, Synergy & Development; *World Development*, 24/6: 1073-1087; reprinted in 1999 as Ch. 15, *Polycentric Governance and Development. Readings from the*

Workshop in Political Theory and Policy Analysis, McGinnis, Michael D. (ed.); Ann Arbor, MI: Univ. of Michigan Press.

Ostrom, E., Ostrom, V., 1971 [1999]; Public Choice: A Different Approach to the Study of Public Administration; *Public Admin. Review*, (March/April) 203-216, reprinted in 1999 as Ch. 1 in *Polycentric Games and Institutions*; M. McGinnis (ed.); Ann Arbor, MI: Univ. of Michigan Press.

Parks, R.B., Baker, P.C., Kiser, L., Oakerson, R., Ostrom, E., Ostrom, V., Perry, S.L., Vandivort, M.B., Whitaker, G.P., (Eds.), 1981 [1999]; Consumers as Co-Producers of Public Services: Some Economic and Institutional Considerations, *Policy Studies Journal*. 9:1001-1011, reprinted in 1999 as Ch. 17 in *Local Public Economies. Readings from the Workshop in Political Theory and Policy Analysis*, McGinnis, Michael D. (ed.); Ann Arbor, MI: Univ. of Michigan Press.

Pestoff, V., 1998. *Beyond the Market & State. Social Enterprise & Civil Democracy in a Welfare Society*. Ashgate, Aldershot, UK & Brookfield, NJ.

Pestoff, V., 2006 [2009]. Citizens and Co-production of Welfare Services; In: V. Pestoff & T. Brandsen (Eds.), *Public Management Review*, reprinted in *Co-production. The Third Sector and the Delivery of Public Services*. London & New York: Routledge.

Pestoff, V., 2008. *A Democratic Architecture for the Welfare State: Promoting Citizen Participation, the Third Sector and Co-production*. London & New York: Routledge.

Pestoff, V., 2009. Towards a paradigm of democratic governance: Citizen participation and co-production of personal social services in Sweden. *Ann. Public. Cooperative Economy 80/2*, 197–224.

Pestoff, V., 2018. *Co-production and Public Service Management. Democracy, Citizenship and Public Service Management*. London & New York: Routledge.

Pestoff, V., Brandsen, T., 2006, [2009]. *Co-production. The Third Sector and the Delivery of Public Service*, Special issue of *Public Management Review*, reprinted in 2009, London & New York: Routledge.

Pestoff, V., Brandsen, T., Verschuere, B. (Eds.), 2012. *New Public Governance, the Third Sector and Co-Production*. London & New York: Routledge.

Pestoff, V., Saito, Y., Vamstad, J., 2017. *Co-production in Health and Elder Care: the Japanese model for better service quality, a project presentation*. Ersta Sköndal Bräcke University College & Osaka University, Stockholm & Osaka.

Pfeffer, J., 2018. *Dying for a Paycheck. How Modern Management Harms Employees Health and Company Performance – and What We Can Do About It*. New York: Harper Business.

Porter, D., 2012. Co-Production and Network Structures in Public Education. Ch. 8 In: Pestoff, V., Brandsen, T., Verschuere, B. (Eds.), *New Public Governance, the Third Sector and Co-Production*. London & New York: Routledge.

Prentice, S., 2006. Childcare, Co-production and the Third Sector in Canada. *Public. Manag. Rev. 8/4*, 830–849, and reprinted in 2009 as Ch. 3 in *Co-production. The Third Sector and the Delivery of Public Services*; V. Pestoff & T. Brandsen (eds); London & New York: Routledge

Schlappa, H., 2012. Co-management and Urban Regeneration. New Perspectives on Transferable Collaborative Practice. Ch. 12 in In: Pestoff, V., Brandsen, T. (Eds.), *Co-production. The Third Sector and the Delivery of Public Services*. London & New York: Routledge.

Scott, W.R., Reuf, M., Mendel, M., Caronna, G., 2000. *Institutional Change and Healthcare Organization: From Professional Dominance to Managed Care*. Chicago, IL: Univ. of Chicago Press.

Spears, R., Cornforth, C., Aiken, M., 2014. Major perspectives on governance of social enterprise. Ch. 7 In: Defourrny, J., Hulgård, L., Pestoff, V. (eds), *Social Enterprise & the Third Sector*. London & New York: Routledge.

United Nations, 1997. *Cooperative Enterprise in the Health and Social Care Sectors – A Global Survey*. New York: United Nations.

Vamstad, J., 2007. *Governing Welfare. The Third Sector and Challenges to the Swedish Welfare State*. Mid-Sweden University Doctoral, Östersund, Thesis 37.

Vamstad, J., 2012. Co-Production and Service Quality: A New Perspective on the Swedish Welfare State. Ch. 16 In: Pestoff, V., Brandsen, T., Verschuere, B. (Eds.), *New Public Governance, the Third Sector and Co-Production*. and reprinted in *Voluntas*, Dec. 2012, London & New York: Routledge.

Vamstad, J., 2014. *Två vägar till individualisering - om kvasi+marknader och medskapande i den svenska välfärdsstaten*. Stockholm: Ersta-Skondal Univ. College paper.

Vancoppenolle, D., Verschuere, B., 2012. The Challenges of Co-management for Public Accountability: Lessons from Flemish Child CareC. Ch. 18 In: Pestoff, V., Brandsen, T., Verschuere, B. (Eds.), *New Public Governance, the Third Sector and Co-Production*. London & New York: Routledge.

Van de Broek, J., Boselie, P., Paauwe, J., 2014. Multiple institutional logics in health care. *Public. Manag. Rev. 16/1*, 1–12.

Vickers, I., Lyon, F., Sepulveda, L., McMullin, C., 2017. *Public Service innovation and multiple institutional logics: The case of hybrid social enterprise providers of health and wellbeing. Journal of Research Policy*; (open access). DOI 10/1016/j.respol.2017.08.003.

Vidal, I., 2013. Governance of Social Enterprises as Producers of Public Services. Ch. 10 In: Valkama, P., Bailey, S., Anttiroiko, A.-V. (Eds.), *Organisational Innovation in Public Services. Forms and Governance*. New York & London: Palgrave.

Vorberg, W., Bekkers, V., Tummers, L., 2015. A systematic review of co-creation and co-production: Embarking on the social innovation journey. *Public. Manag. Rev. 17/9*, 1333–1357.

World Health Organization, 2005. *Ninth Futures Forum on Health Systems Governance and Public Participation*. Copenhagen: WHO.

World Health Organization, 2016. *WHO Global Strategy on People-Centered and Integrated Health Services, Interim Report*. Geneva: WHO.

Part I
Background

2 Third Sector and Cooperative Services

An Alternative to Privatization

This chapter considers the potential contribution of third sector and cooperative organizations to enriching work environment, empowering clients and enhancing public goal achievement. Both consumer and worker cooperatives as well as nonprofit organizations (NPOs) can make unique contributions to renewing the public sector and enriching public services. Consumer co-ops can contribute to empowering the clients and consumers of such services, whereas worker co-ops can contribute to enriching and renewing the work life of the providers of these services. Other types of nonprofit organizations can augment the effectiveness of public services in achieving their goals. After considering the potential advantages and disadvantages of each of the three types of NPOs to enhance public services, it concludes that rather than privatizing public services, there are clear theoretical arguments for "cooperatizing" them and/or involving nonprofit organizations in the provision of social services and healthcare. It provided the theoretical basis for a research project on Work Environment and Cooperative Social Services that was funded in the early 1990s.

A Introduction

In the early 1990s, one of the main proponents of privatization in Sweden was the Confederation of Swedish Employers (SAF). It stepped up its long-term campaign by announcing a detailed timetable for the privatization of all state authorities, except the courts, police and defense, in less than ten years (interview with Ulf Laurin in *Svenska Dagbladet*, 05.11.90). Sweden should be completely 'privatized' by the year 2000, according to SAF's Chairman (*SAF-tidningen*, 06.11.90). This included social and healthcare services associated with the modern welfare state, leaving only an empty shell or 'night watchman state' in its place.

The current Swedish debate in the 1990s over public vs. private provision of social services was highly ideological. It often tended to depict the problems associated with public health and social welfare policy in simple black and white terms. Proponents of public services argued that social services should be provided by the state or municipal governments and definitely not opened to the profit or commercial interests of private firms. Proponents of private services argued that governmental monopoly invariably results in inefficiency, and according to them, privatization of social services not only reduces costs by introducing competition, but also offers customers or clients freedom of choice. The proponents of public and private social welfare services have one thing in common; they both share a lack of interest in the 'third sector' – which is comprised of cooperatives, voluntary associations, non-governmental organizations, popular movements and nonprofit organizations (NPOs).

In spite of their common ignorance of the third sector and its potential contribution to the provision of social welfare services, this debate, nevertheless, underscored the necessity and urgency of renewing the public sector and enriching the welfare state. Third sector alternatives, such as cooperatives and other NPOs, can make a contribution to these goals by giving clients and/or consumers greater influence in the production of social services and by providing them with a plurality of alternatives from which to choose. This chapter explores the theoretical foundation for considering cooperatives and NPOs as viable alternatives to both public and private social service and healthcare providers. Three principal forms or models for cooperation are relevant; they are consumer cooperatives, worker cooperatives and NPOs. Each of these forms provides a conceivable alternative to public or private for-profit provision of social welfare services, but each has different social and political consequences, which are explored below.

First, this chapter provides a theoretical review of third sector organizations – such as cooperatives and NPOs – as alternatives to public and private provision of social services from a 'welfare mix' framework. It then identifies the major potential contribution of each of these alternative forms for providing social welfare services, as well as their respective drawbacks. Considering third sector social services in greater detail helps to reveal their inherent advantages and disadvantages relative to public and private social services. In brief, their advantages include the empowerment of the clients or consumers of these services, the enrichment and renewal of the work life of producers of these services – as well as the enhancement of effectivity and goal fulfillment in public services brought about by involving cooperatives and NPOs in the provision of social services.

Empowerment of consumers can take place in two ways. Either it happens directly in consumer cooperatives, where clients or consumers become involved in the management and production of their own social and healthcare service providers and thus, obtain an institutionalized voice in running it. Alternatively, it takes place indirectly in worker cooperatives, where consumers or clients are indirectly empowered due to the worker-owners' double incentive to promote a dialog with their clients in order to provide the flexible specialization and quality of services necessary for their co-op to compete and survive. The involvement of nonprofit self-help groups in the provision of social services can also give such groups greater influence.

Enrichment and renewal of work life can also take place in two ways. Either it happens directly in worker cooperatives, where the employees own the firm and can decide about their work environment themselves and as employees/owners can influence these and other company decisions. Alternatively, it happens indirectly in consumer cooperatives, which promote a dialog between the consumers and producers of these services which helps to enhance and enrich their work life. Finally, the effectiveness of goal fulfillment in public services can be enhanced in two ways. Either it takes place directly by involving the clients of nonprofit self-help groups in providing such services to themselves. Alternatively, it happens indirectly through being able to reach out to resource poor or crucially afflicted groups and provide them with services that are otherwise outside their reach.

B The Welfare Mix

The welfare mix refers to the interaction of various social institutions and orders. The basic social orders spelled out by Streeck and Schmitter (1985) are community, market, state and associations. Each has its own guiding principles, predominant actors and resources, principal motives and pay-offs. The social institutions normally associated with these four social orders are households, private firms, public agencies and voluntary associations or NPOs, respectively. The welfare mix pertains to the interrelatedness of these social orders and institutions.

It is essential to keep several important distinctions in mind when examining the welfare mix and the interrelatedness of these social orders. These are differences between public/private, for-profit/ nonprofit and formal/informal institutions. Each of these institutions illustrates a unique combination of characteristics. Public agencies are normally formal, NPOs, while private firms are normally formal, for-profit organizations. Households are normally informal, private entities, while voluntary associations are normally formal, private NPOs. Figure 2.1 depicts these distinctions and the interrelatedness of these four social institutions.

Although these distinctions may initially appear trivial, they are fundamental for discussing alternative forms for providing social welfare services. From the perspective found here, it should be noted that the public nonprofit and the private for-profit provision of social welfare services are only two of several possible alternatives and they are not necessarily polar opposites. Moreover, they fail to encompass certain other possibilities, such as services provided by cooperatives, NPOs and/or families. The private nonprofit alternative implies that the delivery of social welfare services does not take place under the auspices of public agencies, although it does not exclude public financing. However, neither does it mean that such provision can be equated with the motives of for-profit organizations.

Much of the debate in Sweden concerns the need for shifting the boundary between public and private social services. Nevertheless and as already pointed out, it overlooks the possible contribution of third sector

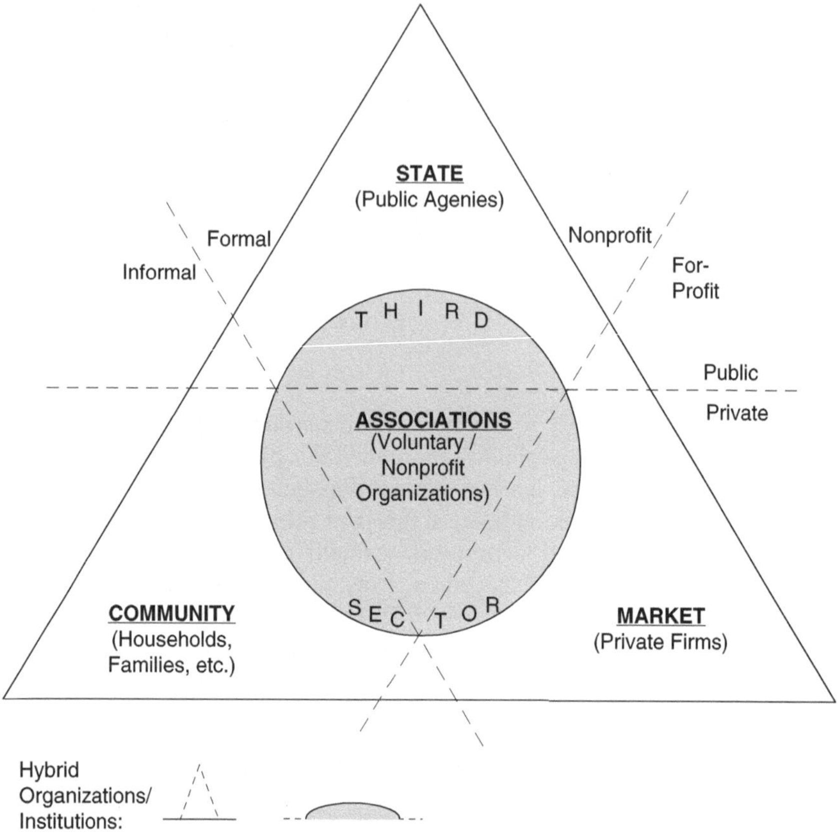

Figure 2.1 The Third Sector and the Welfare Triangle.
Source: Pestoff, 2009.

alternatives as well as individual or family contributions. The third sector – together with families – comprise the civil society, while the market per se falls outside it. Private for-profit firms are thus not included in the civil society, although this need not imply that they are incompatible with it.

The reawakened Eastern European interest in 'civil society' has erroneously led some Western scholars to conclude that everything that is not controlled by the state is a part of civil society. Although such a perspective may seem reasonable at the beginning of a transition from central planning to a market orientation, it lacks validity in democratic, post-industrial societies (Walzer, 1990). Both citizens who live/lived under the command of communist states in the East and those working for anonymous monopoly firms in the West resent being confined to a minor role or being transformed into simple instruments, according to

Vaclav Havel (1978). Transnational firms – some with resources far surpassing the budgets of smaller Western European states – are, for obvious reasons, not germane in the Eastern European debate. However as Havel argues, they must be taken into account in the Western debate on civil society. Thus, privatization of social services in terms of introducing market relationships does not necessarily imply greater control by citizens. In reality, this may result in an absence of consumer influence or in less influence than available through third sector alternatives.

C Cooperatives and Social Welfare Services

The ever increasing needs of citizens for welfare services are reflected by demographic trends in most European countries. Increasing urbanization, growing female participation in the labor force, an increasing number of single-parent families and the rapidly growing ranks of pensioners in most countries are some of the major factors explaining the continual expansion of such needs. Citizens' needs and expectations stand, however, in sharp contrast to the increasing financial constraints facing most European governments as well as the prohibitive costs for ordinary citizens if such services were to be financed solely through private sources.

New or previously unmet needs for welfare services can, under these constraints, help bring the producers and consumers of social welfare services together in untraditional forms. Cooperation among and between producers and consumers can constitute an economically feasible alternative to the public or private provision of social welfare services. Rather than the privatization of the public provision of social welfare services, they may be 'cooperatized'.

Recent developments in the economic and political settings of both Eastern and Western European countries indicate a growing importance of cooperative movements and of the role of cooperatives in the provision of social welfare services. The public sector is being privatized at different rates in many Western European countries, including the public service sector, but 'cooperatization' may provide a viable alternative to privatization. Cooperatives are unique in being able to combine the efficiency of private firms with the social commitments of public services (Pestoff, 1991a).

Understanding the different economic, political and social settings of cooperative movements in both Eastern and Western Europe is necessary for comparing trends in the institutional and organizational transformation of national cooperative movements. The external relations and internal dynamics of cooperatives vary from one country to another; cooperatives can both reflect and influence their environments. The European Community has published a 600-page catalog on cooperatives, mutual benefit societies and NPOs in the European Communities (1986). Cooperative movements are strong in some Western European countries, but weak or nonexistent in others. To illustrate, they are strong in the Nordic countries, but weak in many continental European countries and have collapsed elsewhere. They display a pattern of regional strength and weakness in other countries, such as Italy (Zan, 1982) and Spain (Rovira, 1990).

Established cooperatives are facing new challenges in the final decade of the 20th Century in most European countries, with the erosion of their traditional bases. However, they are rapidly developing in new directions both in the East and West. Although cooperatives do not traditionally provide social services, there are numerous examples of this new type of development now found throughout Europe. In some countries, this new phenomenon is supported by established cooperative movements. In others, it has recently become part of their normal operations, while in others it is condoned if not encouraged by the state. This may reflect a new strategy of survival more than the need to move from stagnant to expanding sectors of the economy (Stryjan, 1989, 1990). It seems reasonable to assume that cooperative alternatives for the provision of social welfare services will more readily develop in favorable institutional and organizational environments.

In Sweden, consumer cooperatives in particular are providing the infrastructural prerequisites necessary for the development of social service cooperatives. For example, small groups of parents wishing to join hands in setting up and running parental daycare cooperatives can turn to the Union of Wholesale and Retail Cooperative Societies (Kooperativa Förbundet, KF) to obtain legal advice on how to proceed (Kooperativa institutet, 1986a). Small groups of parents normally lack the necessary expertise for starting a daycare cooperative or the resources to obtain legal advice on the private market (Kooperativa institutet, 1989). The HSB building and tenant cooperatives are running a project for the cooperative provision of eldercare (HSB, 1988a) as well as daycare (HSB, 1988b). HSB has plans for providing all the social services in a given neighborhood of the city Västerås (Kooperativa institutet, 1986b).

In 1989, the municipality of Västervik decided to turn the integrated operations of social service in an entire neighborhood over to another building and tenant cooperative society, Riksbyggen. The city of Gothenburg decided recently to manage two of its inner-city schools on a cooperative basis by using alternative pedagogics. Starting in 1991, the insurance cooperative – Folksam – is promoting the idea of healthcare cooperatives. It has taken over the management of a local hospital in Åre from the county council and runs a rehabilitation home.

In most of the Swedish examples, social service cooperatives are comprised of the clients or recipients of the services. Clients or consumers are thus empowered vis-à-vis the civil servants or professionals normally providing such services, and they are also involved in the provision of the service. This, in turn, facilitates a dialog between users and providers of social welfare services which can improve the quality of such service.

In Italy, the Lega cooperative movement in the Emilia-Veneto area has assumed the responsibility of creating worker cooperatives for the provision of essential social services (Zan, 1982, 1988). This may concern daycare, health and medical care and similar services. However in this case, it is the providers rather than the consumers or clients who take the initiative to establish cooperatives for the provision of social services.

Throughout Eastern Europe, hundreds of new cooperatives have emerged under policies of economic reform and recent revisions of the laws governing cooperatives. Cooperatives are no longer seen as a socially inferior form of ownership, but rather are now put on equal footing with private ownership. A significant number of these new cooperatives are concerned with the provision of social services (Dellenbrant, 1988). In addition, established cooperative movements are also expressing concern for the development of new forms of cooperatives.

These recent developments in the provision of social welfare services have received scant serious attention by social scientists. This comes as no surprise, since cooperatives are normally studied by economists and political scientists, while social welfare services are studied by sociologists. Moreover, much of the debate about the privatization of social welfare services finds its origin in political concerns associated with neo-liberalism, Thatcherism, etc., which tend to ignore collective solutions provided by cooperatives.

Cooperative welfare services are such a new phenomenon that they have not yet been closely scrutinized by social science researchers and definitely not from the perspective of consumer empowerment nor enrichment of work life. The discussion below of consumer empowerment and enrichment of work life through cooperative social services will therefore be speculative. However, this is necessary in order to derive a number of clear hypothetical expectations to guide further theoretical and empirical research endeavors.

D The Unique Possibilities of Cooperatives in the Provision of Social Services

There are numerous theoretical and practical questions related to the study of the role of cooperatives in the provision of personal welfare services are quite numerous. The discussion here is limited to three main theoretical arguments, each with broad practical implications. The theoretical setting reflects the welfare mix of public, private, cooperative and NPOs in the provision of social welfare services discussed above. The more specific inquiries involve the role of consumer cooperatives in empowering clients or consumers of social welfare services and the role of worker cooperatives in renewing and enriching work life. In addition, the role of NPOs in increasing the effectiveness of the welfare network and social welfare services is also of theoretical importance here. Other considerations, such as entrepreneurship and management of social service cooperatives as well as their effectivity compared with the public and private provision of social services, will be considered at a later stage.

The provision of social welfare services by cooperatives can be divided into three or four main categories which reflect the type of service offered (i.e. services with residence or housing as its starting point; services concentrating on health and other types of personal care; professional or worker cooperatives in the social service sector and cooperatives for leisure, education, culture or tourism). Our interest focuses on all types of cooperatives providing social welfare services, except housing cooperatives per se. Healthcare, rehabilitation societies, various kinds of social cooperatives, handicap, daycare and elderly care, school cooperatives and integrated social service cooperatives will be the subject of future empirical studies.

The two more specific theoretical problems raised in the sections below concern the renewal of the public sector and enrichment of the welfare state as well as the renewal and enrichment of work life associated with the various forms of providing welfare services – in particular, changes between one form of provision and another. What would the most likely impact of a change from public social services to third sector provision on relations with clients and employees of such services be? Financial and strictly economic aspects aside, rather different customer and work relations are implied by each form of provision. Public provision often implies standardization of welfare services according to some publicly agreed upon or politically approved norms. These norms may be determined by relevant experts and applied through political decisions to all providing units within a given territorial jurisdiction. Uniform higher education, particularly for civil servants, ensures the standard application of such norms (William-Olsson, 1988; *Dagens Nyheter Jan*, 18, 1990). However, such standardization has been criticized for resulting in the application of Fordist principles of mass production to the provision of personal welfare services (Christensen, 1990; Tarschys, 1990). This often alienates both the clients and employees. The post-Fordist emphasis on decentralization and flexible specialization rejects such a model of production (Nielsen, 1989; Nielsen and Pedersen, 1989).

The contemporary debate on privatizing public services also influences the goals and constraints of public provision of welfare services. The 1980s the welfare state was subjected to prolonged criticism and severe budget curtailments. This, in turn, has had an impact on the goals of public providers – such as attributing greater priority to economizing resources, rather than expanding or improving the quality of welfare services. The present economic and political climate sharply restricts the possibilities for the renewal of the public sector and the enrichment of the welfare state as well as the renewal and enrichment of work life in the public sector.

Competitive, private provision of welfare services implies greater flexibility and, hence, greater differences between providing units. Standard or uniform norms do not determine all or even most aspects of service, rather only a few basic or strategic ones. Efficiency and profit in providing services are not determined by standardization but rather by market expectations and flexible local solutions. Nor are private providers subject to the same public scrutiny and debate as public ones. Private social services will be relatively small scale, at least at the outset. The greater flexibility and specialization in the services provided will be welcomed by both clients and workers.

There are, however, limits to the renewal of social services via privatization. The flexibility and innovation expected by clients will be limited by the economic constraints of private for-profit firms. Most employees will, moreover, face equal or perhaps even stronger economic constraints in the private sector than in the public sector (Szulkin, 1989). Thus, except for the owners and/or managers of private firms providing social welfare services, possibilities for the renewal and enrichment of work life may be limited to the greater flexibility provided by smaller bureaucratic units.

The discussion below summarizes several of the points in the Swedish debate about new cooperatives (Pestoff, 1990b, 1991b). It considers the main advantages of social service cooperatives in terms of empowerment of consumers, renewal and enrichment of work life, renewal of the public sector and enrichment of the welfare state. They will be addressed separately below. It also mentions some of their drawbacks.

1 *Empowerment of Clients and Consumers*

The first important issue dealt with herein concerns the empowerment of clients or the consumers of social welfare services. Markets and politics are the two main institutions governing the influence of clients and consumers in market-oriented economies (Hirschman, 1970). However, they operate under quite different constraints, according to rather contrasting principles and rely upon quite distinct responses by producers and consumers or clients. Markets respond primarily to market signals which can be initiated or augmented by consumers changing their patronage from one producer or provider to another. Hirschman refers to 'exit' as a reaction by dissatisfied customers or clients. Political decisions, by contrast, are not only subject to voting and elections, but also to protests of one kind or another. Hirschman refers to such responses as 'voice', since they call attention to unsatisfactory conditions in the provision of goods or services. Exit is a typical market response and has the greatest impact on commercial or private firms. Voice is a typical political response and has its greatest impact on public services. The beneficial impact of exit and voice depend, however, upon the type of goods produced or service rendered (Hirschman, 1981, 1982; Pestoff, 1994).

Exit and market responses may provide ample, if not optimal, information in decisions concerning many, if not most, types of goods. In this case, quality can be determined by some combination of objective or general standards. Services, however, are not normally subject to the same general agreement about standards. Voice has one of its most important functions in determining the quality of service. This is true in particular of social welfare services – most of which have been developed and made available to the public-at-large in recent decades – and, therefore, are rarely subject to previously determined general standards of quality. Rather, it is often through a dialog at the local level between the providers and consumers of such services that some agreement upon standards of quality can be derived at all. Market signals alone are, thus, inadequate and inappropriate for determining quality standards of welfare services, since they provide insufficient information concerning the desires of clients.

Most forms of providing social welfare services are governed by either one or the other of these two principles (i.e. exit or voice). Private provision of social welfare services is undertaken on a commercial basis, while public provision depends upon elections and political decisions. The former is primarily subject to exit, the latter to voice. As such, voice may operate at infrequent intervals (e.g. at best, every second, third, fourth or fifth year or more seldom) depending on election periods and the saliency of issues related to welfare services in election campaigns. Not only private providers of social welfare services, but also social service cooperatives run on a worker co-op basis and similarly, though to a lesser extent, NPOs operate under commercial-like constraints. They are primarily subject to exit or market responses if the market is competitive but to little or no voice reactions.

Cooperatives providing social welfare services to members as consumers of these services (i.e. on a consumer co-op basis) can, however, readily combine both exit and voice options among their guiding principles at the level of production. It is their ability to combine both of these guiding principles that makes it possible to discuss the empowerment of clients as consumers, since it makes clients directly responsible for the service produced. By involving members in the day-to-day operations of their cooperatives – in addition to giving them a voice in the running of the co-op as a whole – clients-cum-members obtain an institutionalized voice in the provision of social welfare services. This voice can be employed in determining the standards of quality of the services at the level of production. This type of institutionalized voice is not normally found in other forms of welfare service provision. Thus, clients/customers become empowered with rights and responsibilities by virtue of an institutionalized voice made available to them through membership in the social service co-op.

There are, however, some problems associated with member ownership. Some employees may resent having to deal with clients as members. Certain employees may even consider it an infringement upon their professional prerogatives. Under- and over-consumption of work environment may also become a complication. Members may not always understand the necessity of making investments to improve the work environment. Rather, on the contrary, their investments in the work environment may be to the detriment of the economic well-being or survival of their social service cooperative.

Consumer cooperatives can thus play a unique role in the provision of social welfare services. They alone can directly empower clients or the consumers of these services, and they alone can directly institutionalize a dialog between the producers and consumers of welfare services about the quality of such services. This, in turn, contributes to the renewal and enrichment of the work life of the professional providers of such social services. Employees can gain valuable, direct feedback from clients about the quality of the services provided.

Social welfare services provided by NPOs may, in addition, potentially contribute to the empowerment of consumers. Members who share the group's or NPO's goals might find it easier to engage in a dialog about services and their quality. Common goals may, on the other hand, act to impede criticism of existing routines due to group loyalty. Non-members who subscribe to such services will probably do so with the lower costs made possible by volunteers in mind and, therefore, also avoid open criticism. Thus, although staff resources may facilitate a dialog between volunteer providers and consumers about quality of services, cost considerations will most likely impede overt criticism of existing routines or services.

2 *The Renewal and Enrichment of Work Life*

The second important theoretical issue raised herein concerns the renewal and enrichment of work life associated with the various forms of providing welfare services and, in particular, changes between one form of provision and another. Different work relations are implied by each form of provision, as mentioned above.

In post-communist societies, Havel (1978) recommends that the production and satisfaction of human needs should take place through cooperatives and various forms of self-management. Everybody who works in an enterprise must share in the decisions and in the returns. Cooperative provision of social welfare services in the West also implies greater differentiation than public provision but not significantly so in terms of standards and norms, as in forms for organizing the provision of services (Lindkvist and Westenholz, 1987; Lindkvist, 1990).

Two basic forms or models of cooperative services are apparent. One is the worker co-op model, where all or most of the providers of a social service are also shareholders in the service cooperative but the clients have a formal customer relation with the providers. It is here that we can expect to find the greatest possibilities for the renewal and enrichment of work life (i.e. from a perspective of cooperatization rather than privatization of social welfare services). By combining the roles of owning a firm with that of being an employee, co-determination is also greatly enhanced.

Hirschman (1982) argues that greater participation in work life and the discussions concerning it can help to bridge the gap between instrumental and the expressive attitudes. This would make work less instrumental and introduce more expressive aspects – something which, in turn, renders work more satisfying and enjoyable to most employees.

There are certain problems associated with worker ownership. Either the under- or the over-consumption of work environment is one such problem. The members of social service co-ops of the worker type might ignore some of their own interests as employees, for example, in making investments to improve their work environment. They could be inclined to do this in a highly competitive situation in order to save their jobs. The members/workers of this type of social service cooperative might, on the contrary, make improvements in their work environment at the expense of their clients and/or other financiers of these social services. This should be a greater risk with public than with individual financing of cooperative social services. There is also a risk that members of worker co-ops which provide social services would give preference to their own interests rather than those of their clients. Their preferences for increased salaries may outweigh those of their clients for high-quality services at reasonable prices. This depends, of course, on the competitive nature of the market and on fiscal control, if such services are financed by public funds, on a third-party basis.

The final form of providing social welfare services involves NPOs and bears some of the features of cooperatives but also has some unique characteristics of its own. Great variation is found between countries in terms of the characteristics of NPOs and their role in the provision of personal welfare services (Kramer, 1990a, 1990b). From a Nordic perspective, NPOs often rely on idea-based or purposive groups. They may provide welfare services to members initially and then, perhaps, to non-members on a commercial basis. NPOs do not, however, normally attempt to cater to the public-at-large but only to persons subscribing to, or at least not rejecting, certain of the NPO's basic values. Members of the NPO who are involved in the actual provision of welfare services usually do so on a volunteer basis or for reduced remuneration, thereby lowering the costs of providing such services and, thus, making them more commercially viable or profitable. The surplus derived from the provision of personal social welfare services can be used to finance other activities of the NPO. An equally important point may be contact with non-members and the opportunity of explaining or demonstrating the ideas of the NPO and, thus, gaining new adherents. New souls may be more important than greater income. NPOs will, therefore, provide an uncertain example of the enrichment of work life.

The extent to which NPOs rely upon volunteers diminishes their importance in the renewal and enrichment of work life – in particular, when the active work force includes a large proportion of working-age females. On the contrary, in a society with a lower level of activity in the work force, in particular for women, volunteer work may be the first step out of house work and back into the active remunerative work force. The necessary skills and self-confidence may be gained through volunteering. This aspect is not, however, seen as particularly relevant in countries like Sweden, mainly due to the uniquely high level of female activity in the work force.

3 The Unique Advantages of Nonprofit Organizations in the Welfare Network

Nonprofit organizations have often been praised in the U.S.A. and the U.K. for providing more efficient welfare services than either public or private for-profit channels. The third sector or voluntary associations have not earned the same recognition in Sweden as elsewhere, in spite of recent support by a parliamentary commission (Folkrörelseutredningen, 1986, 1987, 1989; Kulle, 1991). The volunteer aspect of NPOs often gives rise to expectations of less-costly services compared with both public and private provision of such services (Kramer, 1981). They can relieve heavily burdened public budgets, which is often one of the main political reasons for proposing an increased role for NPOs (and privatization) in the implementation of public policy and in the delivery of various social services to the public. A shift to voluntary sector delivery of welfare services in the U.S.A. and the U.K. reinforces, however, the dependence of voluntary organizations on the government for funding such activities (Hall, 1987; Salamon, 1987; Johnsson, 1989). This, in turn, encourages their professionalization and increases their personnel costs in the next phase of development (Salamon, 1987; Kramer, 1990a, 1990b).

Our focus here, however, is not on the issues of efficiency, productivity or costs, but rather on whether and how NPOs contribute to greater effectiveness in achieving the goals of public health and social welfare policy. Thus, it is not the costs of welfare service per se, but rather the ability of NPOs to contribute to the effective achievement of Swedish public health and social welfare goals that deserve attention. Greater effectiveness in public services can be achieved by the unique outreach functions of NPOs.

In a seminal work on voluntary agencies and the welfare state, Kramer (1981) compared the role of NPOs in the U.S.A., the U.K., the Netherlands and Israel that provided services to the handicapped. He argued that voluntary handicap agencies combine three unique functions that are not normally associated with service provision by either public or for-profit agencies in most welfare states: pioneering or innovation through specialization, advocacy and the preservation of specific civic values of participation by clients.

The relationship between governmental and NPOs varies from country to country over time and according to the issue or problem at hand. Kramer (1981) discusses five major strategies of relating government to voluntary agencies in the delivery of personal social services. They range from nationalization, government dominance and 'pragmatic partnership', to 'empowerment' and 'reprivatization'. In the four countries in his study, he characterizes relationships between governments and NPOs for the handicapped according to one or the other of these strategies.

In this way too, the acute case of AIDS helps to bring to light an additional strategy for relating governments to voluntary agencies not initially observed by Kramer. If, for any reason, the government is unable to successfully come into contact with relevant risk groups, then it may actively encourage NPOs to do so in light of their unique outreach function.

A highly topical example was chosen for exploring the role of NPOs in the welfare mix and their outreach functions in the welfare network in Sweden (i.e. the case of 'Managing AIDS') (Marin and Kenis, 1989). It illustrates the interaction of NPOs with the state under dire stress and serves to identify the limits as well as to clarify the essentials of the role played by NPOs in Sweden's welfare mix.

The AIDS epidemic provided clear cut case for examining the functions of NPOs in delivering social services. The acute case of AIDS brought an additional organizational function into focus - namely, reaching out to risk groups that are reluctant to work directly as individuals or in groups with public health or social welfare authorities, partly because of the stigma involved with their group characteristics and special illness. This outreach is the unique feature of NPOs that provide AIDS services (Pestoff and Walden Laing, 1990; Walden Laing and Eads, 1991). Without NPOs, it would be impossible to come into contact with most risk groups, to inform them, test them and provide them with counseling and services, nor would it be possible to provide them with humane conditions and treatment once their HIV-positive situation becomes more acute.

NPOs involved with managing AIDS in Sweden and elsewhere are engaged, to a greater or lesser degree, with one or more of the following functions: Prevention; Care and social services; Control, surveillance or monitoring; Policy advocacy. They collaborate, of course, with public agencies in most of these functions and much of their financing comes from public funds. However, a significant number of NPOs can also be expected to fulfill the unique function of outreach in which both public and for-profit agencies fall short.

Government dominance may be the principal mode of operation in most areas of personal social service in Sweden, as Kramer claims elsewhere (1990a, 1990b). However, 'pragmatic partnership', active encouragement of outreach or 'empowerment' can determine this relationship in other areas of social services. Thus, 'empowerment' would best characterize the Swedish government's relationship with NPOs in the field of consumer policy (Pestoff, 1989, 1990a), while 'pragmatic partnership' or perhaps active encouragement of outreach seems to best capture this relationship when it comes to managing AIDS (Pestoff and Walden Laing, 1990).

By virtue of their unique outreach function, we expect that, in most aspects of managing AIDS, many if not most of Swedish NPOs will function as a supplement or complement to public health and social welfare agencies rather than as an alternative or obstacle to them. In a more general sense, if clients are organized in self-help groups, then they can play a more active role in articulating and promoting the interests of their members in designing and delivering social services. This gives them greater influence in the provision of such social services. Their participation may initially promote some disagreement between such self-help groups and public sector agencies over the quality and quantity of such services. However, in the long run, it should promote a greater dialog among these groups.

Resource-poor clients who lack organizations of their own may be assisted by public servants and/or concerned individuals in forming client groups. Extremely disadvantaged groups may, thus, be reached by these social services via such client groups. However, they are unable actively to articulate their own needs or to promote the provision of services tailored to their needs. Thus, both in the specific case discussed above and in general, NPOs can increase the goal fulfillment of public health and social service policies. Under some circumstances, NPOs may even provide greater client influence on the services provided.

E Summary and Conclusions

Both consumer and worker cooperatives as well as NPOs can make unique contributions to renewing the public sector and enriching the welfare state, if their roles in the provision of social welfare services are better understood. Consumer co-ops can empower the clients and consumers of such services, while worker co-ops can enrich and renew the work life of the providers of such services. Other types of NPOs can contribute to greater effectiveness in achieving the goals of the welfare state. Thus, rather than simply privatizing the welfare state, there are strong theoretical arguments for 'cooperatizing' social services and/or involving other voluntary organizations in the provision of social services.

Figure 2.2 summarizes the advantages of the various institutional alternatives in relation to the goal of renewing the public sector and the enrichment of the welfare state, as well as to the market and political

Org./Response	exit	voice	Enrich work life	Goal fulfillment
Cons co-op	XX(X)	XXX	X(X)	X(X)
Worker co-op	XX(X)	X(X)	XXX	X(X)
NPOs/NGOs	XX(X)	XX	(X)	XX(X)
Public	(X)	X(X)	X	XXX
Private	X(X)	(X)	(X)	X(X)

Figure 2.2 Institutional Alternatives for Exit and Voice, Enrichment of Working Life and Enhancing Public Goal Fulfillment.

Source: V. Pestoff, 1992.

Key: X=weak, XX=medium, XXX=strong, ( ) potential.

reactions characterized as exit and voice and the enrichment of work life. One X indicates that a particular form of social welfare service only meets a particular objective poorly, while two XXs indicates a medium relationship and three XXXs a strong relationship. A parenthesis indicates that the strength of the relationship depends on certain circumstances. Thus, the influence of exit on private providers of social welfare services is highly dependent on the existence of significant market competition. This clearly varies not only from country to country, but also from branch to branch in any given country.

From the outset, the intention has been to consider three often ignored alternatives to public and private social services. Our summary comments will thus primarily be restricted to cooperative and nonprofit alternatives. The main contribution of consumer cooperatives to renewing the public sector and enriching the welfare state comes in terms of directly empowering the clients or consumers of such services by providing them with an institutionalized voice. This also indirectly contributes to the enrichment of work life and public goal fulfillment.

The main contribution of worker cooperatives to renewing the public sector and enriching the welfare state is in terms of directly enriching work life. They also indirectly contribute, under certain circumstances, to the revitalization of the market – exit – alternative and to greater public goal fulfillment.

The main contribution of NPOs to renewing the public sector and enriching the welfare state is in terms of directly enhancing the effectiveness and goal fulfillment of the public sector. Under certain circumstances, they can also make a modest but indirect contribution to client empowerment and the enrichment of work life.

Consumer cooperatives, thus, provide the greatest opportunity for the exercise of voice as an institution of consumer influence and also for some exit influence. Both the public and nonprofit provision of social welfare services potentially allow for some consumer voice, again depending on certain circumstances. Producer cooperatives provide for weak voice, while private provision excludes voice – relying on exit where competition exists.

Worker cooperatives are conceived as the principal alternative for enriching and renewing work life. Given the high degree of economic concentration and hierarchical control in most branches of the Swedish economy, there is no reason to postulate axiomatically that private providers will be competitive (Pestoff and Ronit, 1990; Pestoff, 1992). It is, however, highly unlikely that worker cooperative social welfare services could ever gain an oligopolistic or monopolistic position. Thus, they allow for more exit influence than either private competitors or consumer cooperatives.

Cooperatives and other NPOs can also enhance public goal fulfillment when they serve as a complement and supplement to public social welfare services, rather than as an alternative to it. An additional consideration associated with cooperative social services stems from the possibility of combining the positive features of both types of cooperatives (i.e. worker and consumer co-ops) in the same organizational form. Multi-stakeholder cooperatives were formed and have been run experimentally for a number of years in Canada (Jordan, 1989). The separate interests of the employees and the clients of cooperative organizations have been given institutional representation in a unique fashion in such cooperatives (Pestoff, 1995). Whether this could serve as a model for similar efforts in combining both the interests of workers and consumers of social welfare services in Sweden or other countries remains to be seen. It could, however, provide grounds for undertaking an interesting experiment in certain areas such as healthcare – where multi-stakeholder social welfare service cooperatives could be developed.

The practical ramifications of this discussion of cooperative social services are numerous. An empirical study of the subject provided the first systematic documentation of consumer empowerment and work environment enrichment in cooperative social services in Sweden. It allowed for a direct comparison of consumer empowerment and work environment in consumer and worker forms of cooperative social services as well as nonprofit organizations and municipal services (Pestoff, 1998).

References

Dagens Nyheter, Jan. 18, 1990. Missnöjd personal kartlägges (Dissatisfied staff will be studied); Jan. 23. 1990; A. Christensen, Barnomsorg i den svenska

fabriken (Childcare in the Swedish factory); Jan. 29, 1990, D. Tarschys, Barnomsorgens förlorade år (Childcare's lost years); and Oct. 6, 1991, C. Örtendahl, Director General of Socialstyrelse (National Board of Health and Welfare), on the HIV/AIDS epidemic.
Dellenbrant, J.Á., 1988. *The Changing Role of Co-operatives in Socialist Countries*. University of Umeå, Department of Political Science, Umeå.
European Communities, 1986. *The Cooperative, Mutual and Non-Profit Sector and its Organizations in the European Community*. EC, Luxembourg.
Folkrörelseutredningen, 1986. *Kommitédirektiv till en utredning om ett ökat ansvar för folkrörelser, föreningar och kooperativ (Instructions to a parliamentary commission to consider increased responsibilities for voluntary associations, organizations, and co-operatives)*. Civildepartementet, Stockholm, Directive 1986, p. 17.
Folkrörelseutredningen, 1987. *Ju mer vi är tillsammans, del 1-3 (The more we are together, parts 1–3)*. SOU (Swedish Government Reports), Stockholm, 1987, pp. 33–35.
Folkrörelseutredningen, 1989. *Mål og resultat (Objectives and results)*. SOU (Swedish Government Reports), Stockholm, 1989, p. 39.
Hall, P.D., 1987. Abandoning the rhetoric of independence: Reflections on the nonprofit sector in the post-liberal era. *J. Voluntary Action. Res. 16*, 11–27.
Havel, V., 1978. De maktlösas makt (The power of the powerless). In: Havel, V., *En dåre i Prag (A fool in Prague)*. Symposium, Stockholm.
Hirschman, A.O., 1970. *Exit, Voice, and Loyalty*. Harvard University Press, Cambridge, MA.
Hirschman, A.O., 1981. *Essays in Trespassing*. Cambridge University Press, Cambridge.
Hirschman, A.O., 1982. *Shifting Involvements*. Princeton University Press, Princeton, NJ.
HSB, 1988a. *Boendeservice i HSB – det kooperativa alternativet (Caring for the tenants — the co-operative alternative)*. HSB, Stockholm.
HSB, 1988b. *Kooperativa daghem i HSB - alternativet inom barnomsorg (Cooperative daycare centers in HSB — the alternative childcare)*. HSB, Stockholm.
Johnsson, N., 1989. The privatization of welfare. *Soc. Policy Adm. 23*, 17–29.
Jordan, J., 1989. A multi-stakeholder concept of organizations. In: Quarter, J., Melnyk, (Eds.), *Partners in Enterprise - The Worker Ownership Phenomenon*. Black Rose Books, Montreal, pp. 113–131.
Kooperativa institutet, 1986a. *Föräldrakooperativa daghem en vägledning (Parental daycare cooperatives - A guide)*. Kooperativa institutet, Stockholm.
Kooperativa institutet, 1986b. *Kooperativ stadsdel (The cooperative neighborhood)*. Kooperativa institutet, Stockholm.
Kooperativa institutet, 1989. *Föräldrakooperativa daghem – den tredje vägen inom barnomsorg (Parental daycare co-operatives the third alternative in child care)*. Kooperativa instituet, Stockholm.
Kramer, R., 1981. *Voluntary Agencies in the Welfare State*. University of California Press, Berkeley, CA.
Kramer, R., 1990a. Nonprofit social services and the welfare state: Some research considerations. In: Anheier, H., Seibel, W. (Eds.), *The Third Sector:*

Comparative Studies of Nonprofit Organizations. de Gruyter, Berlin, pp. 255–267.

Kramer, R., 1990b. Voluntary organizations in the welfare state on the threshold of the 90's. Paper presented at the London School of Economics, November 29, 1989

Kulle, S., 1991. *Government and the Voluntary Sector in Norway in the Post War Period*. EGOS Conference Paper, Vienna.

Lindkvist, L., 1990. *Arbetskooperation (Worker cooperatives)*. Nordic Council of Ministers and Kooperativa institutet, Stockholm.

Lindkvist, L., Westenholz, A. (Eds.), 1987. *Medarbetarägda företag i Norden (Employee-owned companies in the Nordic countries)*. Nordic Council of Ministers, Stockholm.

Marin, B., Kenis, P., 1989. *Managing AIDS – A Project Description*. European Centre, Vienna.

Nielsen, K., 1989. Flexible adjustment and political stability: The terms of the debate. *Scand. Political Stud. 12*, 297–313.

Nielsen, K., Pedersen, O.K., 1989. Is small still flexible – An evaluation of recent trends in Danish politics. *Scand. Political Stud. 12*, 343–372.

Pestoff, V., 1989. Organisationernas medverkan och förhandlingar i svensk konsumentpolitik (Organizational participation and negotiations in Swedish consumer policy). In: Nielsen, K., Pedersen, O.K. (Eds.), *Forhandlingsøkonomi i Norden*. DJØF, Copenhagen, pp. 102–139.

Pestoff, V., 1990a. Nonprofit organizations and consumer policy: The Swedish model. In: Anheier, H., Seibel, W. (Eds.), *The Third Sector: Comparative Studies of Nonprofit Organizations*. de Gruyter, Berlin, pp. 77–91.

Pestoff, V., 1990b. Kooperation och sociala tjänster (Co-operation and social services), *Ombyggnad pågår! Om kooperativ utveckling inom den offentliga sektorn*. Kooperative Institutet, Stockholm.

Pestoff, V., 1991a. *Between Markets and Politics. Co-operatives in Sweden*. Campus, Frankfurt.

Pestoff, V., 1991b. *Social service i kooperativ regi — ett alternativ till privatisering (Social service in a co-operative framework — An alternative to privatization)*. Föreningen Kooperativa Studier, Stockholm.

Pestoff, V., 1992. *Towards a new Swedish model: From neo-cooperatist to neoliberal priorities for the welfare state*. Academy of Economics, Cracow.

Pestoff, V., 1994. Beyond exit and voice in social services: Citizens as co-producers. In: Vidal , I. (Ed.), *Delivering Welfare: Repositioning Non-profit and Cooperative Action in Western European Welfare States*. CIES and University Autonomous of Barcelona, Barcelona, p. 6.

Pestoff, V., 1995. Local economic democracy and multi-stakeholder cooperatives. *J. Rural Cooperation*, *23*, 151–168.

Pestoff, V., 1998. *Beyond the Market and State. Social Enterprises and Civil Democracy in a Welfare Society*. Ashgate, Aldershot, UK and Brookfield, NJ, USA.

Pestoff, V., Ronit, K., 1990. *Changing environments and European integration*. University of Stockholm, Department of Business Administration, Stockholm.

Pestoff, V., Walden Laing, D., 1990. *Managing AIDS in Sweden*. University of Stockholm, Department of Business Administration, Stockholm.

Rovira, J., 1990. The role of nonprofit organizations in the Spanish healthcare market. In: Anheier, H., Seibel, W. (Eds.), *The Third Sector: Comparative Studies of Nonprofit Organizations*. de Gruyter, Berlin, pp. 333–345.
SAF-Tidning, Nov. 6, 1990. Interview with SAF Chairman, Ulf Laurin.
Salamon, L., 1987. On market failure, voluntary failure, and third party government: Towards a theory of government-nonprofit relations in the modern welfare state. *J. Voluntary Action. Res. 16*, 20–49.
Streeck, W., Schmitter, P., 1985. Community, market, state – and associations? Streeck, W., Schmitter, P., *Private Interest Government: Beyond Market and State*. Sage, London, pp. 1–29.
Stryjan, Y., 1989. *Why does established cooperation need new cooperation?* University of Stockholm, Department of Business Administration, Stockholm.
Stryjan, Y., 1990. *Cooperatives in a changing world: Membership, organizational strategies, and adaptation*. University of Stockholm, Department of Business Administration, Stockholm.
Svenska Dagbladet, Nov. 5, 1990. Interview with SAF Chairman, Ulf Laurin.
Szulkin, R., 1989. *Privat eller offentlig (Private or public)?*. Swedish Institute for Social Research, Stockholm.
Walden Laing, D., Eads, M., 1991. *Managing AIDS in Sweden*. Conference paper, Vienna.
Walzer, M., 1990. *The civil society*. The Gunnar Myrdal Lecture, Stockholm.
William-Olsson, I., 1988. *Vilka tar ansvar för barnomsorgen (Who takes the responsibility for childcare)?*. Lärarhögskolan, Stockholm.
Zan, S., 1982. *La cooperazione in Italia*. De Donato coop, Bari.
Zan, S., 1988. The social responsibility of consumer co-operatives, Stockholm. Paper presented at *the ICA World Congress*, July 1–4, 1988.

3 Democratizing Medical and Healthcare

The Japanese Example

Nobel Laureate Kenneth Arrow argued that market failure in healthcare leads to societal efforts to fill the gap and regarded nonprofit healthcare in the U.S.A. as an illustration of this. Based on semi-structured interviews, five healthcare providers in Japan were compared in terms of their relationship with the government and the ability to provide a democratic alternative. This overview concluded that Arrow's assumptions about the medical industry in the U.S.A. appeared to hold true in Japan at the beginning of the 21st Century. However, it also showed that society could either act to fill this gap on the behest of the government and public authorities or through citizens' initiatives to engage civil society in healthcare provision. Arrow also noted the asymmetric information relations between users and professionals in the healthcare sector. This study found a unique example of an organization actively engaging its members in maintaining their own health and turning them into co-producers of healthcare. This embodies the potential for better quality services at a lower cost. This chapter previously appeared in *A Democratic Architecture for the Welfare State* (Pestoff, 2008).

A Introduction: Markets or Other Social Institutions

Nobel Laureate Kenneth Arrow maintained that, when markets fail to achieve an optimal state, society will recognize the gap to some extent, and non-market social institutions will arise to bridge it (1963: 947). Furthermore, he contended that the special structural characteristics of the medical-care market in the U.S.A. were largely attempts to overcome the lack of optimality due to the lack of a market for taking suitable risks and the imperfect marketability of information. As a result, there was an overwhelming predominance of nonprofit over proprietary hospitals in the U.S.A. In 1958, only 3% of hospital beds were in for-profit hospitals compared with 30% that were in voluntary nonprofits, while the remaining two-thirds were in federal, state and local hospitals (ibid.: 950, fn. no. 20).

Arrow argued that the special character of the medical industry in the U.S.A. was a result of the necessity of trust in the relationship between the patient and physician, where the latter cannot appear as if they were maximizing their income at every moment. Thus, they avoid the stigma of appearing to profit-maximize in order to maintain trust. Arrow states, that '[t]he very word profit is a signal that denies the trust relations in the medical industry' (ibid.: 965).

Osborne and his colleagues recently analyzed the challenge of change in the contemporary Japanese voluntary and nonprofit sector (2003) with particular reference given to developments after the *Hanshin Awaji* Earthquake in January, 1995 (Makoto, 2003). Osborne emphasizes the importance of distinguishing between old and new style voluntary non-profit organizations in Japan, where the former are institutionalized, but the latter remain non-institutionalized. Referring to Deguchi (2001), Osborne (2003) argues that institutionalization means voluntary non-profit organizations are highly dependent on the state for their very existence, while non-institutionalized voluntary nonprofit organizations are very much a product of local communities and independent initiatives. However, the latter have problems securing stable funding and do not have a formal relationship with the government because of their lack of legal status. Based on Buddhist traditions of mutual aid, the Japanese voluntary sector, nevertheless, has been vertically integrated and inter-dependent with the state. Young argues that Japan, to this day, maintains a nonprofit sector that is mostly guided, controlled or closely coordinated by government, and is therefore often seen as an extension of the public sector (2000). Thus, Japan appears most strongly oriented toward the complementary relationship between the government and nonprofit sector, and nonprofit organizations appear as agents in a principal-agent relationship (ibid.: 168). However, Osborne maintains that the Nonprofit Organization Law of 1998 and the Long-Term Care Insurance Law of 2000 are helping to rectify this situation and provide the newer voluntary nonprofit organizations with greater legitimacy (Osborne, 2003: 8).

Nearly 40 years ago, A. Hirschman (1970) initiated a discussion of 'exit' and 'voice' as alternative consumer responses to decline in the performance of firms, organizations and states, and as alternatives for improving the quality of goods and services. 'Exit' is a typical market response, where disappointed customers change their patronage to other suppliers of the goods or services they purchase. 'Voice' is a typical political response, where customers verbally express their disappointment about poor quality, either individually or collectively (ibid.). Voice can either be expressed as complaints or as suggestions for improvement (Stryjan, 1989; Pestoff, 1994).

In his reflections on the reaction to the initial discussion of exit and voice, Hirschman (1981) notes that consumer and producer ignorance about products or services – particularly, new or very complicated products or services – also motivate voice. Consumers often have clear preferences about their food tastes and readily use exit to express their preferences. However, expressing preferences about welfare services – like childcare, education, eldercare, healthcare, etc. – which are of uncertain quality both for the consumers and producers require more voice.

In this case, an active and constructive dialog between consumers and producers is necessary in order to improve the quality of the goods or services. Similarly, with products or services where there is highly disproportionate knowledge between sellers and buyers of such goods or services, such as medical care, voice has an important role to play in improving service quality. Furthermore, the demand for new services may arise more rapidly than the ability to meet it or the knowledge of how to satisfy it. Under such circumstances, it is not only a question of consumer redress, but also of educating both consumers and producers and providing them with as much information as possible about their expectations and performance. Voice provides much more information about performance and is much richer in detail than exit (ibid.).

Voice, together with the repeated encounter and continuous interaction between consumers and producers, is central to the process of quality improvements. Recognizing consumers as co-producers shifts our focus from the traditional transactions and exchanges between producers and consumers to their interaction (Wickström, 1993: 5–6). The focus on the interactions between producers and consumers also shifts attention to establishing long-term relations between them. This carries with it three major potential benefits (i.e. better quality products and services and a shorter time required to develop new products or services and at lower costs) (ibid.: 8–11).

In complex societies, there is a division of labor, and most persons are engaged in full-time production of goods and services as regular producers. However, individual consumers or groups of consumers may also contribute to the production of goods and services as consumer-producers. This mixing may occur directly or indirectly. If co-production occurs, then it takes place as a result of technological, economic and institutional or political influences (Parks et al., 1981 [1999]). Technology determines whether there are production functions for a service where both regular and consumer-producer activities contribute to the output. Economic considerations determine whether it is efficient to mix regular and consumer-producer activities to provide the service. Institutional considerations determine whether appropriate mixing is permitted in situations where co-production is technically feasible and economically efficient and whether mixing is discouraged where it is inefficient (ibid.: 1002). According to Ostrom (1996 [1999]), all public goods and services are potentially produced by the regular producer and by those who are frequently referred to as the client. However, the term 'client' is a passive term – indicating that they are acted upon. Co-production, by contrast, implies that citizens can play an active role in producing public goods and services of consequence to them (ibid.: 347).

The classical public health model is based on the premise that ordinary people are passive, unknowledgeable and in need of help and guidance from above. The promotion of public health becomes an expert activity and is based on a top-down approach. In this model, it is not the sick, the handicapped, the unemployed and the homeless who are a source of information. Rather, outside experts – like doctors – provide the answers instead. Once the experts say 'what is what', then bureaucrats step in to administer the prescribed solutions. Fountain observes that the private sector makes considerable efforts to condition consumer expectations about the nature of the service encounter (2000). She quotes Heskett et al. (1990) to illustrate that '[t]he medical profession has done a masterful job of enhancing the value of service perception by conditioning prospective patients to expect to be treated as small children, [they are] told little and accept much of what happens to them in faith, and [should] not be disappointed with failures to correct medical problems' (ibid.: 59).

By contrast, a popular health model, according to Starrin (1997), starts with everyone being an expert, each in their own way. In this case, increasing everyone's own resources is most important as well as increasing everyone's competence to help deepen democracy and improve their health conditions. In the former model, negative developments are supposed to be stopped or hindered; in the latter, something positive is developed – resources, competence and equality (Levi, 2000). However, Lundåsen (2005) notes that Sweden initiated a new National Public Health Policy in 2003. Its opening paragraph is devoted to Participation and Influence in Society, which is now considered a basic precondition for public health. Therefore, it deserves to be included as a separate goal in its own right (ibid). Whether this is the start of a new chapter in Swedish public health policy or is merely rhetoric remains, of course, an empirical question.

Healthcare is always problematic, especially for the very poor. A popular health model stresses the primacy of autonomous healthcare. Scientific medicine in very poor areas must be regarded as only one possible approach to health and sickness. Werner's book, *Where There is No Doctor, A Village Healthcare Handbook* (1977 [2003]) is perhaps the best-known manual for healthcare in very poor communities. His approach emphasizes the following:

- Healthcare is not just everyone's right, but it is everyone's responsibility,
- Informal self-care should be the main goal of any health program or activity,
- Ordinary people provided with clear, simple information can prevent and treat most common health problems in their own homes – earlier, cheaper and often better than can doctors,
- Medical knowledge should not be the guarded secret of a select few, but should be freely shared by everyone,
- People with little formal education can be trusted as much as those with a lot, and they are just as clever, and
- Basic healthcare should not be delivered, but encouraged (Werner, 1977 [2003]).

Werner's approach is clearly one of involving all citizens in maintaining their own health to the greatest possible extent. It focuses on trying to rectify the asymmetry of information between doctors and their patients. Given the growing availability of health and medical information on the internet, this may change gradually in the future – at least in the developed world. Dr. Andrew Weil's manual on *Natural Health, Natural Medicine* (1995 [2004]) is also a welcome effort to inform patients about existing healthcare alternatives.

Japan introduced universal healthcare in 1961 when it established compulsory public medical insurance schemes. In 1973, the Ministry of Health and Welfare[1] introduced major reforms to reduce patients' co-payments. In effect, all patients have access to medical services and are insured to cover most of the costs for this, regardless of where they choose to go for medical services. This not only includes all public providers of medical services, but also the medical providers discussed below.

What role does civil society play in filling the gap noted by K. Arrow? What role does it play in promoting cooperation and co-production between the professional staff of hospitals and their patients of publicly financed healthcare? What role does civil society play in attempting to change the information asymmetry noted by K. Arrow? In order to answer these questions, this chapter compares five 'alternative' or third sector providers of health and medical care in Japan at the turn of the century. They will be compared in terms of their purpose, relations with the government and authorities as well as their attempts to change the asymmetry of information between doctors and patients and promoting a more active role for patients in their own healthcare.

B Methods and Materials

Several voluntary nonprofit organizations provide healthcare services and run hospitals and health clinics in Japan. Some are well known from other countries, like the Japanese Red Cross Society, while others are unique – in particular, the medical cooperatives associated with both the agricultural and consumer cooperative movements of Japan. Their reasons for providing such services to their members vary, but there are clear social motives behind their medical entities.

Most of the materials presented herein were collected in a partial survey of the field of alternative medical and healthcare providers in the spring of 1998 during a sabbatical stay in Kanazawa as a research fellow. They are comprised of both written materials from the relevant organizations and other sources and interviews. Semi-structured interviews were carried out with representatives of some alternative medical care providers in the cities of Kanazawa and Hirosaki, in the Prefectures of Ishikawa and Aomori as well as Saitama Prefecture outside Tokyo. The interviews covered three main areas of interest: 1) a brief description of the organization and their resources – like beds and staff, 2) main goals and challenges currently facing their organizations, and 3) their relations with other providers of medical services and with public authorities. Most interviews were conducted face-to-face, some with the help of an interpreter and lasted for about two hours each. Recent figures for the number of hospitals, beds, staff, etc., from 2004 have been included to update this overview.

The alternative providers of medical and healthcare services included in this survey are the following organizations: 1) The Social Welfare Organization *Saiseikai*, or Imperial Gift Foundation, Inc.; 2) The Japanese Red Cross Society, through its representatives at the Ishikawa Red Cross Society, the Kanazawa Red Cross Hospital (KRCH) and the Kanazawa Red Cross Blood Center; 3) The *Koseiren* or National Welfare Federation of Japanese Agricultural Cooperatives, through their branch in Aomori; 4) The health co-ops of the Japanese Consumer Cooperative Union, through their representatives at the Saitama Medical Cooperative Hospital in the greater Tokyo area and the *Sakura-so* Cooperative Hospital in Hirosaki and finally, 5) the Japanese Federation of Democratic (Proletarian) Medical Institutions or *Min-iren*, through its Honorary President at his office in the *Min-iren* nursing home in Kanazawa.

C A Short Presentation of Alternative Medical Care Providers

The five alternative providers of medical care included in this study together represented about seven percent (7%) of the national capacity of hospital beds already in 1997. Taken together, they ran more than 500 hospitals with 144,000 beds in 2004 or 30,000 more beds than in 1997, with an average size ranging from 167 beds to 439 beds. They employed 220,000 staff members in 2004 or 50,000 more than in 1997. This included doctors, nurses, technical personnel and administrative staff. Table 3.A in the appendix provides more information on these five 'alternative' providers of healthcare in Japan. Next, each medical provider included in this overview is presented briefly.

1 Saiseikai, or the Imperial Gift Foundation

Saiseikai was founded in 1911, at a time of great social unrest, on the initiative of the Emperor Meiji to provide medical care to the needy. After World War II, it became a 'social welfare corporation', with its headquarters in Tokyo and with branch offices in each prefecture. *Saiseikai* has the explicit purpose of establishing and running medical institutions to provide free or low-cost medical care for people with lower income, babies and handicapped persons, aged persons, patients of mental disease and for the training of nurses. It has a clear benevolent or charitable goal. In 2004, it ran 79 hospitals, which represents an increase of five hospitals and more than 2,000 beds since 1997, and a staff of 35,000, which went up by more than 7,000 persons since 1997. The average size of its hospitals was 285 beds in 2004. In 1996, its auxiliary medical facilities included: 13 health clinics, one maternity hospital, 17 health facilities for the elderly, 18 home nursing stations, 32 elderly person's nursing help centers, 19 home nursing help stations and *Saiseikai* boat clinics on 65 islands, etc.

2 *The Japanese Red Cross Society (JRCS)*

The JRCS was first established in 1877 and reestablished as a special medical corporation under the Japanese Red Cross Law of 1952. Both individual and corporate donations to it were and are deductible from income taxes, which provided it with a unique privilege that was not available to other NPOs in Japan at the time. Health services and blood services are the two biggest parts of the JRCS, employing 83.2% and 12.2% of the JRCS paid staff respectively in 1997. In 2004, the JRCS ran 90 hospitals or six fewer than in 1997. It employed nearly 57,000 staff and had more than 39,000 beds, for an average of 439 beds per hospital. This represented a growth of more than 5,200 staff and 16,000 more beds since 1997. The large size of its medical services and blood facilities make the JRCS unique when compared with the RCS in other countries. The historical explanation for this was the close ties between the JRCS and the Japanese Army at the time of the Meiji Restoration. The JRCS's activities in 1996 included disaster relief, medical services, nursing training, social assistance services for children, handicapped and the elderly, the junior Red Cross, various courses, blood services, international co-operation and fundraising. In 1996, the JRCS had 18.7 million members and 4.3 million volunteers in Japan.

In 1974, the *Diet* created blood centers in each prefecture and gave the JRCS a monopoly on organizing them. In Ishikawa, it comes under the Prefecture Office of the Ministry of Health and Welfare. According to the director of the Kanazawa Blood Center (KBC), they have enough voluntary donations to meet the needs of Ishikawa Prefecture. The KBC pays a fee for blood.

Red Cross Society hospitals are financed through their own efforts and donations. The blood facilities and hospitals are run on a for-profit basis, while the international and social welfare activities are run on a non-profit basis. The JRCS gets 1.5 billion Japanese Yen per year in donations, but this is decreasing now. This poses big problems to the Red Cross system of medical care, and half of the hospitals may go bankrupt in the future. Patients spend 'too much time' in the hospital in Japan as compared with Europe. For example, they spend 5–7 days for an appendix operation, in Japan as compared with 1–2 days in Europe, and five weeks for a bypass operation in Japan as compared with 5–7 days in Europe. 'Hospital services in Japan need to be rationalized, we are 20 years behind Europe', according to the director of the KRCH.

The KRCH is building a new section with 120 beds. Once finished, the KRCH will have a total of 300 beds. The old section is 30 years old. Red Cross hospitals were unique when first established 50 years ago, but have lost their principles now. The national health insurance covers everyone, and the fee individual patients pay is the same no matter which hospital they go to. However, in the future, each hospital must be unique, and they must provide rooms with individual beds as in the new section of the KRCH. They must all become specialized in certain specific areas – like diabetes, gynecology, etc.

The Ishikawa Red Cross Society maintains few contacts with the KRCH. In fact, it sees little difference between itself and ordinary hospitals. In their opinion, the KRCH works closely with the local and prefecture governments where it gets most of its funds. According to the representative at the Ishikawa Red Cross, it faces no major problems today, but the flow of volunteers could become problematic. The new Nonprofit Organization Law is not a threat, since they are the only disaster relief organization in Japan (i.e. they have their own niche with long experience and knowledge of it).

3 Koseiren *or the National Welfare Federation of Japanese Agricultural Cooperatives*

The Japanese Agricultural Cooperative Movement (JA) can trace its origin to the beginning of the 20th Century. It was reestablished in 1945. Today, gaining the highest return on its capital is the main goal. It has grown into a multipurpose agricultural cooperative offering supply, marketing, credit, insurance and other services, including health and social services. JA set up the National Welfare Federation of Agricultural Co-ops in 1948 with a specialist organization in each prefecture known as *Koseiren*. It developed at a time and in areas where public practices were inadequate and private practices beyond the financial means of most members. It aims to serve the rural community and its residents with medical services. Already in 1951, it was designated by the government as responsible for the implementation of public health programs in rural areas, and as such entitled to public subsidies and tax concessions. It has the purpose of supporting members' health and their financial and social standing by improving their medical welfare. It performs the important function of providing regular annual health examinations for the rural population. It provides health examinations (for tuberculosis) by traveling clinics, lectures and movies to promote members' health, diet and housing conditions. More than three million farmers and their families receive medical checkups every year.

Koseiren provides various kinds of long-term and low-interest funds to promote the modernization of agricultural institutions and equipment and lobbies for the modernization and improvement of medical institutions – particularly in rural areas. In the beginning, JA ran hospitals in all of the provinces of Japan, but now they cover only about half of them. Each regional JA organization decides what kind of social activities to undertake. According to its local representative in Hirosaki, it had a hospital in Aomori in the 1950s but sold it after a few years later to the municipality. He notes that perhaps it isn't JA's main responsibility to provide healthcare to its members, but it has other social activities in most prefectures. If a region is not enthusiastic about providing healthcare, then its health business does not always do well, and it must eventually sell it.

In 1997, more than two-thirds of *Koseiren* hospitals and health clinics were found in rural towns of 50,000 or fewer inhabitants, while it only operated a single hospital in one of the 13 largest Japanese cities, the *Saku* Hospital in Nagano. This gives it a very clear agricultural and rural profile that it maintains today. In 2004, *Koseiren* ran 122 hospitals and 47 clinics with 46,400 beds and 287 mobile facilities which visited rural areas for checkups or remote areas for primary care. This represented an additional 7,400 staff and 100 more beds than in 2002. That year, they employed 4,009 doctors, 23,456 nurses and 11,539 administrative staff (Kurimoto, 2005a, 2005b). On average, *Koseiren* hospitals had 309 beds in 2004.

At the initiative of the Ministry of Health and Welfare, the Agricultural Cooperative Law was changed about five years ago, permitting JA to undertake social welfare activities. Presently, they are developing eldercare services in most provinces. The local authorities could not meet the growing demand in rural areas, so the Minister of Health and Welfare gave JA the right to educate 'home helpers'. Today, about 60,000 women have qualified to provide such services, and they are mostly farmers' wives. They get certified by JA but provide their services through the municipalities in rural areas. By the end of the 1990s, JA ran 28 home helper stations, four daycare centers for the elderly and 15 nursing homes in Aomori Prefecture. Becoming a home helper provides an education, professional status and income for rural women who often previously lacked all such things.

4 Health Co-ops of the Japanese Consumer Cooperative Union

Consumer cooperative health and medical care can trace its roots to the turbulent years of the 1930s and 1940s when it was part of the opposition to the Japanese wars and imperialism in Asia. It was important during the deprivation of the immediate post-war period. It developed at a time and in areas where public medical services were inadequate and private practices beyond the financial means of most of its members. Its aim is to serve the community and its residents with medical and rehabilitative services while emphasizing preventative services including comprehensive and life-long approaches to healthy living. Health co-ops are independent legal persons who are organized under the Consumers' Livelihood Cooperative Society Law. The people in a community form their own health co-op and run their facilities in order to meet their own health and medical needs. The Japanese Consumer Cooperative Union (JCCU) set up a Medical Co-op Committee in the 1980s to bring all the health co-ops together in one organization. The Medical Co-op Committee established a Medical Co-op Charter of Patients Rights in 1991 that includes: the Right to Know about their own health and/or illness, the Right to Decide, Privacy Rights and the Right to Learn about their own health and/or illness as well as the Right to Receive Medical Treatment.

One distinctive feature of the Japanese health co-ops is that members are expected to play an active role in their own healthcare. Therefore, they normally take their own blood pressure when arriving at a clinic or hospital and then inform the nurse and/or doctor on duty what it was that day, rather than passively being informed about it by the professional providers. Most members probably know both what their blood pressure was on their last visit and what it normally should be – something not often known even by well-educated persons in most other OECD countries. At the grassroots-level, members are encouraged to learn about promoting their own health by joining a *han* group, or a small neighborhood group of between nine and ten members. In 2004, nearly one-quarter of a million active health co-op members belonged to one of 26,127 *han* groups, representing one in ten members in health co-ops. *Han* members attend lectures and courses arranged by local health co-ops. Some go on to become health advisors, who can then lead *han* groups. Today, there are more than 40,000 medical advisors.

Members in the *han* groups, initially with the assistance of nurses and health advisors, learn to conduct self-checks in order to monitor their own health conditions. They keep records of their blood pressure, sugar and salt content in their urine, fat content, etc., using simple devices. If irregularities are found, members will have a health checkup and meet a doctor at a health co-op. These self-monitoring activities provide effective early detection and treatment of illness (Kurimoto, 2004). *Han* groups also discuss their members' basic health conditions, determined by self-monitoring, along with their diet and nutrition, exercise habits and lifestyle, in order to bring them closer into balance with each other. Thus, *han* group members are made aware of their health conditions, which enable them to lead a healthier life. Through their learning and acquired knowledge, users can actively collaborate with healthcare providers to prevent or combat disease, rather than passively leaving their health in the hands of professional providers.

The Saitama Cooperative Hospital opened in 1978 with 74 beds. Since then, it has developed into one of the largest hospitals in southern Saitama Prefecture – with 350 beds and 1,000 outpatients daily in the mid-1990s. The total staff was 450 persons, including 50 doctors and 210 nurses. It amalgamated with three other cooperative hospitals, nine medical clinics and four dental clinics in Saitama Prefecture in the late 1990s, with 156,000 members

– making it the largest health cooperative organization in Japan. Members have a share capital of 5,000 Japanese Yen, while that of staff members is five to ten times as much. Share capital is invested in medical buildings and equipment. The employees of the Saitama Cooperative consider themselves a community hospital serving all the residents of Saitama Prefecture.

The board of the hospital is composed of nearly 40 persons, more than two-thirds of which must be chosen from among the resident members. In addition, Saitama Health Cooperative has 42 directors, nine of which are full-time and must have medical training, while 33 part-time directors are chosen from among members. The combination of different member categories, representation of members on the board and use of members as part-time directors qualify the Saitama Cooperative Hospital as a multi-stakeholder organization.

The CEO of the Saitama Cooperative Hospital feels that breaking the paternalistic approach of traditional medical care is an important task. He notes that few members have direct contact with the cooperative health services unless they are ill. Similarly, there are few opportunities for members to become directly involved in the management of the hospital. However, active and conscious members can participate in community health study groups or a *Han*. They are often women in their 50s to 60s. The staff receives the same wages as in public medical facilities. However, they are not only employees, but most are also members of the health co-op and also have share capital. Volunteers are used by the Saitama hospital. They come in for one day a week between 9:00 a.m. and 3:30 p.m. They are usually either housewives or retired men. They perform mostly nonprofessional tasks, like washing patients' clothes, taking them to the bathroom, etc.

The Ministry of Health and Welfare wanted to greatly expand the number of doctors in Japan. The Ministry asked the Saitama Cooperative Hospital in the early 1990s to play a more important role in providing places to train interns and asked them to accept graduate students in its facility. In 1994, the Saitama Cooperative Hospital agreed to comply with this request. Long-term care insurance for the elderly started in April 2000 to provide social support for the elderly. It opened competition among care service providers, including private nonprofit operators. Many hospitals are now attempting to provide long-term care services, thus strengthening their grip on the so-called medico-social care complex. Health co-ops are among those providing such services but they try to get community participation in forming healthcare-medical welfare networks, which also includes the local authorities. This may result in even wider multi-stakeholder approaches to health and medical care (Kurimoto, 2005a), at the municipal level and, thereby, introduce co-management in the medical system.

In 2004, the healthcare co-ops had nearly 2.5 million members, compared with 1.8 million members in 1996. In 1996, it was established in 38 prefectures and ran 336 hospitals and clinics, most of which were affiliated with the *Min-iren* discussed below. By 2004, the healthcare co-ops ran 76 hospitals and 240 clinics in 40 prefectures with 12,660 beds, or an average size of 167 beds. They had over 25,000 employees – including 1,779 doctors, 9,896 nurses and 13,897 administrative staff. Medical professionals – including doctors, nurses and administration officers – are also members of the health co-ops. Health co-ops seek to create synergy effects by involving different stakeholders in the same organization. Multiple membership categories in the health co-ops result in a user-dominated board of directors. Considering all healthcare co-ops together, there were 2,133 lay members and 710 other members representing professional providers. For example, at the Saitama Medical Co-op in the Tokyo area, 27 board members represent users while ten full-time board members consist of three doctors, one nurse and six executive directors (ibid.). In Hirosaki, the board of *Sakura-so* Cooperative Hospital has 41 members. Twelve of them are chosen by the hospital and its staff, while 29 of them represent the 27 local membership districts. Therefore, cooperative healthcare is managed on a multi-stakeholder basis.

The *Sakura-so* Cooperative Hospital in Hirosaki expressed its economic, political and social goals in the following fashion in 1998. In economic terms, after the year 2000 the new law on eldercare insurance will take effect, but there will not be enough facilities. It plans several new activities-building visiting nurse centers, nursing homes, a network of daycare centers for elder persons; training care managers, consultants and home helpers, adding beds to their hospital, etc. In September, 1998, 20 of their care managers passed the test to be certified. All of this means considerable expansion and investments. Although they opposed many details of the new eldercare insurance, it is better than nothing. It will enlarge their sphere of activities, improve the medical system and can help to democratize medical services. The 52,000 members in Hirosaki are divided into 27 geographic areas or districts, but they are unsure how they will meet the new demands under the new law.

In terms of politics, they note that democracy should take into account the will of the people. The representative functions at the local and regional levels of government are not sufficient. Nonprofit organizations and co-ops need to play a role. *Sakura-so* members are divided into 640 *hans* in Hirosaki. They meet regularly, discuss medical problems, provide members daycare, have distance education about medicine and co-ops, discuss patients' rights, etc. *Sakura-so* thinks of the JCCU medical co-ops as a tool of empowerment and not just a medical organization. In terms of their social issues, they noted that their goal is a socially healthy and sound society. They want to democratize medical services and promote citizen/member involvement in them. They want a healthy society in all areas and want to improve the medical status of the whole population (i.e. they want to promote a healthy nation).

The *Sakura-so* Cooperative Hospital in Hirosaki notes that there are no *Saiseikai*, Red Cross nor *Koseiren* hospitals in Hirosaki. The *Sakura-so* Cooperative Hospital is very active in *Min-iren*. After the war, it was for the poor people and many tenant-farmers had no access to medical care, so they turned to *Min-iren* instead. It cooperates with other hospitals in the prefecture, of which there are six (one prefecture, one co-op and four private hospitals) in practical ways. This includes activities such as rotating emergency *jour* services for 24 hours a day or rotating emergency night services.

The *Sakura-so* Cooperative Hospital also collaborates with prefecture authorities to provide medical education, control hospital services and provide subsidies for emergency services. They also provide trainee courses and hold annual meetings, etc. There is also an Association of Doctors at the local and prefecture-level, where doctors from all types of hospitals meet regularly.

5 The Min-iren *or Federation of Democratic Medical Institutions*

The *Min-iren* can also trace its roots to the turbulent years of the 1930s and its opposition to the wars and Japanese imperialism in Asia. It was (re) established in 1953. According to the Japanese Ministry of Health and Welfare's Welfare White Paper in 1990, the *Min-iren* had 1.5% of all sickbeds, 1.3% of the medical doctors, 2.3% of all nurses and 2.2% of all radiographers in the country – making it an important provider of medical and healthcare in Japan. In 2004, it organized 151 hospitals, 592 clinics (including 45 dental clinics), 81 insurance pharmacies and 64 other affiliated organizations, such as nurse training schools, nursery schools, etc. This represents a decrease of three hospitals since 1993, but the number of clinics grew by more than 200 during the past ten years. Nearly half of their affiliates were health co-ops, while the rest of them were public or private medical care providers. Today, *Min-iren* organizes medical facilities employing more than 4,000 doctors, 22,000 nurses, 10,000 administrators, together with other specialists, for a total staff of 62,287 persons. By 2005, the number of beds reached nearly 27,000. The member hospitals and clinics can take a variety of legal forms, but most of them are either medical care corporations or consumer cooperative corporations.

Patients of *Min-iren* are grouped according to their illness – like cancer, rheumatism, etc. – and into 147 groups. They are organized into users associations, called *Kyodo soshiki*, that is comprised of 3 million people – about 70% of which come from the health co-ops in the JCCU. Patients' active participation is encouraged, and they are invited as observers to General Assemblies and district conferences of *Min-iren*. There are also 57,000 patients actively organized for ideological support of the *Min-iren* and its peace movement.

The *Min-iren* faces four important problems in the future: 1) Out of a total staff of 62,000 working in *Min-iren* hospitals, there are 2–3,000 new persons employed each year. How does one educate them into the *Min-iren* principles? 2) Capitalism is unfavorable to *Min-iren* and its principles, but they must survive and must keep in good financial shape. How do they finance the investments needed to improve their service? *Min-iren* borrows money from their patients; 3) There is a shortage of doctors in *Min-iren;* 4) Both doctors and patients must participate in medical care. As its honorary President, Dr. Shozo Azami's motto was: 'Medical activity should be a common or joint activity, involving both the doctors and patients'.

Min-iren has close relations with the HCA of the JCCU. Most health co-ops belong to *Min-iren* (94%). It has no established relations with the Japanese Workers' Cooperative Union, but the JRCS gives *Min-iren* a contribution of 100,000 Japanese Yen per year. They have no relations with *Koseiren* or *Saiseikai*, nor do they have systematic relations with prefecture or municipal medical hospitals or clinics, but they maintain ad hoc relations in case of emergency, like heart attacks. However, their personal relations with the medical corps and individual providers are cordial.

Min-iren emphasizes that they receive no official support from municipal or prefecture authorities, but they are an important provider of medical services, with more outpatients per day than either the Red Cross or *Saiseikai*. They also do not maintain formal relations with any political party, although the medical policy of the Communist Party is close to that of *Min-iren*, especially on eldercare. In general elections, the staff of *Min-iren* generally support the Japanese Communist Party, and many *Min-iren* doctors run as candidates for the JCP at the municipal and county levels.

D Different Social Profiles and Relations with Public Authorities

These five providers of alternative medical care in Japan all have distinct social profiles. The *Saiseikai* was founded by the Emperor at the beginning of the 1900s to provide medical care to poor citizens who could not afford it. Given both its origin and focus group, it maintains a clear social profile related to benevolent and charitable activities. The Japanese Red Cross Society demonstrates a clear managerial approach today in providing healthcare. It emphasizes strategic management and the need for medical providers to find their right niche. The *Koseiren* is a part of the Japanese Agricultural Cooperative Movement (JA), and, unlike other alternative providers herein, medical care does not comprise its main activity. Some of the JA's regional branches provide medical services to members today while others do not. However, eldercare

Relations with:		with special	patient groups
		no	yes
Governmental	strong	JRCS, KRCH, BCs	*Saiseikai, Koseiren*
Authorities	weak	--------	HCA, Min-iren

Figure 3.1 Relations with Governmental Authorities and Patient Groups.
Source: Pestoff, 2008, p. 151.

insurance and services provide a new field of social welfare for JA. Its training courses for women as home helpers to elder persons in rural areas opens new possibilities for rural women to get an education, profession and income of their own. This new development could provide a major impetus to change in otherwise very conservative rural settings.

The health co-ops are unique in the sense that they actively involve their users/members in the healthcare process as agents of change. Users gain knowledge about their own and others' health, which facilitates more effective collaboration between users and medical care providers toward the common goal of enhancing citizens' health and their quality of life. Their users/members become co-producers of their own healthcare. Health co-ops are also governed as multi-stakeholder organizations. Thus, they promote democracy in medical care in two different ways: first by bringing greater parity into the asymmetric relation between users and providers or staff and patients and second in the democratic governing of healthcare co-ops. Finally, *Min-iren* actively promotes values of equality and democracy among its members who are mainly the professional staff of health co-ops and other hospitals.

These five alternative providers of healthcare in Japan demonstrate different relations with public authorities and with healthcare clients or patients. Some of them have strong relations to the Ministry of Health and Welfare or other parts of the government, while others have weak ties to public authorities. A few of them are focused on providing healthcare to specific groups in society, while others serve the public in general. These factors reflect their goals and may impact how they meet future challenges in healthcare, as seen in Figure 3.1.

From the times of the Meiji Reformation, the Japanese Red Cross Society enjoyed a special relation to public authorities. JRCS was recreated through a special law after the war, and it was given a public monopoly to manage blood centers – again through a special law. Moreover, only the JRCS had the right to receive tax-deductible donations until recently. Thus, it could be argued that society has recognized a gap where the market does not achieve an optimal state in providing medical care, and it has taken steps to bridge the gap with other social institutions. However, turning to the other dimension in the figure, the JRCS no longer has a special focus on a particular group in society, as it previously did in the military. Today, it provides medical care to all persons living in Japan.

The *Saiseikai*, on the other hand, was started by the Emperor Meiji in 1911 with a focus on providing medical care to persons with a low or meager income, etc. Therefore, it was also started to fill a gap where healthcare was otherwise unavailable. They have a clear benevolent relation with their patients. Similarly, the *Koseiren* was enlisted by the Ministry of Health and Welfare to provide medical care in rural areas at the end of the war and again, more recently, to help expand provisions for the new insurance in rural areas, as well as home helpers for elderly persons in such areas. It is given a monopoly-like situation in providing healthcare in rural areas of Japan, where the government cannot provide such services and where no market alternatives exist. Both of these organizations have special relations with the authorities and are an institutionalized part of the Japanese nonprofit sector.

All three of these medical providers – the JRCS, *Saiseikai* and *Koseiren* – clearly provide examples of what Arrow referred to as social institutions arising to fill the gap where the market fails to provide an optimal situation. In all three cases, the state, either through the Emperor or more recently the Ministry of Health and Welfare, intervened to fill a gap or took initiative to create and encourage medical institutions to fill a perceived gap in existing medical services. Thus, Japanese society worked through the government rather than civil society to fill the gap left by the market.

Concerning the activities of both the health cooperatives and the *Min-iren* as healthcare providers, the gap was filled by civil society rather than the government. Therefore, they are found in another part of the figure above. They have weak ties with public authorities, and both organizations focus on the same group of clients or patients – the urban working class. They also appear to overlap extensively with each other, at least in terms of their professional or medical members. However, *Min-iren* seems to have more of a macro and ideological perspective on healthcare, while the health co-ops have a more micro perspective. Accordingly, *Min-iren* proposes to reform medical care in Japan at the macro-level, while the health co-ops focus mainly on providing ordinary members with greater information about their own healthcare through relevant education, self-monitoring and discussion in small *han* groups.

Thus, the health co-ops also function as democratic multi-stakeholder organizations that can bring together both patients and professionals in decision-making about the running of the healthcare entities and can facilitate their working together in providing better healthcare, thereby bridging the information asymmetry between them. Providing ordinary members – or patients – with voice in the governance of their own healthcare and the medical institutions they belong to and run jointly also help provide a check on any potential opportunistic behavior by the professionals and the exploitation of existing information asymmetries. In the making, many members of the health co-ops are turned into active co-producers of their own health rather than retaining the status as passive consumers or patients of purely professional medical care. This helps place them closer to the popular healthcare model than the traditional public healthcare model. This is, by all accounts, no simple matter; rather, it is one that clearly facilitates the involvement of ordinary members in their own healthcare and the democratization of medical care.

E Conclusion and Discussion

From this overview of alternative medical care in Japan, we can conclude that Arrow's assumptions about the special structural characteristics of the medical industry in the U.S.A. also appear to hold true in Japan more than 40 years later. Arrow claims that society will recognize the gap in healthcare provision and non-market institutions will arise to fill the gap. However, we found that society could either act to fill this gap on the behest of the government and public authorities – as observed with *Saiseikai*, the Red Cross Society and *Koseiren* – or through direct citizens' initiatives by engaging civil society in medical care provision, as seen in the health co-ops of the JCCU and *Min-iren*.

The distinction made by Osborne (2003) between the older or institutionalized voluntary organizations and the newer or non-institutionalized ones in Japan was partly born out by alternative medical care providers. The three more institutional providers were clearly dependent on the state and appeared to be an extension of the public sector provision of medical care, while the two non-institutional ones were kept at arms-length by public authorities. The type and scope of services provided by the former providers were clearly dependent on the sanction and leadership of the government and their services were vertically integrated into and interdependent with the Ministry of Health, Labor and Welfare. However, neither of the latter providers corresponds closely with the fragmented, local or spontaneous community developments after the *Hanshin Awaji* Earthquake. Rather than view healthcare users as passive consumers who must choose between various alternative service providers, the non-institutionalized providers of medical care promote values clearly related to citizenship and democracy. Moreover, they are dependent on the sanction and leadership of two relatively established and institutionalized popular movements, dating back to before World War II. However, both the

Japanese Consumer Cooperative Union and the Japanese Communist Party belonged to the opposition to the ruling Liberal Party during most of the post-war period.

Concerning the asymmetric information relation between users and professionals in the medical industry as noted by Arrow, we also found a unique case of an organization actively attempting to change this asymmetry by promoting greater member knowledge about their own health and, thereby, also promoting greater member influence and democracy in medical care. Thus, we found that many members of the health co-ops were systematically educated about healthcare issues. This approach emphasizes that healthcare is not just everyone's right, but is also their responsibility. Health co-ops attempt to involve all members actively in maintaining their own health to the greatest possible extent. Members are thereby turned into co-producers of their own healthcare and also provided with an organized voice in the management of co-op medical services. This is based on a medical philosophy that is closer to popular healthcare than the public healthcare approach. This is not a simple matter; rather, it could serve as an inspiration and model for democratizing medical care elsewhere in the world.

In particular, the health co-ops demonstrate that, in a country where mutual aid is an essential component of society, the unitary state has lost the initiative in developing new services demanded by some citizens. The state is unable to respond to all the needs of an increasingly heterogeneous and divergent society. Healthcare co-ops are able to give voice to a growing minority and to other disenfranchised people by expanding the range of services available to meet emerging social needs due to demographic changes. Some citizens want to play a more active role in their own healthcare today. This was also true in part for the agricultural co-ops' provision of training and services for eldercare under the new Long Term Care Insurance Law, even if it was initiated and supported and led by the Ministry of Health, Labor and Welfare.

The voice of members in the health co-ops is institutionalized through democratic channels and multi-stakeholder representation of both producers and consumers of healthcare services. This is central to providing members with influence and participation in the process of quality improvements. Such democratic institutions carry with them the major potential benefits of better quality healthcare services at a lower cost. However, the professional and patient/consumer-members are highly interdependent on each other to achieve high-quality healthcare services. Neither the professional nor the consumer-members can supply high-quality healthcare alone: Inputs from both are necessary. However, without the institutional incentives to both groups of producers, co-production would not be possible.

Note

1 Became the Ministry of Health, Labor and Welfare in January, 2001.

References

a) Published materials

Arrow, K., 1963. Uncertainty and the welfare economics of medical care. *Am. Econ. Review. 53/5*, 941–973.

Deguchi, M., 2001. The Distinction Between Institutionalized and Non-Institutionalized NPOs. New Policy Initiatives and Non-Profit Organizations in Japan. In: Kendall, J., Anheier, H. (Eds.), *Third Sector Policy at Crossroads. An International Nonprofit Analysis*. Routledge, London, pp. 153–167.

Heskett, J., Sasser, W., Hart, C., 1990. *Service Breakthroughs: Changing the Rules of the Game*. The Free Press, New York.

Hirschman, A.O., 1970. *Exit, Voice & Loyalty. Responses to Decline in the Performance of Firms, Organizations and States*. Harvard University Press, Cambridge, MA & London.

Hirschman, A.O., 1981. *Essays in Trespassing*. Cambridge University Press, Cambridge, London & New York.

Fountain, J., 2000. Paradoxes of public service customer service. *Governance: Int. J. Policy Adm. 14/1*, 55–73.

Kurimoto, A., 2004. How Social Economy Can Improve User Access and the Capability of Health Services – the Case of Health Co-ops. *CCIJ N*. No. 43, Dec. 2004 1–7, Tokyo.

Kurimoto, A., 2005a. What Can Co-operative Health and Social Care Offer? Ch. 19 In: Tsuzuki, C. et al. (Eds.), *The Emergence of Global Citizenship: Utopian Ideas, Cooperative Movements and the Third Sector*. Robert Owens Society of Japan, Tokyo.

Kurimoto, A., 2005b. How Health Care Systems Cope with Aging Populations: The Japanese Case. Consumer Co-operative Institute of Japan, Tokyo.

Levi, L., 2000. *Folkhälsa makt o. demokrati*. LO Folk Styr, LOs Demokratiutredning, Stockholm.

Lundåsen, S., 2005. *Frivilliga insatser och hälsa*. Statens folkhälsoinstitut, Stockholm. R2005:47.

Makoto, I., 2003. The voluntary response to the Hanshin Awaji earthquake. A trigger for the development of the voluntary non-profit sector in Japan. Ch. 3 In: Osborne, Stephen (Ed.), *The Voluntary and Non-profit Sector in Contemporary Japan: The Challenge of Change*. Routledge Curzon, Taylor & Francis Group, London & New York.

Osborne, S.P. (Ed.), 2003. *The Voluntary and Non-Profit Sector in Japan. The Challenge of Change*. Routledge Curzon, Taylor & Francis Group, London & New York.

Ostrom, E., 1996 [1999]. Crossing the great divide: Co-production, Synergy & Development. *World Dev. 24/6*, 1073–1087. Reprinted in 1999 as Ch. 15, *Polycentric Governance and Development. Readings from the Workshop in Political Theory and Policy Analysis*, McGinnis, Michael D. (Ed.); Ann Arbor, MI: Univ. of Michigan Press.

Parks, R.B., P.C. Baker, L. Kiser, R. Oakerson, E. Ostrom, V. Ostrom, S.L. Perry, M.B. Vandivort, G.P. Whitaker (Eds.), 1981 [1999]. Consumers as co-producers of public services: Some economic and institutional considerations. *Policy Stud. J.* 9, 1001–1011, reprinted in 1999 as Ch. 17 in *Local Public Economies. Readings from the Workshop in Political Theory and Policy Analysis*, McGinnis, Michael D. (Ed.); Ann Arbor, MI: Univ. of Michigan Press.

Pestoff, V. 1994 [2018]. Beyond Exit & Voice in Social Services – Citizens as Co-Producers. In: P. 6, Vidal, I. (Ed.), *Delivering Welfare – repositioning non-profit and co-operative action in western European welfare states.* CIES, Barcelona. reprinted in 2018, V. Pestoff, *Co-production and Public Service Management. Citizenship, Democracy and Public Service Management.* London & New York: Routledge.

Pestoff, V., 1998. *Beyond the Market and State: Social Enterprises and Civil Democracy in a Welfare Society.* Ashgate, Aldershot, UK, Brookfield, USA and Singapore.

Pestoff, V., 1998a. An Overview of Alternative Medical and Health Care Services in Japan. Stockholm: unpublished report.

Pestoff, V., 2008. *A Democratic Architecture for the Welfare State.* Routledge, London & New York.

Starrin, B., 1997. Empowerment som tankemodell. In: Forsberg, I., Starrin, B. (Eds.), *Frigörande kraft – Empowerment som modell i skola, omsorg och arbetsliv.* Gothia, Stockholm.

Stryjan, Y., 1989. *Impossible Organizations - Self-Management and Organizational Reproduction.* Greenwood Press, Westport, CT.

Weil, A., 1995. [2004]. *Natural Health, Natural Medicine. A Comprehensive Manual for Wellness and Self-Care.* Houghton Mifflin Co, Boston & New York.

Werner, D., 1977. [2003]. *Where There is No Doctor, a Village Health Care Handbook.* The Hesperian Foundation, Berkeley.

Wickström, S., 1993. *The Customer as Co-Producer, Studies in Action and Enterprise.* Dept. of Business Administration, Stockholm, PP1993, 1.

Young, D.R., 2000. Alternative models of government-nonprofit sector relations: Theoretical and international perspectives. *Nonprofit Voluntary Sect. Q.* 29/1, 149–172.

b) Interviews and personal correspondence

Min-iren Nursing Home in Kanazawa on 26 May, 1998, interview with Dr. Shozo Azami, Honorary President of *Min-iren* and Dr. Kawanishi.

Ishikawa Red Cross Society in Kanazawa on 28 May, 1998, interview Mr. Norika Kobayshi, together with Mr. Yasushige Sano.

Kanazawa Red Cross Hospital (KRCH) on 28 May, 1998, interview with Dr. H. Matumoto, Director of KRCH.

Kanazawa Blood Centre on 28 May, 1998, interview with the Director.

Sakura-so Cooperative Hospital in Hirosaki, 1 June, 1998; interview with Dr. Ryoji Arituka, Chair & Psychiatrist at the mental hospital, plus three other

unspecified staff, together with Prof. Kensaku Kanda and Mr. Alvar Hugosson, Faculty of Agriculture, Hirosaki University.
Aomori Prefecture Agricultural Co-op, on 4 June, 1998, interview with Mr. Narita, together with Prof. Kensaku Kanda and Mr. Alvar Hugosson, Faculty of Agriculture, Hirosaki University.
Dr. Alvar Hugosson, Faculty of Agriculture, Hirosaki University, e-mail on 13 March 2006.
Professor Hideo Ishizuka, e-mail on 9 March, 2006.

c) Organizational documents

History of *Min-iren*.
Explanation of the General Principals of *Min-iren*.
Annual General Reports of the Red Cross of Kanazawa, 1984/85–1994/95.

Appendix 3

Table 3.A Comparison of Alternative Medical Care Providers in Japan, 2004

Item/Org.:	*Saiseikai*	*Red Cross*	*Koseiren*	*HeW CO-OP*	*Min-iren***
(Re-)Establ.	1911	1877(1952)	1945	1990*	1953
Prefectures	all	all	Na.	40	all
Hospitals	79	90	122	76	151
Clinics	10	2	47	240	592
Home Visiting Nursing Station	42	50	102	Na.	379
Doctors	Na.	Na.	4,009	1,779	4,059
Nurses	Na.	Na.	23,456	9,896	22,072
Admin. staff	Na.	Na.	11,539	13,897	10,471
Total staff	35,218	56,751	46,400	25,572	62,287
Beds	22,546	39,511	37,734	12,660	26,793
Av. No. Beds	285	439	309	167	177
Members	none	18.7 mil.	Na.	2.5 mil.	3.0 mil.
Volunteers	Na.	4.3 mil.	Na.	40,000+	Na.

Source: Pestoff, 2008, p. 300; *HeW CO-OP Japan was established in 1990 as a separate organization for the health co-ops associated with the Japanese Consumer Co-op Union (JCCU). Some of them had provided healthcare services since before World War II; ** figures for 2005; Na. = not available.

4 Co-production in Public Service Delivery and Healthcare

Attempts to understand and facilitate citizen/user participation in the provision of public services led to an explosion of interest in co-production. Today, it encompasses a variety of phenomena, contexts and levels, and it is studied by different disciplines that employ a variety of approaches. Co-production in public services and patient participation in healthcare have different origins, focus and definitions, and there is a myriad of terms, concepts, definitions and perspectives of this phenomenon. There is no right or wrong approach to studying co-production or putting it into practice. Rather, these diverse perspectives often reflect the underlying cultural, social and political values of researchers and practitioners. However, co-production can either refer to individual patient participation or collective co-production. Much of the literature in healthcare focuses on individual patients and describes the relationship between clinicians and patients as a meeting of two experts. This puts heavy emphasis on the ability and agency of individual patients, but it ignores their limitations. Collective co-production embraces health literacy outreach and the importance of social support for facilitating both the agency and the ability of patients to participate in healthcare.

A Co-production

The concept of co-production was originally developed by Nobel Laureate Elinor Ostrom and her colleagues at the Workshop in Political Theory and Policy Analysis at Indiana University during the 1970s to describe and analyze the role of citizens in the provision of public services (Parks *et al.*, 1981; Ostrom, 1996). They struggled with the dominant theories of urban governance that recommended the massive centralization of public services, but they found no support for claims of the benefits of large bureaucracies. Moreover, they also realized that the production of services was difficult without the active participation of the actual persons receiving them (*ibid.*). Accordingly, they developed the term co-production to describe the potential relationship that could exist between the 'regular producers' – like street-level police officers, school teachers or health workers – and their 'clients' who wanted to be transformed by the service into safer, better educated or healthier people (*ibid.*).

Co-production is often considered a partnership between citizens and public service providers that is essential for meeting a growing number of economic, political and social challenges in the 21st Century. They include, among other things, improving the efficiency and effectiveness of public services in times of financial strain, increasing the legitimacy of the public sector after decades of undermining its ability with the spread of New Public Management, finding viable solutions for meeting the growing needs of aging populations in many parts of the world and renewing democracy at the grassroots level, in light of the growing threat posed by populism in many advanced democracies.

In spite of these serious challenges, neither the government nor citizens can solve them on their own. A seminal OECD report (2011) called for reconsidering traditional public service delivery in a new socio-economic environment. It argued that existing models of public service provision are not only tenuous, but they are also no longer affordable. This lends greater urgency to developing alternative models that focus on citizen participation in the design and delivery of public services. However, it also noted that involving citizens/users in more systematic exchanges with the paid staff who deliver public services can transform the relationship between service users and providers, ensuring the former greater influence and ownership. Thus, the OECD concludes that co-production is more than tokenism, occasional client consultation or focus group discussions. Nevertheless, providing citizens and users with more influence, particularly concerning service quality, may prove crucial for successfully engaging them as co-producers, particularly in enduring, labor-intensive services such as healthcare and social services.

Co-production can make an important contribution to the debate on public management because it goes to the heart of both effective public services delivery and the role of public services in achieving societal ends – like social integration and citizen engagement (Osborne *et al.*, 2012: 145). Co-production is often noted by the mix of activities that both public service agents and citizens contribute to the provision of public services. The former are involved as professionals or 'regular producers', while 'citizen production' is based on voluntary efforts of individuals or groups to enhance the quality and/or quantity of services they receive (Parks *et al.*, 1981; Brudney and England, 1983). Initially, co-production attracted a lot of attention in the U.S.A. in the 1970s and 1980s, but, for a few decades thereafter, New Public Management gained ascendancy, and the idea of involving people and groups outside the government in producing public services only received sporadic attention. However, today there is a renewed interest among academics and practitioners in understanding co-production or citizen participation in the provision of public services. It recognizes that, in many important areas of government activity, it is impossible to deliver services without the contributions of time and effort by citizens. Ostrom emphasized that co-production implies citizens playing 'an active role in producing public goods and services of consequence to them' (Ostrom, 1996.: 347). Alford (2002) specified three different sources of motivation for citizen participation in public sector services: material, solidarity and expressive incentives. Recognizing and promoting non-monetary incentives is important, according to Alford, since material rewards and sanctions are ineffective in eliciting the requisite client contributions in all but the simplest of tasks (*ibid.*).

Co-production clearly implies different kinds of relationships between professional service providers and their clients than those traditionally found in public services. In some cases, both parties are physically present and the production and delivery of the service are inseparable. When an organization cannot produce the service without some customer input, then they are considered interdependent (Parks *et al.*, 1981). Examples of this are found in various types of educational or vocational training programs for the long-term unemployed (Alford, 2002, 2009). Without pupil or student input in educational settings, no learning can take place (Porter, 2012).

Citizen or client participation can either supplement (or replace) professional service providers, or it can complement them at least in some activities. Parent participation in cooperative or associative preschool services in Europe provides a good example of a complementary relationship. The staff retains full pedagogical responsibility for the content and development of the preschool services, so it continues to perform the key or core activities of the organization. Parents, by contrast, are normally in charge of essential and complementary tasks. For example, in France, Germany and Sweden, parent participation in public financed, but third sector provided childcare services is manifested in their responsibility for the management and maintenance of these services (Pestoff, 2006). They decide important issues that have consequences for the economic viability of a parent co-op providing such services. They must weigh individual demands for things such as longer opening hours and/or providing services during holidays or vacation periods against the group needs to balance the facility's budget and retain qualified staff. However, these matters are no longer decided by distant politicians or bureaucrats who are mainly interested in curtailing public expenses, but rather by the parents themselves. Thus, co-production allows service users and the front-line staff to gain more control over daily operations, particularly over issues affecting service quality (Vamstad, 2007; Pestoff, 2009). Moreover, a clear division of labor can help avoid, or at least mitigate, potential conflicts of interest between the staff and their clients. Chapters 7 and 8 in this volume discuss the role of patients and volunteers in co-producing healthcare in Japan.

This research on childcare led to three main conclusions. First, there are different dimensions of parent participation in the provision of publicly financed social services, namely economic, social, political, and service-specific participation. Second, there is a higher level of parent participation in all dimensions of third sector social service, since it is based on collective action and requires direct parent participation. Third, some limited parent participation is also noted in public childcare services, but they are usually encouraged to contribute in a more limited, sporadic fashion – like helping arrange the Christmas or Spring Party. However, those parents seldom have the opportunity to play a more active or significant role in managing the services or sharing decision-making rights and responsibilities for the service provision. Thus, a 'glass ceiling' in public services limits parents to playing a passive role as service users who can make demands, but do not participate in decisions nor take any responsibility for implementing them (Pestoff, 2008; 2009).

An example from a local health clinic in Sweden describes changing annual 'checkups' for municipal residents to one where patients make such appointments themselves when they considered it necessary (Tholstrup, 2012). Patient collaboration in redesigning the scheduling for planned appointments resulted in less staff frustration, allowing them to concentrate on more important tasks, and it reduced patient waiting times. This study concludes that patients do not flood the system when they are in charge of scheduling. They are rational and use the healthcare system responsibly, which decreases unnecessary demands on the time of healthcare professionals (*ibid.*: 98).

Moreover, it seems necessary to distinguish between individual and collective co-production. Individual co-production is the collaboration between individual citizens and public servants to provide public services, and it involves existing citizen-provider interactions at the point of service delivery (Griffiths and Foley, 2009). Collective co-production, by contrast, is more complicated, since it involves the participation of groups of citizens and/or community members with public servants. It implies developing ways to encourage citizens to engage in collective action and fostering these efforts (*ibid.*). However, in practice, co-production often involves a mix of both individual and collective participation by citizens. Both forms of co-production are considered in this study, with the intention of bringing collective co-production into sharper focus.

Furthermore, the term co-production has been used in rather different contexts and for utterly different phenomena; however, these differences are not always made clear. Sometimes, co-production is used as a general or umbrella concept to cover many different types of citizen participation in public service provision – including a variety of ways citizens and/or the third sector participate in public policy-making and/or policy implementation. Other times, it may be used more narrowly to refer to direct citizen or user participation at the site of delivery of publicly financed services and even to group participation in the same. In contrast, co-management refers to the growing diversity or hybridization of welfare service provision and the need to manage it. Finally, co-governance refers to attempts to manage this diversity in a more inclusive fashion by creating city-wide or regional/national bodies where various service providers are represented in deciding the future of a sector –more specifically, its governance. Therefore, in addition to serving as a general term, co-production is a phenomenon found at the micro-level, as well as the meso and macro levels. Accordingly, it is given different names to distinguish between the different levels (Brandsen and Pestoff, 2006).

B From a Buzzword to a Cornerstone of Public Policy Reforms?

In the past 20 years, there has been a flurry of attempts to expand the study of co-production beyond the original focus on active citizen participation in the delivery of public services. Mentioning only a few of these efforts, Brandsen and Pestoff (2006) extended the range of citizen participation by distinguishing between co-governance, co-management and co-production of public services, as noted above; Osborne and Strokosch (2013) called for integrating service-dominant and public administration perspectives; Alford (2014) discussed the unexplored potential of co-production; Pestoff (2014a) focused on the role of the third sector in making co-production more sustainable; Voorberg *et al.* (2015) suggested that co-production and co-creation are similar, if not interchangeable, concepts. Other scholars have proposed various typologies of co-production. The proposal by Bovaird and Löffler (2012) is based on co-commissioned and co-provided services, where 'fully co-produced services' are high both in terms of commissioning and provision, while traditional services are low on both counts. Brandsen and Honingh (2016) distinguished between four different types of co-production in public services based on citizen participation in the design and/or implementation of public services and whether it was undertaken in core or complementary tasks. Nabatchi *et al.* (2017) combine several aspects or dimensions of co-production in an effort to summarize and synthesize much of the recent debate on how to conceptualize co-production. However, this is not an easy task given the growing number of approaches to study this phenomenon and efforts by governments to expand its scope.

1 Co-production – At the Focus of Several Academic Disciplines

Given the renewed interest in the study of co-production, there was a notable increase recently in academic conferences and in the number of books published that include or focus on co-production (Pestoff and Brandsen, 2006; Alford, 2009; OECD, 2011; Pestoff *et al.*, 2012;

Brandsen *et al.*, 2018; Pestoff, 2018) as well as several hundred journal articles recently devoted to co-production in major journals on public administration and management (Voorberg *et al.*, 2015). This research shows that co-production can take place in a variety of different fields and contexts, ranging from local safety and police activities (Parks *et al.*, 1981; Meijer, 2012; Freise, 2012.); childcare (Pestoff, 1998, 2008; Prentice, 2006; Vamstad, 2007, 2012; Vancoppenolle and Verschuere, 2012); basic education (Davis and Ostrom, 1991; Porter, 2012); housing (Brandsen and Helderman, 2012); urban regeneration (Osborne. and McLaughlin, 2004; Schlappa, 2012), etc. In healthcare, citizen engagement in service provision takes different names – such as patient-centeredness, patient experience, patient empowerment and, occasionally, co-production. The focus can range from patient compliance and adherence to professional advice, the role of nonprofits or to reforming entire health systems (Anderson and Funnell, 2012; Batalden *et al.*, 2015; Coutler and Ellins, 2007; Dunston *et al.*, 2009; Fotaki, 2009; Fotaki, 2011; Meijer, 2016; Tholstrup, 2012; Walden-Laing and Pestoff, 1997). Efforts to promote greater patient participation in healthcare are discussed in greater detail, in the section below.

New academic concepts often gain inspiration from real-life phenomena that are not adequately covered or understood by existing concepts. Accordingly and quite naturally, there are different perspectives on similar phenomena in different countries, disciplines and sectors. This means that our understanding of a new concept, like co-production, is heavily influenced by its context – where discipline, service sector and even national setting can easily color it. Moreover, the study of co-production in public services is a complex phenomenon that not only has attracted significant scholarly interest in recent years; it has also gained adherents from several academic disciplines. They include, among others, business administration, economics, health management, political science, policy studies, public administration and management, sociology and third sector studies. Similar to other hot topics – like social enterprise or social innovation – this highly complex phenomenon involves multiple dimensions (e.g. economic, political and social) that require a truly multidisciplinary approach.

Nonetheless, academic disciplines have their own basic understanding or starting point, and, quite naturally, they jostle to promote their own perspective and approach. This can prove challenging in a multi-disciplinary endeavor or field. All of them should be reflected, to a greater or lesser extent, in attempts to develop a generic definition of co-production. However, this can result in growing confusion and a muddled concept that lacks a clear and consistent definition. In particular, many younger scholars may feel compelled to address different, and sometimes conflicting, perspectives of this phenomenon without being able to reconcile or synthesize them.

In addition, in post-modern service societies, citizens have numerous roles, including several different ones vis-à-vis the public sector (Pestoff, 1998). Alford (2009) attributes four different roles to the clients of public sector services: paying customers, beneficiaries, obligates and citizens. Thomas (2012, 2013) distinguished between three principal roles played by the public vis-à-vis the professionals providing public services: citizens, customers and partners. Similarly, Nabatchi, *et al.*, refer to multiple roles of lay actors who interact with the state: citizens, clients and customers (2017: 770). The fact that citizens have multiple roles and a variety of interactions with the public sector should serve as a reminder that not all of them involve co-production.

Therefore, several of the co-production pioneers warned against employing too broad a definition of co-production, where virtually any citizen activity directly or indirectly connected with the public sector or public financed services was identified as co-production. Warren *et al.* (1982) and Rosentraub and Warren (1987) excluded certain types of activities from those considered as co-production. Ancillary actions – such as obeying the law, paying taxes and following regulations or reporting crime – are expected forms of behavior for citizens. Parallel production involves services similar to those provided by public agencies, but they are produced by individuals or groups without any contact or cooperation with public agencies (*ibid.*). Terms like ancillary and/or parallel production help to distinguish co-production from other forms of citizen interaction with the public sector in the design and delivery of public services.

2 Expanding the Public Mandate to Involve Civil Society in Co-production

Academic terms in the social sciences, even relatively well-established ones, are often subject to efforts to use them in ways that do not always contribute to conceptual clarity or the original definition. Both the market and state can demonstrate an interest in adopting and adapting certain key terms for their own purpose. This can result in broader or narrower definitions than the original academic concept. The concept of the social enterprise provides a classical illustration. It is subject both to particularly broad and rather narrow definitions, depending on the perspective or interest of the party defining it. The market and firms usually prefer broad definitions that can shroud business activities with greater legitimacy, especially when compliance is voluntary. The state and public agencies often employ narrower interpretations that suit their particular policy aims (Pestoff and Hulgård, 2016). This clearly illustrates a conceptual risk – too broad a definition of a new phenomenon, like social enterprise, means that almost everything and anything can be included, but then there is nothing left to compare and contrast it with.

On the other hand, too narrow a definition implies the opposite – almost nothing qualifies, and it becomes an empty or stand-alone phenomenon. In both cases, meaningful academic inquiry becomes more difficult, if not impossible (Pestoff, 2014b).

The recent academic discourse about civil society and co-production illustrates similar tendencies. Brandsen and colleagues warned recently that there is a vogue for renewed state-civil society initiatives around the globe (2017). This opens up for the risk that appeals by governments for citizens to participate and self-organize may lead the state to attempt to control such initiatives, resulting in 'engineered' or 'contracted-out' civil society that has little to do with spontaneous citizen initiatives (*ibid.*: 676). Contemporary governments attempt to shift responsibility for public service delivery to civil society. Such ambitions include large-scale efforts to reconstruct images of local communities, civil society and citizenship by giving public responsibilities for providing public services to citizens and civil society organizations. However, the intent may not merely be a way to give citizens more control, but is also considered as a means for governments to cut their costs and guide or steer policies in a particular direction (*ibid.*: 684). This risks delegitimizing the very civil society organizations that the government claims to support in the eyes of their members and citizens at large, thereby undermining the very essence of civil self-organization. This was evident in European Social Fund unemployment policies and projects in the new E.U. member states at the beginning of the century that attempted to engage social enterprises in training citizens with physical and social disabilities (Pestoff, 2011). Examples of similar efforts at promoting civil society provision of social services were recently identified in Denmark, the Netherlands, Japan and the United Kingdom (Andersen *et al.*, 2019; Fehsenfeld, 2019; Nederhand and van Meerkerk, 2018; Ogawa, 2009, 2020; Tsutsui, 2014; Fotaki, 2009, 2011; Slocock, 2015).

They illustrate three intertwined tendencies of public efforts to engage civil society in the co-production of public services. First, it greatly expands the scope of co-production to include new groups and/or reorganize existing phenomena by involving civil society and citizens in the provision of traditional public services. Second, it shifts the responsibility for providing social services from one group or sector of society to another (i.e. from the public sector to civil society and private citizens). Third, sometimes it inadvertently or intentionally turns an existing concept on its head and reverses established roles, like efforts to equate the concepts of co-production and co-creation. Despite the intentions of the government, co-creation may, nevertheless, appear more like a Trojan Horse to many citizens. Promises of 'empowerment',' influence' and 'democracy' can, in reality, mean that public services are turned over to civil society and 'responsibilized citizens' without much public finance or backup from public professionals. This can be illustrated by the policy of Community-Based Integrated Care (CIC) in Japanese healthcare and eldercare that is discussed in greater detail in Chapter 11 of this volume.

3 Enhancing Co-production or Muddying the Waters?

The concept of co-production has become a buzzword in recent years, but this has probably taken place at the cost of clarity. Scholars have different theories and values that lead them, understandably, to attribute different contents and meanings to co-production. There are, in other words, several theories and several worlds of co-production, each of which has different implications for user participation. However, when a concept includes anything and everything involving the client and/or volunteer participation in public service provision, it risks becoming an empty shell. For example, should smiley face machines installed in many service institutions be considered an example of co-production or perhaps co-evaluation? They let clients/customers register their satisfaction with a certain service on a given day, 'How was your experience today? Good, Average or Bad'. Such machines can be found just after security control at many airports and in public restrooms today.

Understandably, there is a lively debate about the concept of co-production. It is probably a healthy sign that we are still discovering new facets of this variegated phenomenon and also that there is still no consensus on a precise, generic definition of co-production. Nevertheless, questions about the 'true' nature of co-production often surface as interest in this relatively new phenomenon grows (i.e. questions about what it is and what it is not, or perhaps what it should be). At a two-day seminar on co-production a few years ago, every second or third author briefed his/her presentation with a comment to the effect 'I wonder if this is really co-production?', but then continued to present her/his theories and data. One young scholar even asked if any kind of citizen participation except voting should be considered co-production.

Today, co-production is one of the cornerstones of public policy reforms across the globe. Among other things, it is seen as a valuable route to public service reform and the planning and delivery of effective services – a response to the democratic deficit and a route to active citizenship and active communities – and as a means by which to lever in additional resources for public service delivery. Despite these varied roles, co-production is actually poorly formulated and has become one of a series of 'woolly words' in public policy (Osborne *et al.*, 2016: 639). A growing chorus of scholars and practitioners has called into question current attempts to define and delimit co-production. They argue that it is ill-defined, poorly formulated or a muddled concept. However, the solution is to propose a new definition that hopefully can encompass more elements and provide a more holistic approach to the study of this phenomenon. On the other hand, there is a growing concern that the possibility of finding or proposing a unifying, generic definition of this multifaceted phenomenon is becoming more elusive as more scholars with different backgrounds and perspectives join this rapidly expanding field of study.

C Three Schools of Co-production?

However, definitions may not be a problem per se, but rather, this might be more of a question of different approaches, models or schools of study that shape and color our understanding of this phenomenon. Accordingly, perhaps it is time to shift focus and consider identifying different schools of co-production. This section will briefly examine the differences between some of these perspectives and explore the implications of their shortcomings for the potential of co-production to reform the public sector. The three main contenders today appear to be a classical political science/public administration, input/output model that emphasizes citizen participation on the output side of the political system; a service management model that focuses on a variety of stages in the value chain approach and growing interest in co-creation based on service marketing and management. Juxtaposing them will help to disentangle the activities of citizens in the provision of public services, and, hopefully, bring greater clarity to the debate among scholars and practitioners. However, these three approaches are more or less developed, but there is also a certain overlap between them, so they are not mutually exclusive. A fourth approach is found in a mix of these three, while a potential fifth approach focuses on third sector management (Benjamin and Brudney, 2018).

Whether we embrace an input/output perspective, a value chain or a service marketing and management approach is crucial for our understanding of co-production, what it includes and excludes, how it works, etc. It also has implications in terms of the different values they represent. This is particularly relevant given the context and setting of the phenomenon at hand (i.e. promoting citizen participation in the provision of public services and facilitating patient participation in healthcare). Ostrom claims that co-production attributes to citizens an active role in providing public goods and services of consequence to them. However, mixing several perspectives, as is sometimes the case, can unwittingly result in a state of confusion by turning co-production into a 'fuzzy' concept that reflects a poorly formulated understanding of the phenomenon at hand.

1 An Input-Output Model

It is important to underline a few of the basic features of public policymaking. Fundamental insights for understanding the public sector are found in the pioneering work of David Easton, *A Systems Analysis of Political Life* (1965). In particular, his input/output model appears germane and provides an appropriate starting point. He differentiates between the input and output sides of public policy-making, emphasizing their different roles and functions. Traditionally, studies of citizen participation focused on the input side and included activities like voting, contacting elected representatives, participating in demonstrations, etc., that are designed to articulate citizens' demands and project their influence in politics and policy-making. However, the work of Elinor Ostrom and her colleagues served to shift the focus of public administration to the output side of the political system by focusing on citizen participation in the delivery of public services.

The distinction between citizen participation on the input or output sides of the political system is not a trivial matter, nor is it academic 'hair-splitting'. The same individuals are not necessarily involved in both the input and output sides. The input side of policy-making is based on discrete activities that are usually limited in time, like promoting the adoption of a new law or reform, while the output side normally comprises continuous activities, where service users can be locked into service provision for several years (Pestoff, 2018). This also implies that participation on the input side is temporally more distant from the service actually provided than participation on the output side, as well as from the final outcome. Moreover, citizens' daily activities in policy implementation usually become intertwined with or even part of the final outcome, and the collective process of achieving them also contributes added value for them and to the outcome (Hirschman, 1982; Pestoff, 1998).

Moreover, the possibility for citizens to influence the design of a service, or to co-design a service, is not limited to the input side of the political system. Given the growing use of 'framework legislation', more and more details are determined during the implementation phase of laws and ordinances. This means that there is an important role for co-producers in fleshing out many of the detailed rules and practices when providing a service that they are co-producing. They are not simply providing their time and effort to produce a service. Often, they must make decisions about how, why and when to produce it, in partnership with the professional providers. However, concentrating on their role in delivering a service often tends to overshadow this aspect of co-production, making it appear that once a law or regulation is passed, citizens have no further role in that process. Nothing could be farther from the truth. Scholars and practitioners promoting a traditional public administration; input/output approach should devote more time to document and explain the role of co-producers in decision-making on the output side of the political system. It is also important to distinguish between the user or patient spokespersons sitting on a user council and the users or co-producers making decisions themselves, in partnership with the professional providers that impact the quality and/or quantity of a certain service.

2 A Value Chain Model

Turning to the service management approach, Bovaird's prolific writings on co-production illustrate his importance in the discourse on co-production. He provided a robust definition of co-production, '[u]ser and community co-production is the provision of services through regular, long-term relationships between professionalized service providers (in any sector) and service users and/or other members of the community, where all parties make substantial resource contributions' (2007: 847). Nonetheless, he also argued that co-production is not only relevant to the '... delivery phase of service management, but can also extend across the full value chain of service planning, design, commissioning, managing, delivering, monitoring and evaluation activities' (*ibid.*: 846), and, therefore, he affixed a 'co' to each of the above terms. In more general terms, Bovarid and Löffler (2012) distinguish between four stages or types of citizen participation in public services: co-commissioning, co-design, co-delivery and co-evaluation of public services (*ibid.*). While a service management perspective does provide some valuable insights that enhance our understanding of co-production, it appears to attribute equal weight or importance to each discrete link or stage in the value chain. However, it fails to clarify whether one link might prove more important than another for evoking sustainable citizen participation in co-production.

The value chain perspective of business administration might be enriched by recognizing that decision-making does not only take place on the input side of the political system. Once a policy is designed, many detailed decisions are left to citizens who help implement framework legislation at the site of service provision. Moreover, not everyone involved in co-designing a public service on the input side of the political system is also involved in co-delivering it on the output side. In fact, probably very few are. Usually, the people who are involved in one phase or link of the value chain are not the same as those persons involved in another phase or link. The links of the value chain as a conceptual model are, in fact, discrete activities that seldom demonstrate an additive relationship with each other. Lumping them together as 'fully co-produced services' seems to miss the point. It does not appear possible to add all the persons or citizens involved in various links of the value chain to determine the level or amount of co-production at any given time or in a given country or policy sector. More attention should perhaps be given to considering the implications of this for the value chain approach.

3 Co-creation: A Public Value Creation Model

Scholars seem rather ambivalent about the concept of co-creation. There are at least three ways of understanding the relationship between the two concepts of co-production and co-creation (Brandsen and Honingh, 2018). Either they mean approximately the same thing, co-creation is more encompassing than co-production or they have distinct meanings that refer to different kinds of citizen inputs (*ibid.* 10). A fourth and perhaps more notable interpretation holds that citizens are the true creators of public value, and the public sector merely helps them co-produce it. Value creation is a core feature of the service marketing and management perspective – in particular, the notion of 'value-in exchange' (Grönroos, 2008). It states that 'value is not created by the service provider, but rather in the customer's value-generating processes' (*ibid.*: 299). Service as business logic, according to Grönroos, means facilitating interactive processes that support customers' value creation in their everyday practices (2008: 300). He maintains that goods and services are consumed in essentially the same type of process and people do not buy goods and services for basically different purposes. Rather, customers buy goods in order to assist them with a service that creates value for them. For example, groceries are not bought for the sake of taking them home and storing them. They are bought in order to provide input resources in the process of 'cooking dinner for the family and having a nice family occasion around the dining table' (*ibid.*: 301). This is designated as the value of the process of shopping and cooking a meal.

The service process can either be actively supported by a service provider by using a full-service concept (i.e. eating at a restaurant or buying takeaway meals) or be only passively supported through a self-service setup (i.e. buying groceries at the store). In the latter situation, the customer is expected to initiate and implement all activities of the service process needed to get the service and subsequent value rendered by it. In this case, the customer merely needs to add his or her skills (*ibid.*: 303). Although value creation is a key concept, Grönroos and Voima (2013: 134) argue that 'value is perhaps the most ill-defined and elusive concept in service marketing and management' (as cited by Hardyman *et al.*, 2015: 99).

However, it is worth keeping in mind that, at the rate of three meals a day, the average person eats more than a thousand meals per year. Given the work and/or school obligations of the average family with children, they eat anywhere between 700-800 meals at home. Most of the breakfasts are probably rushed affairs, while they usually eat lunch at work or school during the week. Therefore, at best dinner on the weekends might occasionally allow enjoying 'a nice family occasion around the dining table', perhaps only once or twice a month.

Therefore, the picture of relaxed family gatherings providing the value gained from grocery shopping and cooking that Grönroos paints seems rather atypical. Perhaps, a more nuanced, systematic analysis of the relationship between consumers and service providers would be appropriate.

The co-creation perspective, particularly if combined with a service-dominant emphasis, should attempt to explain in greater detail what happens to value creation during the other 300+ days a year when it is not possible to enjoy a relaxed meal with the family around the dinner table. How can value be co-created during stressful breakfasts in the morning or rushed lunches at work or school? How applicable is the metaphor of value creation to understanding citizen participation in public service delivery or healthcare? In particular, does it apply to more mundane or daily activities – such as enduring social services, eldercare or treating chronic illness – that are far removed from the value added by enjoying a relaxed family meal around the dinner table? Moreover and if so, how, why and under what circumstances? Delving into the more mundane details of co-construction in enduring public services would help make it more amenable to academic discussion.

D Co-production and Healthcare

Some scholars argue that services are fundamentally different from products, they are always 'co-produced' (Ostrom, 1996; Grönroos, 2008; Osborne *et al.*, 2016; Batalden *et al.*, 2015). Proposals to enable and facilitate patient participation in healthcare are called by a variety of names. We will now turn our attention to a brief overview that covers a variety of approaches to promote patient participation in healthcare. This discussion includes the following topics concerning patient participation in healthcare: 1) Different perspectives; 2) Diversity among patients, health literacy and social support; 3) Manifestations of co-production and co-creation and 4) Hurdles to co-production in healthcare and the way forward.

1 Different Perspectives

The World Health Organization documents show a diversity of perspectives about citizen participation in healthcare. In 2005, the World Health Organization stated that voice, choice and representation were the main channels for citizen participation in healthcare (World Health Organization, 2005). Two years later, the WHO proposed a policy framework called People-Centered Healthcare (World Health Organization, 2007). Ten years later, it adopted a Global Strategy on People-Centered and Integrated Health Services, which recommends five closely connected steps – including one that emphasizes primary and community care services and the co-production of health (World Health Organization, 2016). This represents a gradual expansion of the WHO perspective, which now mentions co-production by name.

The European Health Management Association (EHMA) argued that, given the growing interest in patient participation, they are increasingly expected to participate actively in healthcare and be better informed about clinical decision-making. However, this has been accompanied by an explosion of definitions and interpretations that generate a fuzzy conceptualization of what the various terms related to patient participation really mean (European Healthcare Management Association EHMA, 2013). Understandably, patient participation in healthcare is often called by different names – such as patient-centeredness, patient engagement, patient experience, patient empowerment, shared decision-making, health literacy, healthcare co-creation, collaborative co-production, etc. We will consider the main features of a few of them below.

The People-Centered approach heralded by the 2007 WHO document was designed to humanize the provision of healthcare. Today, there are two somewhat similar approaches that focus on changing the relationship between physicians and patients. The first is called 'Person-centered care' and the second is 'Patient-centered care'; however, the difference between the two is not entirely clear. A comparison of these two terms, based on a systematic literature review, suggests that the main difference between them is related to their ultimate goal. For person-centered care, it is a meaningful life, while for patient-centered care, it is a functional life (Håkansson Eklund *et al.*, 2018; Summer Meranius *et al.*, 2020). In addition, the former represents a psychosocial approach, while the latter provides a more economic and business orientation to healthcare. However, both approaches clearly focus on the individual patient-provider relationship, rather than the structural elements that could either promote or hinder patient participation in healthcare.

The concept of Person-centered care traces its origin back to the early 1960s, thus, predating the work of Ostrom and her colleagues. Rather than being a passive recipient of professional care, the patient actively participates in his/her own medical treatment in close cooperation with health professionals. It argues that many health professionals are traditionally focused on the needs of the patients instead of recognizing their resources. The Person-centered care model allows for the inclusion of the patient and their relatives in making a joint design and reaching mutual agreement about the medical plan and treatments (Tyrell, 2020).

The rise of person-centered care is seen as a response to the traditional biomedical model that prioritizes the basic physiological needs of persons but ignores their psychosocial needs. The prioritization of needs resulted in negative outcomes for persons with chronic illness and their caregivers. This approach basically reduces the chronically ill person to a bearer of an incurable disease, neglecting the personal attributes and qualities of the individual (*ibid*.: 19). Person-centered care promotes a holistic approach to healthcare that takes the whole person into account, instead of a narrow perspective that focuses on the illness or symptoms (*ibid*).

Proponents of the second approach claim that the principle behind the growing movement toward Patient-centered care is simple: It is possible to improve the quality of healthcare and reduce costs at the same time. Physicians practicing this approach can improve their patients' clinical outcomes and satisfaction rates by improving the quality of the doctor-patient relationship while, at the same time, decreasing utilization of diagnostic testing, prescriptions, hospitalizations and referrals (Ricker, 2012). This can save healthcare providers thousands of dollars of unnecessary procedures (Univ. of New Mexico, 2020). Patient-centered care replaces the current physician-centered system with one that revolves around the patient. Effective care is generally defined by or in consultation with patients rather than by physicians who are dependent on traditional healthcare tools and standards. The relationship between a patient and his/her doctor greatly determines both treatment outcomes and a patient's satisfaction with his/her care. Accordingly, practitioners need to employ a set of measurable skills and behaviors in order to help their patients become more compliant with treatment and active in the management of their disease (*ibid*.). This type of care can be employed by physicians in any specialty, and it is effective across disease types.

Collaborative co-production requires patients to be experts in their own circumstances and be capable of making decisions. To be truly transformative, co-production requires relocation of power towards service users. This necessitates new relationships with front-line professionals who need appropriate training and to enable them to take on new roles. Shared decision-making considers that the time patients spend meeting with their physician – the clinical encounter – is the most important moment for them to become engaged in their own health through the process of shared decision making. In the U.S., shared decision-making is being promoted for its potential to improve the health of populations and individual patients, while helping to control care costs. It is based on three essential elements: Recognizing and acknowledging that a decision is required; Knowing and understanding the best available evidence; Incorporating the patient's values and preferences into the decision. To achieve the promise of shared decision making, physicians need more training in the approach, and more practices need to be reorganized around the principles of patient engagement (Legare and Witteman, 2013: 276).

2 *Diversity Among Patients, Health Literacy and Social Support*

It was maintained that 'the 19th Century was an age of acute and infectious disease, whereas today, we battle with lifestyle and chronic disease' (Realpe and Wallace, 2010: 10). However, there is an important difference between an acute health condition and a chronic or long-term condition. The former tends to be episodic and generally treatable, while long-term conditions are ongoing, incurable and need to be managed for life. Nonetheless, chronic conditions occupy up to 80% of consultations in primary care in the U.K. (*ibid.*: 10–11). Batalden, *et al.* confirm that the underlying diversity among patients (acute versus chronic) influences their potential role as co-producers of healthcare and also sets the parameters for adequate care (2015: 6).

Some scholars argue that service co-production has distinguishing characteristics when it is applied to healthcare. First, it is not possible to apply a 'one-size-fits-all' approach. Rather, tailored solutions are necessary to meet the specific needs of different patients. In health services, co-production requires a process of enablement or empowerment, aimed at allowing patients to perform as the partners of healthcare professionals, rather than merely as the recipient of health services (Palumbo and Manna, 2017: 2). However, empowerment faces a basic problem related to the adoption of a new paradigm. In most countries, healthcare professionals are trained and specialized in an approach to healthcare that focuses on the treatment of acute illness. However, this is problematic with chronic diseases like type II diabetes. Much of the literature on diabetes care focuses on reducing patient noncompliance, rather than attempting to understand their lifestyle issues (Anderson and Funnell, 2012).

However, not all patients have the desire or capacity to become active participants in co-producing healthcare. Their ability to do so in part reflects their health literacy. According to Palumbo and Annarumma (2016), health literacy has been usually discussed as an individual trait, concerning the patient's ability to navigate the healthcare service system. Alternatively, the organizational side of health literacy reflects the ability of healthcare organizations to establish comfortable relationships with patients (*ibid.*: 133). However, this requires that healthcare organizations take steps to remove the hurdles to patient participation and empower them. Health literacy should, therefore, be understood as a complex and stratified concept, which affects both the strategic and managerial practices of healthcare organizations (*ibid.*: 134). Healthcare organizations are often not able to establish a setting that empowers patients and enables them to perform as co-producers. On one hand, patients meet significant hurdles in participating in the provision of care. On the other hand, cultural and organizational constraints prevent healthcare professionals from establishing a patient-centered approach to care that discourages patient participation. Thus, structural factors are manifest in a managerial and cultural approach that prevent the transition toward patient-centered care (Palumbo and Manna, 2017: 9).

Moreover, there is growing concern about the adverse consequences of low individual health literacy, and studies have shown significant variation in individual adaptation to health literacy problems. Lee, *et al.* argued that social support can have a positive impact on the relationship between health literacy and health service utilization (2004). The concept of social support is defined as resources provided by a network of individuals and social groups (*ibid.*: 1313). Research suggests that social support may have both direct effects and moderating effects. Structural social support refers to an individual's location in the social structure (e.g. participation in community and voluntary organizations, maintenance of social contact and immersion in close social networks). A sense of belonging and being supported, originating from participation in social groups, may enable an individual to face a stressful situation that would otherwise seem overwhelming (*ibid.*: 1314). Furthermore, healthcare organizations can proactively promote health literacy and embrace a health literacy outreach strategy, as noted in Chapter 7 of this volume.

3 Value, Co-production and Co-creation

The concept of co-creation frequently appears in the literature on healthcare. As noted earlier in section C, co-creation can either be used interchangeably with co-production, or it refers primarily to 'the involvement of citizens in initiation or design of public services' (Voorberg *et al.*, 2017). In healthcare, this might translate into patient-centeredness, patient consultations and patient collaboration. However, Osborne (2017), following Grönroos, maintains that co-creation together with a public service logic implies that the citizen and/or service user is the one who creates the value of a public service for her/himself, while the public agent is merely acting as a facilitator or co-producer of this process. What this implies for healthcare remains uncertain; nevertheless, the co-creation perspective seems to turn Ostrom's concept of co-production on its head.

By contrast, Porter attributes a clear monetary definition to value in healthcare. He argues that improving performance and accountability in any field depends on having a shared goal that unites the interests and activities of all stakeholders. The concept of value refers to the output achieved relative to the costs incurred. Defining and measuring value is, therefore, essential to understanding the performance of any organization and driving continuous improvement (Porter, 2010: 2477). In healthcare, value is defined as the patient's health outcomes achieved per dollar spent. The value should be the preeminent goal in the healthcare system, because it is what ultimately matters for customers (i.e. patients) and unites the interests of all system actors (*ibid.*). When value improves, patients, payers, providers and suppliers can all benefit, and the economic sustainability of the healthcare system improves. Moreover, he contends that value encompasses many of the other goals already embraced in healthcare, such as quality, safety, patient-centeredness and cost containment, and it integrates them (*ibid.*: 2478).

However, both the value chain and co-creation approach to co-production discussed earlier reflect a transaction cost approach employed by economists and business administration that seems informed by New Public Management (NPM). In the service management discourse and co-creation, the patient is seen as a customer who actively makes choices, seeks information and creates value him/herself. However, it is debatable how suitable this approach is for healthcare. Imported terminology, like customer and value creation stem from economic thought. It differs considerably from the dominant ideas in healthcare that prefer terms like medical needs, diagnoses, prioritizing, indication and care. Differing perspectives that are represented by different terms reflect the tensions that importing new models represent (Nordgren and Åhgren, 2013: 106). By contrast, they note that the most prominent values expressed by patients in their study were 'receiving professional care' and 'a good level of service when in hospital'. Furthermore, there was an expectation by patients to be acknowledged and respected as an individual (*ibid.*: 114).

Moreover, Mintzberg warns that several myths impede the effective management of healthcare (2012). The prevailing business model stems from industry and manufacturing that comprises a top-down, control-oriented, numbers-driven and outputs-standardized focus. However, a different model – the professional organization – is more common in healthcare. It is expert-driven, skills-oriented and focused on getting the patients into the right box, so the most appropriate interventions can be applied (*ibid.*). It relies mainly on professional values based on knowledge and experience.

4 Hurdles to Co-production in Healthcare and the Way Forward

Studies show that patients want to be more involved in their own healthcare. However, many patient-physician interactions still follow the traditional office visit format where the patient is passive, trusting and compliant (Bernadeo and Holmboe, 2013: 250). One recent study shows that, while physicians may advocate the rhetoric of shared decision-making, they often fail to adopt it when communicating with patients. Physicians do not necessarily have the skills required to put this rhetoric into practice, or they may lack an appropriate context in which they can practice such skills (*ibid.*: 252). For example, diabetes is a complex chronic illness requiring substantial engagement by patients and their healthcare teams to maintain control of blood sugar and blood pressure and to prevent complications (*ibid.*: 253). This involves much more than simply complying with doctors' orders (Söderholm Werkö, 2008). In particular, this reflects the failure to recognize the unique character of a service, as opposed to goods, and the implications of this shortcoming may limit our success in partnering with patients to improve healthcare (Batalden *et al.*, 2015: 1). Moreover, engaging professionals and patients as partners in co-production is difficult and time-consuming. They lament that, years after introducing the idea of shared decision-making, these principles are rarely employed in patient-clinician encounters. Conversations between them easily revert to professional-centric priorities and professionals too often slip into providing healthcare service as a product rather than a service requiring co-production (*ibid.*: 7).

However, there are some valid reasons for a lack of equity and reciprocity between professionals and patients. Professionals are trained to be experts and expected to be the authority by offering advice and providing solutions. Service users are often viewed, both by themselves and others, as passive recipients of this expertise with problems waiting to be solved (Dineen, 2017). Without the development of appropriate health literacy policies and strategies, patient participation is often neglected by healthcare organizations, and healthcare professionals are not supported to achieve patient engagement. Rather, Palumbo and Manna argue that, in most cases, the inclusion of health literacy within organizational planning is prevented by the lack of policy and managerial tools to establish a health literate environment in healthcare (2017: 12).

Moreover, citizens and patients often may not share a common understanding of the aims and scope of efforts to promote public participation with state officials, professionals and managers. This difference seems to reflect basic beliefs by professionals about the proper relationship between their knowledge and authority and the public's view and wishes. Such differences are likely to resist policy prescriptions for a larger role for public participation. For example, two initiatives were popular in the U.K. and the NHS at the beginning of the century – public and patient engagement (PPE) and patient and public involvement (PPI). However, bringing patients and professionals together in genuine collaborative relationships proved more challenging than anticipated. Consultative, rather than partnership approaches, became common and replaying divisions and asymmetries between healthcare professionals and patients (Martin, 2009). A growing sense of public disillusionment with PPE/PPI initiatives and consultation fatigue are considered key hurdles to sustaining collaborative relationships. Therefore, healthcare professionals in the U.K. often became weary of PPE/PPI reforms (Renedo *et al.*, 2015: 18, Hudson, 2015: 3).

Bernadeo and Holmboe (2013) recognized the realities of clinical practice, but believe that the healthcare system cannot increase patient engagement in decision-making without overcoming the underlying obstacles that impede patients' access to and understanding of needed information. Effective and shared decision-making takes time to deliver proficiently (*ibid.*: 255). Coutler and Ellins (2007) state that a substantial evidence base exists for building strategies to strengthen patient engagement. Any strategy to reduce health inequalities must promote health literacy and engagement. Patients could help in selecting treatments, managing long-term conditions and increasing the safety of drug use and infection control. Interventions can improve patients' knowledge and experience, use of health services, health behavior and health status (*ibid.*: 26). However, unless the management includes the front-line staff in the co-production approach, they will be inclined to make decisions about what can be done based on established clinical hierarchies, ignoring the vital skills of communication, building trust, empathy and the capabilities and potential that the staff possesses but have not been given enough thought or acknowledgment (Dineen, 2017). Chapters 6 and 9 in this volume explore the work environment of the hospital staff and the governance models that guide their daily work.

Co-production requires a shift from a hierarchical, provider-driven network to one in which all stakeholders work as partners in improving individual health, clinic healthcare service and network operations (Batalden *et al.*, 2015: 5). Co-production challenges existing hierarchical forms of healthcare – in particular, expert-based practice – that informs professional identity defines and differentiates expert knowledge from lay knowledge and shapes the roles and rules that typically govern the ways healthcare professionals and consumers interact (Dunston *et al.*, 2009: 42). By contrast, the partner-in-co-production approach provides a different location, status and role for health consumers within the system and service development process. In this case, consumers become co-participants, co-designers and co-producers as part of the process of service provision. Choice and voice may be important, but they are not enough to significantly alter the dominant culture and practices of provider-centric and expert-based health service production (*ibid.*: 45). 'Experience and relationships are recurring themes in co-production that happen at *the point of delivery* and through conversations and dialog. The site of the *relationship* is the interface between health consumers and health professionals' (*ibid.*: 47).

Hudson (2012) introduced a U.K. framework for analyzing the relationship between changing paradigms of healthcare and the 'modes of production'. The three paradigms he proposed are mass production, mass customization and mass collaboration. Mass production characterized the early phase of the NHS, where the focus was on acute diseases and infections. Passive patients gratefully received treatments based on expert professional knowledge. The mass customization paradigm focuses on patient needs and the notion of 'personalization' of care, especially for those with complex long-term conditions. This favors individual co-production with an emphasis on choice and assumes that patients are rational consumers in a market of healthcare choices. Healthcare is co-designed between professionals and patients but tends to be delivered according to the prescriptions of professionals. A more transformative model – mass collaboration – is based on ideas of participatory governance and collective co-production (*ibid.*: 76). A potential expression of the latter is discussed in Chapter 7 in this volume.

E Summary and Conclusions

In recent decades, co-production has become one of the cornerstones of public policy reform across the globe. With the explosion of interest in understanding and facilitating citizen/user participation in the provision of public services, co-production now encompasses a variety of different phenomena, contexts and levels, and it is studied by a variety of disciplines that employ a variety of approaches. Nonetheless, a growing chorus of scholars and practitioners has called into question current attempts to define and delimit co-production. They argue that it is a poorly defined and formulated concept. It has become one of a series of 'woolly words' that risks becoming an empty signifier. This troubling development can perhaps be considered normal when different disciplines with different approaches attempt to reach a common generic definition and understanding. Moreover, many states are actively attempting to expand the scope of co-production to include civil society and volunteers for policy reasons. However, neither the rapid growth of the field nor the political efforts to enlarge the scope contribute to clarifying this key concept. Much of the growing confusion could be resolved by separating various approaches into different schools. Comparing the three schools of study, each with a unique understanding of this phenomenon, can contribute to understanding this development. They include a political science/public administration, input/output model; a business administration, a value chain approach; and a service marketing and management, co-creation approach. This implies that there is no single, unique or correct definition or approach to the study of co-production in public service provision.

Co-production in public services and patient participation in healthcare have different origins, focus and definitions. Patient participation in healthcare faces a familiar variety of terms and understandings to describe the need for and forms of patient participation in healthcare. However, much of this seems to focus on individual patient participation rather than collective co-production. An emphasis on either the consultative or the collaborative on both the individual and organizational side of health literacy, on the diversity of patients and their needs or on the hurdles to co-production all seem to suggest a similar conclusion.

This overview of co-production in public services and healthcare reveals that there is a myriad of terms, concepts, definitions and perspectives of this phenomenon. There is no single dominant approach, but rather a number of clusters that suggest the existence of different schools of co-production in public services in general and, most likely, in healthcare as well. While this underlines the ambiguity of co-production as a concept, it also means that there is no right or wrong approach to studying co-production or putting it into practice. Rather, these diverse perspectives often reflect the underlying cultural, social and political values of researchers and practitioners. However, it is also indicative of the paradox of co-production. It can either refer to individual and aspirational values in relation to patient participation or to collective co-production with a more transformative capacity.

Much of the literature on patient participation in healthcare is aspirational. It focuses on individual patients and describes the relationship between clinicians and patients as a meeting of two experts, each with their respective knowledge and skills. This challenges the traditional relationship between them, and it requires patients to become experts in their own circumstances and therefore capable of making decisions and having control as responsible citizens. This literature puts heavy emphasis on the ability and agency of individual patients, but it seems to ignore the shortcomings of many patients in this respect and, therefore, the importance of social support for facilitating both their agency and ability. Chapter 7 on patients and Japanese healthcare explores the contribution of membership in health co-ops to promote the agency and ability of individual patients to achieve health literacy and well-being, together with others.

At the same time, much of this literature also implies a change in the role of the professionals from being the fixers of problems to facilitators who find solutions by working with their clients. This underlines the importance of front-line staff. When co-production is transformative, there is a relocation of power by the development of new joint mechanisms where professionals and patients collaborate in the planning, delivering and management of healthcare. Two chapters in this volume consider those mechanisms in greater detail. Chapter 6 explores the relationship between work environment and service quality and demonstrates how staff satisfaction is related to improved service quality. Chapter 9 discusses the impact of governance models on staff control and influence, as well as possibilities for promoting a multi-stakeholder approach to healthcare. Chapter 8 is devoted to the tasks performed by volunteers, which can either be essential or complementary to the core tasks of the professional staff. Chapter 10 compares the perspective of the staff, patients and volunteers on the social values of their hospital, and documents the unique profiles of the three hospital groups in this study.

Considered together, the chapters in this volume allow us to compare and contrast two widely different approaches to co-production (i.e. aspirational and transformative co-production). The former focuses on individual interactions between patients and professional healthcare providers and it promotes incremental change. The latter demonstrates a more collective, transformative approach to promoting patient participation in healthcare. However, this study also shows that these two different approaches can satisfy different healthcare needs. Therefore, the patients' evaluations of the hospitals serving them show that they appear equally satisfied with the service they receive. Thus, both the aspirational and transformative approach has its advantages, and hopefully, they can learn from each other.

Finally, before presenting the Japanese data, it is important to clarify my own understanding of co-production, since it guides much of the text in the remaining chapters in this volume. As a professor of political science and public administration, I build on the role played by citizens in the provision of publicly financed services – regardless of whether the provider is public, private, NGO/NPO or a social enterprise. Therefore, the focus is on service delivery and the role played by citizen/service users in providing such services for themselves and others and, eventually, in modifying them to better suit their needs and improve the service quality. This perspective adheres more to the public administration and public management school of study than the value chain or service-dominant approach of business administration. I trust that readers of this volume will see what unique insights this perspective reveals about co-production and patient participation in healthcare. I trust that the journey will be both enriching and rewarding in terms of new knowledge and insights gained from studying co-production and Japanese healthcare.

References

Alford, J., 2002. Why do Public Sector Clients Co-produce? Towards a Contingent Theory. *Adm. Soc. 34/1*, 32–56.

Alford, J., 2009. *Engaging Public Sector Clients. From Service Delivery to Co-production.* Palgrave Macmillian, Houndmills, Hamps., UK & New York, NY.

Alford, J., 2014. The multiple facets of co-production: Building on the work of Elinor Ostrom. *Public. Manag. Rev. v. 16/3*, 299–316.

Andersen, L.L., Espersen, H.H., Tortzen, A., 2019. *Civil Society Organizations and municipalities in changing times: potentials and pitfalls in the collaborative turn.* SDU conference on Civil Society Organizations and Municipalities, Copenhagen, Aug., 2019.

Anderson, R.M., Funnell, M.M., 2012. Patient empowerment: myths and misconceptions. *Patient Educ. Counseling 79/2*, 277–282.

Batalden, M., Batalden, P., Margolis, P., Seid, M., Armstrong, G., Opipari-Arrigan, L., Hartung, H., 2015. *Coproduction of healthcare service. British Medical Journal: Quality & Safety*. DOI: 10.1136/bmjqs-2015-004315.

Benjamin, L., Brudney, J., 2018. What do Voluntary Sector Studies Offer Research on Co-Production?. Ch. 6 In: Brandsen, T., Steen, T., Verschuere, B. (Eds.), *Co-production and Co-creation. Engaging Citizens in Public Services.* Routledge, London & New York.

Bernadeo, E., Holmboe, E.S., 2013. Patients, Providers, and System Need to Acquire a Specific Set of Competencies to Achieve Truly Patient-Centered Care. *Health Aff. 32/2*, 250–258.

Bovaird, T., 2007. Beyond Engagement and Participation. Users and community co-production of public services. *Public. Adm. Rev. 67/5*, 846–860.

Bovarid, T., Löffler, E., 2012. From Engagement to Co-production. How users and communities contribute to public services. Ch. 2 In: Pestoff, V., Brandsen, T., Verschuere, B. (Eds.), *New Public Governance, the Third Sector and Co-Production.* Routledge, London & New York.

Brandsen, T., Helderman, J.K., 2012. A Case Study of German The Conditions for Successful Co-Production in Housing Cooperatives. Ch. 9 In: Pestoff, V., Brandsen, T., Verschuere, B. (Eds.), *New Public Governance, the Third Sector and Co-Production.* Routledge, London & New York.

Brandsen, T., Honingh, M., 2016. Distinguishing Different Types of Co-production. A Conceptual Definition Based on a Classical Definition. *Public. Manag. Rev. 76/3*, 427–435.

Brandsen, T., Honingh, M., 2018. definitions of Co-production and Co-creation. Ch. 2 In: Brandsen, T., Steen, T., Verschuere, B. (Eds.), *Co-production and Co-creation. Engaging Citizens in Public Services.* Routledge, London & New York.

Brandsen, T., Pestoff, V., 2006. [2009]; Co-production, the Third Sector and the Delivery of Public Services. An Introduction; special issue of *Public Management Review*, reprinted in 2009 in *Co-production, the Third Sector and the Delivery of Public Services*; London & New York: Routledge.

Brandsen, T., Steen, T., Verschuere, B. (Eds.), 2018. *Co-production and Co-creation. Engaging Citizens in Public Services.* Routledge, London & New York.

Brandsen, T., Trommel, W., Verschuere, B., 2017. The state and the re-construction of civil society. *Int. Rev. Adm. Sci. 83/4*, 676–693.

Brudney, J., England, R., 1983. Towards a Definition of the Co-production Concept. *Public. Adm. Rev. 43/1*, 59–65.

Coutler, A., Ellins, J., 2007. Effectiveness of strategies for informing, educating and involving patients. *Br. Med. J. 335*, 24–27.

Davis, G., Ostrom, E., 1991. A Public Economy Approach to Education: Choice & Co-Production. *Int. Political Sci. Rev. 12/4*, 313–335.

Dineen, R., 2017. *Co-producing prudent healthcare: putting people in the picture.* Co-production Wales.

Dunston, R., Lee, A., Boud, D., Brodie, P., Chiraella, M., 2009. Co-Production & Health System Reform – From Re-imaging to Re-Making. *Australian J. Public. Adm. 68/1*, 39–52.

Easton, D., 1965. *A Systems Analysis of Political Life.* J. Wiley & Sons, New York.

European Healthcare Management Association (EHMA), 2013. *Empowering the Patients: antecedents and consequences from a systematic literature review*; Milano: EHMA Annual Conference, book abstract 122.

Fehsenfeld, M., 2019. *Politisering af frivillighed i samspellet mellem den offentligt og den firvillige sektor: 'Vi ska tänke gadekäret ind'/Politicizing volunteering in the collaboration between the voluntary and public sectors*. SDU, Research Gate, Odense.

Fotaki, M., 2009. Patient Choice in Healthcare in the UK & Sweden: From Quasi-markets and back to markets? A Comparative analysis of the Failure of Unlearning. *Public Adm. 84/4*, 1059–1075.

Fotaki, M., 2011. Towards Developing New Partnerships in Public Services: Users as consumers, Citizens and/or Co-Producers in Health & Social Care in England & Sweden. *Public. Adm. 89/3*, 933–955.

Freise, M., 2012. Co-Producing Safety or Participative Window Dressing? Regulative Partnerships in German Local Governance Arrangements. Ch. 14 In: Pestoff, V., Brandsen, T., Verschuere, B. (Eds.), *New Public Governance, the Third Sector and Co-Production*. Routledge, London & New York.

Griffiths, S., Foley, B., 2009. *Collective Co-production: Working together to Improve Public Services - LARCI Commissioned Summary Report*. Local Authorities & Research Council Initiative, London.

Grönroos, C., 2008. Service logic revisited: who creates value? And who co-creates? *Eur. Bus. Rev. 4*, 298–314.

Grönroos, C., Voima, P., 2013. Critical Service Logic: Making Sense of Value Creation and Co-creation. *J. Acad. Mark. Sci. 41*, 133–150.

Håkansson Eklund, J., Holmström, I.K., Kumlin, T., Karminsky, E., Skoglund, K., Höglander, J., Sundler, A.J., Conden, E., Meranius, M.S., 2018. *"Same of different?" A review of reviews of person-centered and patient-centered care. Science Direct*; doi.org/10.1016/j.pec2018.08.029.

Hardyman, W., Daunt, K., Kitchner, M., 2015. Value Creation through Patient Engagement in Health Care A micro-level approach and research agenda. *Public. Manag. Rev. 7/1*, 90–107.

Hirschman, A., 1982. *Shifting Involvements*. Princeton University Press, Princeton, NJ.

Hudson, B., 2012. Competition or co-production? Which way for governance in health and wellbeing? Loeffler, E., *et al.* (Eds.), *Making Health and Social Care Personal and Local. Moving from Mass Production to Co-Production*. Governance International & Local Government Information Unit, London.

Hudson, B., 2015. Public and Patient Engagement in Commissioning in the English NHS. An idea whose time has come? *Public. Manag. Rev. 17/1*, 1–16.

Isett, K.R., Miranda, J., 2015. Watching Sausage Being Made. Lessons learned from the co-production of governance in behavioral health systems. *Public. Manag. Rev. 17/1*, 35–56.

Lee, S.Y., Arozullah, A.M., Ik Cho, Y., 2004. Health literacy, social support and health: a research agenda. *Soc. Sci. Med. 58*, 1309–1321.

Legare, F., Witteman, H.O., 2013. Shared Decision Making: Examining Key Elements and Barriers to Adoption into Routine Clinical Practice. *Health Aff. 32/2*, 276–284.

Malan, N., 2017. *The Patient Empowerment Self-Care Solution.* EHMA, European Health Management Association.

Martin, G.P., 2009. Public and User Participation in Public Service Delivery: Tensions in Policy and Practice. *Sociol. Compass 3/2*, 310–326.

Meijer, A., 2012. Co-Production in an Information Age. Ch. 10 In: Pestoff, V., Brandsen, T., Verschuere, B. (Eds.), *New Public Governance, the Third Sector and Co-Production.* Routledge, London & New York.

Meijer, A., 2016. Coproduction as a structural transformation of the public sector. *Int. J. Public. Sect. Manag. 29/6*, 596–611.

Mintzberg, H., 2012. *Managing the myths of health care. World Hospitals and Health Services 48/3.*

Nabatchi, T., Sancino, A., Siclia, M., 2017. Varieties of Participation in Public Services: The Who, When and What of Coproduction. *Public. Adm. Rev. 77*, 766–776.

Nederhand, J., van Meerkerk, I., 2018. Co-production of care services: co-opting citizens in the reform agenda. Ch. 4.1 In: Brandsen, T., Verschuere, B., Steen, T. (Eds.), *Co-production and Co-creation: Engaging Citizens in Public Services.* Routledge, New York & London.

Nordgren, L., Åhgren, B., 2013. The value creation-concept in hospitals. Health values from the patients' perspective. *Nordisk Sygeplejeforskning 3/2*, 105–116.

OECD, 2011. *Together for Better Public Service. Partnering with citizens and civil society.* OECD, Paris.

Ogawa, A., 2009. *The Failure of Civil Society. The Third Sector and State in Contemporary Japan.* State University of New York Press, Albany.

Ogawa, A., 2020. Japanese NPOs and the State Re-examined –Reflections eighteen years on. Ch. 9 In: Chiavacci, D., Grano, S., Obinger, J. (Eds.), *Civil Society and the State in Democratic East Asia.* Amsterdam University Press, Amsterdam.

Osborne, S.P., 2017. *Editorial: From public service dominant logic to public service logic: are public service organizations capable of co-production and value co-creation? Public Management Review.* DOI:m10.1080/1479037. 2017.1350461.

Osborne, S.P., McLaughlin, K., 2004. The Cross-Cutting Review of the Voluntary Sector. What next for local government voluntary sector relationships. *Regional Stud. 38/5*, 573–582.

Osborne, S.P., Radnor, Z., Nasi, G., 2012. A new theory for public service management? Towards a (public) service dominant approach. *Am. Rev. Public. Adm. 43/2*, 135–158.

Osborne, S.P., Radnor, Z., Strokosch, K., 2016. Co-production and the Co-creation of Value in Public Services: A suitable case for treatment? *Public. Manag. Rev. 15/8*, 639–653. 10.1080/14719037.2015.1111927.

Osborne, S.P., Strokosch, 2013. It Takes Two to Tango? Understanding the Co-production of Public Services by Integrating the Service Management and Public Administration Perspectives. *Br. J. Manag. 24*, 31–47.

Ostrom, E., 1996 [1999]. Crossing the Great Divide: Co-production, Synergy & Development, *World Dev. 24/6*, 1073–1087. reprinted in 1999 as Ch. 15, *Polycentric Governance and Development. Readings from the Workshop in*

Political Theory and Policy Analysis, McGinnis, Michael D. (ed.); Ann Arbor, MI: Univ. of Michigan Press.

Palumbo, R., Annarumma, C., 2016. Empowering organizations to empower patients: An organizational health literacy approach. *Int. J. Healthc. Manag. 11/2*, 133–142. 10.1080/20479700.2016.1253254.

Palumbo, R., Manna, R., 2017. *What if things go wrong in co-producing health services? Exploring the implementation problems of healthcare co-production. Policy and Society*, 1–18; DOI.org/10.1080/1449035-2018.141872.

Parks, R. B., P.C. Baker, L. Kiser, R. Oakerson, E. Ostrom, V. Ostrom, S.L. Perry, M.B. Vandivort, G.P. Whitaker (Eds), 1981 [1999]. Consumers as Co-Producers of Public Services: Some Economic and Institutional Considerations. *Policy Stud. J. v.9*, 1001–1011. reprinted in 1999 as Ch. 17 in *Local Public Economies. Readings from the Workshop in Political Theory and Policy Analysis,* McGinnis, Michael D. (ed.); Ann Arbor, MI: Univ. of Michigan Press.

Pestoff, V., 1998. *Beyond the Market & State. Social Enterprise & Civil Democracy in a Welfare Society*. Ashgate, Aldershot, UK & Brookfield, NJ.

Pestoff, V., 2006 [2009]. Citizens as Co-Producers of Welfare Services: preschool services in eight European countries. *Public. Manag. Rev.* vol. *8/4*, 503–520 and reprinted in 2009 as Ch. 2 in *Co-production. The Third Sector and the Delivery of Public Services*; V. Pestoff & T. Brandsen (eds); London & New York: Routledge.

Pestoff, V., 2008. *A Democratic Architecture for the Welfare State*. Routledge, London & New York.

Pestoff, V., 2009. Towards a Paradigm of Democratic Governance: Citizen Participation and Co-Production of Personal Social Services in Sweden. *Ann. Public. Cooperative Economy 80/2*, 197–224.

Pestoff, V., 2011. Lost in Translation or What's not included in the Polish Social Economy?, paper presented at the *ISTR International Conference*, Siena, Italy.

Pestoff, V., 2012. Co-production and Third Sector Social Services in Europe: Some concepts and Evidence. *Voluntas 23*, 1102–1118.

Pestoff, V., 2014a. Collective Action and the Sustainability of Co-production. *Public. Manag. Rev. 16/3*, 383–401.

Pestoff, V., 2014b. The Role of Participatory Governance in the EMES Approach to Social Enterprise. *J. Entrepreneurial Organ. Diversity, JEOD 2/2*, 48–60.

Pestoff, V., 2018. *Co-production and Public Service Management. Democracy, Citizenship and Public Service Management.* Routledge, London & New York.

Pestoff, V., 2019. Promoting Co-production in Japanese Healthcare: A tale of two cooperative healthcare providers and two kinds of co-production. *EMES conference paper*. Sheffield, UK.

Pestoff, V., Brandsen, T. (Eds.), 2006. [2009]. *Public Management Review* (vol. 8/4). and reprinted in 2009 *Co-production. The Third Sector and the Delivery of Public Services*, Routledge, London & New York.

Pestoff, V., Brandsen, T., Verschuere, B. (Eds.), 2012. *New Public Governance, the Third Sector and Co-Production*. Routledge, London & New York.

Pestoff, V., Hulgård, L., 2016. Participatory Governance in Social Enterprise. *Voluntas 27/4*, 1742–1759. 10.1007/s11266-015-9662-3.

Porter, D., 2012. Co-Production and Network Structures in Public Education. Ch. 8 In: Pestoff, V., Brandsen, T., Verschuere, B. (Eds.), *New Public Governance, the Third Sector and Co-Production.* Routledge, London & New York.

Porter, M.E., 2010. What is value in health care? N. *Engl. J. Med. 363*, 2477–2481. Suppl. Appendix 1.

Prentice, S., 2006. Childcare, Co-production and the Third Sector in Canada. *Public. Manag. Rev.* vol. *8/4*, 830–849 and reprinted in 2009 as Ch. 3 in *Co-production. The Third Sector and the Delivery of Public Services*; V. Pestoff & T. Brandsen (eds); London & New York: Routledge.

Realpe, A., Wallace, L.M., 2010. *What is co-production?.* The Health Foundation, London.

Renedo, A., Marston, C.A., Spyridonidis, D., Barlow, J., 2015. Patient and Public Involvement in Healthcare Quality Improvements. How organizations can help patients and professionals to collaborate. *Public. Manag. Rev. 17/1*, 17–34.

Ricker, J., 2012. *Patient-centered care: What it means and how to get there. Health Affairs*; blog on Jan. 24, 2012.

Rosentraub, M., Warren, R., 1987. Citizen Participation in the Production of Urban Services. *Public. Product. Rev. 41*, 75–89.

Schlappa, H., 2012; Co-management and Urban Regeneration. New Perspectives on Transferable Collaborative Practice; Ch. 12, In: V. Pestoff & T. Brandsen (Eds.), *Co-production. The Third Sector and the Delivery of Public Services.* London & New York: Routledge.

Slocock, S., 2015. *Whose society? The Final Big Society Audit.* Civil Change, London.

Söderholm Werkö, S., 2008. *Patient Patients? Achieving Patient Empowerment through active participation, increased knowledge and organization.* School of Business, Stockholm.

Summer Meranius, M., Holmström, I.K., Håkansson, J., Breitholz, A., Moniri, F., Skogevall, S., Skoglund, K., Rasoal, D., 2020. *Paradoxes of person-centered care: A discussion paper. Nursing Open.* Wiley; DOI: 10.1002/nop2.520.

Tholstrup, J., 2012. Empowering patients to need less care and to do better in Highland Hospital, South Sweden. In: Loeffler, E., *et al.* (Eds.), *Making Health and Social Care Personal and Local. Moving from Mass Production to Co-Production.* Governance International & Local Government Information Unit, London.

Thomas, J.C., 2012. *Citizen, Customer & Partner. Engaging the Public in Public Management.* M.E. Scharp, Armonk, NY.

Thomas, J.C., 2013. Citizens, Customers, Partners: Rethinking the Place of the Public in Public Management. *Public. Adm. Rev.* 73, 786–796.

Tsutsui, T., 2014. *Implementation process and challenges for the Community-based Integrated Care system in Japan. International Journal of Integrated Care*, Jan-Mar, 2014 e002, 20 Jan., 2014. Doi: 10.5334/ijic.988.

Tyrell, M., 2020. *Voices to remember: Persons' and family members' experiences of living with neurocognitive disorders and related symptoms.* Karolinska institutet, Master's thesis, Stockholm.

Univ. of New Mexico, 2020. What is Patient-Centered Care? Accessed on 6 July, 2020.

Vamstad, J., 2007. *Gov. Welf. Third Sect. Chall. Swed. Welfare State*. Mid-Sweden University Doctoral Thesis 37, Östersund.

Vamstad, J., 2012. Co-Production and Service Quality: A New Perspective on the Swedish Welfare State. Ch. 16 In: Pestoff, V., Brandsen, T., Verschuere, B. (Eds.), *New Public Governance, the Third Sector and Co-Production*. Routledge, London & New York and reprinted in *Voluntas*, Dec. 2012.

Vancoppenolle, D., Verschuere, B., 2012. The Challenges of Co-management for Public Accountability: Lessons from Flemish Child Care. Ch. 18 In: Pestoff, V., Brandsen, T., Verschuere, B. (Eds.), *New Public Governance, the Third Sector and Co-Production*. Routledge, London & New York.

Voorberg, W., Bekkers, V., Tummers, L., 2015. A Systematic Review of Co-creation and Co-production: Embarking on the Social Innovation Journal. *Public. Manag. Rev. 17/9*, 1333–1357.

Voorberg, W., Bekkers, V., Fleming, S., Timeus, K., Tornrist, P., Tummers, L.G., 2017. Does Co-creation Impact Public Service Delivery?. *Public Money Manag. 37/5*, 365–373.

Walden-Laing, D., Pestoff, V., 1997. The Role of Non-Profit Organizations in Managing AIDS in Sweden. Ch. 4 In: Kenis, P., Marine, B. (Eds.), *Managing AIDS: Organizational Responses in Six European Countries*. Ashgate, Aldershot & Brookfield, NJ.

Warren, R., Harlow, K., Rosentraub, M., 1982. Citizen Participation in the Production of Services: Methodological and Policy Issues in Coproduction Research. *Southwest. Rev. Manag. Econ.* 2, 41–55.

World Health Organization, 2005. *Ninth Futures Forum on Health Systems Governance and Public Participation*. WHO, Copenhagen.

World Health Organization, 2007. *People centered health care: a policy framework*. WHO, Regional Office for the Western Pacific, Manila.

World Health Organization, 2016. *WHO Global Strategy on People-Centered and Integrated Health Services, Interim Report*. WHO, Geneva.

Part II

Co-production and Japanese Healthcare

5 Research on Japanese Healthcare

Background, Data and Methods

This chapter provides a technical overview of this project on Co-production and Japanese Healthcare. It introduces the data collection and the procedures for collecting it. First, the Organization Study was based on interviews conducted with the CEOs and board members of eight cooperative hospitals. Second, the Staff Study was based on questionnaires developed to explore the relationship between work environment and service quality at these eight cooperative hospitals in 2016, plus two public hospitals in Osaka in 2017. Third, the Patient Study and Volunteer Study collected questionnaire data in 2017 at four of the cooperative hospitals. The presentation begins with a brief background of cooperative healthcare in Japan. Then it discusses planning of the survey data collection and the phases involved in the project, followed by a brief overview of the data and questionnaires, the sampling procedures for each study; and finally, there is a short note on some of the project's shortcomings.

A Introduction

This research project[1] relies on several data sources to address a variety of questions that explore different aspects of co-production in Japanese healthcare. This project began in 2013 with onsite visits to nine co-operative hospitals in different parts of Japan. They were proposed by a reference committee made up of the umbrella organizations of co-operative healthcare providers that operate hospitals, clinics and elder-care facilities. We interviewed the president, managing director and board members of these hospitals and employed semi-structured open questions to gain insights into the hospital, its operations and to explain the purpose of our project. The results of these onsite meetings comprise the Organizational Study. We then developed questionnaires for the main stakeholders included in this study: the staff, patients and volunteers. Eight out of the nine cooperative hospitals agreed to participate in our study, and two public hospitals were added later. The Staff Study employed a work environment approach and collected 6,859 completed staff answer sheets in the summer of 2016 from four Medical Co-ops and four *Koseiren* hospitals and eldercare facilities, and the following spring from two public hospitals. We continued with the Patient Study and Volunteer Study in the Spring of 2017 and collected 631 respective 236 completed answer sheets from the patients and volunteers at two of the Medical Co-ops and two *Koseiren* hospitals.

Data from these studies describes and analyzes several different aspects of co-production, work environment, governance, service quality and social values in Japanese healthcare. Having access to data from four separate sources – the leaders, staff, patients and volunteers – allows us to compare and corroborate the details and dimensions of one study in relation to another. For example, if the staff indicates that it provides high-quality services to its clients or patients, what do the patients think about it and what do the volunteers say? Similarly, if the staff at hospital A or hospital B claims that it promotes certain social values, we need to ask what do the patients or volunteers think about the hospital's social contribution to the community? Using different sources allows us to cross-check facts and explore different dimensions of the phenomenon at hand. This study benefits from a comparative approach, and Chapter 11 compares the staff, patient and volunteer perspectives on the hospitals' social values and mission as well as their willingness to recommend the service to friends and acquaintances.

Exploring models that promote public participation in healthcare poses a challenge – the lack of good examples or 'best practices'. A theoretical sample would focus on 'user-owned' healthcare providers, but there are very few examples of user-owned and controlled healthcare services in Europe. According to the United Nations global survey (1997), Japan has a unique healthcare system with not just one, but two user-owned healthcare providers. Therefore, we turned our attention to Japan.

There was a serious problem of accessibility to healthcare in Japan before World War II, particularly in rural areas. As noted earlier in Chapter 3, civil society can help fill the gap in healthcare provision. The first health co-op was founded in Aohara Village, Shimane Prefecture in 1919. Local people worked together to start a small clinic and hired a medical doctor from town. This movement spread to other rural areas in Japan. Later, it became easier to start new clinics in rural areas and poor towns because of national insurance. In 1961, the National Health Care Insurance was expanded to provide universal coverage, similar to the German model, for the entire population. It not only included employees, but also farmers, owners of small shops, among others. However, service provision is poorly coordinated, mainly through non-public hospitals/clinics. Free access to healthcare resulted in imbalanced healthcare provision in terms of locality or specialty and severe congestion at large hospitals. Among the service providers, medical corporations are set up as nonprofits and they occupy a dominant position today (e.g. 68% of hospitals and 42% of primary care clinics). However, their nonprofit status is questionable, since the non-distribution constraint is not evenly enforced. Public hospitals were set up to serve the specific needs of public interest, but they have decreased in number due to a persistent deficit in their operations (Kurimoto, 2015).

Today, there are two user-owned healthcare providers in Japan. First is *Koseiren* (Federation of Agricultural Cooperatives for Health and Welfare), which is affiliated with Japanese Agriculture (JA) and provides healthcare for JA members and the public mainly in the rural areas, but *Koseiren* has no individual members. In 2019, it provided healthcare services at 107 hospitals and 59 clinics, 99 home nursing stations, 33 rehabilitation facilities, nine nursing homes. It has a nationwide capacity of 33,483 beds and nearly 55,000 employees (Koseiren homepage, 2020). Historically, *Koseiren* played the role of a core hospital in rural areas, and today, nearly 40% of them are located in municipalities with populations of less than 50,000 people. It is the only option in one quarter of the towns and villages where they are located (Kurimoto, 2015, 2018).

The second are the health co-ops that mainly provide healthcare in urban areas. In 2010, the health co-ops associated with the Japanese Consumers' Cooperative Union (JCCU) joined together to form the Japanese Health and Welfare Co-op Federation (HeW CO-OP JAPAN). In 2018, it consisted of 105 health and welfare cooperatives with nearly 3 million individual members. It managed 75 hospitals with 12,000 beds nationwide. In addition, it operated 345 primary health centers, 79 dental clinics, 175 visiting nurse stations, 24 nursing care facilities and 195 home helper stations. Together, they have nearly 40,000 employees nationwide, including more than 2,000 doctors (HeW CO-OP JAPAN homepage, 2020). Both these cooperative healthcare providers were discussed in greater detail in Chapter 3.

B The Japanese Project Plan

This project focuses on co-production, work environment, governance, service quality, social values and organizational logics in multi-stakeholder organizations that provide healthcare. This involves eight cooperative hospitals in six different prefectures of Japan. Table 5.A in the appendix has a list of participating healthcare providers. This includes four medical or consumer co-op healthcare providers in urban areas and four agricultural co-op or *Koseiren* healthcare providers in rural and suburban areas, plus two public hospitals in Osaka. This research project was conducted within the framework of established collaboration between senior researchers at Ersta Sköndal Bräcke University College in Stockholm (Prof. V. Pestoff and Doc. J. Vamstad) and the Graduate School of Human Sciences, Osaka University (Prof. Y. Saito). This interdisciplinary group of Swedish and Japanese researchers was supported by a reference group of the relevant cooperative health and eldercare providers in Japan, *Koseiren* (Agricultural Cooperatives of

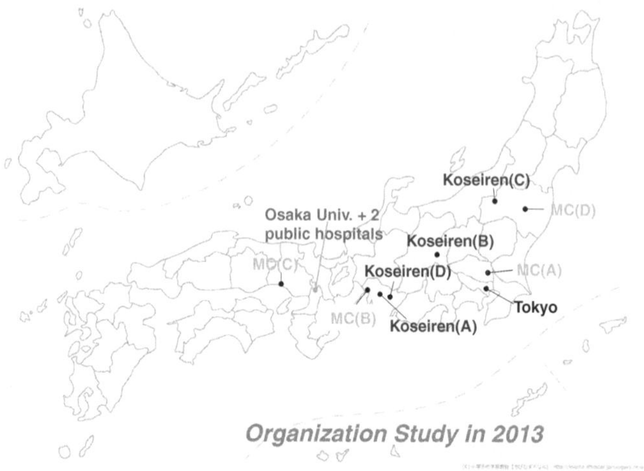

Figure 5.1 Map of Participating Hospitals.

Health and Welfare) and the Japanese Health and Welfare Co-operative Federation, HeW CO-OP JAPAN. The Consumer Cooperative Institute of Japan (CCIJ, Mr. Akira Kurimoto and Ms. Y. Yamazaki) also collaborated in this project.

A brief description of the four participating Medical Co-ops (A, B, C and D) and four *Koseiren* hospitals (A, B, C and D) is found in Table 5.A in the appendix to this chapter. Figure 5.1 shows the location of the hospitals.

The empirical materials in this project were collected in four different phases. Currently, we are in the fifth and final data analysis phase. These phases are/were:

Phase One – Field Mapping Study: In May 2013, the management and directors of nine cooperative hospitals were interviewed on-site using a structured interview schedule to obtain necessary background data about these organizations. Written records – like annual general reports, budgets and other relevant documents – were also collected at this time. Together, they comprise the Organization Study that provides information about their organizational conditions and complexity, governance models and organizational logics, as well as some important insights into their institutional and environmental conditions.

Phase Two – Questionnaires and Pilot Study: In 2014 and 2015, the information collected by the Organizational Study contributed to constructing relevant interviews and survey instruments for the staff, patients and volunteers. The staff questionnaire was tested in a pilot study at three hospitals to determine if major adjustments were required in the measurement instruments, but this was not deemed necessary.

Phase Three – The Staff, Patient and Volunteer Studies: During the summer of 2016 and spring of 2017, these questionnaires were employed at a wider range of hospitals in order to gain a more nuanced understanding of how co-production was perceived in Japanese healthcare, as well as the importance of work environment and institutions, that promote a multi-stakeholder dialog. The survey studies were carried out with three different questionnaires for the staff, patients and volunteers at the relevant cooperative healthcare providers.

Phase Four – Repeating the Staff Study at Two Public Hospitals: In the summer of 2017, similar materials were collected from the staff of two public hospitals in Osaka, and they were merged with materials gathered from the eight cooperative hospitals participating in this study of Co-production and Japanese Healthcare.

Phase Five – Analysis of the Data: This phase involves analyzing the data collected in the Staff Study, Patient Study and Volunteer Study. The analytical model of this project primarily focuses on the surveys to measure the output and outcome, while a study of documents and interviews from the hospitals help to provide the necessary context in which to analyze the findings from the surveys.

C Methods, Data and Questionnaires

A brief word about the two main methods employed in this study of Co-production and Japanese Healthcare is due. First is the comparative method of political science, and there are two varieties of this method. One can choose relatively similar countries, institutions or organizations and search for differences between them. Alternatively, one can choose rather different countries, institutions or organizations and search for similarities among them. In this case, we will focus on healthcare organizations operating in the same sector or field and country, so we will explore differences between them. The benefits of this method are considered in Chapter 12.

Second, this study has a strong focus on work environment, which allows us to evaluate questions about influence and control. Employing a work environment approach contributes to understanding how healthcare providers function in Japan and how they can contribute to improving service quality – particularly, in highly complex social services like healthcare. Comparing these two user-owned healthcare groups with public providers of healthcare in Japan will, hopefully, allow us to identify and isolate the factors that can facilitate greater staff control over their work life and promote active patient participation in their healthcare.

The initial premise of the Staff Study was rather simple and straightforward: More satisfied employees produce more satisfactory results than less satisfied employees. In our study, 'more satisfactory results' means less stress, fewer health issues for the staff and better quality services for the patients. To evaluate the contribution of work environment to healthcare provision in Japan, we included the following work-related aspects of their daily life: social support, influence, personal development and the classical Karasek and Theorell Demand/Control variables as well as staff contact with clients and other relevant stakeholders.

D Sampling Procedures and Response Rates

The data collection was financed by the Japanese Society for the Promotion of Science (JSPS, #15K03913), the Mitsubishi Foundation and the International Joint Research Program of Osaka University. It was supervised by Prof. Yayoi Saito, Osaka University. The Staff Survey was approved (#2015035) by the Ethics Review Board at the Department of Sociology at the Graduate School of Human Sciences, Osaka University.

In 2013, we visited nine cooperative healthcare providers in different parts of Japan to enlist their support for our project. We presented our project plans and interviewed their directors, board members and managers at that time. Eight of them agreed to actively participate in this study, and their staff would contribute to it. In 2014 and 2015, we developed the measurement instrument for the Staff Study in the form of a questionnaire adapted from the biannual Swedish SCB Work Environment Study. These healthcare organizations also agreed to assist us in distributing and collecting the anonymous staff questionnaires. In order to ensure the study's confidentiality, we provided the healthcare organizations with the staff questionnaire, an answer sheet and a sealable envelope in the same number as the total number of employees at each hospital in the spring of 2016. These healthcare organizations, in turn, provided the staff with information about the importance of filling in the questionnaires, and a central place at the hospital for returning their sealed, anonymous answers. Once the staff had completed the survey, their answer sheets in sealed envelopes were shipped in bulk to a separate data company, where they were coded and recorded. We received the coded staff answers in the form of an Excel file and then converted it into an SPSS file.

In 2016, we added a Patient and Volunteer Study to the project and developed an appropriate questionnaire for each of these groups. In the spring of 2017, four of the co-op hospitals assisted us in distributing and collecting the patient and volunteer questionnaires which were once again in sealed envelopes. We received 631 completed patient questionnaires and 236 completed volunteer questionnaires. Finally, in the fall of 2017, we replicated the Staff Study at two public hospitals in Osaka and solicited their responses in a similar fashion – in sealed envelopes. We received 1,445 completed staff questionnaires from the staff at these two public hospitals in Osaka. Neither the patient nor the volunteer survey was conducted at the public hospitals.

1 *Staff Survey*

Below is a short description of the process for obtaining access to the hospitals, gaining their participation, distributing questionnaires and collecting answer sheets. In the spring of 2016, Professor Yayoi Saito contacted the respective national organizations for cooperative healthcare providers, HeW CO-OP and Zenkoren (the national organizations for *Koseiren*). She met with their leaders, elicited their support for the Staff Study and obtained their agreement with the data collection procedures. The HeW CO-OP Federation sent a letter to five presumptive co-op healthcare providers to secure their participation in the Staff Survey, and four of them agreed to do so. Later, Professor Saito and the Chief of the Management Consulting of Zenkoren visited each of the four *Koseiren* hospital directors involved in the Organizations Study to explain the Staff Study and necessary survey procedures and met the contact person at each hospital.

Following these agreements, a discussion about the actual procedure of the survey began with the appropriate contact people at each participating health co-op and *Koseiren* hospital. The number of answer sheets was calculated for the entire staff at each participating hospitals, clinics and eldercare facilities – both at the Medical Co-ops and *Koseiren* hospitals – and a decision was made about how best to distribute and collect them. Then questionnaires and survey answer sheets were sent to a contact person at each participating health co-op and *Koseiren* hospital at the beginning of July, and the initial requested date for returning the answer sheets was set for one month later, but additional answer sheets were accepted until the end of August, 2016 (Table 5.1).

For three of the health co-ops, Medical Co-ops B, C and D and for all four *Koseiren* hospitals, the questionnaires, answer sheets and plain envelopes were sent to the contact person at each healthcare organization and distributed to the staff. Respondents put their answer sheet in the envelope and sealed it before returning it to the contact person or dropping it in the collection box. The contact person was provided a prepaid transmittal form and instructions to send the answer sheets to the data processing company by the end of August at the latest. However, one health co-op – Medical Co-op A – preferred to use a different procedure. To insure anonymity, the staff was provided with stamped envelopes addressed directly to the Consumer Co-operative Institute in Tokyo. Unfortunately, the return rate for this health co-op was rather low, partly because it had recently just participated in another major staff survey in July and partly because they chose a different return procedure.

Table 5.1 Respondents and Response Rate for the Staff Study

*Organization**	*No. Sent*	*No. Returned*	*Response Rate*	*% Per Hosp. Gp.**
Medical Co-ops:	4,500	2,852	62.8%	100%
A	1,960	735	37.5%	25.7
B	1,250	988	79.0%	34.6
C	860	714	83.0%	25.1
D	430	415	96.5%	14.6
Koseiren:	2,990	2,562	85.7%	100%
A	1,500	1,356	90.4%	52.9
B	790	595	76.3%	23.2
C	390	334	85.6%	13.0
D	310	277	89.4%	10.8
Public:	1,980	1,445	73.0%	100%
A	700	418	59.7%	28.9
B	1,280	1,027	80.2%	71.1
Total (All Hospitals.)	9,510	6,859	72.1%	

*Adds column-wise and group-wise.

A data processing company (Tokai Kyodo Printing Company, Ltd. in Aichi Prefecture) processed all the returned answer sheets and produced raw data by early September, 2016. Prof. Yayoi Saito, Ms. Yukiko Yamazaki and a research assistant at the Consumer Cooperative Institute of Japan (CCIJ) cleaned the raw data from September to October of the same year. See Pestoff (2017a) for a brief presentation of the Staff Study.

2 *Patient and Volunteer Survey*

The following describes the process of distributing questionnaires and collecting answer sheets. After consulting with HeW CO-OP JAPAN in early January, 2017, we intended to conduct the Patient and Volunteer Surveys at two out of four health co-ops that participated in the Staff Survey. Medical Co-ops A and B agreed to join this effort. The research target was outpatients both at the hospitals and primary care clinics. Together with HeW CO-OP, it was determined how many questionnaires and answer sheets would be necessary and how best to distribute and collect them. In general, a contact person at each healthcare provider would be in charge of distributing these to the patients and volunteers. Both Medical Co-ops A and B participate in the annual Patients' Satisfaction Survey of the Hew Co-op Federation, and, therefore, have experience with survey management. Questionnaires and answer sheets for both volunteers and patients were sent to the two participating co-op healthcare providers in mid-February, and they distributed these to the hospitals and certain clinics via the contact person. They were requested to return the answer sheets by the end of March, but the late ones were accepted until April 10.

An appropriate predetermined number of questionnaires, answer sheets and plain envelopes was sent to the contact person at each hospital. Envelopes allowed the respondents to put their answer sheet in and seal before returning it to the volunteers or dropping it in the collection box. The staff at the hospitals of Medical Co-ops A and B divided the questionnaires between the hospital and some clinics. Volunteers, co-op members and the staff worked together to distribute these at the hospital outpatients waiting rooms, and respondents returned the questionnaires in sealed envelopes to them or a central point.

A similar procedure was followed for the *Koseiren* hospitals. Prof. Saito visited Zenkoren to request their participation in the Patient and Volunteer Surveys in early January, 2017 (Table 5.2). They decided that *Koseiren* Hospitals A and D would join the survey, and Prof. Saito sent a letter to the hospital directors requesting their participation. Questionnaires and answer sheets for both volunteers and patients were sent to the two participating *Koseiren* hospitals early in March. However, the distribution and collection of the answer sheets followed different procedures at the two hospitals. At Hospital A, the administrative staff asked outpatients in the hospital waiting room to answer the questionnaire, but very few did. They noted that there were not sufficient staff to support the patient survey during the research period. This, unfortunately, resulted in a lower participation rate by patients. At *Koseiren* Hospital D, the staff distributed the questionnaire at the monthly patient meeting. Most of the patients live far from the hospital, so the staff asked them to take them home and send them back to the hospital by regular mail. This resulted in different participation rates for the two *Koseiren* hospitals. Both hospitals were requested to return the answer sheets by the end of March, but late ones were accepted until the middle of April.

The contact person at those four healthcare organizations gathered the sealed patient and volunteer answer sheets and sent them back to Prof.

Table 5.2 Participation Rate in the Patient* and Volunteer** Surveys***

Organization	*Patients*	*Per Hosp. Gp.****	*Volunteers*****	*Per Hosp. Gp.****
Medical Co-ops:	517	100%	172	100%
A	333	64.4%	99	57.6%
B	184	35.6%	73	42.2%
***Koseiren*:**	114	100%	64	100%
A	32	28.1%	35	54.7%
D	82	71.9%	29	45.3%
Totals	632		236	

*Respondents are only outpatients at the hospitals or clinics. No inpatients or eldercare patients are included; **Volunteers mean people who worked at the hospital or clinic in a voluntary capacity at the time of this survey; ***Period: February-March, 2017. Adds column-wise.

Saito at Osaka University. A paid transmittal form was provided. A data processing company (Tokai Kyodo Printing Company, Ltd. in Aichi Prefecture) processed all of the returned answer sheets and produced the raw patient and volunteer data in April, 2017. A research assistant at the Consumer Cooperative Institute of Japan cleaned the raw data in early May and sent it to Prof. Saito at Osaka University. See Pestoff (2017b) for a brief presentation of the Patient Study and Pestoff (2017c) for a brief presentation of the Volunteer Study.

3 Staff Survey for Public Hospitals

At the beginning of June, 2017, Prof. Saito solicited permission from the hospital directors at two public hospitals in Osaka to participate in the Staff Survey. They agreed but requested to exclude some information about the staff's social background (e.g. age, family status and income). The survey at the two public hospitals was conducted in a fashion similar to the one noted above for the cooperative healthcare providers. Questionnaires and survey answer sheets were sent to a contact person at both participating public hospitals at the end of August, 2017, and the initial requested return date for answer sheets was set for one month later; nonetheless, additional answer sheets were accepted until the end of September, 2017. However, due to time constraints, it was not possible to undertake a patient survey or volunteer survey at the public hospitals at this time.

E Data Presentation

Many of the questions included in the three surveys are based on five-point ordinal scales of agreement that range from 1) agree to 5) disagree. However, most of the tables found here only include the proportion of positive answers in order to simplify the presentation of an extensive amount of data. Other questions allowed respondents to choose up to three alternatives that best reflected a diversity of views. Some of these responses have been combined, reducing the number of alternatives reported for the sake of simplicity. Combined answers are indicated in *italics*. Most of the tables in this book indicate the difference in the percentage of positive answers for staff at the Medical Co-ops, *Koseiren* and public hospitals, as Dif. (h-l). This is obtained by subtracting the lowest positive score from the highest. Most of the time, this favors the Medical Co-ops, but, when it favors *Koseiren* or public hospitals, it is followed by the letter K or P. If the difference between the highest and lowest score remains at 5% or below, it is considered low, while rates between 5% and 10% are moderate. Above that level, it is considered high. Most of the comments and comparisons focus on questions or variables when the difference between them is 10% or more. Finally, the analysis of patient and volunteer data only includes the Medical Co-ops and *Koseiren* hospitals. Often, the Medical Co-ops rank highest in tables, but, when it favors the *Koseiren* hospitals, it is followed by the letter K.

Moreover, several work environment indices are employed in the tables and chapters of this volume. They usually summarize information from three to five similar items in the Staff Study – like social support, work demands, control, among others. They provide a more robust measure of such items than a single question could. This also saves space and simplifies the presentation. They were calculated and corroborated with the help of the Cronbach's Alfa. Table 6.A in Chapter 6 provides a list of the questions included in each index as well as the Cronbach's Alfa values. Another step taken to streamline the extensive data presented herein is dividing these in dices into three roughly equal parts – high, medium and low. However, in general, only the proportion of responses that belongs to the high category is presented – once again to simplify the data presentation and save space. A clear deviation from a high score of 33% is, therefore, noteworthy.

Furthermore, a few of the questions in each of the studies were multiple response questions – where respondents could choose more than one answer, or they could choose up to three items from a list of 8–10 items. Usually, the percent of respondents choosing an alternative is equal to the number of responses, unless missing data are excluded, but that is not the case with multiple response sets. In fact, SPSS tabulations of multiple response data provide two alternative sets of figures: one for the proportion of cases or respondents who choose a particular item and another for the proportion of the total responses. The first set of figures adds to 100%, while the second frequently exceeds that. After careful consideration, it was decided to report the percentage of respondents in these multiple response sets rather than the proportion of responses. While this procedure clearly underestimates support for a particular item, perhaps, by as much as a factor of two and a half, it nevertheless allows for a more pedagogical approach, since it avoids the confusion when percent figures frequently exceeded 100%. Reporting the lower set of figures is limited to the tables found in Chapters 10 and 11 on hospital social profiles.

Finally, correlations between variables that are calculated with the help of Spearman's Rho were used to establish the existence of an association between them. These statistics were considered preferable to regression coefficients, since this study involves several interrelated aspects or dimensions of co-production and healthcare. Given the complexity of the potential interrelationships between the concepts and variables employed in this study as noted in Figure 1.1, it behooves us to focus more on understanding the relations or interaction between the variables than on exploring the possibility of determining causality between them. Producing a full-page printout with several dozen figures of varying significance, where only a few followed by three stars are considered important enough to discuss, seems questionable if the intention is to better understand how one concept or variable is related to another. It is easy to imagine a complex print-out with several dozen figures on a page and three stars following a variable like gender, age or education. This is not uncommon in academic journals today. However, what would that tell us, if anything, about the relationship between work environment and governance, work satisfaction and service quality or occupational status and social values? In order to explore the interaction between the key concepts employed in this study, we intend, therefore, to focus on the association or relation between them, rather than exploring and explaining the possible causality between them while ignoring all the rest of the potential associations. Therefore, this effort should perhaps be considered more like weaving a tapestry than needlework. Rather than focusing on the color of each thread, we hope to show the bigger picture.

F Some Limitations

This study, like most empirical studies in the social sciences, is subject to some limitations. The most important ones are briefly presented below.

Not all of the ten hospitals in the Staff Study followed the proposed sampling procedure for distributing the questionnaire nor the same process for returning the answer sheets. This was unavoidable, since one hospital had just completed another major survey study shortly before ours arrived, which probably resulted in survey fatigue. Also, this hospital preferred to return the answer sheets in individual stamped prepaid envelopes rather than collecting the sealed response envelopes centrally, as was the case for the other hospitals. This resulted in a much lower response rate.

There were an insufficient number of questions about health issues and stress symptoms among the 110 questions and sub-questions in the Staff Survey. This is clearly a deviation from a classical work environment study. This was motivated by the desire to include questions about other items – such as hospital values, and social missions, the staff's relations with stakeholder groups, etc. As a result, we cannot adequately discuss the staff's health outcomes nor their typical stress symptoms. This is unfortunate, since this is an important aspect of work environment studies.

A lack of resources prevented us from collecting patient and volunteer surveys at all ten of the participating hospitals. Only two of the four cooperative hospitals in each healthcare group participated in the Patient Study and Volunteer Study, while none of the public hospitals did. In particular, the lack of patients and volunteers at the public hospitals limits the possibility to compare them with either or both cooperative hospital groups and to draw any conclusions about the attitudes and behavior of patients and volunteers at public hospitals.

The importance of local social capital for cooperative healthcare was underestimated at the outset, particularly concerning the role of volunteers. Volunteering was discussed with the directors and boards of the cooperative hospitals in 2013 as part of the Organization Study. However, it seems important to distinguish between in-house or in-hospital volunteering and community volunteering. The Volunteer Study, developed after the interviews with the directors of the co-op hospitals, did not clearly reflect this distinction. The potential contribution of community volunteering to provide local social capital and/or promote community development was not adequately documented. The volunteer questionnaire was only distributed on-site to in-hospital volunteers and not to community volunteers. The latter are much harder to reach, since they often reside in remote towns and rural villages. Accordingly, the Volunteer Study underestimates the importance of volunteering – in particular, community volunteering. An ethnographic study would be necessary to do justice to this topic.

A few of the questions included in all three surveys resulted in a high level of missing data or a high proportion of 'neither agree nor disagree' responses. This might indicate a respondent's inability and/or unwillingness to reply to a given question. In such cases, we note the missing data in a separate table in the appendix of the relevant chapters. However, when missing data was high, we were reluctant to include such questions or variables when constructing an index related to these questions.

SPSS was employed for the statistical analysis of all three studies – for the staff, patients and volunteers. However, the completion of some of the more advanced analyses was not possible at the time of publication of this volume. Hopefully, additional results from this unique data collection will appear in articles submitted to reputable academic journals that will eventually help to compensate for this shortcoming.

This volume only represents the 'tip of the iceberg' of user-owned healthcare providers in Japan. It would require another 200 pages to provide a deeper understanding of this fascinating phenomenon, but neither the time nor resources are available. In addition, some facts and details were, most likely, 'lost in translation', and the author assumes full responsibility for such shortcomings.

Finally, time and resources have also ruled out a comparison of the hospitals in each hospital group with each other. That might provide some interesting differences, but such efforts will have to wait for younger researchers to take up the challenge.

Note

1 The data collection was financed by the Japanese Society for the Promotion of Science (JSPS), the Mitsubishi Foundation and Osaka University, supervised by Prof. Yayoi Saito, Osaka University. The project is conducted within the framework of established cooperation between senior researchers at Ersta Sköndal Bräcke University College in Stockholm (Prof. V. Pestoff and Doc. J. Vamstad) and the Faculty of Human Sciences, Osaka University

(Prof. Y. Saito). This interdisciplinary group of Swedish and Japanese researchers is supported by a reference group of the relevant cooperative healthcare providers in Japan, *Koseiren* and the Japanese Health and Welfare Co-operative Federation HeW CO-OP JAPAN.

References

HeW CO-OP JAPAN homepage, accessed on 22 July, 2020.

KOSEIREN homepage, accessed on 22 July, 2020.

Kurimoto, A., 2015. *Social Enterprise Models Providing Health and Social Services in Japan*. ICSEM Working Paper, Liege, pp. 2005–2007.

Kurimoto, A., 2018. Chapter 4 Japan: Health and Elderly Care Cooperatives. In: IHCO, EURICSE (Eds.), *Co-operative Health Report: Assessing the worldwide contribution of cooperatives to healthcare*. IHCO and EURICSE, Geneva & Trento.

Pestoff, V., 2017a. *Staff Study: A preliminary overview of the results from 10 hospitals*. Ersta Sköndal Bräcke University College & Osaka University, Stockholm & Osaka.

Pestoff, V., 2017b. *The Patient Study: A preliminary overview of the questions and answers*. Ersta Sköndal Bräcke University College & Osaka University, Stockholm & Osaka.

Pestoff, V., 2017c. *Volunteer Study: A preliminary overview of the questions and answers*. Ersta Sköndal Bräcke University College & Osaka University, Stockholm & Osaka.

United Nations, 1997. *Co-operative Enterprise in the Health and Social Care Sectors*. United Nations, New York.

Appendix 5

Table 5.A Main Characteristics of the Participating Hospitals

1) Medical Cooperatives

Medical Co-op A: It was created nearly 30 years ago with the amalgamation of six small health cooperatives in a suburb of Tokyo, in Saitama Prefecture. It has four hospitals, eight primary care clinics, three dental clinics, two long term care facilities and 17 homecare service stations. Its largest hospital has 450 beds. It has nearly 2,000 employees. It participated in the pretest, Staff, Patient and Volunteer Surveys.

Medical Co-op B: Residents established a local clinic in 1962, after a typhoon killed more than 5,000 people. It is located in a suburb of Nagoya City in Aichi Prefecture. Today it has two hospitals, with nearly 400 beds, five primary care clinics, a group living for persons with dementia and a service house for the elderly, home visit nursing stations, day care service centers for seniors, etc. Its new hospital was built without any municipal funds, but 20% of the investment was paid for by contributions and donations from its members. It has approximately 1,250 employees. It participated in the pretest, Staff, Patient and Volunteer Survey.

Medical Co-op C: It is located in a small city in Hiyogo Prefecture. There were three big hospitals in the area, but residents wanted one where they could participate. In 1975 they build a clinic and eventually completed a small hospital in 1985, with fewer than 60 beds. Rather than trying to build a new hospital, with all the expensive investment in medical equipment, it is rapidly expanding in providing eldercare services. Now it also runs two primary care facilities, a dental clinic, seven home help stations, seven home nursing stations, four day service centers and two day care centers for seniors, with a staff size of under 900 employees. It participated in the pretest, Staff, Patient and Volunteer Surveys.

Medical Co-op D: It is located in a suburb of Fukushima City, Fukushima Prefecture. It does not have a hospital, but runs four primary care facilities, with 'state of the art' equipment, plus a group home, three home visit nursing stations and other outreach facilities, with a staff size of approximately 450 employees. The authorities won't let them build a hospital, so they are increasing their capacity in long term eldercare. It provided local residents with essential services after the earthquake, tsunami and nuclear disaster of 2011. With the help of the JCCU, it obtained four radiation scanning machines for testing the members' homegrown food, and a full body scan machine. It participated in the Staff Survey.

2) *Koseiren* hospitals

Koseiren hospital A: JA Aichi runs eight hospitals in Aichi Prefecture. The one we studied is located in a suburb of Nagoya City, where it completed a 606 bed facility in the early 2000s, with a staff size of 1,500 employees. It is a general hospital, open to all inhabitants living nearby, with its own helipad. It participated in the Staff, Patient and Volunteer Surveys.

Koseiren hospital B: It was established in 1944 and specializes in providing medical services in rural areas from a medium sized town of Nagano Prefecture. It runs three hospitals, the largest with over 800 beds and two long term care facilities with nearly 200 additional beds. Its staff size is nearly 800 employees. It recently inaugurated a new research hospital. It participated in the Staff Survey.

Koseiren hospital C: It started a small 60 bed facility in the late 1960s in a geographically isolated part of Fukushima Prefecture, but later expanded to nearly 200 beds and its staff is nearly 400 employees. The hospital is more than 45 years old and it needs to build a replacement, but the regional JA prefers to invest in more urban concentrated areas than isolated, declining rural ones. It participated in the Staff Survey.

Koseiren hospital D: It is located in a small town in a remote mountain area of Aichi Prefecture. In the 1950s local farmers wanted to gain access to medical care, so they founded a hospital to recruit a doctor and improve the local medical infrastructure. Today it has a newly refurbished hospital with 190 beds, 140 for general patients and 50 in a long term care facility next door. Its staff size is over 300 employees. It participated in the Staff, Patient and Volunteer Surveys.

3) Public hospitals:

Public hospital A: It is a municipal hospital located in Osaka and has approximately 700 employees and slightly more than 300 beds.

Public hospital B: It is a municipal hospital located in Osaka and has nearly 1,300 employees and slightly more than 600 beds.

Source: Pestoff, 2021.

6 Work Environment and Service Quality in Japanese Healthcare

This chapter discusses the demand/control model of work environment that is comprised of four work life categories: Low Strain, Passive, Active and High Strain. The Staff Study provides information about the work environment, work satisfaction and service quality at 10 Japanese healthcare providers. First it considers all of them together and then it compares the three hospital groups. It has three main conclusions. First, the Demand and Control model is a robust theoretical model, but it provides little practical guidance for enlightened HR experts on how to improve a toxic work environment. Exploring the situation at the three hospital groups points to some notable disparities between the Low and High Strain categories among hospital employees. In particular, nurses and care workers experience an adverse situation in their daily work life. Second, the data confirms that hospital staff with a higher evaluation of their work environment and greater work satisfaction also rate their service quality higher. Third, direct comparisons between the hospitals in terms of work satisfaction and service quality might be somewhat misleading, since they operate in a different setting and context. This is particularly true in rural areas where there are seldom any alternative healthcare providers.

A Background

Peters (1996) notes that mobilizing and harnessing resources beyond the command and control of leaders in the public and private sectors become increasingly crucial for the sustainability of society and the achievement of both public and private goals. Citizens provide critical resources today, so we need to consider how best to mobilize and harness their resources – both in their role as professional service providers and as users/citizens or co-producers of publicly financed services. Peters notes that a participatory administration model focuses on the lower echelons of the service providers and clients. It decentralizes much of the decision-making to them (ibid.).

This project explores the interplay of four main variables in the provision of Japanese healthcare: work environment, service quality, governance models and co-production. However, this chapter only deals with the first two of them, while governance and co-production will be studied in more detail elsewhere. This chapter proceeds in the following fashion. First, we will discuss our assumptions about work environment and introduce previous research based on the Demand, Control, Support model. Second, we will explore the combined effects of the Demand/Control model for the ten Japanese hospitals that participated in this study. We will also consider the ramifications of the four Demand/Control work life categories in terms of work satisfaction and the other work life indices developed for this project. Third, we will examine work environment, work satisfaction, and their health implications and relation to service quality, as well as potential alternative perspectives on service quality. Fourth, we will introduce the three hospital groups included in this study and repeat steps two to three above. This allows us to differentiate the ideal-typical 'demand and control' model from the reality of different healthcare providers in Japan. Fifth, we will identify the staff categories that experience the most detrimental work life situation at the three hospital groups in this study. Finally, we will reach certain conclusions.

B Previous Research on Work Environment

Human resource guru Pfeffer, in his recent book on management and work life, laments the fact that management practices literally sicken and kill employees, yet they fail to improve organizational profitability or performance (2018). He states that ill health from workplace stress adversely affects productivity and drives up voluntary turnover that costs employers and society more than half a trillion dollars per year in the U.S. (ibid., 3). He notes that the physical work environment is closely regulated and inspected in most countries, but the psychosocial work environment usually is not. Therefore, the costs of toxic workplaces result in 'social pollution' that is passed on to various parts of the public health and welfare systems, as well as to individual employees in the form of ill health. His list of the ten most hazardous work life stressors includes three that are the focus of our project, high work demands, the lack of control at work and receiving little social support at work (ibid., 39). Pfeffer emphasizes the enormous toll of toxic workplaces and states that 'the lack of job control is the single most important predictor for developing heart disease' (ibid., 154).

To rectify this dismal situation, Pfeffer proposes several positive steps. First is measuring employee health and well-being both at the company level and the national level on an annual basis; Second is highlighting and shaming the companies that are 'social polluters'; Third is capturing and recuperating the externalities they create (i.e. making companies pay for the individual and social costs of their social pollution) (ibid., 202). He concludes that all work organizations have a choice: They can continue providing workplaces and implementing management practices that

Demands & Control	Low	High
High	*Low strain*	*Active*
Low	*Passive*	*High strain*

Figure 6.1 Psychological Demand and Control Model.
Source: Modified from Karasek & Theorell, 1990, p. 32, taken from Pestoff, 1998.

create physical and mental ill-heath, literally kill people and drive up healthcare costs in the process, or they can make different choices that result in the opposite outcomes (ibid., 211). He asks whether their governance model should only encompass the interests of a single stakeholder – the firm's owners or perhaps it can comprise several of them, including the workers and even their clients? He suggests that such choices become part and parcel of their corporate governance. Hospital governance models are the focus of Chapter 9 in this volume.

Nearly three decades earlier, Karasek and Theorell (1990) noted that work life stress is related both to physical illness and lower productivity. They developed a two-dimensional demand/control model to understand, analyze and explain work environment and its physical and psychosocial impacts on workers and organizations. Combining these two dimensions results in a fourfold classification of jobs illustrated in Figure 6.1, where demands are expressed by the columns and control by the rows. Low demands combined with high control result in 'low-strain jobs', while low demands and low control lead to 'passive jobs'. High demands combined with high control result in 'active jobs', but when control is low it produces 'high strain jobs'. The latter is usually considered most debilitating in work life.

This model was expanded by adding a third dimension – 'social support' at work. This refers to overall levels of helpful social interaction available on the job from both co-workers and supervisors (ibid.:69). Karasek and Theorell note that social support appears to provide buffering mechanisms between psychological stressors at work and adverse health outcomes. Thus, social contact and social structure affect the basic physiological processes important both to the maintenance of long-term health as well as the acquisition of new knowledge. Accordingly, they state that '... together, these three dimensions of work activity – demand, control and social support – are capable of predicting much of the range of total variation in depression symptoms in the U.S. population'. Such symptoms increase in probability from 6% to 41%, given the right or wrong combination of these factors. (ibid.: 72).

Elsewhere, Pestoff and Vamstad (2014) explored the contribution of social enterprises to enriching work environment and their ability to provide 'good work'. The empirical data was taken from two separate studies of Swedish childcare facilities – one from 1994 to 1995 and another one, more than a decade later, from 2006 to 2007. They note that work environment conditions in the public sector deteriorated radically in Sweden about 30 years ago and that these effects were still apparent in public service. However, the empirical part of their study demonstrated third sector organizations (TSOs) and social enterprises (SEs) that provide alternative preschool services in Sweden have good jobs in the fullest meaning of the word, and continue to do so today. In Karasek and Theorell's terms, work in these organizations is psychologically demanding, but it provides high decision latitude and high social support for the workers. These work life attributes stand in sharp contrast with those found in the services provided by the large hierarchical bureaucratic organizations often associated with the public sector services in Sweden. In this sense, the TSO/SE model can not only help to transform social services jobs into active, participative and interactive jobs, but it can also help to enrich the work life of employees. They conclude that enriching the work environment can make a major contribution to improving the quality of the services an organization provides for its clients and/or members (ibid.). A fourth work life dimension concerning the nature and intensity of contact with clients is introduced in Chapter 7 of this volume in relation to the discussion of patients and co-production. Based on previous research, the model in Figure 6.2 captures the relation between work environment, work satisfaction and service quality explored by this chapter.

The initial premise of the Staff Study was rather simple and straightforward: More satisfied employees produce more satisfactory results than less satisfied employees. In our study, 'more satisfactory results' means less stress, fewer health issues for the staff and better quality services for the patients. Given the relational nature of many welfare services – including healthcare – our study is based on the assumption

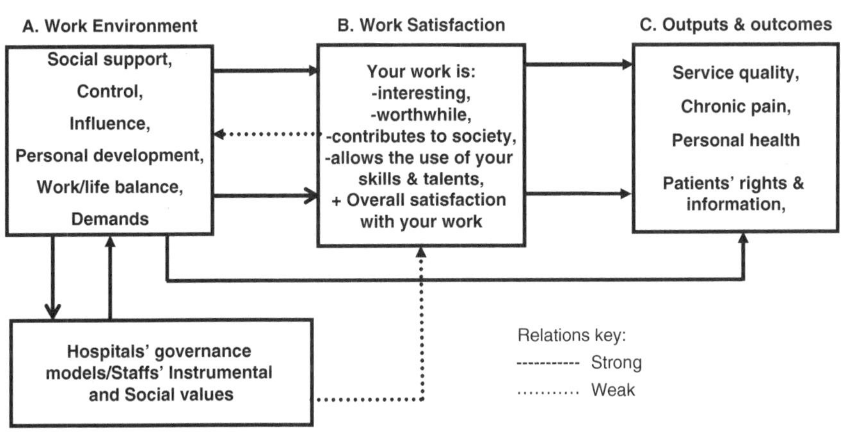

Figure 6.2 Work Environment, Work Satisfaction and Service Quality.

that work environment and service quality are closely related or linked to each other. An employee who has tossed and turned all night worrying about work-related problems, who feels tired and exhausted when they wake up in the morning, who dreads the idea of going to work because they have little or no control or influence on the what, when, why, where and how of their daily routines, who has little chance to learn new things or advance at work – such an employee will not provide as good quality service as one who has the opposite experiences and feelings about their work. Likewise, a client who experiences an unhappy, stressed or disgruntled service professional will not experience as good service quality as one being served by an employee with the opposite feelings.

To evaluate the contribution of work environment to healthcare provision in Japan, we included the following work-related aspects of their daily life: Social support; Influence; Personal development and the classical Karasek and Theorell Demand/Control variables; Contact with clients and other relevant stakeholders. We felt that when any of these aspects of daily work life is present and positive, it will result in a good work environment. When they are absent or negative, it will result in the opposite situation. A poor work environment is related to several negative symptoms – such as psychosocial stress, physical strain, chronic pain, absenteeism and ill health. The data presented here helps to shed light on the importance of such mechanisms for the relations between the staff and their clients and how this is reflected in service quality in healthcare.

C Exploring the Combined Effect of the Demand/Control Model for Japanese Hospital Staff

The empirical materials for the Staff Study[1] come from questionnaire data collected in 2016 from eight cooperative hospitals across Japan and it is compared with similar data from the staff at two public hospitals in Osaka in 2017. The staff sample from these ten hospitals reaches a total of 6,859, with an overall response rate of 72.1%. Differences between the hospital response rates are documented in Chapter 5. The results of the Staff Study will be considered at the general level before introducing the three hospital groups in section 6.D.

Demand and control are the key variables in the Karasek and Theorell model, so exploring their interaction is crucial. An index for workplace demands was constructed from six items and another one for staff control is comprised of four items. Both of the indices were then divided into roughly equal parts. Tables 6.A and 6.C in the appendix provide more details on the construction of the indices employed in this chapter. Combining the two main variables in the Demand/Control model allows us to explore their joint effect on the work environment of these hospitals as seen in Table 6.1. The proportion and number of respondents/staff is indicated for each work life category.

Table 6.1 Combined Demand and Control Categories at Japanese hospitals

Demands/Control	*Low*	*High*
High	*low strain* 35.2% (2,371)	*active* 17.2% (1,161)
Low	*passive* 14.4% (973)	*high strain* 33.2% (2,239)

In general, about one-third of the staff/respondents working at these ten Japanese hospitals are classified as having Low Strain jobs, another third as having High Strain jobs while the remaining third is divided between Passive and Active jobs. As noted earlier, Low Strain jobs mean that low job demands are combined with high control or discretion over the execution of daily job tasks. By contrast, High Strain jobs mean that there are high job demand but low control over the execution of daily job tasks. High Strain jobs are the most problematic in terms of negative health consequences for individual employees. The latter can also have negative effects in terms of service provision and service quality. In addition, more than one out of eight respondents are classified as having a Passive job – which is characterized both by low demands and low control over daily tasks – while less than one of five has an Active job. In the latter category, high demands are combined with high discretion or control over the execution of daily tasks. This is considered the most beneficial work life situation, and it usually results both in good working conditions and also a healthier and longer life (Karasek and Theorell, 1990).

1 *Hospital Occupations and Job Types*

We expect that differences in work environment will be reflected in differences between the occupations found at Japanese hospitals, as well as staff with and without managerial responsibilities. Table 6.2 addresses this for the six main occupation categories employed by this study. In this and in the following pages, we will primarily concentrate attention on the contrast between staff found in the Low Strain and High Strain categories.

The most notable difference in Table 6.2 is between doctors and nurses; both groups deviate notably from the average. Doctors are clearly overrepresented among staff in a Low Strain situation, while nurses are in the opposite situation. They experience unusually high levels of High Strain work. The other occupation categories do not show as much difference compared with the average for all hospitals. We will return to the difference between occupations at the end of this chapter when we look at this from the perspective of the three hospital groups. However, one of the most significant lessons from the Karasek and Theorell model is the importance of giving the staff more autonomy over the contents of their daily work tasks as a way of improving the work environment. Thus, from a work environment perspective, the goal of management and human resource officers should,

Table 6.2 Occupation and Management, by the Demand and Control Categories*

Occupation	*Low Strain*	*Active*	*Passive*	*High Strain*
Doctor	57.0	13.7	12.8	16.6
Nurse	23.3	21.2	10.7	44.8
Care Worker	37.2	16.9	13.7	32.1
Other Medical Specialist	42.3	16.5	17.4	23.8
Administration	46.0	13.4	18.4	22.2
Other Support Staff	42.4	6.4	23.2	28.0
Manager/Non-Manager				
Manager	34.0	31.0	5.6	29.4
Non-Manager	35.4	14.2	16.3	34.1
Average	35.2	17.2	14.4	33.2

*Adds row-wise to 100.0%.

therefore, be to move staff out of a High Strain into Active and then, if possible, into a Low Strain work life situation. This can most easily be achieved by providing them with more control over the 'nuts and bolts' of their daily work tasks (i.e. control over what they do and how and when they do it). Organizations that meet this challenge will not only provide the staff with a better and healthier work environment, but they will also have a more satisfied staff and healthier staff members.

Finally, we also want to consider differences between staff with management responsibilities and those without. Table 6.2 shows that the greatest difference for them is not between staff in the High and Low Strain categories, rather it is between staff in the Active and Passive job categories. As might be expected, staff with management responsibility are primarily found in the Active category and significantly fewer are in the Passive category than the average for all ten hospitals. The situation for staff without managerial responsibilities is much closer to the average for all ten hospitals.

2 *The Impact of Work Life Categories on the Hospital Work Environment*

In order to explore the relationship between various aspects of work life, we constructed several indices to summarize information from between three to six relevant questions on a given topic in the staff survey – such as work satisfaction or social support at work. Staff responses to such questions ranged on a five-point scale from agree, agree somewhat, neither agree nor disagree, disagree somewhat and disagree. Index construction was similar in most cases. An additive index was calculated that combines the responses to these questions and the new combined value was then divided into three roughly equal parts – high, medium and low, with approximately one-third of the respondents in each of them. However, the Index of Service Quality was only divided into two, since it proved impossible to divide it into three categories. Tables 6.A and 6.C in the appendix include more details about the construction of the work life indices.

Table 6.3 provides information about the relationship between the four demand/control, work life categories and the indices of work environment employed by this study. Please consult the appendix for the items included in each index. The table also includes some information about the expected outcome of a good or poor work environment (i.e. some health indicators for the staff and their evaluation of service quality). Please note that only the proportion of the staff that receives a 'high' score on any given index is reported in this table. A score well above or below one-third is noteworthy. For example, nearly half of the staff in the Low Strain category claim a 'high' score in terms of Work Satisfaction, while merely one-eighth of the staff do so in the High Strain category.

Two general patterns are found in the data. First, the proportion with a 'high' score decreases systematically from left to right – or from the Low Strain to High Strain categories – except for chronic pain which shows the opposite pattern. Second, the difference between the highest and lowest score on these indices noted at the far right (dif. h-l) is greatest for the staff in the Low respective High Strain categories. Therefore, the discussion will focus mainly on those two work life categories.

A closer look shows that the 'high' score for Low Strain staff reaches nearly 50% or more on most work life indices, while it is barely one-quarter or less for High Strain staff. The Low Strain category has much higher than average scores on the following work life indices: Work Satisfaction, Social Support, Influence, Professional and Personal Development, Work/Life Balance, Service Quality and their Own Health rating. Moreover, Low Strain staff also have a much lower score for Chronic Pain. The High Strain category, by contrast, has much lower scores on the same indices. They are often only half of those noted for

Table 6.3 Staff Scoring 'High' on Work Environment Indices, by the Demand and Control Categories

WE Index, etc.[*]	*Low Strain*	Active	*Passive*	*High Strain*	*Dif. (h-l)*[**]
Work Satisfaction	48.7	34.5	25.4	13.6	35.1
Social Support	54.2	36.5	32.1	19.3	34.9
Influence	57.1	41.2	19.0	12.9	44.2
Pers & Prof. Dev.	54.6	48.1	28.9	24.3	30.3
Work/Life Balance	47.1	32.5	30.2	19.5	27.6
Service Quality[a]	62.6	46.8	44.8	27.0	35.6
Chronic Pain[b]	80.0	59.0	74.5	50.0	30.0
Own Health[c]	80.8	57.3	71.2	46.7	34.1

*Only shows the 'high' scores for each work environment index;
**The difference between staff categories with the highest and lowest scores on work life indices, etc.; a=dichotomous index; b=rarely & never; and c=healthy.

Low Strain staff, including Work Satisfaction, Social Support, Influence, Personal and Professional Development, Work/Life Balance. In particular, their score on Service Quality and their Own Health is noteworthy. High Strain staff rate their hospital's Service Quality less than half of what Low Strain staff do, and their evaluation of their Own Health is also very low. The pressure they experience from High Strain at work is expressed in their lack of satisfaction with the quality of the service that they provide, as well as in their own well-being, judging by the degree of chronic pain they experience. Thus, the work life experience of the Low Strain staff is much more favorable than for the High Strain staff in every aspect covered by these work environment indices.

3 Work Environment, Work Satisfaction and Service Quality in Japanese Healthcare

Our expectation is that work environment is closely related to work satisfaction. Work satisfaction is comprised of the following items: You are generally satisfied with your work; your work is interesting and stimulating; your work is worthwhile; you are able to use your skills and talents; you feel needed at your workplace; your work contributes to society. Satisfied staff will, most likely, not only be more enthusiastic and positive about their work, but they will also have more positive relations with their fellow workers and equally important, with their clients. Accordingly, a good work environment will, therefore, not only result in less stress, but it will also augment their work satisfaction and personal well-being and, hopefully, improve service quality.

Table 6.B in the appendix indicates the Spearman's Rho correlation between six work environment indices and the Indices of Work Satisfaction and Service Quality. Spearman's Rho is used to evaluate the relationship between two variables without saying anything about causality. It is considered strong when it varies between .60-.79, moderate between .40-.59 and weak between .20-.39. Four of these indices had a moderate Spearman's Rho correlation with the Index of Work Satisfaction that ranged between .526 for Influence and .439 for Control, while two of them had a weaker correlation. Turning to the Index of Service Quality, only two of the work environment indices had a moderate correlation with Service Quality. The strongest one was .49 between the Indices of Work Satisfaction and Service Quality. Therefore, given the moderate correlation between several of the work environment indices and the Index of Work Satisfaction, the latter will be employed as a replacement or surrogate for the other work environment indices in order to reduce the number of tables and variables necessary to explore these relations more fully.

First, we will consider the impact of the two key work environment indices – Demand and Control on Work Satisfaction and then the relationship between Work Satisfaction on Service Quality in Table 6.4.

Table 6.4 Control and Demands, Work Satisfaction and Service Quality

Control	*Work Satisfaction**	*Percent*	*Dif. (h-l)*
High	High	51.7	
Low	High	15.3	36.4
Work Demands	Work Satisfaction	Percent	
High	High	17.4	
Low	High	46.9	29.5
Work Satisfaction	Service Quality*	Percent	Dif. (h-l)
High	High	71.0	
Low	High	22.0	49.0

*Only shows the high values for Work Satisfaction and Service Quality.

In order to simplify the presentation, only the high value for the Index of Work Satisfaction and the high and low values of indices for Demand and Control are included. The Index of Service Quality was calculated on the basis of two questions and is divided into two roughly equal parts – high and low – rather than the usual three categories – high, medium and low. These questions are based on an evaluation of the healthcare provider's overall service quality and whether they would recommend it to a friend or acquaintance. It has a Cronbach's Alpha of .706.

Going from high to low Control, we can note a drop of 36% points in Work Satisfaction. Contrary to the other work environment variables, demands at work often lead to stress, so we expect higher demands will have a negative impact on Work Satisfaction. High workplace demands result in a situation where less than one-fifth of the staff express high satisfaction with their work, while low demands mean nearly half of them are satisfied, for a difference of 29% points. Furthermore, healthcare is considered a typical relational service, so the service the staff provides to their clients will depend to a large extent on the relationship between them, as the perceived service quality also is. Therefore, it is anticipated that more satisfied staff will provide better quality services to their clients than stressed staff or those suffering from chronic pain or struggling with ill health. For two levels of Work Satisfaction (high and low), only the 'high' category of Service Quality is taken into account. Going from the 'high' level of Work Satisfaction to the 'low', there is a dramatic reduction in the percentage of staff who claim that they are providing a 'high' level of Service Quality. It decreases from 71.0% to 22.0% – a drop of almost 50% points. This is a rather sharp drop, and the Spearman's Rho correlation is .480.

4 An Alternative Perspective on Service Quality

There are, of course, many different and sometimes conflicting perspectives on service quality (Vamstad, 2012, 2018). A final consideration recognizes that an alternative interpretation of service quality can focus on technical aspects and the equipment used in most hospitals and clinics. Is it new and 'cutting-edge', or is it old and perhaps 'outdated'? It was decided, therefore, to check whether something important was missed by not including the staff's evaluation of this dimension in the Index of Service Quality. Three questions on hospital standards allow us to look closer at this. The staff was asked to evaluate whether the standards at their hospital were higher than other providers, if they used high-quality equipment and whether the staff's technical skills were high. These questions imply comparisons with other healthcare providers that might be difficult for some staff to make, particularly given the low level of labor market mobility in Japan. Unfortunately, there was an unusually high degree of 'neither agree nor disagree' answers for these questions, ranging from a third to half of the responses. This is unusually high; normally, it would be less than five to ten percent for most other questions in our survey. This suggests a lack of willingness or ability for most of the staff to answer these questions about hospital standards. This made us reluctant to include these items in the Index of Service Quality. Nevertheless, the positive answers to these items can provide some valuable insights into a more technical perspective on service quality. We will consider these from the perspective of the work life categories employed by the Demand/Control model (Table 6.5).

In general, the Low and High Strain categories once again show the greatest difference in all three of the items related to hospital standards. Staff in the Low Strain category give the strongest support to statements about their hospital having higher standards than other hospitals, having high-quality equipment and the staff having high technical competence. These items receive support from nearly half of them. The High Strain staff, by contrast, provide much less support – only a quarter to a third of them agree or agree somewhat, while a third to half or more claim

Table 6.5 Hospital Standards, by Demand and Control Categories

Hospital Standards	*Low Strain*	*Active*	*Passive*	*High Strain*	*Dif. (h-l)*
Higher than other hospitals	51.4	44.6	37.4	31.2	20.2
High-quality equipment	46.9	38.9	41.3	33.4	11.5
High technical skills of staff	47.6	36.9	33.1	25.2	22.4

*Only shows the percent stating they 'agree' or 'agree somewhat'.

they 'neither agree or disagree'. The difference between the support from these two work life categories is greatest for the first and last item and smallest for the item about high-quality equipment.

D Comparing Three Japanese Hospital Groups

Before introducing the three hospital groups at the center of this study, the social background and employment profiles of staff at the three hospital groups will be briefly presented. More details are found in Table 6.D in the appendix. The public hospitals requested us to remove some social background questions that they felt might infringe on the personal integrity of the staff. No information is available about the age, family composition and household income for them. Women comprise between three-fourths to over four-fifths of the staff at these three hospital groups. Between 60% and 70% of the staff at the Medical Co-ops and *Koseiren* hospitals are 50 years of age or younger. More than half of the staff at public hospitals have attended a junior college, vocational college or the university, while less than two-fifths of the staff at the Medical Co-ops and *Koseiren* hospitals have done so. About 30% of the staff at the Medical Co-ops and *Koseiren* hospitals are single or live with a spouse, while nearly 70% live in a three-person or larger household. The household income of two-thirds of the staff at the Medical Co-ops is less than 6 million Japanese Yen, while nearly half of the staff at *Koseiren* hospitals earn more than 6 million Japanese Yen. The most notable differences between the three staff groups are found in terms of their age, where *Koseiren* staff are somewhat younger; education, where public hospital staff are somewhat better educated; and household income, where *Koseiren* staff claims a higher income level. Please consult Pestoff (2017) for more details on the Staff Study.

Table 6.E in the appendix shows the distribution of professions, and Table 6.F indicates the employment conditions at the three hospital groups. An employment profile of the staff at the Medical Co-ops shows that there are fewer doctors and nurses than there are at the other two hospital groups, but there are many more care workers. More than two out of five are part-time employees, which is well above the other two hospital groups. Nearly half of them have been employed for five years or less. More than half work less than 40 hours per week, and they have a shorter workday than their colleagues at the two other hospital groups. Finally, less than one out of five works in acute medicine, and more than four of five work daytime hours.

An employment profile of the staff at *Koseiren* hospitals shows that there are more doctors and nurses and many fewer care workers than at the Medical Co-ops. More than three quarters are employed full-time, and three out of five have worked for a *Koseiren* hospital for five years or more, suggesting that they have more secure, long-term employment.

However, they also have the longest work week of all hospital groups – two-thirds work 40 hours or more per week, and more than two out of five work eight hours or more per day. More than two out of five work in acute medicine, and more than three-fourths work daytime hours.

An employment profile of the staff at public hospitals shows that an equal number of doctors are employed as *Koseiren,* and there are more nurses than the other hospital groups but no care workers. Two-thirds of the staff work full-time and more than half have worked for a public hospital for five years or longer. More than three-fifths work 40 hours or more per week, and many claim that they work eight hours or longer per day for the longest workday of all hospital groups. More than two-thirds work in acute medicine, and a similar proportion work daytime hours.

Returning to the main focus of this study allows us to explore the difference between hospital groups in a given demand/control category. Table 6.6 introduces the specific patterns found when including them in the Demand/Control model. A separate noting exists for the difference between the highest and lowest figures, dif. (h-l) for each work life category.

A brief overview shows that there is not much difference between the staff at these ten hospitals in terms of either Passive or Active jobs. A nearly equal proportion of staff at all three types of hospitals are classified as having Passive or Active jobs, and the difference between hospital groups is rather small at only 0.7% or 2.8% points. By contrast, the difference between hospitals is much larger when it comes to Low Strain and High Strain jobs. In the former category – Low Strain jobs – we note a difference of 19.7% points between the highest and lowest hospital group, while a similar difference is noted for High Strain jobs at 19.3% points. In both of these situations, the staff at Medical Co-ops is clearly in the most preferential and beneficial situation in terms of their work environment. Two of five claim Low Strain jobs and barely one-quarter claim High Strain jobs. By contrast, the staff at

Table 6.6 Combined Demand and Control Categories, by Hospital Group

Demands/Control	*Low*	*High*
High	*low strain* MC: 42.8% K: 33.8% Pub.: 22.6% Dif. (h-l) 19.7%	*active* MC: 17.1% K: 17.0% Pub.:17.8% Dif. (h-l) 0.7%
Low	*passive* MC: 13.3% K: 16.1% Pub.: 13.6% Dif. (h-l) 2.8%	*high strain* MC: 26.7% K: 33.1% Pub.: 46.0% Dif. (h-l) 19.3%

Key: MC = Medical Co-ops, K = *Koseiren* and Pub = Public Hospitals.

Table 6.7 Staff Scoring 'High' on Work Environment Indices, by Hospital Group

*Index name**	*Cronbach's*	*Med Co-ops*	*Koseiren*	*Public*	*Dif (h-l)***
Work Satisfaction	.877	37.2	28.2	24.7	12.5
Demands	.748	28.6	34.3	48.5	20.2
Social Support	.833	42.6	34.1	22.7	19.9
Discretion/Control	.855	39.7	33.1	22.8	16.9
Influence	.912	41.9	31.4	23.7	16.4
Pers/Prof. Development	.758	45.5	35.1	36.4	9.4
Work/Life Balance	.811	39.9	28.9	26.4	12.9
Service Quality[a]	.706	52.4	41.2	39.6	12.8
Chronic Pain[b]	Nr	63.8	67.9	65.4	4.1
Own Health[c]	Nr	63.4	66.6	62.1	4.5/K

*Only shows the 'high' scores for each work environment index;
**Difference between staff categories with the highest and lowest scores on work life indices, etc.; a=dichotomous; b=rarely & never; c=healthy; Nr=not relevant.

public hospitals are much less fortunate. Less than one-quarter claim Low Strain jobs, while nearly half claim High Strain jobs. Staff at the *Koseiren* hospitals fall in between the Medical Co-ops and public hospitals both in terms of Low Strain and High Strain jobs.

Table 6.7 provides an overview of seven work environment indices that were calculated from three to six items each, for a total of 29 work environment items employed in our questionnaire. These indices were divided into three roughly equal parts, where a score well above or below 33.3% is noteworthy. It provides the Cronbach's Alpha and the proportion of the staff providing a high score on each of the seven work life/ work environment indices for the three hospital groups included in this study. The Cronbach's Alpha for these indices varies from .748 to .912, so they all show a high degree of commonality between the items included in each index. It also indicates the difference in percentage points between hospital groups in terms of the highest and lowest proportion of staff taking a strong stance on a given index.

While the difference between hospital groups in this table is only half of that found in Table 6.3, there are nevertheless some clear differences. The Medical Co-ops rate highest on all these indices; *Koseiren* comes much lower, while the public hospitals rank lowest on all but one of them. *Koseiren* comes last on the Index of Personal and Professional Development, which probably reflects the nature of the labor market in rural areas where *Koseiren* is often the only healthcare provider or at least the largest. Accordingly, fewer opportunities exist in rural areas for changing jobs and/or climbing a career ladder.

The difference between the Medical Co-ops and public hospitals ranges from a low of 12.5% points to a high of 19.9% points. It is least for Work

Satisfaction and greatest for Social Support. Moreover, the difference is above 15% points for four out of these seven work environment indices (i.e. Demands, Social support, Control and Influence). Considered together, these seven work environment indices provide solid evidence for the idea that the staff at Medical Co-ops has much more autonomy in their daily work life than the staff at *Koseiren* and public hospitals. The work life experience of the staff at the Medical Co-ops appears much more favorable than for the staff at public hospitals in every aspect covered by these work environment indices. Attempting to improve the conditions for public hospital workers should, therefore, be an important goal for the human relations sections at public hospitals in Japan and elsewhere.

Turning to the expected outcome of the work environment for the three hospital groups, some additional information is included about service quality and health indicators in Table 6.7. The Index of Service Quality shows a clear difference that follows the pattern previously noted for the indices of work environment. The Medical Co-ops come highest and the public hospitals lowest, while the difference between the *Koseiren* and public hospitals is rather small here. Halvarsson (2019) noted elsewhere that there is little difference between the hospital groups in this study in terms of the health outcomes. However, this may reflect one of the limitations of this data set. It included too few questions about traditional work environment indicators and ailments. See Chapter 5 for more details.

Returning briefly to the possibility of an alternative perspective on service quality, Table 6.8 presents the staff's evaluation of their hospital's standards at the three hospital groups.

It is noteworthy that the staff at public hospitals rate their hospitals higher on all three of these items than the staff at the two other hospital groups. In general, more than a third of the staff at all three hospital groups rate their technical skills high and two out of five or more rate their hospital's standards higher than other hospitals. Differences between hospital groups are rather small on these two items. However, given the importance of stable employment and lack of job mobility in Japan, it remains uncertain how many employees have experience of more than one hospital that would allow making comparisons of hospital standards. Moreover, the rate of 'neither agree or disagree' answers were unusually high for these three items, which is why they were not included in the service quality index. Finally, concerning the hospital's technical equipment, there is a somewhat different pattern. More than half of the staff at public hospitals 'agree' or 'agree somewhat', while barely one-quarter do so at Medical Co-op hospitals. This may reflect the fact that the former have easier access to public funding for purchasing expensive 'cutting-edge' equipment than the latter. This finding carries two important messages. First, the staff at all three of these hospital groups can distinguish between different dimensions of hospital standards, and they do not appear to rate them without discrimination.

Table 6.8 Staff Perspective on Hospital Standards, by Hospital Group

Comparing Hospital Standards	*Med Co-ops*	*Koseiren*	Public	*Dif. (h–l)*
Higher than other hospitals	41.7	39.2	45.6	6.4/P
High-quality equipment	27.1	49.5	53.7	26.6/P
High technical skills of staff	35.7	36.3	38.9	3.2/P

*Only shows the percent stating they 'agree' or 'agree somewhat'.

Therefore, the staff at the Medical Co-ops is well aware that technical equipment is not their strong point. Second, this lends greater validity to their staff's answers to other questions in this survey and their ability to discriminate between alternatives presented to them.

E Occupation and Stress by Hospital Group

Table 6.2 presented data about the work environment, the six occupation categories employed in this study and the Demand/Control work environment categories for all ten hospitals. The biggest differences noted were between the Low Strain and High Strain categories for doctors, nurses and care workers. Doctors had a more favorable work environment than their colleagues at the ten hospitals, while nurses and care workers had a less favorable work environment. It was noted earlier that the simplest remedy for improving negative work environment would be to allow the staff in question more control over the execution of their daily tasks.

We will now return to the issue of work environment by presenting data concerning the situation about occupations and the demand/control work environment categories for each hospital group. Table 6.G in the appendix presents the data for four out of the six hospital occupations – doctors, nurses, care workers and the hospital administration – by hospital group. Two other categories – 'other medical specialists' and 'other support staff' – were excluded for the sake of simplicity. Each of the four occupations included can be compared with the average for that particular hospital group. Attention will be reserved for cases where an occupation differs by more than 8% points from the average for the High Strain category at that hospital group. This is the most adverse or debilitating work life situation. The hospital groups are also compared in terms of the most adversely impacted occupations. This helps identify cases where the human resource officers at the hospitals need to pay much closer attention to the work environment of a particular group of employees and develop a viable, long-term strategy for improving the work life situation for them.

First, the Medical Co-ops will be examined, followed by *Koseiren* and then the public hospitals. Nurses at the Medical Co-ops experience more High Strain than the average for Medical Co-ops (34.6% versus 26.5%).

Both many more nurses and even more so care workers experience more High Strain than the average for *Koseiren* hospitals (42.4% and 54.8% versus 33.0%). Nurses at public hospitals experience more High Strain than the average for public hospitals (57.9% versus 45.8%). No care workers were included at public hospitals in our survey. Thus, nurses and care workers are either over-represented or strongly over-represented among staff experiencing high strain. It should be obvious from these figures that the nurses and care workers at these hospitals would benefit from decisive measures to relieve them from the adverse conditions they experience at work. The Demand/Control model clearly suggests allowing them more control or discretion about the what, where, when and how of their daily tasks would be an important step in rectifying their stressful situation. Moreover, Chapter 9 suggests that this is probably facilitated by the governance model practiced by a healthcare provider.

F Summary and Conclusions

The Karasek and Theorell Demand/Control model of work environment, presented in Figure 6.1 appears very relevant for this study of work environment and service quality in Japanese healthcare. It has both a strong heuristic and predictive value. By combining Work Demands and Control in Table 6.1, we discovered a clear pattern where nearly one-third of the staff at these ten Japanese hospitals have Low Strain jobs, one-third High Strain jobs, while the remainder is divided between Passive and Active jobs. Table 6.2 noted that the Demand/Control model had a differential impact on different occupations. In particular, a greater proportion of doctors claimed Low Strain jobs, while more nurses claim High Strain jobs.

Table 6.3 documented the impact of the four work life or job categories on the work environment indices employed by this study, along with some additional work life indicators. A much larger proportion of the Low Strain staff scored 'high' on the work life indices than the High Strain staff. In particular, they have a clear impact on Service Quality – where three of five staff members with Low Strain jobs claim high Service Quality, while only one of four staff with High Strain jobs make the same claim. Table 6.4 showed that higher Discretion and Control at work leads to greater Work Satisfaction, while higher Demands have the opposite effect. It also showed that Work Satisfaction was also closely related to Service Quality. More than two-thirds of the staff that were highly satisfied said that service quality was high, while less than one-fourth of those who were least satisfied claimed high service quality. Table 6.5 documented the results of alternative perspectives on service quality by considering the staff's evaluation of hospital standards. It showed some discrepancies with the Index of Service Quality employed in this study. However, technical issues discussed earlier prevent us from including responses about hospital standards in our Index of Service Quality.

A brief discussion of the social background of the staff and their work conditions introduced the three hospital groups at the heart of our study. Next, the Demand and Control model was revisited from the perspective of the three hospital groups employed in our study. Table 6.6 showed that the staff at Medical Co-ops were clearly over-represented among Low Strain jobs and under-represented in the High Strain category. The staff at public hospitals recorded the opposite pattern, while the *Koseiren* staff came in between them. After, the focus shifted to how the hospitals relate to the seven work environment indices in Table 6.7. The Medical Co-ops often rank highest in terms of positive aspects of these work environment indices, while the public hospitals ranked lowest in all but one. It also showed that staff at the Medical Co-ops rated their service quality notably higher. Half of the staff at Medical Co-ops claimed high Service Quality, while fewer than two out of five did so at public hospitals. Thus, the data demonstrate that work environment and service quality are positively related. A healthy work environment results in greater work satisfaction and it promotes better service quality. Tables 6.5 and 6.8, however, shed some light on alternative perspectives on service quality.

Finally, Table 6.G in the appendix considered hospital occupations and stress. For example, doctors at all three hospital types are over-represented in the Low Strain category and under-represented in the High Strain category, compared with the average for all ten Japanese hospitals. This over/under-representation is most notable at *Koseiren* hospitals. Similarly, administrators are over-represented in the Low Strain category and under-represented in the High Strain category for the staff at Medical Co-ops and *Koseiren* hospitals but not the public hospitals. However, the situation is quite different for nurses and care workers. Nurses are clearly over-represented in the High Strain category and under-represented in the Low Stain category at public hospitals, somewhat over/under-represented in the same work life categories at *Koseiren* hospitals and more closely distributed with the average at the Medical Co-ops. Similarly, care workers are closely distributed with the average at the Medical Co-ops, but clearly over/under-represented at *Koseiren* hospitals, while there are too few care workers at public hospitals to comment on their over/under-representation. This suggests that the human resource departments have their work cut out for them in terms of efforts at improving the work environment of certain groups of employees. In particular, nurses and care workers at *Koseiren* hospitals and nurses at public hospitals are in acute need of viable plans to improve their situation and allow them more discretion in the performance of their daily tasks.

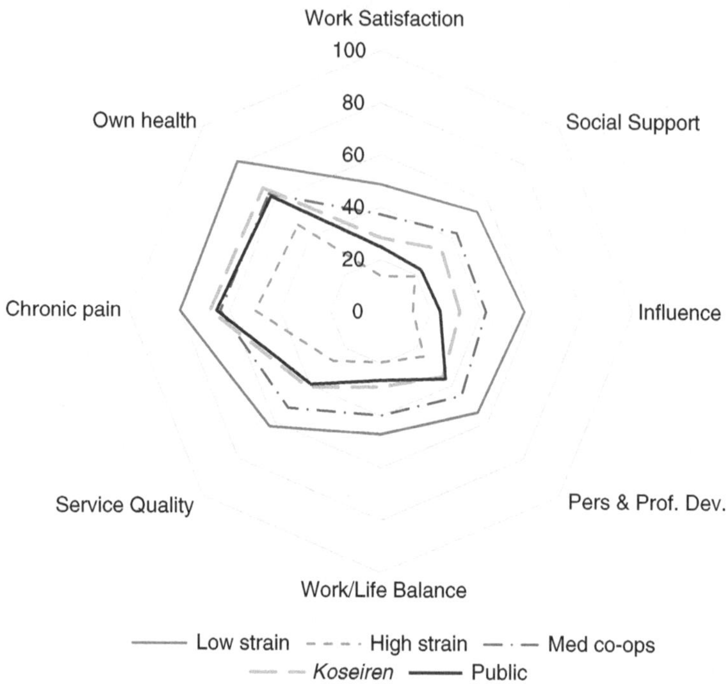

Figure 6.3 Plot of Work Environment Indices and Outcomes.

Figure 6.3 provides a graphic overview of the work environment indices and outcomes for two of the work life categories – Low and High Stress – and the three hospital groups. The three hospital groups fall in between the two work life categories. The five work environment indices only report the 'high' scores, so anything above or below one-third is noteworthy. The Index of Service Quality is dichotomized, while the two health outcome questions report the percent of positive answers. The graph shows a stark difference among the work life categories and the three hospital groups for most of the work life categories and service quality, but almost no difference among the three hospital groups in terms of health outcome. Staff at the Medical Co-ops come closest to the Low Strain category in most respects of work life, whereas staff at the public hospitals are closer to the High Strain category, with staff at Koseiren hospitals somewhere in between.

The three main takeaways for the analysis of the Staff Study are the following. First, in spite of the clear heuristic and predictive value of the Demand and Control model, it is primarily a theoretical model about 'the best of possible worlds'. Nevertheless, on its own, it provides little practical advice or guidance about how enlightened HR experts could proactively expand Low Strain and/or Active jobs to all or most employees and eliminate significant aspects of the toxic work environments and social pollution discussed by Pfeffer. The information gained by including the hospital groups points to notable disparities between them in terms of the Low and High Strain categories among the employees. The final table confirms that nurses and care workers are particularly subject to adverse situations in their daily work life. A general rule of thumb might be, therefore, to give all the staff more control or 'say so' over their everyday tasks. By considering the situation at the three hospital groups, we gain a better understanding where to begin making important improvements in the work environment of the professional healthcare staff. Exploring the situation at individual hospitals is possible, but, unfortunately, it goes well beyond the scope of this book. Moreover, discussions of governance and work environment in Chapter 9 will help to develop a better understanding of what is necessary to enrich the work environment.

Second, continuing on the previous point, we expected that if the staff was more satisfied with their work environment they would also be more satisfied with the quality of the services they provided. This was clearly the case for the work life categories in the Demand/Control model where there was a large difference between the High and Low Strain categories. It also held true in the empirical world with respect to the hospital groups. The differences between them were not as sharp as at the theoretical level, but they were nevertheless discernable. The staff with the highest evaluation of their work environment and work satisfaction also rated their service quality higher. However, what about the patients – what do they say about service quality? Would they be willing to recommend their hospital to a friend or acquaintance? This will be explored in the next chapter on patients and co-production.

Third, direct comparisons between the hospitals in terms of work satisfaction and service quality might be somewhat misleading, since they operate in a different setting and context. This is particularly true in rural areas where there are seldom any alternative healthcare providers. Moreover, these hospitals employ different governance models, promote different social values and have different social profiles, including different approaches to patient dialog and participation. Thus, each hospital group needs to be judged by its own values, in addition to some general or abstract values related to work environment and service quality. Chapter 10 explores the social and instrumental values that the staff associate with their hospitals.

The next chapter studies issues related to patient participation and co-production and is followed by a discussion of the role of volunteers in the succeeding chapter. Data from the Patient Study and Volunteer Study can help to confirm or challenge the staff perspective on service quality. Then hospital governance models are discussed, followed by hospital social values and mission and, finally, the consideration of the impact of public administration regimes and organizational logics on co-production and healthcare.

Note

1 The data collection was financed by the Japanese Society for the Promotion of Science (JSPS), the Mitsubishi Foundation and Osaka University, and it was supervised by Prof. Yayoi Saito, Osaka University. The project is conducted within the framework of an established cooperation between senior researchers at Ersta Sköndal Bräcke University College in Stockholm (Prof. V. Pestoff and Doc. J. Vamstad) and the Faculty of Human Sciences, Osaka University (Prof. Y. Saito). This interdisciplinary group of Swedish and Japanese researchers is supported by a reference group of the relevant co-operative healthcare providers in Japan, *Koseiren* and the Japanese Health and Welfare Co-operative Federation HeW CO-OP JAPAN.

References

Halvarsson, N., 2019. *Does the co-production healthcare model correlate with improved health for healthcare workers? A cross-sectional study comparing healthcare models in Japan*. Stockholm: Karolinska institute: Master's thesis.

Karasek, R., Theorell, T., 1990. *Healthy Work: Stress, Productivity and the Reconstruction of Working Life*. Basic Books, New York.

Pestoff, V., 1998. *Beyond the Market and State*. Ashgate, Aldershot, UK & Brookfield, NJ.

Pestoff, V., 2017. *The Staff Study. A preliminary overview of the results from 10 hospitals*. Ersta Sköndal Bräcke University College / Osaka University, Stockholm & Osaka.

Pestoff, V., Vamstad, J., 2014. Promoting Good Work & Enriching Work Environment: The Case of Social Enterprises in Swedish Childcare. *Ann. Public. Co-op. Econ. 85/3*: 353–370.

Peters, G., 1996. *The Future of Governing. Four Emerging Models*. University Press of Kansas, Lawrence, KS.

Pfeffer, J., 2018. *Dying for a Paycheck. How Modern Management Harms Employees Health and Company Performance – and What We Can Do About It*. Harper Business, New York.

Vamstad, J, 2012. Co-production and Service Quality: New Perspective for the Swedish Welfare State Pestoff, V., Brandsen, T., Verschuere, B. eds, *New Public Governance, the Third Sector and Co-production*. Routledge, London & New York.

Vamstad, J, 2018. Co-production in Japanese healthcare – for Service Quality or for Something Else? ICSEA conference paper: Osaka, Japan.

Wikipedia, Spearman's rank correlation coefficient, Rho. Accessed on 1 June, 2018.

Appendix 6

Table 6.A Reliability Scaling for Work Environment Indices and Cutting Points for High, Medium and Low or High/Low Categories

Index	*Variables**	*Cronbach's Alpha*	*Cut Points for 3 Parts*	*% High*	*% Med.*	*% Low*
Work Satisfaction	10.3, 11.1, 11.2, 11.3, 11.4, 11.5	.877	2.00 & 2.83	31.2	34.6	34.2
Work Demands	12.1, 12.2, 12.3, 12.4 & 17.1, 17.2	.748	2.67 & 3.33	34.9	30.9	34.2
Soc. Sup.	13.1, 13.2, 13.3, 13.4	.833	1.75 & 2.25	36.3	33.2	30.6
Control	14.1, 14.2, 14.3, 14.4	.855	2.25 & 3.00	33.7	31.6	34.7
Influence	15.1, 15.2, 15.3	.912	2.00 & 3.00	34.1	39.9	25.9
Pers. Dev.	16.1, 16.2, 16.3	.758	2.33 & 3.33	39.7	32.4	27.9
Wk/life bal.	18.2.1, 18.2.2	.811	2.00 & 3.50	33.3	39.8	27.2
Instrm. Vals	9.3, 9.4, 9.5, 9.8	.701	1.25 & 2.00	30.5	40.4	29.1
Social Vals	8.2, 9.2, 9.7, 11.5, 23	.757	2.00 & 2.80	30.7	39.0	30.3
			Cut points	**for 2**	**parts****	
Demands	12.1, 12.2, 12.3, 12.4 & 17.1, 17.2	.748	3.0/3.17	50.4	---	49.6
Control	14.1, 14.2, 14.3, 14.4	.855	2.75/3.00	52.4	---	47.6
Serv. Qual.	23 & 27	.706	2.00/2.50	45.5	---	54.6

*Variables refer to the question number; **these indices were only divided into two categories, high and low.

Table 6.B Spearman's Rho for Work Environment Indices with Work Satisfaction and Service Quality

Index Name	*Work Satisfaction*	*Service Quality*
Work Satisfaction	1.000	.490
Social Support	.496	.375
Influence	.526	.394
Prof./Pers Development	.523	.434
Work/Life Balance	.256	.283
Range	.526 - .256	.490 - .283
Service Quality	.490	1.000

Table 6.C Questions Included in the Work Environment Indices

1) Work satisfaction (Qs 10.3, 11.1, 11.2, 11.3, 11.4 and 11.5) (Cronbach's Alpha .877)
Q 10.3. How satisfied are you with your overall work? (from very satisfied to very dissatisfied)
Q 11. Do you agree with the following (from agree to disagree)?
1. Your work is interesting and stimulating;
2. Your work is worthwhile;
3. You are able to use your skills and talents;
4. You are needed in your workplace;
5. Your work contributes to society.

2) Work demands (Qs 12.1, 12.2, 12.3, 12.4 + 17.1 and 17.2) (Cronbach's Alpha .748)
Q 12. Do you agree with the following statements about your current workload and working hours? (from agree to disagree)
1. Your workload is appropriate;
2. You have too much overtime work (inverted to read 'not too much overtime');
3. You have sufficient time to talk with your colleagues at work;
4. Staff numbers are sufficient.
Q 17. How much physical and mental burden do you get from your work? (from little to much)
1. Physical burden (carrying heavy things, noises and odors);
2. Mental burden (stress from work).

3) Social support (Qs 13.1, 13.2, 13.3 and 13.4) (Cronbach's Alpha .833)
Q 13. Do you agree with the following statements about human relations at your workplace? (from agree to disagree)
1. You have good relations with your boss/supervisor;
2. You have good relations with your colleagues and subordinates;
3. There is someone you can talk with about problems at work;
4. You do not experience gender discrimination;
5. Everyone is treated fairly at your workplace.

4) Control (Qs 14.1, 14.2, 14.3 and 14.4) (Cronbach's Alpha .855)
Q 14. How much discretion do you have over your work? (from agree to disagree)

(*Continued*)

Table 6.C (Continued)

1. You are able to adjust your workload;
2. You can work at your own pace;
3. You have control over the order and manner in which you perform tasks;
4. You are given sufficient authority to fulfill your duties.

5) Influence (Qs 15.1, 15.2 and 15.3) (Cronbach's Alpha .912)
Q 15. Do you agree with the following statements about your workplace? (from agree to disagree)
1. Sufficient structures and opportunities are in place for expressing your opinion;
2. Your suggestions and opinions are reflected in decisions;
3. It is easy to express your opinion.

6) Personal and professional development (Qs 16.1, 16.2 and 16.3) (Cronbach's Alpha .758)
Q 16. Do you agree with the following statements about opportunities for professional and personal development at your workplace?
1. Good education and training opportunities/programs are provided;
2. You have good prospects for promotion and career advancement;
3. You feel you developed through your work.

7) Work/life balance (Qs 18.2.1 and 18.2.2) (Cronbach's Alpha .811)
Q 18. How easy is it to take childcare/eldercare leave at your workplace? (from agree to disagree)
1. It is easy to take childcare leave;
2. It is easy to take eldercare leave.

8) Service quality (Qs 23 and 27) (Cronbach's Alpha .706)
Q 23. How would you rate the overall quality of health and eldercare of your workplace? (from good to bad), and
Q 27. Would you recommend your hospital to your friends and acquaintances? (from agree to disagree).

Source: Pestoff, 2020.

Table 6.D Social Background of the Staff

Gender	*Male*		*Female*		*MD*
Medical Co-ops	19.5		78.0		2.5
Koseiren	24.0		74.0		2.0
Public	17.6		82.4		--
Age[a]	**20–30s**	**40s**	**50s**	**60s+**	**MD**
Medical Co-ops	13.8	22.5	27.3	31.3	5.2
Koseiren	26.8	23.5	23.4	21.7	4.6
Education	**B**	**C**	**D**	**E**	**MD**
Medical Co-ops	21.2	35.4	14.4	25.6	3.4
Koseiren	12.1	43.9	11.5	30.0	2.5
Public	8.0	39.0	15.2	37.7	0.1
Family Composition[a]	**single**	**couple**	**3 pers.**	**4+pers.**	**other**
Medical Co-ops	14.6	14.0	56.8	10.9	3.6
Koseiren	19.7	11.0	49.4	17.0	3.1
Household Income[a]	**<2mil.**	**2–4 mil.**	**4–6 mil**	**6+ mil**	**MD**
Medical Co-ops	9.9	27.9	25.0	32.2	5.1
Koseiren	6.5	24.6	23.3	46.3	5.2
Member of Cooperative[a]	**health**	**consumer**	**JA agr.**	**other**	**MD**
Medical Co-ops	92.1	33.3	8.3	0.5	4.8
Koseiren	2.2	18.1	71.9	1.4	20.3

adds to 100% row wise. a = this information not available for public staff; B = Jr. high school and high school; C = vocational/technical school & college; D = Jr. college; E = university & grad school.

Table 6.E Occupations and Hospitals

Current Occupation	*Med Co-ops*	*Koseiren*	*Public*	*Dif. (h-l)**
Doctor[a]	2.4	7.1	7.1	4.7/K&P
Nurse	26.4	47.7	56.2	29.8/P
Care Worker[b]	33.7	4.2	0.6[c]	29.5
Other Medical Specialist	17.0	17.9	14.3	3.6/K
Administrator	16.1	14.3	19.5	5.2/P
Other Support Staff	4.6	8.7	2.4	6.3/K
Total (n)	2,852	2,562	1,445	--

adds to 100% column wise. *difference between high and low; a The average for doctors includes two strong outliers, *Koseiren* A with 10.0% doctors and Med Co-ops C with only 0.7% doctors; b The average for care workers includes the same two outliers, *Koseiren* A with only 2.4% care workers and Med Co-ops B with 55.7%; and c the public hospitals do not employ care workers.

Table 6.F Employment Conditions at Japanese Hospitals

Q2: Employment	*Med Co-ops*	*Koseiren*	*Public*	*Dif. (h-l)**
Full-Time, Permanent	57.2	77.6	69.9	20.4/K
Other and Part-Time[a]	42.8	22.4	30.1	20.4
Manager[b]	18.9	17.3	19.9	2.6/P
Non-Manager	81.1	82.7	80.1	2.6/K
Five Years or Less[c]	46.2	38.6	47.5	8.9/P
More than Five Years	53.8	61.4	52.5	8.9/K
Less than 40 Hours/Wk.[d]	53.5	33.4	37.5	20.1
40 or More Hours/Wk.	46.5	66.6	62.5	20.1/K
8 Hours or Less a Day[e]	70.3	57.8	47.6	22.7
More than 8 Hours a Day	29.7	42.3	52.4	22.7/P
Acute Medicine[f]	17.1	42.3	70.5	53.4/P
Mostly Daytime[g]	84.1	77.8	68.8	15.3

adds to 100% pair wise and column wise, except for f and g. *difference between high and low; a other and part-time includes fixed-term contract and commissioned staff; persons from temporary agencies and those working as part-time temporary staff; b manager includes persons who are managers, 'staff with title' and board members; c length of employment; d hours worked per week; e average hours per day; f percent that work mainly in acute medicine; g percent that works mostly daytime.

Table 6.G Occupation and Demand and Control Categories, by Hospital Groups*

	Low Strain	*Active*	*Passive*	*High Strain*
Medical Co-ops (n)				
Doctor (67)	46.3	23.9	9.0	20.9
Nurse (746)	33.4	21.2	10.9	34.6
Care Worker (946)	40.3	16.9	13.7	29.1
Administration (453)	52.0	16.1	11.9	20.0
Med Co-ops, Average	43.1	17.1	13.4	26.5
***Koseiren* (n)**				
Doctor (177)	64.8	8.0	14.8	12.5
Nurse (1,215)	23.1	22.1	12.5	42.4
Care Worker (106)	12.5	17.3	15.4	54.8
Administration (365)	48.8	12.2	22.2	18.9
Koseiren, Average	33.9	16.9	16.2	33.0
Public (n)				
Doctor (101)	50.5	16.8	11.9	20.8
Nurse (803)	14.2	19.8	8.0	57.9
Care Worker (8)	Na	Na	Na	Na
Administration (280)	32.9	10.5	23.8	32.9
Public, Average	22.6	17.6	14.0	45.8

*adds row-wise to 100%.

7 Two Patterns of Patient Participation in Japanese Healthcare

Both the Medical Co-ops and *Koseiren* embrace health literacy outreach, but the Patient Study suggests that being a patient in a Medical Co-op or a *Koseiren* hospital does not mean the same thing. Patients at the Medical Co-ops are also members of a healthcare co-op, and this provides the social glue that enables and facilitates their working together for a common goal (i.e. the health and well-being of all members). The Medical Co-ops promote active participation by patients in ways that facilitate, foster and institutionalize their inclusion in the internal workings of the healthcare provider, which is a key to active patient co-production. Thus, there are two kinds of co-production – an aspirational and a more participatory kind. The latter has the potential to transform traditional relationships in healthcare. However, these two different approaches also represent the differing needs of their patients. In rural areas, instrumental needs to alleviate local shortages in healthcare services and create qualified jobs are much greater. *Koseiren* patients express a similar high level of satisfaction with the traditional healthcare services provided in rural areas as Medical Co-op patients do with their healthcare services in urban areas.

A Introduction

Healthcare systems in Europe and many other developed countries are facing a complex and partly contradictory mix of challenges. Fiscal strains combined with a New Public Management agenda have caused cutbacks and calls for improved efficiency in publicly funded social services and healthcare. This has significantly contributed to the growing concern about service quality in health and eldercare. Other developments, such as increased demand due to an aging population and an increased level of individualization of services, also add to the mix. Proposed solutions to these challenges in European healthcare help to illustrate the diversity of views. One solution suggested by market proponents is to further concentrate resources and increase efficiency in order to provide more care with better quality. Lean production and just-in-time models that are borrowed from industry and manufacturing are not always well suited for public services – particularly, not healthcare. Another problem with this solution is that the Scandinavian countries already have some of the most streamlined healthcare sectors in the world, and there is probably a limit to how 'efficient' one can make healthcare services while maintaining acceptable service quality levels. A second possible solution would be to increase public funding, but most European healthcare systems are financed by some of the highest taxes in the world. They try to find a way to provide high-quality services to a greater number of patients at a reasonable and socially acceptable cost.

A different kind of solution is reflected in the growing interest in and practice of public participation in healthcare. A decade ago, the World Health Organization (WHO) maintained that there were basically three ways or mechanisms to channel public participation in healthcare governance: 'choice', 'voice' and 'representation'. 'Choice' mostly applies to individual decisions in selecting insurance and/or service providers. 'Voice' tends to be exercised at the group or collective level for expressing public or group views. 'Representation' implies a formal, regulated and often obligatory role in the process of healthcare governance (2005). Co-production can potentially combine choice, voice and representation by actively engaging citizens in the provision of public services – including healthcare services – at the site of service delivery (Pestoff, 2009, 2008). Calls for greater public participation were reflected in the United Kingdom and the National Health Service (NHS), where it was argued that public and patient engagement in healthcare is 'an idea whose time has come' (Hudson, 2014). The Office of Public Management also stated that 'co-production is the new paradigm for effective health and social care' (Alakeson, et al., 2013). The WHO subsequently broadened its perspective by adopting a 'Global Strategy on People-Centered and Integrated Health Services' that mentions co-production. It recommends five closely connected steps: 1) Engaging and empowering people; 2) Strengthening healthcare governance and accountability; 3) Reorienting healthcare through models that prioritize primary and community care services and the co-production of health; 4) Coordinating services; 5) Creating an enabling environment (World Health Organization, 2016).

B Co-production – Some Lessons

The Demand/Control model (Karasek and Theorell, 1990) discussed in Chapter 6 was expanded to include an additional dimension based on the degree of interaction with service users (Pestoff, 1998). It can be divided into a high and low category, similar to the other work life dimensions noted in Chapter 6. Focusing on the level of interaction between the staff and clients suggests using the categories 'sporadic' and 'enduring' to describe differences in their relationship. They are combined in Figure 7.1 with two salient stress categories identified earlier – Low and High Strain.

High/Low strain & clients	High strain	Low strain
Enduring	*Semi-personal staff*	*Empathetic co-producer*
Sporadic	*Reserved bureaucrat*	*Sympathetic professional*

Figure 7.1 Client Relations – a Fourth Dimension in the Psychosocial Work Environment Model.

Staff with High Strain jobs but with only sporadic relations with numerous clients will probably display the typically bureaucratic distance to their clients by remaining impersonal. Staff members with a High Strain job but with enduring contact with their clients will most likely develop a semi-personal relation with them, yet will also probably experience increased stress from such frequent interaction. Staff members with a Low Strain job but with only sporadic contact with their clients may develop a sympathetic professional relation with them. Finally, staff with a Low Strain job and enduring interactions with their clients will most likely develop an empathetic relationship with them and try to involve them in both the design and delivery of the services being provided – which can help turn them into co-producers.

The term co-production was developed in the 1970s by Nobel Laureate Elinor Ostrom and her colleagues to describe the potential relationship that could exist between the 'regular producers' (e.g. street-level police officers, school teachers or health workers) and their 'clients' who desire to be transformed by the service into safer, better educated or healthier people (Parks, et al., 1981, Ostrom, 1996). Co-production is often considered a partnership between citizens and public service providers that is essential for meeting a growing number of economic, political and social challenges in the 21st Century. They include, among other things, improving the efficiency and effectiveness of public services in times of financial strain; increasing the legitimacy of the public sector after decades of questioning its ability with the spread of New Public Management; finding viable solutions for meeting the growing needs of aging populations in many parts of the world; facing the growing threat posed by populism in many advanced democracies today. The latter can be seen, at least in part, as a reaction to the persistent cutbacks in public services – particularly, under NPM policies after the Great Recession of 2008 – 2010.

However, neither the government nor citizens can solve these challenges on their own. Co-production can make an important contribution to the debate on public management, because it goes to the heart of both effective public services delivery and the role of public services in achieving societal ends, such as social integration and citizen engagement (Osborne, et al., 2013: 145). A seminal OECD report (2011) on co-production called for reconsidering traditional public service delivery in a new socio-economic environment. It argued that existing models of public service provision are not only tenuous, but are also no longer affordable. This lends greater urgency to developing alternative models that focus on citizen participation in the design and delivery of public services. However, it also noted that involving citizens/users in more systematic exchanges with the paid staff who deliver public services can transform the relationship between service users and providers, hence ensuring the former greater influence and ownership. Thus, the OECD concludes that co-production is more than tokenism, occasional client consultation or focus group discussions. Moreover, providing citizens and users with more influence over public services – particularly concerning service quality – may prove crucial for successfully evoking their participation as co-producers, notably in enduring, labor-intensive services like healthcare and social services.

Co-production is often noted by the mix of activities that both public service agents and citizens contribute to the provision of public services. The former are involved as professionals or 'regular producers', while 'citizen production' is based on voluntary efforts of individuals or groups to enhance the quality and/or quantity of services they receive (Parks, et al., 1981; Brudney and England, 1983). Initially, co-production attracted a lot of attention in the U.S.A. in the 1970s and 1980s, but, for a few decades thereafter when New Public Management gained ascendancy, the idea of involving people and groups outside the government in producing public services only received sporadic attention. However, today, there is a renewed interest among academics and practitioners in understanding co-production and greater citizen participation in the provision of public services. Ostrom argued that co-production implies that citizens can play an active role in producing public goods and services of consequence to them (1996: 347). Alford (2002) distinguished between three sources of motivation for citizen participation in public sector services: material, solidarity and expressive incentives. He noted that material rewards and sanctions are ineffective in eliciting the requisite client contributions in all but the simplest of tasks (*ibid.*).

As discussed earlier in Chapter 4, several scholars have argued that services are always 'co-produced' (Ostrom, 1996; Grönroos, 2008; Osborne, et al., 2013; Batalden, et al., 2015). Proposals to ensure patient participation in healthcare are called by a variety of names, like patient-centeredness, patient engagement and patient experience. While many of these proposals embrace patient participation, they are often limited in scope. They quite often pay lip-service to participation, but actually, fail to go beyond consultation. Typically, governments select the issues for consultation, set the questions and manage the process, while citizens are invited to contribute their views and opinions on prepackaged options rather than having a say about the contents of the services. Thus, the OECD argues that co-production is something more than consultations with clients. It implies changed relations between the providers and consumers of services (OECD, 2011). It is appropriate, therefore, to distinguish between individual and collective co-production and consider the role of organizations and organizational culture in providing the social support necessary to promote health literacy and co-production.

C Collective Co-production and Social Support

Griffiths and Foley contrasted individual and collective co-production (2009). Individual co-production involves a 'vertical' partnership, and negotiations take place between the individual service users and the front-line service provider responsible for helping them. This form of co-production is easiest to implement, since it builds on existing citizen-provider interactions at the point of service delivery. Collective co-production, by contrast, involves expanding this interaction to encompass groups of citizens in shaping and administering public services or public financed services. This implies fostering 'horizontal' relationships between active citizens, in addition to the existing 'vertical' relations that they have with the state. This can take a variety of forms (*ibid.*: 5). Thus, collective co-production attempts to move public services away from a centralized, standardized, competitive agenda, towards a model of provision that is more localized, flexible and collaborative. It also expands the concept of 'service users' to encompass local communities and wider societal networks. However, they note that this is not equated with self-help or philanthropic efforts – both of which were considered parallel production rather than co-production by the pioneers of the 1980s, nor is it synonymous with a model where the third sector or citizens themselves take primary responsibility for areas previously overseen by the state (*ibid.*: 4). The latter development promotes a Communitarian regime, and it is compared with other public administration regimes in Chapter 11.

Hudson (2012) distinguished between individual and collective co-production with reference to developments in healthcare in the United Kingdom. He sketched a shift in the National Health Services from mass production to mass collaboration (*ibid.*). The latter, known as participatory healthcare, relies on sustained patient engagement to deal with complex and chronic conditions. Efforts at augmenting the sustainability of citizen/user participation in the provision of public services were analyzed in terms of collective action (Pestoff, 2014). Co-producing public services promises to limit the cost of public services, but it also requires a change in the relations and behavior of public servants and citizens/users in order for the latter to make a long-term commitment to co-production. Olsen proposed two types of logic for collective action not just one (1965). Focusing on small group interaction can provide an important strategy for achieving sustainable co-production, particularly for enduring social services and healthcare. Ostrom identified seven structural variables for resolving social dilemmas (2009) that also facilitate sustainable citizen participation in co-production. Certain additional factors are considered crucial for making co-production more sustainable, including the nature of the service itself, promoting a dialog between the staff and clients and facilitating small group interactions in large organizations (Pestoff, 2014). This suggests that governments need to develop more flexible, service-specific and organization-specific approaches for promoting co-production rather than looking for simple 'one-size-fits-all' solutions to the challenges facing public service delivery. This is notably relevant for enduring services – like healthcare – where sustainable patient participation is crucial for resolving the mounting challenges posed by chronic illness.

Both of these forms of co-production are associated with a number of important benefits derived by citizens and the state that can roughly be divided into two categories – instrumental and intrinsic values or benefits. On the instrumental side, co-production can significantly improve service quality and facilitate better service outcomes. On the intrinsic side, co-production serves as a means of coupling public service provision with broader concepts of citizenship and facilitates easier identification of problems and challenges in service delivery. Moreover, individualized co-production often delivers instrumental benefits, while collective co-production can also foster trust and communication between service users and providers that help to develop community networks and social capital (Griffiths and Foley, 2009: 6).

Despite its crucial benefits, collective co-production does not share the same recognition or support from government initiatives as individual co-production. This is largely due to the fact that collective co-production is very difficult to implement from the center alone; it requires a local strategy. Individual co-production can incorporate opportunities for direct negotiation between the service users and providers at the point of delivery, while collective co-production requires a more localized approach to fostering or tapping into local networks (*ibid.*: 7). Moreover, it represents a significant challenge to traditional models of centralized public service provision. It is a more diverse approach – encompassing a variety of methods and forms that rely on collaboration between local government and local community groups (*ibid.*: 17). This type of collaboration reflects a government's willingness to engage in something more than individual co-production. Whether it is willing to do so is, in turn, influenced by the type of public administration regime (PAR) that dominates in a particular service sector or country. Differences between PARs are discussed in Chapter 11.

Although citizens are increasingly called upon to participate in healthcare improvements worldwide, it is not often clear how this can be made to work in practice at the micro-level or for the individual healthcare provider. Renedo, et al. (2015) found that engaging patients and professionals in real collaborative relationships is challenging. Consultative arrangements are common, but they tend to replay traditional divisions and asymmetries between healthcare professionals and patients. This can lead to growing public disillusionment with narrow patient initiatives as well as to consultation fatigue – both of which undermine the sustainability of collaborative relationships (*ibid.*: 29). However, they have also shown how organizational culture can become an enabling resource for active and meaningful participation in healthcare improvements. Patients can adopt the cultural elements that they find within the organizational context and use them in new ways to support their participation and collaboration with healthcare professionals (*ibid.*: 31). A key element in their study was the organizational emphasis on non-hierarchical, multidisciplinary collaboration, which is reflected in an organization's governance model. Governance models in Japanese healthcare are discussed and compared in Chapter 9.

Health literacy is a key aspect of approaches to increased patient participation in healthcare, as discussed earlier in Chapter 4. Given increased concerns about the adverse consequences of low health literacy, some studies have shown significant variation in individual adaptation to health literacy problems. Little attention has been given to the impact of social support on the relationship between health literacy and health service utilization. However, empirical studies of health literacy reveal an individualistic premise of current literature where individuals are treated as isolated and passive actors. Thus, low health literacy is usually considered an individual trait that is independent of the support and resources that individuals can mobilize in their social environment. Nonetheless, Lee, et al., argue that it is necessary to take social support into account, since people can draw on it when faced with problems due to limitations in their health literacy (2004: 1309).

The concept of social support is defined as resources provided by a network of individuals and social groups (*ibid.*: 1313). Research suggests that social support may have both direct effects and moderating effects on health status and health service utilization. Following the common distinction in the literature, they differentiated two aspects of social support –

structural and functional. Structural social support refers to an individual's location in the social structure (e.g. participation in community or voluntary organizations, maintenance of social contact and immersion in close social networks). A sense of belonging and being supported may originate from participation in social groups. It can enable an individual to face a stressful situation that would otherwise seem overwhelming (*ibid.*: 1314). Finally, healthcare providers can also play an active role in promoting health literacy. Rather than considering health literacy as an individual attribute that motivates informed individuals, it can also be conceived as an organizational attribute of healthcare providers. They can actively engage in health literacy outreach by contacting citizens in the communities where they live and attempt to bring health literacy to them. Examples of this are discussed below.

Keeping these distinctions in mind will be important for analyzing the Patient Study. Differences between an organization culture that pays lip-service to patient participation and one that actively fosters and institutionalizes it and provides support for health literacy are crucial considerations. Examined together, they suggest that, perhaps, there is more than one type of co-production. Durose, et al. (2013) distinguished between the role played by clients of public services in terms of describing, recognizing and transforming co-production. Rather than a public agent presenting standardized, mass-customized or 'finished products' to the citizen, collaboration between professionals and citizens can produce the desired changes. However, this process demands 'mutual readjustment' where actions taken by both parties are based on their joint consideration of a problem and where both share responsibility for deciding what action to take. Therefore, each actor must recognize the legitimacy and responsibility of the other party to contribute to their joint service production. This, of course, challenges the traditional power relations, control and expertise in public services (*ibid.*). This suggests the existence of two kinds of co-production: aspirational and transformative co-production, which are illustrated in Figure 7.2.

Aspirational co-production favors citizen participation, but it ignores the structural hurdles to it and, therefore, often results in marginal or minimal changes in existing structures and social relations rather than the transformative changes called for by the OECD. Therefore, it seems associated with New Public Management (NPM) with an emphasis on economic values and efficiency. Transformative social innovations, by comparison, challenge, alter, and/or replace dominant institutions in the social context (Avelino et al., 2019). Transformative co-production is, consequently, considered a social innovation that requires new social relations, involves new ways of doing, organizing, framing and knowing (Hartley, 2005). Thus, it appears closer coupled to New Public Governance (NPG) and efforts to balance economic pursuits

Aspirational	Transformative
Describing	Encouraging
Recognizing	Facilitating
Pay lip service	Fostering
Accepting	Institutionalizing

Figure 7.2 Two Kinds of Co-production.

with other important social and political values. The two types of co-production are also related to the distinction between individual and collective co-production noted above. Individual co-production is restricted to the aspirational type, while collective co-production seems necessary to promote transformative co-production. This is discussed in more detail in Chapters 10 and 11.

Returning briefly to patient representation in decision-making Wright reminds us that descriptive and substantive representation of patients on the boards of healthcare providers are not the same thing (2015). His study of Community Health Clinics in the U.S. demonstrates that consumer governance is extremely difficult to implement. Common challenges include the dominance of social elites, low levels of patient participation, disparities in working knowledge between patients and professionals and unanswered questions about the impact of patient governance on desired outcomes (*ibid.*: 64). Moreover, while patient representatives can express their experiences and desires, they cannot replace accountants, lawyers and other professional skills necessary for effective organizational governance (*ibid.*: 66). This brings us to critical differences between standardized and flexible services in healthcare and the role of patient uncertainty.

D Standardized and Flexible Services in Healthcare

Healthcare, as a service, is not only subject to a high degree of asymmetry in knowledge between the professional providers and the service users. There is also a high degree of uncertainty in terms of service quality and how to define this, both from the patient/user and provider perspective (Hirschman, 1970). This is due to two main trends – technical advances in service provision particularly in the advent of ICT solutions and increasing patient/citizen uncertainty about their own needs. Their needs may change with new diagnostic and treatment options, as well as changing life cycle circumstances or different stages in the development of a given disease and its treatment. Citizen/user involvement in service provision also depends on the degree of complexity and uncertainty in terms of achieving good service quality. Standardized services often require a less complex form of citizen involvement in service provision, while services that involve a high degree of user/citizen uncertainty may demand a higher degree of involvement in service provision (Blandi, 2018).

For example, the community and home safety services studied by Ostrom and her colleagues in the 1970s can easily be standardized. The police can meet with local residential groups once or twice a year – organized as Neighborhood Watch Groups – to exchange information, instruct homeowners how to mark their possessions and advise them about devices that can help secure their homes. They can also initiate a 'hotline' to ensure easy and rapid reporting of suspicious activities. ICT solutions can also facilitate such matters with online sites (Meijer, 2012). However, the contribution of homeowners remains at the aspirational level of citizen involvement in service provision. It does not require a major change in how local community safety services are organized nor in the nature of the interaction between citizens and community safety professionals.

By contrast, patient/citizen involvement in healthcare services – particularly chronic care – involves much more uncertainty on the part of citizens, since these services are highly complex and subject to rapidly changing technology. In this case, service quality requires much greater patient interaction with the front-line staff in order to identify and define the patient's needs, to discuss the alternatives available to them and, finally, to agree on the best and most realistic treatment. The need for greater citizen involvement in more complex services can, therefore, acquire an economic-political dimension not usually associated with simpler or less complex services. This has clear ramifications on how to best organize healthcare services and promote efficiency and effectiveness. In particular, Blandi (2018) distinguishes between internal and external efficiency.

High internal efficiency may require standardization or mass customization of services, yet some degree of flexibility may be necessary to achieve external efficiency. Under such circumstances, the staff needs to interact with external actors (i.e. their clients) in a flexible fashion in order to help clients identify and define their needs – including their changing needs. In cases of high user/citizen uncertainty, a service provider's efforts to achieve internal efficiency can, in fact, diminish its efforts to achieve high external efficiency and, thus, reduce the overall efficiency and effectiveness of a service (*ibid.*). This implies a dual or split approach to organizing healthcare between the back and front office. Back-office staff can provide standardized services (e.g. booking visits and billing services) while front-office staff (e.g. nurses and care workers) require much greater autonomy in their daily tasks to achieve the flexibility required for promoting external efficiency (*ibid.*). This flexibility reflects both the complexity of the service provided and the degree of patient uncertainty. Moreover, this requires adopting a systems approach to complex issues involving feedback loops to guarantee appropriate organizational flexibility that can promote greater patient participation in healthcare design and delivery. An attempt to understand patient participation in and influence on hospital services is proposed in Figure 7.3. It will guide the presentation of the Patient Study.

Reasons for patients to choose a hospital are either based on their expressive or institutional needs. Patient needs are then filtered by hospital structures that reflect the status attributed to patients as passive recipients of or active participants in healthcare as well as the governance models designed to accommodate patient needs and promote hospital social values. These enhancing structures can promote patient participation in hospital activities and provide them various ways to express their opinion about hospital services. How does this model impact service quality? Notably, the healthcare provided by both hospital groups in this study achieves similar levels of approval from their patients. This suggests that there are probably two different types of co-production – an aspirational and a transformative kind. It is time to introduce the empirical materials will allow us to explore these ideas in greater detail.

E The Patient Study

In 2017, two Medical Co-ops and two *Koseiren* hospitals participated in the Patient Study that resulted in 631 completed questionnaires[1]. Table 5.2 in Chapter 5 provided an overview of the data collection and procedures. There were 517 respondents from the Medical Co-ops and 114 respondents from *Koseiren*, resulting in just over four-fifths of the respondents from the Medical Co-ops and under one-fifth from *Koseiren* hospitals. Many of the questions included are based on five-point ordinal scales of agreement that range from 1) agree to 5) disagree. Some of the tables found here only include the proportion of positive answers to questions about being an active client/patient. Usually, the difference between the percentage of positive answers for patients at the Medical Co-ops and *Koseiren* hospitals is noted on the

Patient needs &	Hospital	Enhancement	Patient	Type of
---------1-------→	---------2-------→	---------3-------→	---------4-------→	---------5---
hospital values	institutions	structures	satisfaction	co-production

Figure 7.3 Exploring Two Models of Patient Participation in Healthcare.

far right as Dif. In most cases, the Medical Co-ops patients were more positive, but, when patients at *Koseiren* hospitals were more positive, it is followed by 'K'. If the difference remains at five percent or below, then it seems low, while rates between 5% and 10% are moderate and above that level, it seems high. Most of the comments and comparisons will focus on questions or variables where the difference between them is 10% or more. Note that, however, there is a high level of missing data (MD) for a few questions. Intuitively, if MD remains at 5% or below, then it seems low, while rates between 5% and 10% are moderate, but above that level, it is considered high. Table 7.A in the appendix summarizes the missing data for the Patient Study when it reaches 10% or more. For a more detailed discussion of the questions included in the Patient Study please consult the Preliminary Overview of the Patient Study (Pestoff, 2017). The discussion of the results also includes some comments and observations from the Organization Study when appropriate (Pestoff, 2016).

1 Patients' Social Background and Reason for Visiting Their Hospital

Table 7.B in the appendix contains data about the social background of patients. The difference between them is generally rather small. About two-thirds of the patients are female in both hospital groups. Three out of five patients at the Medical Co-ops are 70 years and older, while over half of the patients at *Koseiren* hospitals are 70 years and older. Less than one-third of the patients at both hospital groups claim to have achieved a higher educational level (i.e. they have attended a vocational or technical college or the university). Three out of five patients at the Medical Co-ops live alone or with a partner, while more than half of them at *Koseiren* hospitals live in a family of three or more persons. In terms of their employment status, more than two out of five state that they are pensioners at both hospital groups, but they differ somewhat in terms of whether they are employed. Less than one out of five is employed at the Medical Co-ops, while more than one in four is at *Koseiren* hospitals. More than half of the patients at the Medical Co-ops state that their household earned less than 3 million Japanese Yen in 2016, while two out of five made the same claim at *Koseiren* hospitals. However, the most striking difference between these two patient groups is found in terms of the type of cooperative memberships they claim. The dominant membership form is considered their primary membership, while the next most frequent membership form is regarded as their secondary membership. More than four out of five Medical Co-op patients claim membership in a health co-op, and more than two out of five claim membership in a consumer co-op. By contrast, more than three-fourths of the patients at *Koseiren* hospitals claim membership in a JA co-op, while one in five also claim membership in a consumer co-op. More details on the social background of patients can be found in the Preliminary Overview of the Patient Study (Pestoff, 2017). The membership pattern of the staff, patients and volunteers is compared in Chapter 10.

Chapter 9 in this volume considers governance models associated with the respective hospital groups in greater detail. However, briefly, Koseiren is a secondary organization that is owned and managed by the primary, multipurpose agriculture cooperatives affiliated with Agricultural Japan (JA). Farmers can join a local branch of JA, but they do not become a member of Koseiren. It has no direct individual membership and, therefore, lacks user/patient representation on its supervisory committees or its executive boards. By contrast, Medical Co-op patients, as well as the medical and administrative staff, are members of their local health co-ops and therefore, they are represented on the board of the Medical Co-op hospitals. Direct membership in a health co-op makes a major difference in terms of a hospital's ability to channel and institutionalize patient influence.

2 *Reasons for Choosing their Current Healthcare Provider*

The overwhelming majority of patients visited their local hospital or clinic for one of three types of treatment on the day of the interview: internal medicine, orthopedics and/or ophthalmology. Significantly more of the *Koseiren* patients sought treatment for the latter two issues than patients at the Medical Co-ops. In addition, *Koseiren* patients indicated having more than one treatment on the day of their visit. On average, there were 1.91 treatments for *Koseiren* patients and 1.37 for Medical Co-op patients. Patients were asked to indicate the reasons for choosing their healthcare provider. In an effort to simplify the data in Table 7.1, the ten original answers were reduced to three main alternatives and are noted by *italics*: the reputation of the staff and/or hospital, utility or instrumental reasons and their membership. For more details about the ten original answers, please consult Pestoff, 2017.

Two very distinct patterns are found in patient reasons for choosing their hospital. Patients in both hospital groups agree that the reputation of the staff and hospital is an important factor for choosing a hospital, and the difference between them in this respect is smaller than for two other key issues. In addition, Medical Co-op patients are clearly motivated by their membership in a health co-op, while *Koseiren* patients are strongly motivated by utilitarian or instrumental considerations – such as the ease of access, having special services or it being the only local hospital available. Thus, patients have widely divergent reasons for choosing their respective hospitals.

Table 7.1 Why did you choose this hospital? (Choose more than one alternative when relevant)

Reasons for Choosing	*No. resp.***	*Med Co-ops*	*Koseiren*	*Dif.****
Membership[a]	417	76.9	26.5	50.4
Reputation[b]	415	70.8	55.7	15.1
Utility/ Instrumental[c]	384	53.2	103.5	50.3/K
Other Reasons	48	9.2	2.8	6.4
Total Responses (*av.*)	1,264	1,007 (*1.95*)	221 (*1.94*)	--

*Multiple responses; patients could name more than one reason.
Number of responses, the average per patient was 1.95 for the Medical Co-Ops and 1.94 for *Koseiren*; * Difference between Medical Co-ops and *Koseiren*; a *Membership* combines three answers: member of a co-op, recommended by my local co-op and wanted to participate more actively; b *Reputation* combines four answers: the staff is kind and helpful, recommended by a friend, has a good reputation and the staff is competent; and c *Instrumental* combines three answers: ease of access, has special medical services and only one available.

3 Hospitals and Health Literacy Outreach

Some Japanese healthcare providers actively engage in what might be called health literacy outreach. *Koseiren* Hospitals B and C, as well as Medical Co-op B, actively promote health literacy for residents in small towns and villages through a variety of activities designed to animate and engage the residents in their own and others' healthcare. *Koseiren* Hospital B is located in a sparsely populated prefecture and, for several decades, it has sent healthcare teams to remote villages on Sundays, holidays and a few days each summer. It employs a variety of means to engage local residents to think and learn about issues related to their own individual and collective healthcare. These methods include performing plays and promoting village drama about important healthcare issues, arranging discussions and seminars, etc. This is usually combined with annual tuberculosis screenings and other basic health checks for all village residents. In addition, it arranges a two-day health festival at the hospital that draws a crowd of more than 20,000 residents each year. Considered together, these health literacy outreach activities illustrate the claim that, over several decades, their commitment to promote rural medicine has contributed to reducing overall healthcare costs in the Nagano prefecture from the highest per capita at the end of World War II to the lowest in the nation today (Pestoff, 2016).

Medical Co-op B and *Koseiren* Hospital D in Aichi Prefecture both described their outreach efforts in terms of encouraging local neighborhood patrols by members/volunteers. They notice who is 'out and about' and who has not been seen for a few days. They pay a visit to 'absent neighbors' to make sure that everything is okay with them or to see if they need any help (*ibid.*). These neighborhood patrols also assist in searching for suitable premises for new social activities, like meeting weekly for tea or monthly for lunch. Such social events provide a good opportunity for discussing relevant healthcare issues – such as diet and exercise or providing accurate information about the spread of new diseases, among other things. (Yamasaki, 2018). These efforts also contribute to creating and replenishing social capital. Medical Co-op B also arranges an annual health festival, patterned on the model of *Koseiren* Hospital B. In addition, Medical Co-op B prints a monthly newspaper that is distributed by hand to the home of all its members by health co-op volunteers. This is a rather common practice for local health co-ops in Japan (Pestoff, 2016). These newspapers can make a valuable contribution to increasing health literacy among members as well as providing an opportunity for exchanges between the volunteers and members that can contribute to the social capital in the health co-op movement. Thus, there are a variety of activities that healthcare organizations can embrace if they want to actively engage in health literacy outreach. This also reflects a healthcare provider's commitment to embracing preventative medicine.

4 Participation in Hospital Events and Influencing Hospital Services

We will now turn our attention to patient participation in various types of activities related to or promoted by their hospital – including networking or internal channels of communication and their influence on hospital services. Table 7.2 addresses patient participation in hospital activities, while Table 7.3 explores how they express their opinion about hospital services. Data in Chapters 6 and 9 suggest that the Medical Co-ops have an organizational culture and social support structures that facilitate and promote a more active, participatory role for their patients/members. Patient data shows that members/patients at the Medical Co-ops respond appropriately; they appear more or significantly more active in various types of hospital events. Referring to the column of differences in Table 7.2, some forms of participation appear more specific for the Medical Co-ops, like participating in community activities, attending local co-op member meetings, volunteering and making investments and donations. They are mentioned much more frequently by patients at the Medical Co-ops.

Annual health festivals arranged by some *Koseiren* hospitals and Medical Co-ops are very important activities, particularly in rural areas, as noted previously in the section on health literacy outreach. Data in Table 7.2 indicate that half or more of patients at both hospital groups attend this type of hospital event. Given the information

Table 7.2 Participation in Hospital Activities

*Participation in Hospital Events**/**	*Med Co-ops*	*Koseiren*	*Dif.****
1. Hospital events (health festival)	57.5	49.5	8.0
2. Community activities (flea markets)	51.0	34.5	16.5
3. Local co-op member meetings	47.9	17.5	30.4
4. Study groups for health issues	48.8	54.7	5.9/K
5. Volunteer activities	40.0	11.4	28.6
6. Make investments and donations	82.5	11.7	70.8
7. Others, please specify...	2.3	0.9	1.4

*Only the proportion of positive answers that combine the 'often' and 'sometimes' answers are included here;
**Consult Table 7.A in the appendix for missing data; and
***Difference between Medical Co-ops and *Koseiren*.

asymmetry in healthcare and specific knowledge of professionals, these festivals play an important function. They help to demystify both the hospital and the persons in white lab coats (i.e. the medical professionals) and to humanize them in the eyes of visitors. They can see several dozen stalls or exhibits at an annual hospital festival, many of which are interactive. They can look through a small hole to see how robotic surgery could be performed. They can see different stages of development of ulcers in the stomach, etc. They can sample different kinds of green tea or even buy some at another stall. There are puppet performances that carry a health message for small visitors. Annual health festivals are usually two-day events held on weekends. Hospital staff and volunteers work the stalls and answer visitors' questions. Annual health festivals are an important part of their community-building activities (Pestoff, 2016).

Moreover, a distinctive feature of the health co-ops that was noted previously in Chapter 3 is that members are encouraged to play an active role in their own healthcare on a routine basis. For example, members/patients are normally expected to take their own blood pressure when they arrive at a clinic or hospital and to inform the nurse and/or doctor on duty what it is on that day. This helps to make them aware of the importance of keeping track of their blood pressure. Members are also encouraged to actively participate in a *han* or a small community wellness or health study group consisting of between eight to ten neighbors, often women in their 50s to 60s. In 2020, there were 140,540 health co-op members enrolled in 26,270 *han* groups with an average size of 5.35 members per group (E-mail from Y. Yamasaki, 2020). *Han* members attend regular lectures and courses arranged by local health co-ops. Some go on to become health advisors and can subsequently lead *han* groups. Today, there are more than 40,000 health advisors. Members in the *han* groups learn to conduct self-checks in order to monitor their own health condition, usually with the assistance of a nurse or health advisor. They keep records of their blood pressure, the sugar and salt content in their urine, fat content, etc. by using simple devices and methods. These self-monitoring activities provide effective early detection and treatment of illness (Kurimoto, 2015). *Han* groups also discuss each members' basic health conditions as determined by self-monitoring in relation to their diet and nutrition, exercise habits and lifestyle. Through their learning and acquired knowledge, members/patients can actively collaborate with professional healthcare providers to combat or prevent chronic disease rather than passively leaving most health issues in the hands of healthcare professionals. Data in Table 7.2 indicate that half or more of patients at both hospital groups often or sometimes participate in health study groups. In fact, this is one activity where *Koseiren* patients have a slightly higher noting than Medical Co-op patients. It would be very interesting to compare the health study groups and their activities at different hospitals. For Medical Co-ops, *han* groups also help to generate social capital, particularly among older health co-op members, by arranging monthly lunches, exercise groups, hikes, etc. (Yamasaki, 2018).

Table 7.2 also indicates that more than three times as many Medical Co-ops patients volunteer at their healthcare provider as *Koseiren* patients, and nearly three times as many patients attend local member meetings at Medical Co-ops. Volunteering is considered in greater detail in the next chapter. Concerning the last form of participation – making investments and donations – both members and staff are required to hold a share in the medical co-op where they are regular patients or work. Becoming a member and having a share helps create stronger bonds with their healthcare provider than simply being a patient. For example, Medical Co-op B opened its new 303-bed hospital in 2010 that employed 54 full-time and 75 part-time doctors and 228 full-time nurses. They explained the role of their members in planning and financing the hospital that involved 45 meetings and over 1,000 people/members for three years to discuss the new hospital. Health co-op members also contributed financially, partly through their 1,000-yen membership contribution and partly by taking personal bank loans toward the new hospital. Together, members contributed nearly 1 billion Japanese Yen, while the remaining 10 billion Japanese Yen for completing this came from bank loans; however, the government contributed nothing toward the new hospital (Pestoff, 2016).

Turning now to the issue of patient influence, Table 7.3 addresses various ways patients are able to express their opinion about hospital services.

Given the differences noted in their activity patterns, we should expect to find some differences between them in terms of the internal channels of communication that reflect their different governing

Table 7.3 How can you express your opinion about the services? (Choose more than one if necessary)

*Ways to Express Your Opinion**	*No. resp.***	*Med Co-ops*	*Koseiren*	*Dif.****
Talking to the professional staff	285	44.5	48.2	3.7/K
Voicing opinion in com. Meetings	138	26.1	2.6	23.5
Attending local co-op meetings	117	22.1	2.6	19.5
Talking to the administrative staff	116	19.5	13.2	6.3
Participating in hospital activities	110	18.2	14.0	4.2
Using the suggestion (rainbow) box	88	12.8	19.3	6.5/K
Talking with board members	40	7.4	1.8	5.6
No way to communicate my opinion, never tried to do so, or other.....	115	16.8	24.5	7.7/K
Total responses (*av.*)	1009	865 (*1.67*)	154 (*1.35*)	--

*Multiple responses, respondents could choose more than one alternative for expressing their opinion;
**Number of responses; and
***Difference between Medical Co-ops and *Koseiren*.

structures and styles (i.e. inclusive versus exclusive). Talking with the professional staff clearly outweighs the other alternatives as a natural resource for patients at both hospital groups. It garners nearly twice as many responses as any of the next four alternatives, and there is very little difference between patients at the respective hospitals on this issue. Smaller differences are noted for some other alternatives – like talking with the administrative staff or board members and using the Rainbow or suggestion box, etc. However, there are some stark contrasts between two other alternatives preferred by patients at these two hospital groups. In particular, voicing an opinion in a committee meeting and/or attending a local co-op meeting are much more widely used channels for patients at the Medical Co-ops. This reflects a more participatory organization culture and a more inclusive governance model that will be discussed in Chapter 9.

How does the existence of more inclusive channels impact their perception of having influence? The data shows that patients at the Medical Co-ops appear more confident that they can influence hospital services than *Koseiren* patients. Two-fifths of Medical Co-op patients (39.9%) feel that their opinions are reflected in hospital activities, while barely one-fourth of them (27.1%) do at *Koseiren* hospitals. Note that, however, there was a lot of missing data (17.2% and 21.9% respectively), and 'neither agree nor disagree' answers (35.0% and 40.4% respectively). This suggests that some patients are unwilling to express themselves on this issue. However, very few patients stated that the hospitals did not consider their opinions.

5 Satisfaction with the Staff and Service Quality

Our attention will now turn to questions about patient satisfaction with the staff and hospital services and, finally, their willingness to recommend it to their friends and neighbors. It begins with patient evaluations of the hospital and its services in Table 7.4.

Patients at both hospital groups show rather high levels of appreciation for the staff and hospital. They are most satisfied with the administrative staff and least satisfied with the management. The difference between patient groups is marginal, and patients at the Medical Co-ops appear slightly more satisfied on most issues, except for accessibility. The latter item emphasizes *Koseiren* patients' main reasons for making their initial choice of a healthcare provider (i.e. reasons of access). This is the item that gets the highest level of support from *Koseiren* patients. See Table 7.A in the appendix for more details about missing data.

Finally, concerning their willingness to recommend the hospital to a friend or acquaintance, the data shows that more than two-thirds of the patients at both hospital groups are willing to do so. Medical Co-op patients responded positively at a rate of 73.6% and 70.1% did so at *Koseiren* hospitals. However and once again, there is a larger than normal rate of 'neither agree nor disagree' responses in this case (22.5% and 26.2% respectively), suggesting a high degree of uncertainty for some patients.

F Summary and Conclusions – Two Kinds of Co-production

The analysis of data from the Patient Study was based on a model of patient needs, hospital structures and enhancing institutions that can promote patient participation and influence and their service

Table 7.4 How satisfied are you with the staff and hospital services in general?

Are you satisfied with the hospital and staff/**	*Med Co-ops*	*Koseiren*	*Dif.****
Administrative Staff[a]	83.2	79.2	4.0
Professional Staff[b]	80.5	71.3	9.2
Healthcare Services (In General)	72.2	67.3	4.9
Accessibility	68.6	80.0	11.4/K
Management	66.7	57.4	9.3

*Combines the 'satisfied' and 'somewhat satisfied' answers;

**Consult Table 7.B in the appendix for missing data in this table; and

***Difference between the Medical Co-ops and *Koseiren*; a = Reception, accounting, information, etc. and b = Doctors and nurses.

satisfaction. It was argued that the results from the Patient Study suggest the existence of two different kinds of co-production, aspirational and transformative. Table 7.1 showed that instrumental motivations weigh heavily for *Koseiren* patients in the choice of their healthcare provider. Ease of access and necessity are mentioned by virtually all of them. The reputation of the hospital or staff for being 'kind and helpful' or considered 'competent' motivated more than half of the patients at *Koseiren* hospitals and two-thirds of patients at the Medical Co-ops. In addition, Medical Co-op patients attach greater importance in their co-op membership when choosing a healthcare provider.

Table 7.2 showed that Medical Co-op patients participated more actively in most types of hospital events. It also illustrated some features of health literacy outreach that both the Medical Co-ops and *Koseiren* share. In addition, the Medical Co-op patients noted several channels that facilitate member participation in running the health co-ops. In particular, this included making investments in their healthcare provider via a membership contribution, participating in community activities, attending local membership meetings and participating in volunteer activities. Table 7.3 underlined that Medical Co-op patients also felt more capable of and willing to express their opinion about the hospital and its services. They also found additional channels for expressing their opinions through committee meetings and by attending local co-op meetings. Table 7.4 demonstrates that patients at both hospital groups were generally quite satisfied with the hospital's staff and services, but Medical Co-op patients were slightly more satisfied than *Koseiren* patients on all matters except for accessibility to the hospital or clinic itself. Finally, nearly the same proportion of patients at both hospital groups – more than two-thirds of them – stated they would recommend it to friends or acquaintances.

The Patient Study addresses issues related to the importance of membership. Does being a patient in a Medical Co-op mean the same thing as being a patient at a *Koseiren* hospital? Data presented in the Patient Study suggest that it does not. Patients at the Medical Co-ops are more than just patients; they are also members of their healthcare co-op. Being a member creates ties that bind. It also provides them with a feeling of ownership that gives them certain rights and responsibilities that are not shared by non-members. Thus, membership provides the social glue that enables and facilitates their working together for a common goal (i.e. their individual and collective health and well-being).

The comparison of patient participation in Medical Co-ops and *Koseiren* healthcare providers demonstrates that there are different levels and different kinds of patient participation when patients are members in health co-ops rather than simply patients or clients at a hospital. Although, both hospital groups seem to embrace an active stance in terms of health literacy outreach. Patients at both hospital groups note similar levels of participation in hospital festivals and study groups for health issues. This begs the question: What can hospitals do to encourage and facilitate patient participation? Direct membership in health co-ops seems to comprise the key of an active organizational culture that, combined with social support structures, can promote patient activism in addition to high health literacy via the health study groups. Thus, both organizational culture and social support appear to enable and facilitate the manifestation of transformative co-production at the micro-level of single healthcare providers.

The Medical Co-ops promote active participation by patients in a variety of ways, and they have institutions that can facilitate and foster their inclusion in the internal workings of their healthcare provider. By expecting patients to become a member of the health co-op, the Medical Co-ops are able to extend the rights and responsibilities of membership in a very different fashion than in *Koseiren*, since it lacks direct individual patient members. Thus, membership in a health co-op provides a key to facilitating and fostering active patient participation at the Medical Co-ops. Patients who are direct members of health co-ops have more positive attitudes about several aspects of the healthcare services, and they are more active in the provision of their own healthcare.

These two different approaches to co-production not only express two different patterns of patient involvement in the provision of healthcare. They also represent the differing needs of their patients. In rural areas, utilitarian or instrumental needs to alleviate local shortages in healthcare services and create qualified jobs locally are understandably much greater. Therefore, members of agricultural co-ops are satisfied with the traditional healthcare services provided by *Koseiren*. In urban areas, however, the need for more engagement and activity by some groups manifests itself, and health co-op members appear equally satisfied with the services provided by the Medical Co-ops. Nevertheless, they have the possibility of challenging traditional relationships of power, control and expertise in healthcare, rendering it the joint product of the activities of both patients and professional healthcare providers.

Thus, the Patient Study illustrates that there are two kinds of co-production: aspirational and transformative. Aspirational co-production is limited to describing and recognizing the potential benefits of co-production, paying lip service to it and accepting some marginal or ad hoc contributions by citizens to public services. This may include finding ways to gradually increase the input of citizens to the provision of healthcare in one fashion or another. However, it does not call into question or challenge the power asymmetry between the professional service providers and citizens. Transformative co-production, on the other hand, includes encouraging co-production by actively facilitating, fostering and institutionalizing it. This leads to the conclusion that, if a healthcare provider wants to embrace transformative co-production in the 21st Century, then it must develop a proactive strategy for encouraging patients to participate actively in their own healthcare, both individually and collectively, and a sustainable policy to facilitate and implement it. However, there is no quick fix, since opening an organization for transformative co-production can be a lengthy and complicated process.

Whether transformative co-production at the level of an individual healthcare provider is sufficient to facilitate co-production at the meso and/or macro levels remains to be seen. This will be given more attention in Chapter 11. However, studies of citizen participation in the provision of publicly financed services in Sweden and Japan help illustrate the breadth and depth of the steps necessary to achieve transformative co-production. In Sweden, parents in parent co-op childcare and voluntary organizations with a special pedagogical profile are responsible for the management and maintenance of the childcare facility and balancing its budget, or they can share these responsibilities with the staff. By contrast, parents at worker co-ops and public childcare facilities can contribute to the Christmas or Spring party and make ad hoc suggestions for daily activities or improvements at the facility. Sometimes, they are represented on a parent council that meets every second or third month to discuss issues or make suggestions for changes. However, they have no vote and cannot decide such matters. Thus, there is a 'glass ceiling' that limits their participation (Pestoff, 1998); their influence is rather limited, and it does not challenge or change the power balance between the professional service providers and service recipients. However, including parents on the board of worker co-ops and giving them both a voice and vote would provide a means to transform them into multi-stakeholder organizations and imply adopting a different governance model.

Similarly, patients at Medical Co-op hospitals share the rights and responsibilities of membership in a health co-op that gives them a privileged position vis-à-vis that of simply being a patient. They value their Medical Co-op mostly in terms of expressive rather than instrumental values as will be seen in Chapter 10 They are involved in a variety of the manifestations and inner workings of their health co-op – in particular, community activities and local membership meetings. They also volunteer at the hospital and they make donations to and investments in its health promotion activities. Moreover, in addition to talking with the professional staff and using the suggestion box, they can gain influence by voicing their opinion at a committee meeting, attending a local health co-op meeting, etc.

Furthermore, health co-op members are encouraged to join *han* study groups in order to bring their diet, exercise and lifestyle into balance as part of their effort to promote preventive medicine. Members are also recruited to relevant hospital committees, and many of them are board members and/or even lay hospital directors. Such opportunities both foster and institutionalize the role of members as co-producers of their own and others' healthcare. These opportunities are not available to the patients at hospitals lacking these structures. They do not have the rights and responsibilities of health co-op members, rather they are simply hospital patients. Lacking the features of transformative co-production, they are part and parcel of an incremental and instrumental approach to co-production. Moreover, given the hierarchical command and control model of governance found in public healthcare, co-production in public hospitals will most likely be limited to lower levels of the aspirational variety of co-production (McMullin, 2020). Nevertheless, these two different approaches to co-production might have something to learn from each other in terms of best practices. This points to the importance of the governance models employed by hospital groups and the social values they promote in their activities in order to more fully understand their unique contribution to Japanese healthcare. Governance is the topic of Chapter 9, while social values and hospital missions are the focus of Chapter 10.

Finally, this suggests that governments need to develop more flexible, service-specific and organization-specific approaches for promoting co-production in healthcare – particularly, collective co-production – rather than looking for simple 'one-size-fits-all' solutions to the challenges facing public service delivery. This is notably relevant for enduring services, like healthcare, where sustainable patient participation is crucial for resolving the mounting challenges posed by chronic illness.

Note

1 The data collection was financed by the Japanese Society for the Promotion of Science (JSPS), the Mitsubishi Foundation and Osaka University; and it was supervised by Prof. Yayoi Saito, Osaka University and the Consumer Co-operative Institute of Japan (CCIJ). The project is conducted within the framework of established cooperation between senior researchers at Ersta Sköndal Bräcke University College in Stockholm (Prof. V. Pestoff and Doc. J. Vamstad) and the Faculty of Human Sciences, Osaka University (Prof. Y. Saito). This interdisciplinary group of Swedish and Japanese researchers is supported by a reference group of the relevant cooperative healthcare providers in Japan, *Koseiren* and the Japanese Health and Welfare Co-operative Federation HeW CO-OP JAPAN.

References

Alakeson, V., Bunnin, A., Miller, C., 2013. *Coproduction of Health and Wellbeing Outcomes. The New Paradigm for Effective Health and Social Care*. Office of Public Management, London.

Alford, J., 2002. Why do Public Sector Clients Co-Produce? Towards a Contingency Theory. *Adm. Soc. 34/1*, 32–56.

Avelino, F., et al., 2019. Transformative social innovations and (dis)empowerment. *Technol. Forecast. Soc. Change 145*, 195–206.

Batalden, M., Batalden, P., Margolis, P., Seid, M., Armstrong, G., Opipari-Arrigan, L., Hartung, H., 2015. *Coproduction of health care service. BMJ Quality & Safety*, 10.1136/bmjqs-2015-004315.

Blandi, V., 2018. *Customer Uncertainty: A source of organizational inefficiency in the light of Modularity Theory of the Firm.* Ph.D. Dissertation Trento & Florence.

Brudney, J., England, R., 1983. Towards a Definition of the Coproduction Concept. *Public. Adm. Rev. 43*, 59–65.

Durose, C., Mangan, C., Needham, C., Rees, J., Hilton, M., 2013. *Transforming local public services through co-production.* Univ. of Birmingham & Arts & Humanities Research Council. (PPT slides), Birmingham.

Griffiths, S., Foley, B., 2009. *Collective Co-production: Working together to Improve Public Services - LARCI Commissioned Summary Report.* Local Authorities & Research Council Initiative, London.

Grönroos, C., 2008. Service logic revisited: who creates value? And who co-creates? *Eur. Bus. Rev. 4*, 298–314.

Hartley, J., 2005. *Innovation in Governance and Public Services. Past and Present; Public Money & Management*, 26/2: 101–108.

Hirschman, A., 1970. *Exit, Voice and Loyalty.* Harvard University Press, Cambridge, MA and London.

Hudson, B., 2012. Competition or co-production? Which way for governance in health and wellbeing? Loeffler, E., Taylor-Godby, D., Bovaird, T., Hine-Hughes, F., Wilkes, L. eds, *Making Health and Social Care Personal and Local. Moving from Mass Production to Co-production.* London Governance International & Local Government Information Unit.

Hudson, B., 2014. Public and Patient Engagement in Commissioning in the English NHS. An idea whose time has come? *Public. Manag. Rev. v. 17/1*, 1–16.

Karasek, R., Theorell, T., 1990. *Healthy Work: Stress, Productivity, and the Reconstruction of Working Life.* Basic Books, New York.

Kurimoto, A., 2015. *Social Enterprise in Japan: The Field of Health and Social Services'* No. 7 *ICSEM Working Paper.*

Kurimoto, A., 2018. *Chapter 4 Japan: health and elderly care cooperatives; IHCO and EURICSE ed.. Co-operative Health Report: Assessing the world-wide contribution of cooperatives to healthcare.*

Lee, S.Y., Arozullah, A.M., Cho, Y.I.k, 2004. Health literacy, social support and health: a research agenda. *Soc. Sci. Med. 58*, 1309–1321.

McMullin, C., 2020. Co-production of Public Services: Institutional Barriers to the Involvement of Citizens in Policy Implementation. In: Sullivan, H., Dickinson, H., Henderson, H. (eds), *The Palgrave Handbook of the Public Servant.* Palgrave Macmillan, Cham.

Meijer, A., 2012. Co-production in an Information Age; Ch. 10. In: Pestoff, V., Brandsen, T., Verschuere, B. eds, *New Public Governance, the Third Sector and Co-production.* Routledge, London & New York.

OECD, 2011. *Together for Better Public Services. Partnering with Citizens and Civil Society.* OECD Public Governance Reviews, Paris.

Olsen, M., 1965. [1971] *The Logic of Collective Action.* Harvard University Press, Cambridge MA & London.

Osborne, S.P., Radnor, Z., Nasi, G., 2013. A New Theory for Public Service Management? Towards a (Public) Service Dominant Approach. *Am. Rev. Public. Adm. 43/2*, 135–158.

Ostrom, E., 1996. Crossing the Great Divide: Coproduction, Synergy, and Development, *World Development*, 24/6: 1073-1087; reprinted in 1999 as Ch. 15. In: McGinnis, M.D. (ed.), *Polycentric Governance and Development. Readings from the Workshop in Political Theory and Policy Analysis*. Univ. of Michigan Press, Ann Arbor, MI.

Ostrom, E., 2009. *Social Cooperation in Collective-Action Situations*. Rösner, H.J. Schulz-Nieswandt, F. Neue Kolner Genossenschaftswissenschaft, Cologne.

Parks, R.B., Baker, P.C., Kiser, L., Oakerson, R., Ostrom, E., Ostrom, V., Perry, S.L., Vandivort, M.B., Whitaker, G.P., 1981. Consumers as Co-Producers of Public Services: Some Economic and Institutional Considerations; *Policy Studies Journal*, 9: 1001-1011; reprinted in 1999 as Ch. 17. In: McGinnis, M.ichaelD. (ed.), *Local Public Economies. Readings from the Workshop in Political Theory and Policy Analysis*. Univ. of Michigan Press, Ann Arbor, MI.

Pestoff, V., 1998. *Beyond the Market & State: Social enterprises and civil democracy in a welfare society*. Ashgate, Aldershot UK, Brookfield USA.

Pestoff, V., 2008. *A Democratic Architecture for the Welfare State: Promoting citizen participation, the third sector and co-production*. Routledge, London & New York.

Pestoff, V., 2009. Towards a Paradigm of Democratic Governance: Citizen Participation and Co-production of Personal Social Services in Sweden. *Ann. Public. Cooperative Economy 80/2*, 197–224.

Pestoff, V., 2014. Collective Action and the Sustainability of Co-production. *Public. Manag. Rev. 16/3*, 383–401.

Pestoff, V., 2016. *Cooperative health and eldercare in Japan – a brief overview of eight co-op hospitals*. Stockholm: Ersta Sköndal Bräcke University College.

Pestoff, V. 2017. *The Patient Study: A Preliminary Overview of the questions and answers*. Stockholm & Osaka: Ersta Sköndal Bräcke University College & Osaka University.

Pestoff, V., 2018. *Co-production and Public Service Management. Citizenship, Governance and Public Service Management*. Routledge, London & New York.

Renedo, A., Marston, C.A., Spyridonidis, D., Barlow, J., 2015. Patient and Public Involvement in Healthcare Quality Improvements. How organizations can help patients and professionals to collaborate. *Public. Manag. Rev. 17/1*, 17–34.

United Nations, 1997. *Co-operative Enterprise in the Health and Social Care Sectors*. United Nations, New York.

World Health Organization, 2005. *Ninth Futures Forum on Health Systems Governance and Public Participation*. WHO, Copenhagen.

World Health Organization, 2016. *WHO Global Strategy on People-Centered and Integrated Health Services, Interim Report*. Geneva: WHO.

Wright, B., 2015. Voices of the Vulnerable. Community health centers and the promise and pearl of consumer governance. *Public. Man. Rev. 17/1*, 57–71.

Yamasaki, Y., 2018. *Various types of voluntary activities by Japanese Health Cooperative Members*. Osaka: paper presented at the ICSEA conference on social enterprise.

Yamasaki, Y., 2020. e-mail communication on 12 Aug., 2020.

Appendix 7

Table 7.A Missing Data for Some Tables

Table 7.2	2.1	2.2	2.3	2.4	2.5	2.6	2.7
MC	13.9	17.0	17.2	17.2	19.2	11.8	92.3
K	18.4	26.3	29.8	16.7	30.7	32.5	86.8

Key: Table and item number, 2.1 means Table 2, item 1 and 4.4 means Table 4, item 4.

Table 7.4	4.1	4.2	4.3	4.4	4.5	4.1	4.2	4.3	4.4	4.5
MC	10.1	8.3	14.3	13.7	13.5	14.3	17.6	26.0	28.3	30.6
K	15.8	11.4	14.0	16.7	17.5	15.1	24.6	30.6	29.0	42.6

Key: the first half is % missing data, second half is % 'neither agree or disagree' answers.

Table 7.B The Social Background of Patients

	Male		*Female*		*MD*
Medical Co-ops	33.3		62.9		3.9
Koseiren	30.7		67.5		1.8
Age[a]	**30s-50s**	**60s**	**70s+**		**MD**
Medical Co-ops	9.2	25.6	61.1		4.1
Koseiren	14.9	26.3	55.2		3.5
Education	**B**	**C**	**D**	**E**	**MD**
Medical Co-ops	17.0	42.9	14.7	16.6	8.7
Koseiren	35.1	27.2	21.9	7.0	8.8
Family Composition[a]	**single**	**couple**	**3 pers**	**4+ pers**	**other**
Medical Co-ops	17.0	42.4	22.6	12.4	5.6
Koseiren	15.8	30.7	16.7	34.2	2.6
Occupation	**employed**	**housewf**[f]	**pensioner**	**other**	**MD**
Medical Co-ops	19.8	25.5	43.9	3.7	5.6
Koseiren	28.9	16.7	44.7	5.3	2.6
Household Income[a]	**<2mil.**	**2–3mil.**	**3–4mil.**	**4–15mil.**	**MD**
Medical Co-ops	25.5	29.6	13.2	21.8	9.9
Koseiren	26.3	17.5	14.9	26.3	14.9
Member of Cooperative[a]	**health**	**consumer**	**JA agr.**	**other**	**MD**
Medical Co-ops	85.5	42.0	15.7	1.0	9.3
Koseiren	3.5	20.2	76.3	6.1	15.8

a = this information not available for public staff;
B = Jr. high school;
C = high school;
D = vocational/technical college;
E = university & grad school,
f = housewife/man.

8 Volunteering and Co-production in Japanese Healthcare

This chapter problematizes both the tasks and actors involved in healthcare co-production. Tasks can either be core, essential or complementary and they can be performed by professionals, patients or volunteers. Core tasks are reserved for the staff with professional training. The tasks studied in the Volunteer Study include both the essential and complementary types. Most of the complementary tasks require little or no special training to perform and having volunteers perform them is routine. However, several of the other activities are deemed essential and closer to features related to membership in a health co-op than complementary healthcare tasks. Establishing an ancillary organization allows the health co-ops to mobilize community stakeholders and benefit from the resources they bring with them, as well as allowing them to engage members in the provision and management of their own and others' healthcare and well-being.

A Volunteering and Co-production

Nearly 200 years ago, De Tocqueville regarded voluntary organizations as a 'school of democracy' (1835). It is frequently noted that there is a growing role for volunteers in delivering public services (UN Volunteers, 2011), but what role do they play in healthcare? Typically, they guide patients and visitors by helping them to find the right clinic or ward both in public and private hospitals in many parts of the world. This chapter relates the tasks volunteers perform to two key issues for co-production (i.e. the 'who' and 'what' of co-production). Who are the main actors in co-production, and what kinds of tasks do they perform?

The classical stance is that citizens or service users and the professional staff are the two main actors in co-production (Ostrom, 1996; Parks et al., 1981). In the traditional configuration, the professional staff provides all the core services, and users perform some complementary tasks (Pestoff, 1998, 2006; Brandsen and Honingh, 2016) like guiding patients and visitors to the correct ward. Facilitating co-production becomes a question of finding ways to evoke user participation in complementary tasks without encroaching on the core ones. If, however, citizens performed core tasks, then they would supplement the staff as service providers, and this could pose a threat to the staff's status and job security. On the other hand, if users mainly performed complementary tasks, then they could augment service provision and/or improve service quality (Ostrom, 1996). Which tasks citizens or users performed and which ones the paid staff undertake, therefore, becomes an empirical question.

Nonetheless, recent research suggests that this relationship might be more complex than previously thought. Concerning the 'what' of co-production, it may prove necessary to go a step further by distinguishing between core, essential and complementary tasks, not simply the core and complementary tasks. Core tasks are at the heart of the service provided; essential tasks are necessary activities, but not part of the core functions of a service, while complementary tasks are often tertiary ones that improve the quality of the service and give it a more personal or human touch. The importance assigned to these tasks may, however, shift with time, changing political preferences and economic necessities as well as vary among countries, service sectors and providers.

Moreover, with the growth of different public administration regimes, especially those anchored in prolonged austerity of public finances, we can note the spread of volunteering in the provision of public services. For example, in the 2010s, Denmark adopted a broader definition of co-production/co-creation in a variety of social services that include volunteers and voluntary organizations (Fehsenfeld, 2019). A similar development was noted in the Netherlands (Nederhand and van Meerkerk, 2017). Elsewhere in Europe, there is a growing use of volunteers in the delivery of various public services. In the United Kingdom, local fire and rescue services not only include volunteers; now they have job descriptions, work alongside the professional staff and even wear the uniforms of firemen, but they receive no pay (Schlappa and Imani, 2016). Accordingly, even the 'who' of co-production seems to be evolving with the increasing presence of the third category of service providers – volunteers – alongside the service users and paid staff. Thus, we can observe the development of a new constellation of roles and tasks with three main categories of providers and three kinds of tasks present in many types of co-production arrangements, as seen in Figure 8.1.

Roles/tasks	Professional staff	Volunteers	Users
Core	M	N	N
Essential	C	C	C
Complementary	N	S	M

Figure 8.1 An Enhanced Configuration of the Roles and Tasks in Co-Producing Public Services.

Source: Pestoff, 2018, Figure 11.1, p. 167. Key: M = main provider, S = secondary provider, N = none, C = contested task or role.

The mix of actors and roles involved in citizen participation in the provision of public services can be illustrated by some examples mentioned above. In firefighting services in the U.K., the paid staff provides core services, but, due to cutbacks in public funding, some essential services like home safety inspections are now provided by volunteers. This is an example of substitutive rather than complementary co-production. However, these volunteers also provide some services not usually associated with home inspections by salaried fire and safety services. During a home visit, they can help to identify socially isolated citizens, elders in need and other pressing social issues that can be reported to the appropriate social authorities for assistance (*ibid.*). In other E.U. countries, volunteers have replaced the paid, professional firefighters, and they are now responsible for all the firefighting services. In Estonia, for example, volunteers have substituted or replaced the paid staff in rural areas (Tõnurist and Sruva, 2017). This type of citizen participation seems like parallel production and should not be confused with co-production, since there are no longer any professionals with whom citizens can interact or co-produce (Ostrom, 1996; Parks et al., 1981). By contrast, the staff in parent co-op childcare in Sweden provide the core pedagogical services, while parents provide both essential and complementary services. The latter includes the management and maintenance of the facility, arranging social events, etc. (Pestoff, 1998). Therefore, an approach that takes into account an enhanced or more nuanced understanding of the actors and/or tasks than a simple dichotomy seems more appropriate for future research into co-production.

The above discussion of 'who' co-produces helps to identify a closely related consideration (i.e. the difference), if any, between volunteers and co-producers in delivering public services. As noted earlier in Chapter 4, some authors suggest volunteering and co-production are more or less the same thing, and they use these concepts interchangeably. Others take the recent expansion of volunteering in the provision of public services as an example of the growth of co-production (Tõnurist and Sruva, 2017). This is probably a mistake. However, before rushing to judgment, perhaps more analysis is necessary. We will, therefore, briefly note some similarities between volunteering and co-production and then discuss the differences between them.

Alford argued that there are some basic differences between volunteers and co-producers in terms of providing inputs to and/or consuming outputs from public goods and services (2009). Volunteering and co-production often have a similar organizational base, and their participants may share similar values although with a different emphasis (Pestoff, 1998, 2008). Volunteers provide service to others without expecting a direct material reward for their efforts and without benefiting directly or personally from the service provided (UN Volunteers,

2011). They may, of course, receive indirect benefits – such as job training, skills development, increased social status and contact and/or personal satisfaction (*ibid.*) – but they are not direct service recipients. Co-production, by contrast, is based on participation by service users both in the provision and consumption of a service. Thus, co-producers are the direct beneficiaries of their own and others' activities in providing public services (Alford, 2009: 24).

How can these seemingly contrary perspectives on the relationship between volunteering and co-production be reconciled? One possible explanation for both volunteering and co-production being present and considered relevant concepts in public service provision at the same time is gleaned from the early findings of research on public administrations regimes (PARs) (Pestoff, 2018, Ch. 9). Volunteers only play a marginal role in traditional public administration and New Public Management (NPM). By contrast, New Public Governance (NPG) relies more heavily on citizen participation in the provision of public services, and co-production is considered a key component or aspect of this PAR. In this case, it corresponds closely with the idea of dual roles of co-producers who make unpaid inputs to public service provision by contributing their time and effort to improve the quality and quantity of public services and, at the same time, who receive or consume the same public services as service users.

Finally, a Communitarian type of regime, also calls for much greater citizen input to public service provision, primarily to compensate for public budget cutbacks, but their role is mainly confined to being 'coerced' volunteers rather than individual public service users (Pestoff, 2018, Ch. 6). The withdrawal of public support leaves them with little choice, as seen with rural firefighting in Estonia. Accordingly, the lack of clarity about the different roles played by volunteers and co-producers stems, at least in part, from the institutional context of public sector reforms. Failing to distinguish between PARs and the role attributed to various actors – like volunteers and co-producers – by different PARs creates unnecessary confusion. Both NPG and a Communitarian type of regime call for more citizen participation in the provision of public services, but citizens participate in rather different ways. In NPG, they participate as co-producers, while in a Communitarian type of regime they participate mainly as 'coerced' volunteers. Chapter 11 in this volume discusses competing Public Administration Regimes in more detail.

B The Volunteer Study

Two cooperative hospitals from the Health and Welfare Co-op Federation of Japan (HeW CO-OP) that are affiliated with the Japanese Consumer Co-operative Union (JCCU) and two cooperative hospitals from the social welfare branch of Japanese Agriculture (JA) participated in this study in the spring of 2017, and it resulted in 236 completed questionnaires. The former hospitals are called Medical Co-ops herein, while the latter is known as *Koseiren*. Table 5.2 in Chapter 5 provides an overview of the data collected by the Volunteer Study[1]. Volunteers at the Medical Co-ops contributed nearly three-fourths of the completed questionnaires, while those from *Koseiren* made up just over one-quarter of the total answers received. The response rate was 31.6% for the Medical Co-ops and 56.2% for *Koseiren*. Many of the questions included in the Volunteer Study are based on five-point ordinal scales of agreement that range from 1) agree to 5) disagree. Most of the tables found here only report the proportion of positive answers to a variety of questions about volunteering. Usually, the difference between the percentage of positive answers for volunteers at the Medical Co-ops and *Koseiren* hospitals is noted as Dif. Most of the time, it favors the Medical Co-ops, but, when it favors *Koseiren,* it is followed by the letter K. If the difference remains at five percent or below, then it seems low, while rates between 5% and 10% are moderate. Above that level, it seems high. The comments and comparisons will mostly focus on questions or variables where the difference between them is 10% or more. Some questions allowed respondents to choose up to three alternatives that best reflected their views on certain issues. Some of the comments to the tables are derived from the Organizational Study (Pestoff, 2016).

This chapter focuses on the most substantially and theoretically relevant variables included in the Volunteer Study. For a more detailed presentation of the questions included, please consult the Volunteer Study: a preliminary overview of the questions and answers (Pestoff, 2017). There is some missing data (MD) in a few the agreement questions in this survey; however, the figures in most of the tables presented in this case exclude missing data. Intuitively, if MD remains at five percent or below, then it seems low, while rates between 5% and 10% seem moderate. Above that level, it seems high. Table 8.A in the appendix summarizes the missing data for questions where it is high.

We will begin by providing some background to volunteering at these two cooperative healthcare providers. This includes a brief overview of the social background of volunteers, then we will consider the importance of membership in a healthcare co-op and its implications for co-production in Japanese healthcare, followed by information about the degree of volunteering at these four hospitals – where and how much they volunteer and their reasons for volunteering at these cooperative hospitals. After, we consider their participation in the hospital's activities and discuss the type of tasks they perform, their relations with the staff, contact with various groups and their perceived benefit from volunteering. Finally, we will discuss their evaluation of the service quality and reach certain conclusions.

Table 8.B in the appendix contains data about the social background of volunteers. It covers the following items: their gender, age, education, family composition, family income and cooperative memberships. Concerning the gender division, 85% or more of the volunteers are female at both hospital groups. The Medical Co-ops volunteers are somewhat older, 70 years old and above, than *Koseiren* volunteers. Concerning their educational achievement, more of the volunteers at *Koseiren* have not completed high school, while more volunteers at the Medical Co-ops have a college degree. In terms of their civil or family status, most of the volunteers at the Medical Co-ops are single or live with a partner, while most volunteers at *Koseiren* hospitals live in three or more person families. Considering occupation, more of the volunteers at Medical Co-ops are pensioners, while more of them claim full or part-time employment in *Koseiren*. In terms of family or household income, more volunteers at the Medical Co-ops fall in the income bracket of 1–3 million Japanese Yen annually, while more of the *Koseiren* volunteers are found in the bracket of 4–10 million Japanese Yen per year.

However, similar to the staff and patients, the most significant difference between the social background of volunteers at these two hospital groups is found in terms of their cooperative memberships. More than nine of ten volunteers at the Medical Co-ops are members in a health co-op, and more than half of them are also members of a consumer co-op. By contrast, four out of five *Koseiren* volunteers are members of a JA affiliate, while more than one-quarter of them are also members of a consumer co-op. The memberships of the staff, patients and volunteers will be compared in Chapter 10. Finally, before proceeding, it is worth remembering that the Patient Study discussed in Chapter 7 noted that two out of five patients (40.0%) at the Medical Co-ops were volunteers, while less than one out of eight (11.4%) was at *Koseiren* hospitals. Accordingly, volunteering is considerably more prevalent among patients at the Medical Co-ops than at *Koseiren* hospitals.

1 *Where and When They Volunteer*

The Volunteer Study starts by asking how long and how often they volunteer. Table 8.1 provides the following picture about their length of volunteering at the Medical Co-ops and *Koseiren* hospitals.

About two out of five have volunteered for five years or less at both the Medical Co-ops and *Koseiren* hospitals. Most *Koseiren* volunteers claim to have done so between 5–10 years, but considerably more Medical Co-ops volunteers claim to have done so for ten years or longer. Volunteering at cooperative healthcare providers in Japan does not,

Table 8.1 How long have you been a volunteer?

How long have you volunteered?	*Med Co-ops*	Koseiren	*Dif.**
Less than one year	11.6	6.3	5.3
1–5 years	30.9	35.9	5.0/K
5–10 years	19.2	37.5	18.3/K
10 years or more	37.2	12.5	18.4
Missing Data	1.2	1.6	0.4/K
Total (236)	100% (172)	100% (64)	–

*Difference between Medical Co-ops and *Koseiren.*

Table 8.2 How many hours do you volunteer per month?

Hours per Month	*Med Co-ops*	Koseiren	*Dif.**
Less than 10 hrs/mo.	52.3	90.6	38.3/K
More than 10 hrs/mo.	45.9	7.8	38.1
Missing Data	1.7	1.6	0.1
Total (236)	100% (172)	100% (64)	–

*Difference between Medical Co-ops and *Koseiren.*

therefore, appear to be a short-term or ad hoc activity for either hospital group; rather, volunteers appear committed for the long-term.

They were also asked if they volunteered regularly or only occasionally. Between 70% and 80% of the volunteers at both of the hospital groups claim that they do so regularly. Somewhat more of them volunteer regularly at the Medical Co-ops (80.2%), but more do so occasionally or they are on call at the *Koseiren* hospitals (28.1%). Table 8.2 shows the average of how many hours they volunteer per month.

Nearly two-thirds of *Koseiren* volunteers contribute five hours or less of their time per month, and another 25% of them give between 5–10 hours per month, but very few volunteer more than that. By contrast, more than half of the Medical Co-ops volunteers give between 5–10 hours of their time per month, while nearly half of them give between 10–50 hours per month. Thus, volunteers at the Medical Co-ops contribute more hours of their time every month than *Koseiren* volunteers. However, as seen in Table 8.6, more *Koseiren* than Medical Co-op volunteers state that they would like to volunteer more than they do currently. Thus, it seems that the Medical Co-ops are able to mobilize an important resource that remains largely unexplored or untapped by *Koseiren* hospitals, and this can have clear economic and social consequences.

Respondents were also asked whether they currently volunteered elsewhere or had previously done so. More than half of the volunteers at the Medical Co-ops (56.4%) claim they do or did, while nearly three-quarters of them (73.4%) make the same claim at *Koseiren* hospitals. However, getting more *Koseiren* patients to volunteer or to volunteer longer hours may prove difficult, given their other voluntary commitments.

2 *Reasons for Volunteering at a Healthcare Facility*

Turning to the central question of why they volunteer, respondents could name one or more of five reasons for doing so. These five alternatives are presented in Table 8.3 below in order of support that they received from the volunteers.

Four main motives for volunteering supported by one-third to one-half of the volunteers at both hospitals: 1) Wanting to learn more about medical care and a healthy lifestyle, 2) Agreeing with the purpose of the hospital, 3) Wanting to be involved in the local community and 4) Wanting to help people in need. The relative importance of these motives varies somewhat, but the difference between the two hospital groups is modest, except for the first one – wanting to learn more about medical care and leading a healthy lifestyle – that received more support from volunteers at the Medical Co-ops. The average number of responses by volunteers is nearly equal in both hospital groups, 2.1 for the Medical Co-ops and 1.9 for *Koseiren*. Volunteers were also asked whether they receive any compensation for their voluntary work. If they get some kind of compensation, then it usually covers the cost of local

Table 8.3 Why do you volunteer? (Choose more than one alternative when relevant)

*Reasons for Volunteering**	*No. Resp.***	*Med Co-ops*	Koseiren	*Dif.****
To learn more about medical care and a healthy lifestyle	117	48.8	35.9	12.9
Agreement with the purpose of this hospital	114	50.0	43.8	6.2
Want to be involved in improving the community	100	42.2	42.2	–
To help people in need	99	40.1	46.9	6.8/K
Because of family, friends & acquaintances, or others, ...	66	29.7	23.4	6.3
Total responses/(*av.*)	486	363 (*2.1*)	123 (*1.9*)	

*Multiple responses; volunteers could name more than one reason;
**Number of responses for a given item; and
***Difference between Medical Co-ops and *Koseiren*.

transportation to and from the hospital along with a free meal when they arrive. However, Medical Co-ops have different policies on compensating volunteers. One of them no longer provides any financial support to volunteers, while the other still does (Pestoff, 2016). Nearly half of volunteers at the Medical Co-ops (48.3%) claim that they pay all of their own costs, while three-fourths of the *Koseiren* volunteers (75.0%) claim that they receive some form of compensation for volunteering.

3 Tasks Performed by Volunteers

We discussed volunteering with the directors and boards of the co-operative hospitals in 2013 as part of the Organization Study. Unfortunately, these interviews did not clearly reflect the distinction between in-house or in-hospital volunteering and community volunteering, nor did they fully explore the potential of the latter for contributing to local social capital and/or promoting community development. The volunteer questionnaire was only distributed to in-hospital volunteers, and the Volunteer Study, therefore, underestimates the importance of community volunteering.

Medical Co-op A has several committees and councils that include volunteers or ordinary members. The Council for Information publishes a monthly newspaper in 120,000 copies that is distributed by volunteers to every member's household. This is a typical health literacy outreach activity for Medical Co-ops in Japan. Volunteers supervise the Rainbow or comment box and the Council publishes a newsletter with patient feedback on hospital services intended to improve their services. There are several committees that include volunteers. To become a volunteer, they must be a member of the local health co-op and take volunteer courses. They are unpaid, except for transportation and lunch. Volunteers observe what the staff does; they perform many essential secondary or tertiary tasks at Medical Co-op A. For example, they help care for newborn babies, and train new mothers on how to feed them and prepare infant food, and they help at the childcare center, etc. At the residential eldercare center, volunteers help residents vote in elections and provide them with entertainment and help lead their exercise. Volunteers make small handicraft items, display and sell them on the hospital premises that help support it. They also help with gardening at the hospital. There was a separate room for volunteers at Medical Co-op A, and the day we visited, 11 volunteers were present – two men and nine women (Pestoff, 2016).

The Committee for Hospital Construction included members/volunteers and, once the new 401-bed hospital was completed in 2003, this group became the Committee for Management. The Ethical Committee, comprised of volunteers, focuses on everyday issues and publishes a homepage. They encourage patients not to be too critical of doctors, but, rather, to support them so they can retain them, which is very difficult in a Tokyo suburb. In the post-operation or rehabilitation section, patients can remain for a maximum of 60 days. Volunteers help care for post-stroke and leg fracture patients by assisting them in their physiotherapy and exercises. Medical Co-op A also mentioned community volunteering, where active members can participate in exercise classes together, take walks together, etc. Such activities also include the active health and lifestyle study groups or *han* groups affiliated with Medical Co-ops (*ibid.*).

At the Medical Co-op B, members are such a mainstay and contribute so much volunteer work that the Director for Volunteering described it as 'the basis of their existence'. It provides a channel for the staff to learn more about members' needs and interests. In 2013, Medical Co-op B had 447 volunteers, but, contrary to Medical Co-op A, they receive no help with transportation costs nor a free lunch. Medical Co-op B also engages community volunteers for essential functions in rural villages – like keeping track of elder inhabitants, visiting them regularly to make sure that they are okay and participating in bicycle patrols to look for suitable houses for developing new facilities or activities (*ibid.*).

Directors at *Koseiren* Hospital A said that most volunteers provide support to outpatients. The Volunteer Committee has 30 members, and two or three of them come to the hospital every day to guide patients to the correct ward, etc. However, they noted that it is difficult for them to use volunteers from JA or their home helpers at the hospital due to their lack of specialization. They need more training to be useful. Moreover, in an aging society, hospitals need more volunteers, but at the same time, the supply of volunteers is decreasing (*ibid.*).

The director at *Koseiren* Hospital D pointed out that they provide a free daily bus service for the surrounding villages that allows elder inhabitants to come to town and spend the day. Once there, they are engaged in various activities. The hospital has 20 regular volunteers who are mostly women on weekdays and a few men from JA on weekends. Male volunteers clean the wheelchairs, while females guide visitors and patients in the hospital and serve them tea. The director considers them a link between the medical section and long-term care at the nursing facility next door. He also mentioned community volunteering in remote mountain villages. Volunteers keep an eye on local residents, note who is missing or has not been seen recently, visit them regularly to make sure they are okay, etc. They also look for suitable houses or premises for new facilities or activities, etc. (*ibid.*).

Table 8.4 combines the information from two questions in the volunteer survey – one about the tasks performed by volunteers (Q8) and another about additional activities they participate in at the hospital (Q9). Like most tables, the items are listed in order of frequency, going from the most often named to the least often. Certain answers have been combined into a new item which is indicated in *italics*. The 'other things ...' category combines this alternative from both questions (Q8 and Q9). The 'not involved' category also includes missing data from both questions, and the simple manual tasks combine two different kinds of manual tasks. Table 8.4 includes six tasks or activities that are considered complementary and six that are essential. The complementary tasks will be discussed first and then essential tasks.

Table 8.4 What do you do as a volunteer? (Choose more than one alternative when relevant)

*Tasks/Activities Performed by Volunteers**	*No. of Resp.***	*Essential/ Compl.****	*Medical Co-ops*	Koseiren	*Dif.*****
Guide people in the facility[a]	87	compl.	25.6	68.8	43.2/K
Other things[x], please specify[a+b]	*87*	*compl.*	*43.3*	*23.5*	*19.8*
Read to or talk with patients[a]	84	compl.	41.1	23.4	17.7
Donate or invest in a project[b]	83	essential	45.9	6.3	39.6
Participate in a committee[b]	73	essential	37.8	12.5	25.3
Facilitate a local activity[b]	72	essential	32.0	26.6	5.4
Simple manual tasks[y]	*70*	*compl.*	*32.6*	*21.9*	*10.7*
Recruit volunteers[b]	68	compl.	29.7	26.6	3.1
Simple care tasks[a/c]	63	essential	33.3	10.9	22.4
Not involved or missing data[d]	*62*	–	*23.2*	*34.4*	*11.2/K*
Help at events, health festival[a]	48	compl.	11.6	43.8	32.2/K
Plan events, like health festival[b]	47	essential	23.3	10.9	12.4
Distribute h-c newspaper[a+e]	21	essential	12.5	–	12.4
Total responses a+b (*av.*)	834	–	645(*1.9/1.9*)	189(*1.9/1.1*)	–

*Multiple responses; volunteers could name more than one reason;
**Number of responses;
***Essential or complementary tasks; and
****Difference between Medical Co-ops and *Koseiren*; x = Other things include serving tea, reading books to patients or children, pushing the book trolley to patients rooms, etc.; y = Simple manual tasks include the following activities: labor tasks (weeding or carpentry) and perform simple tasks (cleaning, folding towels); a = tasks (Q8); b = activities (Q9); c = simple care tasks are pushing a wheelchair, help with dressing, etc.; d = not involved or missing data comes primarily from Question 9 about participation in hospital activities; and e = distributing a health co-op newspaper is an important part of their health literacy outreach policy.

Focusing on the difference column, we observe that the volunteers at the Medical Co-ops participate at a much higher rate in some complementary tasks and *Koseiren* volunteers do so in others. Two-thirds of the *Koseiren* volunteers participate in guiding visitors and patients to the correct ward or room at the hospital, while only one-fourth of the Medical Co-op volunteers do so. Two-fifths of the Medical Co-op volunteers read to or talk with patients, while one-fifth of the *Koseiren* volunteers do so. Nearly a third of the Medical Co-op volunteers participate in simple manual tasks and one-fifth of the *Koseiren* volunteers do so. More than two out of five *Koseiren* volunteers help at events like the annual health festival, but barely one in ten do at the Medical Co-ops. Finally, both hospital groups received similar support from volunteers for things like facilitating local activities and recruiting new volunteers.

Medical Co-ops demonstrate a preference for using volunteers for talking with or reading to patients and other simple tasks like cleaning or folding towels. The *Koseiren* hospitals, by contrast, engage volunteers in guiding patients and visitors to the correct ward or helping at special events like the annual health festival. The average number of responses to the question about tasks (Q8) was the same at both hospital groups – 1.91. There was very little missing data for questions about performing tasks. For more details, consult Pestoff, 2017.

Six of the activities in this table are considered essential for a hospital's operations. They include making financial donations, participating in a committee, facilitating local activities, executing simple care tasks, planning a healthcare event like the annual healthcare festival and distributing the health co-ops newspaper. Volunteers at the Medical Co-ops participate in them at a higher rate, but several of them seem specific to the unique character of the Medical Co-ops as membership organizations. One noteworthy aspect of the Medical Co-ops is the existence of a modest financial commitment associated with membership in a health co-op. Members are expected to contribute economically by purchasing a basic share that is between 1,000 to 5,000 Japanese Yen or $10.00 to $50.00 U.S. Dollars and they are encouraged to make additional contributions, if they can afford it. This allows the Medical Co-ops to be partially self-financing in terms of constructing or expanding their medical facilities, as the Medical Co-op B's new hospital illustrates. Moreover, the inclusive democratic governance practiced by the Medical Co-ops encourages and institutionalizes member participation in hospital committees, so it is not surprising to see more than one-third of the Medical Co-op volunteers mention this alternative. Between one-fourth and one-third of the volunteers at both hospital groups contribute their time and efforts to facilitating local health activities like health study circles, etc.

Finally, there is a slight overrepresentation of *Koseiren* volunteers among those who either state that they are not involved in any additional activities or (Q9) failed to answer the question about participation in these activities and, therefore, are classified as missing data. There were differences in the response rate to this part of the table. There were 1.9 answers on average for Medical Co-op volunteers but only 1.1 for *Koseiren* volunteers.

In terms of the tasks performed by volunteers, there was a higher level of participation in some complementary tasks by Medical Co-op volunteers and by *Koseiren* volunteers in others. However, when it came to the additional hospital activities (Q9), there was a higher level of participation by Medical Co-op volunteers, particularly in essential activities that contribute to defining the special character of health co-ops. Finally, this table also confirms that volunteers can be engaged in more than simple menial or mundane tasks, like guiding visitors at the hospital, gardening or folding towels. They can contribute essential tasks that allow the professional staff to concentrate on providing more technical or advanced core tasks of healthcare.

4 Relations, Networking, Feelings about and Benefits from Volunteering

Table 8.5 presents the volunteers' view of their own role and influence. Most volunteers claim to have good relations with the staff and that the latter is competent. This helps make them feel like they are members of the hospital rather than occasional visitors. Support for these three items ranges from three-fourths to three-fifths. More Medical Co-op volunteers express such feelings of belonging than *Koseiren* volunteers. This reflects the fact that they are, in fact, members of a health co-op that is the base for their local Medical Co-op healthcare provider.

Moreover, volunteers state that they can communicate patients' needs, and make proposals for improvements, that the staff listens to their suggestions and their proposals can help improve services at the hospital or clinic. Yamazaki's study of volunteers at the Medical Co-op eldercare facilities confirms this (2018, 2019). She argues that volunteers make a positive impact on service quality, due to the longevity of their role as volunteers at Medical Co-op eldercare facilities. They often get to know the residents better than the staff. Moreover, elder residents might be reluctant to complain directly to the staff, but they talk more freely with volunteers, especially those who they know well. Accordingly, volunteers can serve as a bridge, and they make suggestions for changes and improvements (*ibid.*, 2018: 11). Furthermore, Table 8.5 shows that between three-fourths and one-half of the volunteers express feelings of having influence at the hospital where they volunteer. More volunteers at Medical Co-ops share such feelings than volunteers at *Koseiren* hospitals. Thus, volunteers at both hospital groups do not seem to feel that they merely provide inexpensive labor for a variety of menial tasks and

Table 8.5 Relations with the Staff/Hospital

*Relations with the Staff/Hospital**	*Med Co-ops*	Koseiren	*Dif.***
Relations between staff and volunteers are good	76.8	62.3	14.5
The staff is competent	71.1	65.6	5.5
I feel like a member of this organization	71.1	56.7	14.4
The staff listens to and considers my suggestions	73.6	65.6	8.1
Volunteers' proposals can help improve services	68.7	70.0	1.3/K
Volunteers can communicate patients' needs to staff	64.4	52.5	11.9
Volunteers can propose improvements	52.9	49.2	3.7

*Combines the 'agree' and 'somewhat agree' answers;
**Difference between Medical Co-ops and *Koseiren*. Consult Table 8.A for details about missing data.

Table 8.6 What are your feelings about volunteering?

*Your Feelings about Volunteering**	*Med Co-ops*	Koseiren	*Dif.***
I enjoy volunteering here	89.8	77.8	12.0
I want to invite my friends to vol.	46.6	35.0	11.6
I want new experiences as a vol.	29.3	30.0	0.7/K
I would like to volunteer more	23.0	33.3	10.3/K

*Combines the 'agree' and 'somewhat agree' answers; and
**Difference between Medical Co-ops and *Koseiren*. Consult Table 8.A for details about missing data.

social activities. Rather, they state that they can augment service quality by helping to communicate the patients' needs and wishes, etc. Together, this gives volunteers at both hospital groups a feeling that they can make a positive contribution to the hospital and its services and can influence it in several respects. Then, their personal evaluation of the volunteering experience was explored in Table 8.6.

Three-fourths or more of the volunteers in both hospital groups say they enjoy volunteering. A third to half of them would like to invite a friend or acquaintance to join them as volunteers; a quarter or more look forward to new challenges and experiences in their volunteering, but fewer of them want to volunteer more than they do now. There is a somewhat higher level of those who want to volunteer more at *Koseiren* hospitals than at the Medical Co-ops. As noted in Table 8.2 above, 90% of *Koseiren* volunteers do so less than ten hours per month. Therefore, the desire to volunteer more indicates a potentially untapped resource, as does the possibility to engage

Table 8.7 What are the personal benefits experienced by volunteering?

*Benefits from Volunteering**	*Med Co-ops*	Koseiren	*Dif.***
It keeps me healthy and fit	86.6	84.1	2.5
It gives me a wider perspective on society	81.0	78.7	2.3
I learn new things and skills	76.6	78.0	1.4/K
It gives me a network in the community	69.3	63.9	5.4
It promotes my attachment to the community	60.0	56.7	3.3
I feel I can change the community for the better	46.3	49.2	2.9/K

*Combines the 'agree' and 'somewhat agree' answers; and
**Difference between Medical Co-ops and *Koseiren*. Consult Table 8.A for details about missing data.

more volunteers at *Koseiren* hospitals. Shifting focus to personal benefits perceived from volunteering, respondents could note their agreement with six statements found in Table 8.7.

Positive answers range from just under one-half of the volunteers to nearly nine out of ten. The differences between volunteers at the Medical Co-ops and *Koseiren* hospitals are very modest in terms of the personal benefits they perceive from volunteering. More than four-fifths claim that it keeps them healthy and fit, while three-fourths or more say that it gives them a broader perspective on society and/or they learn new things and skills. More than half of them claim that it helps them to network in the community and promotes their attachment to it. Finally, nearly half of them assert that they feel they are able to change the community for the better by volunteering. Most of these aspects of volunteering would seem to promote their self-esteem as volunteers and citizens which also help to keep them sound in body and in mind.

Finally, considering the volunteers' willingness to recommend their hospital to friends and acquaintances, we found that nearly three-fourths of the volunteers at both hospitals agree that they would do so; 76.8% agreed for the Medical Co-ops and 73.0% did so for *Koseiren* hospitals. It is worth noting that this question is similar to one posed to both the staff and patients, which allows us to compare the answers of these three different stakeholder groups in Chapter 10.

C Summary and Conclusions: The Importance of Membership in a Healthcare Co-op

Tables 8.1 and 8.2 are related to how long and how much volunteers engage with cooperative healthcare providers. We noted some differences between the two hospital groups concerning how long and how much they volunteered. More *Koseiren* volunteers have done so between 5–10 years, while Medical Co-op volunteers have done so for ten years or more. The overwhelming majority of volunteers at both hospital groups volunteer regularly, yet three in ten do so occasionally at *Koseiren* hospitals. Regarding how much they volunteer, we saw a big difference between the two cooperative hospital groups. Nearly all *Koseiren* volunteers do so for ten hours or less per month, but nearly half of them do so for ten hours or more at Medical Co-ops and some for more than 20 hours per month.

Table 8.3 explored their reasons for becoming volunteers at their co-operative healthcare provider. The four most popular reasons given by respondents were: 'wanting to learn more about medical care and a healthy life style', 'agreeing with the purpose of this hospital', 'wanting to be involved in improving the community' and 'wanting to help people in need'. They gain support from two out of five to half of the volunteers at both hospital groups. However, the first one gets somewhat more support from volunteers at Medical Co-ops than *Koseiren* hospitals. In addition, three-quarters of the volunteers receive symbolic financial compensation for travel and a meal at *Koseiren* hospitals, while half of them do not at Medical Co-ops.

Table 8.4 showed a varied picture concerning the tasks and activities of volunteers at these hospitals. Volunteers at the Medical Co-ops participated at higher rates in some complementary tasks and volunteers at *Koseiren* hospitals participated more in others. However, many of the activities classified as essential were part of the unique profile of health co-ops as membership organizations with inclusive, democratic governance structures. Therefore, volunteers at the Medical Co-ops, understandably, mentioned them more frequently.

Tables 8.5 to 8.7 deal with relations, contact, perceived benefits from volunteering. Table 8.5 on volunteers' relations with the staff and hospital express their feelings of belonging and having influence on the hospital. The positive answers by *Koseiren* volunteers range from one-half to three-quarters, while Medical Co-op volunteers are somewhat more positive. However, there is more missing data for Medical Co-op volunteers than *Koseiren* volunteers, as seen in Table 8.B in the appendix. Table 8.6 about volunteers' feelings concerning volunteering shows that between three-fourths and nine-tenths claim to enjoy it. However, Medical Co-op volunteers hold somewhat more positive feelings than *Koseiren* volunteers. One-third of *Koseiren* volunteers state that they would like to volunteer more than today, while less than one-fourth do so at Medical Co-ops. Finally, Table 8.7 concerns the perceived benefits of volunteering. Positive answers range from more than four-fifths of the volunteers at both hospital groups who claim that volunteering helps keep them fit and healthy to just under one-half who consider it a way to change the community for the better. Medical Co-op and *Koseiren* volunteers are quite similar in acclaiming the personal benefits of volunteering.

What then does the Volunteer Study have to say about the potential role of volunteers as co-producers of healthcare? Do volunteers help to co-produce healthcare at these two hospital groups and if so, how? These questions will be considered from the perspective of Figure 8.1 mentioned in the introductory section of this chapter. First, how do the tasks undertaken by volunteers at these four cooperative hospitals relate to the tasks and roles discussed earlier? The tasks listed in Table 8.4 includes essential and complementary tasks in the provision of healthcare. Most of the complementary tasks require little or no special training or competence to perform, although the quality of the service may vary. Guiding people in the facility, talking with or reading to patients, recruiting new volunteers, performing simple manual tasks and/or helping out at events like the annual health festival fall into the complementary category. Having volunteers perform such tasks therefore, is routine and not unusual. However, several of the other activities seem essential and closer to the features related to membership in a health co-op than complementary healthcare tasks. Donating to build a new hospital, as in the case of Medical Co-op B; participating in a hospital committee, like the building and maintenance committee at Medical Co-op A; and helping plan a hospital event, like the annual health festival at most Medical Co-ops, seem like essential tasks for a member-based, participatory healthcare provider like the Medical Co-ops.

Finally, we noted that more than nine of ten Medical Co-op volunteers claim that they are members of a healthcare co-op, and more than four out of five *Koseiren* volunteers state that their principal cooperative affiliation was with an agricultural federation of Japanese Agriculture (JA). Establishing an ancillary organization, like the health co-ops, can mobilize and engage its members in the management of their own and others' well-being. The Medical Co-ops can provide a unique 'best practice'. They are able to mobilize outside of stakeholders and benefit from the resources and engagement they bring with them. It could be argued, therefore, that volunteers at Medical Co-ops do so for the benefit of themselves and other members of the healthcare co-op. Nonetheless, it seems more likely that *Koseiren* volunteers do so for the JA federation that creates the basis of their financial existence as farmers and for the healthcare it provides them in rural areas, but not necessarily for their own direct personal benefit. If this is correct, then it would be more difficult to regard them as co-producers in their own right. However, this does not mean that there are no notable differences between the *Koseiren* healthcare providers participating in our study. Some of them show greater affinity with the Medical Co-ops in terms of mobilizing local social capital than others. However, they do so without the advantage of having an ancillary organization or branch that can mobilize and engage outside stakeholders. Thus, it seems that membership in a local health co-op provides a key to access to external resources that can increase the possibility to engage patients and volunteers. Furthermore, as noted earlier in Chapter 7, volunteers who are members of a health co-op have all of the rights and responsibilities associated with belonging to it, while *Koseiren* volunteers lack these rights and responsibilities. Considered together, they seem more like traditional volunteers than co-producers.

Note

1 The data collection was financed by the Japanese Society for the Promotion of Science (JSPS), the Mitsubishi Foundation and Osaka University; and it was supervised by Prof. Yayoi Saito, Osaka University and the Consumer Co-operative Institute of Japan (CCIJ). The project is conducted within the framework of established cooperation between senior researchers at Ersta Sköndal Bräcke University College in Stockholm (Prof. V. Pestoff and Doc. J. Vamstad) and the Faculty of Human Sciences, Osaka University (Prof. Y. Saito). This interdisciplinary group of Swedish and Japanese researchers is supported by a reference group of the relevant cooperative healthcare providers in Japan, *Koseiren* and the Japanese Health and Welfare Co-operative Federation HeW CO-OP JAPAN.

References

Alford, J., 2009. *Engaging Public Sector Clients. From Service Delivery to Co-production.* Palgrave Macmillian, Houndmills, Hamps., UK & New York, NY.

Brandsen, T., Honingh, M., 2016. Distinguishing Different Types of Co-production. A Conceptual Definition Based on a Classical Definition. *Public Management Review* 76 (3), 427–435.

De Tocqueville, A., 1835/40. [2000], *On Democracy in America/American Democracy.* Chicago University Press, Chicago.

Fehsenfeld, M., 2019. Politisering af frivillighed i samspellet mellem den offentligt og den firvillige sektor: 'Vi ska tänke gadekäret ind'/Politicizing volunteering in the collaboration between the voluntary and public sectors, *Researchgate.* Syd Dansk Uiversitet, Odense.

Nederhand, J., van Meerkerk, I., 2017. *Activating citizens in Dutch care reforms: framing new co-production roles and competences for citizens and professionals, Policy & Politics*, on line.

Ostrom, E., 1996. Crossing the Great Divide: Coproduction, Synergy, and Development, *World Development*, 24/6: 1073–1087; reprinted in 1999 as Ch. 15. In: McGinnis, M.D. (ed.), *Polycentric Governance and Development. Readings from the Workshop in Political Theory and Policy Analysis.* Univ. of Michigan Press, Ann Arbor, MI.

Parks, R.B., Baker, P.C., Kiser, L., Oakerson, R., Ostrom, E., Ostrom, V., Perry, S.L., Vandivort, M.B., Whitaker, G.P., 1981. Consumers as Co-Producers of Public Services: Some Economic and Institutional Considerations; *Policy Studies Journal*, 9: 1001–1011; reprinted in 1999 as Ch. 17. In: McGinnis, M.D. (ed.), *Local Public Economies. Readings from the Workshop in Political Theory and Policy Analysis.* Univ. of Michigan Press, Ann Arbor, MI.

Pestoff, V., 1991. *Between markets and politics. Co-operatives in Sweden.* Campus, Frankfurt.

Pestoff, V., 1998. *Beyond the Market & State: Social enterprises and civil democracy in a welfare society.* Ashgate, Aldershot UK, Brookfield USA.

Pestoff, V., 2006. Citizens as Co-Producers of Welfare Services: preschool services in eight European countries, *Public Management Review*; 8/4: 503–520, reprinted 2006 as a hardback & 2009 as a paperback. In: Pestoff, V.,

Brandsen, T. (eds.), *Co-production. The Third Sector and the Delivery of Public Services*. Routledge, London & New York.
Pestoff, V., 2008. *A Democratic Architecture for the Welfare State: Promoting citizen participation, the third sector and co-production.* Routledge, London & New York.
Pestoff, V., 2016. *Cooperative health and eldercare in Japan – a brief overview of eight co-op hospitals.* Ersta Sköndal Bräcke University College, Stockholm.
Pestoff, V., 2017. *The Volunteer Study: A preliminary overview of questions and answers.* Ersta Sköndal Bräcke University College & Osaka University, Stockholm & Osaka.
Pestoff, V., 2018. *Co-production and Public Service Management. Citizenship, Governance and Public Service Management.* Routledge, London & New York.
Schlappa, H., Imani, Y., 2016. *Leading Service Co-production. Preliminary Findings from the Hertfordshire Fire and Rescue Services.* IIAS Conference paper, Tampere.
Tõnurist, P., Sruva, L., 2017. Is Volunteering Always Voluntary? Between Compulsion and Coercion in Co-production. *Voluntas 28*, 223–247.
UN Volunteers, 2011. notes from the North American Consultation Meeting: State of the World's Volunteerism Report (SWVP).
Yamazaki, Y., 2018. Various types of voluntary activities by Japanese Health Cooperative members. 5th *ICSEA Conference, paper,* Osaka.
Yamazaki, Y., 2019. Case of Co-production in Japanese Health Cooperatives: Qualitative approach. 7th *EMES Conference, slides,* Sheffield.

Appendix 8

Table 8.A Missing Data in the Volunteer Study

Tab. 5	**5.1***	**5.2**	**5.3**	**5.4**	**5.5**	**5.6**	**5.7**				
MC	9.9	11.6	11.6	14.0	14.5	16.3	19.8				
K	4.7	4.7	6.3	4.7	6.3	4.7	7.8				
Tab. 6	**6.1**	**6.2**	**6.3**	**6.4**	Tab. 7	**7.1**	**7.2**	**7.3**	**7.4**	**7.5**	**7.6**
MC	3.5	14.0	14.5	14.0		8.7	11.0	12.8	11.0	12.8	13.4
K	1.6	6.3	6.3	6.3		1.6	4.7	7.8	4.7	6.3	4.7

*Table and item in order of presentation, so 5.1 stands for Table 5 item 1 and 7.3 for Table 7, item 3. When missing data equals or surpasses 10%, it seems necessary to report it in a systematic fashion for tables where it is present. More missing data is found in answers from volunteers at the two Medical Co-op hospitals than in answers from Koseiren hospitals. Why this should be the case for volunteers is not evident, but it, nevertheless, has an impact on the figures found in some of the tables included in this chapter. SPSS eliminates the missing data in the frequencies for a given item, so more missing data in one hospital category than another inflates the figures somewhat where the missing data is greatest. This is unavoidable when missing data is excluded, but we need to be aware of this phenomenon.

Table 8.B The Social Background of Volunteers

(*continued on next page*)

Table 8.B (*continued*)

Gender	*Male*		*Female*		*MD*
Medical Co-ops	14.0		86.0		–
Koseiren	12.5		84.4		3.1
Age[a]	**20s–50s**	**60s**	**70s+**		**MD**
Medical Co-ops	9.9	31.4	55.8		2.9
Koseiren	18.6	32.8	40.7		7.8
Education	**B**	**C**	**D**	**E**	**MD**
Medical Co-ops	11.6	45.9	20.9	18.0	3.5
Koseiren	10.9	56.3	20.3	7.8	4.7
Family composition[a]	**single**	**couple**	**3 pers**	**4+ pers**	**other**
Medical Co-ops	19.8	39.0	25.6	13.4	3.2
Koseiren	6.3	37.5	31.3	18.8	6.3
Occupation	**employed**	**housewf.**[f]	**pensioner**	**other**	**MD**
Medical Co-ops	13.9	34.4	45.3	2.9	3.5
Koseiren	39.1	34.4	25.0	–	1.6
Household Income[a]	**<2 mil.**	**2–3 mil.**	**3–4 mil.**	**4–15 mil.**	**MD**
Medical Co-ops	23.9	26.2	15.1	22.1	12.8
Koseiren	17.9	10.9	21.9	28.2	21.9
Member of Cooperative[a]	**health**	**consumer**	**JA agr.**	**other**	**MD**
Medical Co-ops	91.3	53.5	19.2	0.6	5.2
Koseiren	1.6	28.1	81.3	-	12.5

a = this information not available for public staff; MD = missing data
B = Jr. high school;
C = high school;
D = vocational/technical college; E = university & grad school, f = housewife/man.

9 Participatory Governance and Japanese Healthcare

This chapter contrasts three models of healthcare governance in relation to external efficiency in Japanese healthcare. They embody different levels of staff autonomy and patient inclusion in decision-making. The first is a hierarchical command and control model that allows for little autonomy or discretion to either the staff or clients. The second is a stewardship model involving more autonomy and inclusion, but the leaders make decisions on their behalf of the group that they serve. The third is a more horizontal, multi-stakeholder model that attributes greater autonomy to both the staff and their clients to resolve some key issues about service provision and quality together. Governance models clearly interact with the work life situation of the hospital staff. A democratic multi-stakeholder model promotes greater staff control and influence than either of the other two. The staff also has more frequent and inclusive discussions about hospital affairs with key stakeholders than at the other two hospital groups. A governance model that makes an important impact on a hospital's work environment and service quality also contributes to the external efficiency of healthcare providers.

A Introduction – Participatory Administration

Weber's ideal of modern public bureaucracy was based on a military-like hierarchical command and control model that became the central point of reference for the development of the public sector for most of the 20th Century (1947). It was also adopted as a key organizational concept by industry and manufacture in advanced countries and dominated business administration until recently. However, it is increasingly apparent that it is both inadequate and inappropriate in the 21st Century when services and work in the service sector have become the predominant form of production and employment. Unlike goods, public services often require the input or active contribution of the users or clients in the production process itself, making them co-producers of such services (Ostrom, 1996; Osborne et al., 2013). Personal social services are considered 'relational goods' by economists. If they are long-term or 'enduring welfare services', dissatisfied users will seldom find redress by using exit. Accordingly, voice becomes a more viable alternative for gaining influence (Pestoff, 2018). However, staff and client voice is channeled and amplified differently by different governance models.

At about the same time as the renewed academic and professional interest in co-production, Peters (1994) discussed the emergence of four alternatives to the traditional model of public administration: the market model, the participatory state, flexible government and deregulated government. Here, the focus will be on a participatory state, or participatory governance, where groups usually excluded under more hierarchical models are permitted greater involvement. This approach concentrates power in the lower echelons of the administration – the workers as well as the clients of an organization – rather than on the managers. It recognizes that the workers and clients found closest to the actual production of public goods and services have the greatest amount of information about these programs. If the energy, talents and ideas of those groups are harnessed, then the government will work more efficiently and effectively. However, this calls for greater empowerment and self-governance for such groups, which has clear implications for managing the public sector as a whole. Both the staff and clients become more directly involved in managerial decisions and governance of the service (ibid: 13), often through a greater dialog between them. A multi-stakeholder dialog between the front-line staff and service users helps to place the experience and knowledge of both groups at the heart of effective public service design and delivery and can promote collaboration between them (Vidal, 2013).

The 'participatory state' model is still less familiar than the market approach in terms of its political ideology, but some of its recommendations, nevertheless, appear similar. Hierarchy is considered a severe impediment to effective public service management and governance. The participatory state proposes much flatter structures, since better quality goods or services would require fewer controllers from above. As noted, the participatory approach concentrates on the lower echelons of workers, as well as on the clients of public service organizations to provide the solution (Peters, 1994: 11), rather than on the managers of public services, as is the case with New Public Management (NPM). It, therefore, emphasizes the need for new structures to channel participation, especially for clients and front-line employees. This calls for the creation of a variety of councils, advisory groups, etc., to promote a dialog between front-line staff and their clients. This model enhances the role of the citizen and attempts to induce democratic participation in public management by means other than voting (ibid.: 13).

Moreover, the participatory state is dependent upon citizens themselves becoming involved in making some choices about policy, particularly its implementation, both in their role as users or clients and as providers of publicly financed services. It would give citizens more consumer choice and direct control over programs, similar to the market model. On the other hand, the manner in which consumer choices would be exercised in the participatory state would be through some sort of political process. Their participation might take the form of referenda on policy or it may be in local structures, like parent involvement in school committees, etc. (ibid.: 15). It could also include their direct participation in collaboration with the professional staff at the site of the provision of a particular service, as noted earlier for parents in parent co-op preschool services in Europe.

Although the prescriptions of neoliberals and those proposing a participatory administration appear to bear some similarities, they are definitely not the same. Rather than being a means for creating competition among service providers in order to facilitate the market, decentralization in the participatory model is intended primarily to channel control to a different set of professionals and/or to the clients (ibid., 16) through new direct democratic or participatory institutions. While Peters discusses distinct models or alternatives for organizing the entire public sector, it is possible to study its development in more limited sectors of service provision (see also Peters, 1996). The study of social enterprises providing childcare in Europe and user-owned healthcare providers in Japan provide good opportunities to explore this. Social enterprises providing childcare in Europe demonstrated that giving parents and staff more influence cannot only enrich the work environment (Pestoff, 2000; Pestoff and Vamstad, 2014), but this can also renew the public sector and improve service quality both in the perspectives of users and the staff (Vamstad, 2012). A similar interpretation stems from data presented earlier in Chapters 6 and 7 in this volume. In order to understand what makes this kind of collaboration between the staff and clients possible, attention will now shift to the issue of governance.

B Governance at the Macro, Meso and Micro levels

The concept of governance gained extensive attention about 25 years ago and became a buzzword in the social sciences. It is used in a wide array of contexts with widely divergent meanings. Van Kersbergen and van Waarden's (2004) survey of the literature identified no fewer than nine different definitions of the concept, and Hirst (2002) attributes it five different meanings or contexts. These include economic development, international institutions and regimes, corporate governance, private provision of public services in the wake of NPM and new practices for coordinating activities through networks, partnerships and deliberative forums (*ibid.* 18–19). The latter is referred to as New Public Governance (Osborne, 2010). Hirst argued that the main reason for promoting greater governance is the growth of 'organizational society' (2002). Big organizations on either side of the public/private divide in advanced post-industrial societies leave little room for democracy or citizen influence. This reflects the lack of local control and democratic processes for internal decision-making in many large organizations. The concept of governance points to the need to rethink democracy and find new methods of control and regulation that do not rely on the state or public sector having a monopoly of such practices (*ibid.* 21).

Today, governance is used in many different contexts, and it is employed differently at the macro, meso and micro levels, yet there are some notable similarities between the usage at different levels. From a macro perspective, participatory governance is related to concepts like network governance, New Public Governance, co-governance and it concerns public policy-making at the highest level. In a multilevel European context, it is seen as 'a method or mechanism for dealing with a broad range of problems or conflicts in which actors regularly arrive at mutual satisfactory and binding decisions by negotiating with each other and cooperating in the implementation of these decisions' (Schmitter, 2002: 53). It is based on horizontal forms of interaction between actors who are '… sufficiently *independent* of each other so that neither can impose a solution on the other and yet sufficiently *interdependent* so that both would lose if no solution were found' (ibid.: 53; *italics* in the original). Their regular participation results in trust and mutual accommodation. It implies flexible combinations of both public and private authority by representatives of those groups that will be affected by the policy adopted, many of whom will be found in civil society. However, roles other than citizenship come into focus in participatory governance, including those of rights-holders, stakeholders, shareholders, etc. (ibid.: 56).

At the meso level, interactive governance refers to jointly managed networks and/or collaborative governance, co-management, etc. Sicilia et al. (2016) provide an illustration of co-planning in a multilevel setting between different authorities providing services to parents with autistic children in Italy. Eldenbos and van Meerkerk (2016) introduce three perspectives on interactive governance, particularly in an 'Era of Big Society'. They comprise an *instrumental perspective* found in public administration literature, with a focus on effective governance and efficiency; a *cultural perspective* found in sociology and social psychology, with a focus on group dynamics and relationships; and a *democratic perspective* grounded in political science, with the objective of promoting legitimacy, democratic control and accountability in decision-making. However, they note that interactive governance is often subject to the 'push and pull' of processes between citizens and governments. This leads them to distinguish between two main forms of interactive governance (i.e. government-induced and citizen initiatives). The former is a top-down process that relies on 'citizen participation', but is strongly organized and constrained by governments, while the latter is based on bottom-up citizen initiatives and civic engagement that often stems from their dissatisfaction with government policy and action (ibid.: 3). Chapter 3 employed a similar perspective on alternative provides of healthcare in Japan.

At the micro level or governance at the point of service delivery, the concepts multi-stakeholder and co-production are relevant. Governance at the micro level refers to systems and processes concerned with ensuring the overall direction, supervision and accountability of an organization (Cornforth, 2004). Six different models of corporate governance for nonprofit organizations include principle-agent theory, democratic theory, stakeholder theory, resource dependency theory and managerial hegemony theory (Spears et al., 2014). Both control and collaboration are essential elements of these theories. Accordingly, control helps to overcome human limitations through vigilance and discipline, while collaboration taps individuals' aspirations via cooperation and empowerment. However, there is always a tension between them and a need to balance them (ibid.). See Chapter 11 on the need to balance social and economic values in Japanese healthcare.

Ostrom maintains that citizenship was confined for too long to voting and the consumption of public services. She notes that limiting citizens either to being voters or clients constrains them to passive roles that leave them in the hands of others, rather than being something which they can control. The latter can be achieved when citizens are attributed with a more active role as co-producers of public services (1993). Therefore, she proposes a more collaborative and functional governance model that emphasizes a horizontal, two-way relationship among various participants in the community-local process, in contrast to the traditional hierarchical command and control model of traditional public administration (ibid.: 230).

Sacchetti (2013) argues that both governance and decision-making practices can be divided into inclusive and exclusive categories. Inclusive governance coordination structures embody an awareness of the effects generated on specific stakeholders or 'publics' and on society more broadly. Therefore, they take into account both outcomes and impacts of decisions on these 'publics'. By extending impacts to encompass broader society, inclusive governance structures can activate resources from participating 'publics' and produce durable networks based on reciprocity and trust, as well as produce innovative outcomes (ibid.: 16). The combination of the inclusive/exclusive categories results in four different types of organizations that correspond roughly with three of the four types of healthcare providers found in this study of Japanese healthcare. The inclusive/inclusive type is found in the Medical Co-ops; the inclusive/exclusive type is seen in *Koseiren;* the exclusive/inclusive type is seen in the medical corporations (which is not included in this study), while the exclusive/exclusive kind is illustrated by public sector hospitals.

Governance can play an important role in developing new methods and models to improve work environment and promote co-production in healthcare in Japan. The three most central and relevant governance models for studying cooperative and public healthcare in Japan are the command and control model, the stewardship model and the democratic, multi-stakeholder model. The command and control model is based on the Weberian ideal for public bureaucracy. The stewardship model assumes that managers want to do a good job and will act as effective stewards of an

Figure 9.1 Staff Autonomy and Stakeholder Inclusiveness in Three Models of Governance.

organization's resources, in collaboration with the main stakeholders. The role of the board is primarily strategic: to add value to important decisions and improve organizational performance. Board members are selected on the basis of their professional expertise, skills and contacts, and they should receive proper training. By contrast, the democratic model includes ideas of open elections on the basis of one member one vote, pluralism, representation of different interests and accountability to its members. The board is often recruited from lay members and its main function is to represent the diverse interests of the organization's members (Cornforth, 2004).

From a business administration and leadership perspective, governance models usually focus on the relationship between the board and top management of a nonprofit or cooperative. However, employing a more holistic or encompassing approach based on different academic perspectives – like political science, social work or sociology – would call for broadening the focus. Although important, the CEO and board do not provide the whole picture, so other major stakeholders – like the staff and clients – will be included in this purview. However, the CEO and board provide a natural starting point, and they were interviewed with a semi-structured interview schedule in May, 2013. Preliminary results suggest that agricultural co-ops and the *Koseiren* adhere to a stewardship model of governance, while the consumer and Medical Co-ops embody a democratic model (Pestoff, 2016). However, it is worth noting that these concepts were initially considered heuristic tools, and it remains an empirical question of how they actually differ in terms of the governance of their healthcare organizations and the role they attribute to key stakeholders, like the staff, patients and volunteers. The three governance models are sketched in Figure 9.1.

These three models can be distinguished by the degree of autonomy given to the staff in terms of their everyday work life and the degree of inclusiveness of various stakeholders in discussions and decision-making. Differences between them can be visualized and summarized by the step-stool figure, where staff autonomy is represented by the vertical axis and inclusiveness by the horizontal axis. The higher up a governance model is on the stool, the more autonomy it gives to the staff, while the lower down on the stool, the less autonomy given to the staff. The first step is a hierarchical command and control top-down model that allows little autonomy or discretion to either the staff or clients. Traditional public services embody the hierarchical model. The middle step is a corporatist model based on a 70-year public-private partnership in Japanese healthcare that started at the end of World War II. It provided healthcare for more than seven decades to large groups of citizens in rural areas residing well beyond the reach of public services. Finally, the top step represents the highest level of autonomy and greatest inclusiveness. It embodies a bottom-up democratic, multi-stakeholder model of governance that has evolved in Japan for nearly 80 years. It is worth noting that differences between these three steps or models do not simply involve the staff or the service users separately, but, rather, both groups together.

Moreover, as a service, healthcare is not only subject to a high degree of asymmetry of knowledge between professional healthcare providers and service users. There is also a high degree of uncertainty about what comprises service quality, both from the patient/user and provider perspective (Hirschman, 1970). As noted earlier in Chapter 7, Blandi (2018) argued that this is due to two main factors – technical advancements in service provision, particularly with the advent of Internet, computer technology (ICT) solutions, and increasing patient/citizen uncertainty about their own needs. The latter reflects new diagnostic and treatment options, as well as changing life cycle circumstances or different stages in the development of a given disease and its treatment. Under such circumstances, the staff needs to interact with clients in a more flexible fashion in order to help clients identify and define their needs, including their changing healthcare needs (ibid.). However, this has clear ramifications on how to best organize healthcare services in order to garner active patient participation in defining and determining appropriate health promotion or treatment plans, and thereby increasing the efficiency and effectiveness of healthcare.

This requires much greater patient interaction with the front-line staff in order to identify and define the patient's needs, discuss alternatives with them and agree on the best and most realistic treatment. The need for greater citizen involvement in more complex services can, therefore, acquire an economic-political dimension not usually found in simpler or less complex services. It implies a divided or split approach to organizing healthcare. Back-office staff can provide standardized services, while front office staff – such as nurses and care workers – require much greater autonomy in their daily tasks to promote the flexibility required for increasing external efficiency and at the same time reflect the complexity of the services provided and the degree of patient uncertainty. This implies adopting a systems approach to complex issues that involve feedback loops to guarantee the organizational flexibility necessary to promote patient participation in healthcare design and delivery. More inclusive models of governance can facilitate this.

C Advantages of a Participatory Model of Governance: Staff, Patients and Volunteers

All three key stakeholders surveyed in this project[1] demonstrate the advantages of a participatory model of governance that can potentially increase an organization's external efficiency. Below, we will briefly consider some of the main advantages for the staff, patients and volunteers attributed to participatory governance.

1 Staff and Participatory Governance

A quick overview of the data presented in Chapter 6 shows that there is not much difference between the staff at these ten hospitals in terms of having passive or active jobs. A nearly equal proportion of staff at all three types of hospitals are classified as having Passive or Active jobs, and the difference between hospital groups is rather small at only 2.8% and 0.7% points respectively for these two types of work environments. By contrast, the difference between hospitals is much larger when it comes to Low Strain and High Strain jobs. In the former category of Low Strain jobs, there is a difference of 19.7% points between the highest and lowest hospital group, while a similar difference for High Strain jobs is 19.3% points (see Table 6.6). In both of these situations, the staff at Medical Co-ops is clearly in the most beneficial situation in terms of their work environment. More of them claim Low Strain jobs, and fewer claim High Strain jobs. By contrast, the staff at public hospitals is much less fortunate. Fewer of them claim Low Strain jobs, while many more claim High Strain jobs. Staff at the *Koseiren* hospitals fall in between the Medical Co-ops and public hospitals, both in terms of Low Strain and High Strain jobs.

Similarly, Chapter 6 provided an overview of five work environment indices that were calculated from three to six items each, for a total of 29 work environment items (see Table 6.7). The Medical Co-ops rated highest on all these indices; *Koseiren* came much lower, while the public hospitals ranked lowest on all but one. Considered together, these five work environment indices provide strong evidence that the staff at Medical Co-ops have much more autonomy in their daily work life than the staff at *Koseiren* and public hospitals. The anticipated outcome is seen in the Index of Service Quality by hospital groups. It shows a clear difference between these hospital groups that follows the pattern previously noted for the work environment indices. The Medical Co-ops came highest on Service Quality and the public hospitals lowest, while the difference between the *Koseiren* and public

Table 9.1 Staff Perception of Having Discretion or Control at Work

*Control at Work**	*Med Co-ops*	Koseiren	*Public*	*Dif. (h-l)***
Have lots of control over the order and way tasks are performed	59.0	50.9	44.8	14.2
Can work at your own pace	47.7	39.4	29.6	18.1
Can adjust your workload	46.9	38.0	29.1	17.8
Sufficient authority to fulfill duties	41.2	37.4	30.8	10.4

*Indicates percent of positive answers, 'agree' and 'somewhat agree';
**Difference between high and low.

hospitals was rather small. Thus, participatory governance clearly contributes to improving staff autonomy and service quality of the Medical Co-ops.

2 *Staff Control and Influence*

It is time to take a closer look at staff autonomy and influence, since these are the key aspects of the governance model presented in Figure 9.1. We expect that different governance models will promote more or less staff autonomy. In order to explore this, we will examine the two sets of questions from the Staff Study that comprise the Index of Control at Work and the Index of Influence.

The staff answered four questions about how much discretion they had over their work. This comprises the 'nuts and bolts' of workplace control, being able to decide the what, when, where and how they fulfill their daily tasks at work. It includes questions like having lots of control, being able to work at their own pace, being able to adjust their workload and being given sufficient authority to fulfill their duties. Table 9.1 explores this. Note that only the proportion of 'high' answers is included here.

The difference between the highest and lowest scores on the questions about staff discretion is rather large. It ranges from 10.4% to 18.1% points. The staff at Medical Co-ops appear to have the most control over all of these items. Their support ranged from three of five to two of five staff members, while staff at public hospitals have the least control. Turning to staff influence, three items found under the heading of influence at the workplace include the existence of sufficient structures and opportunities for expressing their opinion, perceived ease of expressing their opinion and having their suggestions and opinions reflected in hospital decisions. The results are presented in Table 9.2.

Once again the difference between the hospital groups seems rather large. Support for these items ranges from the high 50s and low 40s to the high or mid-30s on most items, and we note some clear differences between the staff at the hospital groups. The staff at the Medical Co-ops

Table 9.2 Staff Perception of Having Influence at Work

*Influence at Work**	*Med Co-ops*	Koseiren	*Public*	*Dif. (h-l)***
Sufficient structures and opportunities for expressing my opinion	59.1	47.3	38.1	21.0
It is easy to express my opinion	55.0	42.1	34.1	20.9
My suggestions and opinions are reflected (in decisions)	48.1	38.9	28.9	19.2

*Indicates percent of positive answers, 'agree' and 'somewhat agree';
**Difference between high and low; na=not available.

express most support for these items, followed by the staff at *Koseiren* hospitals, while the staff at public hospitals come last on all aspects of staff influence. This is not an unexpected finding and reflects differences between the bottom-up, democratic decision-making structures at Medical Co-ops and the hierarchical top-down model practiced by public hospitals.

3 Networking: Contact with Key Stakeholders

At this point, we now turn to the network activities of the staff and hospitals. The staff were asked about their interactions with key stakeholders, including patients, other healthcare providers, volunteers, members of the co-ops, local community members, local government officials and others. This question asks how often they talk with various groups about issues related to their hospital. This reflects the existence of channels for engaging in a dialog with various stakeholders, both inside

Table 9.3 Staff Discussions with Stakeholders about Hospital Affairs

*Talk with...**	*Med Co-ops*	Koseiren	*Public*	*Dif. (h-l)***
Patients	68.8	53.7	50.9	17.9
Other Healthcare Providers	35.3	32.2	31.4	3.9
Volunteers	31.1	19.3	16.2	14.9
Members of JA or Med. Co-ops	19.8	10.0	Na	9.8
Members of the Local Community	18.6	11.5	7.7	10.9
Local Government Officers	9.0	5.7	6.1	2.0
Others, specify***	11.7	7.0	7.1	4.7

*Indicates percent of positive answers, 'often' and 'sometimes';
**Difference between high and low; and
***Missing data was over 75%, so these answers will therefore not be included in our analysis. Na = not available, this question/alternative was not available for staff at public hospitals, so the difference only reflects the Medical Co-ops and *Koseiren*.

and outside the hospital. This reflects the second main dimension of governance models – the inclusiveness of key stakeholders (Table 9.3).

There seems to be a high degree of consensus concerning who are the most important stakeholders for the staff at all the hospitals. Patients, other healthcare providers and volunteers are the three most important groups, but the strength of contacts with each of these stakeholders varies considerably among hospital groups. Patients comprise a unique type of stakeholder, since they are also hospital clients, and it is natural to expect staff to talk with them more or less regularly. Frequent contact with patients is mentioned by two-thirds of the staff at Medical Co-ops, while it is mentioned by half of the staff at *Koseiren* and public hospitals. All three hospital groups show a similar rate of contact with other healthcare providers. Turning to volunteers, frequent contact with them is mentioned more often by Medical Co-ops than the other two healthcare providers, as too are contacts with members of the local community. This demonstrates that staff at the Medical Co-ops are more actively engaged in networking with key stakeholders than the staff at *Koseiren* or public hospitals. This shows that Medical Co-ops are more inclusive than the other two hospital groups.

4 Patients and Participatory Governance

The Patient Study included Medical Co-ops and *Koseiren* hospitals but not public hospitals. It demonstrated that the patients at these two hospital groups have different reasons for choosing their healthcare provider (see Chapter 7 for more details). Either they are motivated by instrumental reasons or by values related to their membership in a health co-op. In general, it showed that patients in Medical Co-ops participate more in community activities; more of them volunteer at their healthcare provider and in different types of activities. Moreover, as members of a health co-op, they can voice their opinion on important issues in several different ways. Not only can they talk directly with the professional staff or make suggestions in the appropriate box, but they also sit on hospital committees and participate in their meetings as well as participate in local meetings of the health co-op. This demonstrates that patients are highly integrated into the institutions of Medical Co-op hospitals. This not only contributes to a multi-stakeholder dialog between the professional staff and clients or patients, but this also implies that patients are actively helping to achieve two of the Medical Co-ops main goals – specifically, 'promoting preventative care' and 'promoting user/patient participation in healthcare' (see Chapter 10 for details). This shows how patients can actively contribute to the Medical Co-ops' external efficiency.

In section 8.C, it was maintained that front-line staff would reasonably have more contact with patients than back-office staff. This should give them a chance to discuss matters concerning the hospital with patients. This will be briefly explored below. However, deciding who works as front-line staff and who works in the back office is not always easy. This study employs six occupation categories. Two of them are thought to have more daily contact with patients than the other four. In particular, nurses and care workers are expected to have more contact with patients than other staff categories. They are, therefore, considered the front-line staff, since they provide hands-on care to patients. Table 9.4 explores how much the staff talks with patients about issues related to the hospital for all six occupation categories by hospital group.

The results of Table 9.4 show that different staff categories do, in fact, demonstrate different levels of contact with patients. The data suggests three levels of interaction with patients for two of the hospital groups – the Medical Co-ops and *Koseiren* – while the impression is more mixed for public hospitals. Care workers and nurses have more frequent discussions with patients about important matters for their hospital than other occupational groups; other medical specialists and doctors have a medium level of discussions about the hospital; and the administrative staff and other support staff have the lowest frequency of such discussions. There are also differences between hospital groups. Staff at the Medical Co-ops have the highest level of contact with patients, followed by staff at *Koseiren* hospitals, while staff at public hospitals show the lowest level of discussions with patients.

Such discussions can function like a double-edged sword that cuts in two directions. They can provide social contact that helps to relieve stress, but they can also increase stress, since the front-line staff can feel that they have greater responsibility for the final outcome of the healthcare provided to patients as the de facto hands-on service providers. Whether these discussions result in more or less stress will depend, in part, on the governance model practiced by the hospital. However, the results concerning contact between front-line staff and patients confirm the expectation that a democratic, multi-stakeholder governance model is more inclusive than either a stewardship or a 'command-and-control' model of governance.

Table 9.4 Staff Discussions* with Patients, by Occupation and Hospital Group

Hospitals/Occupations	*Medical Co-ops*	Koseiren	*Public*	*Dif. (h-l)*
Care Workers	74.1	69.5	Na**	4.6
Nurses	71.9	61.7	62.2	10.2
Doctors	65.2	54.8	49.0	16.2
Other Medical Specialists	69.4	52.4	59.2	17.0
Administration	55.9	42.6	26.1	29.8
Other Support Staff	56.3	24.2	44.1	32.1
Average	68.8	53.7	50.0	18.6

*Indicates percent of positive answers, 'often' and 'sometimes';
**Na = not available. Care workers were not included in the public hospital sample.

Furthermore, this implies that a democratic multi-stakeholder model of governance can make a positive contribution to achieving the necessary flexibility, through a dialog between front-line staff and key stakeholders and thereby augmenting external efficiency.

Moreover, as noted earlier in Chapter 7, many patients felt that they could express their opinions about hospital services by talking with the staff. Nearly half of the patients at both hospital groups felt that they could discuss hospital services with the professional staff. Between a fifth of the Medical Co-op patients and an eighth of the *Koseiren* patients said the same about the hospital administration (see Table 7.3 for more details.). Many patients felt that their opinion/s were reflected in hospital matters. Nearly half of the Medical Co-op patients (48.2%) agreed that they were, while one-third of the *Koseiren* patients (34.8%) did so. This is significant, since it underlines the extent to which the Medical Co-ops were successful in integrating their patients into the formal institutions of their healthcare system and in eliciting their support to achieve some of their most important goals.

5 Volunteers and Participatory Governance

Two out of five patients claim that they volunteer at Medical Co-op hospitals (40.0%), while less than one out of eight do so at *Koseiren* hospitals (11.4%). More Medical Co-op volunteers tend to do so for longer periods (i.e. ten years or more) and for more hours per month (i.e. ten hours or more per month) than *Koseiren* volunteers (see Chapter 8 for details). The reasons that they give for volunteering also differ. Nearly half of the Medical Co-op volunteers (49%) do so for personal benefit – specifically, 'to learn about medical care and a healthy lifestyle' – rather than 'to help others' (40%). The opposite is true for *Koseiren* volunteers – just over one-third (36%) do so for their own personal benefit, while nearly half of them do so 'to help others' (47%). However, more than four out of five (87% versus 84%) volunteers in both organizations claim that volunteering 'keeps me fit and healthy'. These figures suggest that the Medical Co-ops are more successful in integrating their volunteers into the organizational life of their healthcare provider. Volunteers who are motivated by wanting to 'learn more about medical care and a healthy lifestyle' are also helping achieve two of the Medical Co-ops main goals – specifically, 'promoting preventative care' and 'promoting user/patient participation in healthcare' (see Chapter 10 for details). This shows that volunteers can actively contribute to the Medical Co-ops external efficiency.

Moreover, nearly two-fifths of the volunteers at the Medical Co-ops (38%) claim that they have a committee position at the hospital, and nearly half of them (46%) state that they make donations and investments in their health co-op. By comparison, only one out of eight volunteers at *Koseiren* hospitals claim to have a committee appointment (12%), while very few claim to make donations or investments in their co-op healthcare (6%). These comparisons serve to drive home the extent to which the Medical Co-ops succeed in integrating their volunteers into the formal institutions of their healthcare system and elicit their help in achieving some of their most important goals.

Table 9.4 supported the assumption that front-line staff would have more daily contact with patients than back-office staff. Nurses and care workers did, in fact, have more frequent contact with patients than other staff categories. Currently, we want to examine if this pattern holds true for staff contacts with volunteers. Table 9.5 explores how much the staff talks with volunteers about issues related to the hospital for all six occupation categories by hospital group.

Contrary to the patterns for staff discussions with patients noted earlier, the results of Table 9.5 are inconclusive concerning differing levels of staff contact with volunteers. There is very little difference among the staff categories concerning contacts with volunteers, but there are, however, clear differences between hospital groups. The Medical Co-op staff have significantly more discussions with volunteers about hospital issues than the staff at *Koseiren* or public hospitals. This can be explained by the fact that volunteers at the Medical Co-ops are also members of the health co-op.

Moreover, as noted earlier in Chapter 8, between three-fourths and three-fifths of the volunteers claim that relations with the hospital staff are good. In addition, between three-fourths and two-thirds of the volunteers feel that the staff listen to their suggestions for improvements (see Table 8.5 for more details). Thus, all three stakeholder groups – the staff, patients and volunteers – provide evidence suggesting an inclusive and democratic model of governance is found at the Medical Co-ops, while evidence from the same sources suggests the existence of a stewardship model of governance at *Koseiren* hospitals. Public hospitals have

Table 9.5 Staff Discussions* with Volunteers, by Occupation and Hospital Group

Hospitals/Occupations	*Medical Co-ops*	Koseiren	Public	*Dif. (h-l)*
Care Workers	32.4	19.0	Na**	13.4
Nurses	31.1	20.0	18.1	13.0
Doctors	31.8	18.8	13.9	17.9
Other Medical Specialists	27.3	19.4	11.7	15.6
Administration	37.4	22.9	10.7	26.7
Other Support Staff	21.8	8.8	5.9	15.9
Average	31.1	19.3	15.2	15.9

*Indicates percent of positive answers, 'often' and 'sometimes'; and
**Na=not available. Care workers were not included in the public hospital sample.

the least inclusive model, which is logical given the professional oriented organizational culture of a command and control governance model.

D Hospital Structures and Implementing Governance Models

In general, the Agricultural Cooperatives in Japan favor the existence of two separate governing bodies – a supervisory committee and a managing or executive board – while the Consumer Cooperatives rely on a single or unitary board of directors. However, the consumer co-ops also have an annual general meeting (AGM) of several hundred district delegates who decide policy, elect representatives to the board and approve the budget. Starting on the agricultural co-op side, *Koseiren* is a secondary organization, owned and controlled by the primary, multi-purpose agricultural cooperatives affiliated to the Agricultural Cooperatives of Japan (JA). 20 out of the 34 regional *Koseiren* organizations have adopted a governance model with dual governing bodies. The supervisory committee makes policy and is comprised of representatives of the regional agricultural co-ops in a given prefecture, while the management board is comprised of a few executive members entrusted to run the day-to-day business operations. This dual governance system was introduced to guarantee professional management, while reflecting the collective interests of its farmer-owners (Kurimoto, 2015, 2018).

For example, the Supervisory Committee for *Koseiren* Hospital C is comprised of 21 members – one each from the 17 JA districts in Fukushima Prefecture plus two top executives from JA and two other related organizations, an economic federation and the insurance federation. 20 of them are male, and one is female. Together, they also comprise the AGM of the Fukushima *Koseiren* that approves the annual budget. *Koseiren* Hospitals A and D are both located in Aichi Prefecture, and, therefore, share the same Supervisory Committee and the same Board of Directors. The latter is comprised of five persons – the chair, two managing directors from JA and two hospital directors, one from each of the hospitals. In addition, each *Koseiren* hospital has its own local management – for example, *Koseiren* Hospital A has a Council of Hospital Management to meet with representatives of the local community and a Board of Hospital Operations that meets annually to approve the hospital budget (Pestoff, 2016).

Given its special relation to JA, it comes as no surprise that *Koseiren* has no direct individual membership nor user/patient representation on its supervisory committees or its executive boards. There may be a users' council to promote consultations with patients, but they have no voice in or vote on decision-making bodies. Moreover, the medical staff is not usually represented on the supervisory committees or executive boards (ibid.). Thus, the governance of *Koseiren* hospitals has all of the trappings of a corporatist-like stewardship governance model.

On the Medical Co-op side, a hospital's Board of Directors is dominated by users. Nationwide, there were 2,133 lay members of the boards of Medical Co-ops in 2015, together with 710 board members who represent professional providers – both medical staff and management (Kurimoto, 2015). Incomplete figures for the year of 2020 indicate that there are 2,510 lay board members – 1,109 of whom are women (44.2%) (E-mail information from Yamazaki, 2020). For example, the Board of Directors at Medical Co-op A is comprised of ten males and 27 females. Ten of them are full-time, and 27 are part-time board members. The former includes three doctors, one nurse and six executive directors. In addition, Medical Co-op A has 42 directors, nine of whom are full-time and must have medical training, while 33 part-time directors are chosen by delegates to the AGM. Moreover, there are several committees that include ordinary members as volunteers. For example, Medical Co-op A's Hospital Construction Committee included several ordinary members, and, when the new 401-bed hospital was completed, it became the hospital's Management Committee with the same composition.

The Board of Directors at Medical Co-op C has 31 members, nine of whom are full-time (seven males and two females), and 22 are part-time (12 males and ten females). In addition, there are 34 territorial boards in Medical Co-op C and 22 members of the Board of Directors are chosen from these areas (Pestoff, 2016). The combination of different membership categories, both patients and staff, the representation of members on the board of directors and engaging members as part-time directors illustrates the Medical Co-ops' efforts to include several stakeholders in the direction and management of their hospitals and demonstrates their multi-stakeholder nature. Thus, health cooperatives practice a multi-stakeholder, democratic model of governance. They, nevertheless, experience some tensions between a managerial logic of cost containment and a professional logic of caring. In order to empower members, they have created several internal organizations between the board and members that encourage and foster patients/members to participate in the governance of their healthcare organizations (Kurimoto, 2015).

Based on the discussion earlier in section B, we expect that command and control governance institutions are hierarchical and exclusive in their nature. They leave little room for staff autonomy and allow very few degrees of freedom for the staff to take their own initiative to solve everyday problems and/or improve service quality. Moreover, there is little need for a dialog with clients or making efforts to obtain their input, since 'the experts know what is best' for their clients. Stewardship governance institutions are more inclusive and can be found in user-owned organizations that allow more room for staff autonomy and accept more degrees of freedom for the staff to take their own initiative to solve everyday problems. However, the long-term public-private partnerships with the government may erode some of their autonomy, and these governance institutions can gradually begin to assume the character of command and control governance structures (Brandsen et al., 2017). Furthermore, democratic, multi-stakeholder governance institutions are most inclusive; they allow the staff greatest autonomy and permit them more degrees of freedom to take their own initiative in solving everyday problems and/or improve service quality. Various stakeholders have both a voice and vote in deciding important strategic matters and everyday issues as well as improving service quality.

Finally, we expect that an inclusive, democratic governance model will result in greater staff satisfaction. The question about staff satisfaction with their work, in general, allows us to evaluate if this holds for Japanese hospitals, but staff satisfaction varies among healthcare providers. Positive staff satisfaction reached 54.4% for the Medical Co-ops, 42.9% for *Koseiren* and 41.4% for public hospitals. As shown in Chapter 6, staff satisfaction is positively related to service quality. Therefore, governance models appear to have a clear positive impact on staff satisfaction and service quality.

E Summary and Conclusions

At the outset of this chapter, it was maintained that a participatory state could decentralize power and influence to groups normally excluded under more hierarchical models. It would promote greater involvement by the front-line staff and clients, or the nurses and care workers, as well as the patients. It was also argued that governance systems can help explain some of the most notable differences in work environment, work satisfaction, and service quality as well as patient participation or co-production. Governance systems can be viewed from various angles. A key perspective adopted here is the degree of autonomy given to staff and clients to interact and resolve certain issues related to service provision and service quality by themselves. Also, the degree of inclusiveness of various stakeholders is important to consider. The three governance models employed in this case embody different levels of autonomy and inclusion in decision-making for both the staff and clients, as illustrated by Figure 9.1. The first is a hierarchical command and control model that is normally associated with traditional public administration and that was articulated by Max Weber. It allows for little autonomy or discretion to either the staff or clients. Traditional public services embody the hierarchical model. The second is a stewardship model where the leaders and representatives of the group served to make decisions on their behalf. It clearly involves more autonomy and inclusion than the first model, though not as much as the last one. It is a corporatist model based on a 70-year public-private partnership in Japanese healthcare that started at the end of World War II to provide healthcare to large groups residing well beyond the reach of the public services. The third is a more horizontal, multi-stakeholder model that attributes greater autonomy to both the staff and their clients to resolve some key issues about service provision and quality together by themselves. It embodies a bottom-up democratic model of governance that has existed and evolved in Japan for nearly 80 years. It is worth noting that differences between these three models do not simply involve the staff or the service users separately, but both groups together.

Tables 9.1 and 9.2 considered control and influence at Japanese hospitals in relation to governance models. The democratic multi-stakeholder model promoted greater control and influence than either the stewardship or command and control model. This chapter also presented data about the frequency of contact between three key stakeholder groups: staff, patients and volunteers in Tables 9.4 and 9.5. They demonstrate that the staff at a democratic multi-stakeholder model has more inclusive discussions with its key stakeholders about hospital affairs than the staff at the other hospital groups. An inclusive, democratic governance model not only allows the staff more autonomy. It also promotes a multi-stakeholder dialog and greater patient participation in their own healthcare which contributes to external efficiency. This suggests that there is more than one model for organizing healthcare. The participatory democracy practiced by some cooperatives and social enterprises can serve as a 'best practice' for other public and private healthcare providers in Japan and elsewhere.

It follows from this analysis of the data that a governance model can make an important impact on a hospital's work environment and service quality. An inclusive, democratic governance model allows the staff more autonomy, and it promotes a multi-stakeholder dialog that facilitates greater patient participation in healthcare. This, in turn, contributes to the external efficiency of healthcare providers. We noted in Chapter 6 that staff with greater autonomy were more satisfied with their work and service quality than those with less autonomy. This suggests that governance models are an important contextual or intervening variable between work environment and service quality. Thus, governance models, rather than ownership per se, appear to require closer attention in research on work environment and service quality in healthcare and other public financed services. Moreover, different ownership constellations might learn from the best practices found in these separate governance models. However, as Kurimoto warns, there are some unresolved tensions between a managerial logic and a professional logic of caring that require closer attention to prevent organizational drift from a democratic multi-stakeholder governance model to a stewardship model (2015). This is discussed further in Chapter 11.

Note

1 The data collection was financed by the Japanese Society for the Promotion of Science (JSPS), the Mitsubishi Foundation and Osaka University; and it was supervised by Prof. Yayoi Saito, Osaka University and the Consumer Co-operative Institute of Japan (CCIJ). The project is conducted within the framework of established cooperation between senior researchers at Ersta Sköndal Bräcke University College in Stockholm (Prof. V. Pestoff and Doc. J. Vamstad) and the Faculty of Human Sciences, Osaka University (Prof. Y. Saito). This interdisciplinary group of Swedish and Japanese researchers is supported by a reference group of the relevant cooperative healthcare providers in Japan, *Koseiren* and the Japanese Health and Welfare Co-operative Federation HeW CO-OP JAPAN.

References

Blandi, V., 2018. *Customer Uncertainty: A Source of Organizational Inefficiency in the Light of Modularity Theory of the Firm*. Ph.D. Dissertation. Trento & Florence.

Brandsen, T., Trommel, W., Verschuere, B., 2017. The state and the reconstruction of civil society. *International Review of Administrative Sciences 83* (4), 676–693.

Cornforth, C., 2004. The governance of co-operatives and mutual associations: A paradox perspective. *Annals of Public and Co-operative Economics 75* (1), 11–32.

Eldenbos, J., van Meerkerk, I., 2016. Introduction: three reflective perspectives on interactive governance. In: J. Eldenbos, J., van Meerkerk, I. (eds.), *Critical Reflections on Interactive Governance: Self-Organization and Participation in Public Governance*. Edward Elgar Publishing, Cheltenham, UK & Northampton, MA, USA.

Hirschman, A.O., 1970. *Exit, Voice & Loyalty. Responses to Decline in the Performance of Firms, Organizations and States*. Harvard University Press, Cambridge, MA & London.

Hirst, P., 2002. Democracy & Governance. In: Pierre, J. (ed.), *Debating Governance, Authority, Steering and Democracy*. Oxford University Press, Oxford.

Kurimoto, A., 2015. *Social Enterprise in Japan: The Field of Health and Social Services*. ICSEM Working Paper No. 7, ISCEM, Liege.

Kurimoto, A., 2018. Chapter 4 Japan: Health and Elderly Care Cooperatives. *Co-operative Health Report: Assessing the Worldwide Contribution of Cooperatives to Healthcare*. IHCO and EURICSE (eds), Geneva & Trento.

Osborne, S.P., 2010. Introduction. In: Osborne, S.P. (ed.), *The New Public Governance?* Routledge, London & New York.

Osborne, S.P., Radnor, Z., Nasi, G., 2013. A new theory for public sector management? Towards a (public) service dominant approach. *American Review of Public Administration 43* (2), 135–158.

Ostrom, E., 1993. *A communitarian approach to local governance*. National Civic Review, 226–233.

Ostrom, E., 1996. Crossing the great divide, coproduction, synergies and development. *World Development 24* (6), 1073–1087.

Pestoff, V., 2000. Enriching Swedish women's work environment: The case of social enterprises in daycare. *Economics & Industrial Democracy 21* (1), 39–70.

Pestoff, V., Vamstad, J., 2014. Promoting good work & enriching work environment: The case of social enterprises in Swedish childcare. *Annals of Public and Co-operative Economics 85* (3), 353–370.

Pestoff, 2016. *Cooperative healthcare in Japan – a brief overview of eight co-op hospitals*. Ersta Sköndal Bräcke University College, Stockholm.

Pestoff, V., 2018. *Work Environment and Service Quality in Japanese Healthcare*. Paper presented to the ICSEA Conference, Osaka, Japan.

Peters, G., 1994. *Alternative Models of Governance: the Changing State of Public Service*. IPSA Congress paper, RC27, Berlin.

Peters, G., 1996. *The Future of Governing. Four Emerging Models*. University Press of Kansas, Lawrence, KS.

Sacchetti, S., 2013. Inclusive and exclusive social preferences: A Deweyan framework to explain governance heterogeneity. *Journal of Business Ethics* 10, 1007s/10551-013-1971-0.

Schmitter, P., 2002. Participation in Governance Arrangements. Is there any reason to expect it will achieve "Sustainable and Innovative Policies in a multilevel context"? Grote, J.R., Gbikpi, B. (eds.), *Participatory Governance. Political and Societal Implications*. Leske & Budrich, Opladen.

Sicilia, M., Guarini, E., Sancino, A., Andreani, M., Ruffini, R., 2016. Public services management and co-production in multi-level governance settings. *International Review of Administrative Sciences 82* (1), 8–27.

Spears, R., Cornforth, C., Aiken, M., 2014. Major perspectives on governance of social enterprise: Ch. 7. In: Defourrny, J., Hulgård, L., Pestoff, V. (eds.), *Social Enterprise & the Third Sector*. Routledge, London & New York.

Vamstad, J., December, 2012. Co-production and service quality: A new perspective on the Swedish welfare state, Ch. 6. In: Pestoff, V., Brandsen, T., Verschuere, B.(eds.), *New Public Governance, the Third Sector and Co-Production*, Routledge and reprinted in Voluntas, London & New York.

Van Kersbergen, K., van Waarden, F., 2004. Governance as a Bridge between Disciplines. *European Journal of Political Research 5* (3), 227–243.

Vidal, I., 2013. Governance of Social Enterprises as Producers of Public Services, Ch. 10. In: Valkama, P., Bailey, S., Anttiroiko, A.-V. (eds.), *Organisational Innovation in Public Services. Forms and Governance*. Palgrave, New York & London.

Weber, M., 1947. In: Parsons, T., Henderson, A.M. trans., *Theory of Social and Economic Organizations*. Oxford University Press, New York.

Yamazaki, Y., 2020. e-mail on 12 Aug., 2020.

10 The Social Values and Mission of Cooperative and Public Healthcare Providers in Japan

Comparing the Perspectives of the Staff, Patients and Volunteers

Hospitals need to balance a variety of goals – cultural, financial, political and social. An organization's social values reflect its preference for how to allocate its resources, both financial and human, between or among its goals. This chapter compares the social values and missions of Japanese hospitals from the perspective of the staff, patients and volunteers. Each hospital group has a distinct mission based on a different set of social values. In general, the staff, patients and volunteers share a similar view about what is most important and less important for each hospital. Although these values are found in the profiles of the other hospitals, they do not carry the same weight. Moreover, information about membership in cooperative organizations from the staff, patients and volunteers shows that it provides the institutional structure that can unite a unique set of social values, and both inform their mission and make it possible to realize this.

A Introduction

This research project on Co-production and Japanese Healthcare has several main focuses or questions, and it relies on several different data sources. First, came the Organization Study in 2013, second, the Staff Study 2016 and 2017 and third, the Patient Study and Volunteer Study in 2017. Chapter 5 presents the data and collection procedures for this research. These four studies allow us to describe and analyze different aspects of co-production, work environment, governance, service quality and social values of Japanese healthcare. Having data from four separate sources – the leaders, staff, patients and volunteers – also allows us to compare their answers in a fashion that can corroborate the details and dimensions of one study in relation to another study. If the staff claims that hospital A or hospital B promotes certain social values, then what do the patients or volunteers at these hospitals think about the relative salience of these values? Also, comparing the staff's evaluation of service quality with that of the patients and volunteers provides a chance to corroborate our data sources. Comparisons of this type provide the main content of this chapter.

B Hospitals as Hybrid Organizations with Multiple Goals and Stakeholders

Japan has a unique healthcare system with not just one, but two different user-owned healthcare providers, according to the United Nations global survey (1997). The Agricultural Co-ops or *Koseiren* provides healthcare services for its members primarily in rural areas, while the Japanese Health and Welfare Co-op Federation (HeW CO-OP) serves urban areas. Given these differences, we would expect them to promote different social values and cater to different population needs. The data in Chapter 7 corroborated this. Efficiency is a very important societal goal but is far from being the only one. In a society that primarily focuses on a single goal – such as efficiency – other important societal goals involving cultural, ethical, political and social values, may be crowded out, and, eventually, it risks becoming a one-dimensional society (Marcuse, 1964). In this chapter, we intend to explore other societal goals than the traditional or standard economic and financial ones. An organization's social orientation can be defined as its preference for how to allocate its resources – both financial and human – between or among its goals. In other words, it is the weight that an organization attributes to promoting its goals and achieving the outcomes.

Resource husbandry is, of course, important for realizing a variety of goals both in times of scarcity and surplus. Sound financial management and prudent goal fulfillment can help sustain an organization in the long run. However, making a surplus can be considered a means to achieve a variety of organizational goals and is not an end in itself. No single goal or value should be allowed to dominate an organization for too long, lest it atrophies and transforms itself into a different organization. It is, therefore, necessary for the leaders and management to recognize the importance of balancing various goals. For example, hospitals in most countries are not established, nor do they operate simply to make a profit, although a healthy surplus is necessary for maintaining their operations, activities and for their survival. Hospitals need, therefore, to balance a variety of goals – cultural, financial, political and social – in conjunction with their healthcare objectives.

1 A Dynamic Model of Cooperative Development

Given the prominence of hybrid organizations in this study of Co-production and Japanese Healthcare, an interactive model of cooperative development is introduced below. Unlike public agencies or for-profit firms that have a single goal, as hybrid organizations, cooperatives are challenged by having to pursue separate and often conflicting logics. This interactive model of cooperative development underlines the importance of adapting and adjusting to major changes in society and their environment. It also points to the need for cooperatives, as hybrid organizations, to balance the demands of various stakeholders or strategic groups so that no single group dominates permanently. Otherwise, there is a risk that it may ignore the claims of some important stakeholders and might pursue a single goal, like maintaining its market shares or increasing its efficiency, at the expense of other goals. This could turn a cooperative into a different type of organization that risks losing the support of some of its original stakeholders. This dynamic model helped analyze and explain the development of the Swedish agricultural, building and tenant and consumer cooperatives in the post-war period (Pestoff 1991, 2012).

The four most important environments for cooperatives in industrial and post-industrial societies are: the market, their members, their employees and the public authorities. Together, they set clear limits on the actions and decisions of cooperatives and their managers. Each of them can potentially act as a major constraint on the freedom of cooperative leaders to make decisions. Each of them promotes its own particular values and represents its own particular goals, which, at times, may come in conflict with each other. Each of them is based on a separate logic, making it possible to speak of four competing logics or principles of cooperatives: the logic of (efficient) competition, the logic of (democratic) membership, the logic of (political) influence and the logic of (personnel) management. Figure 10.1 illustrates this.

Both members and employees comprise the internal environment of cooperatives, as they are part of the organization; while markets and authorities comprise the external environment of cooperatives, since they are outside the organization itself. At the same time, cooperatives can also be analyzed in terms of their commercial and social/political dimensions. In this case, markets and employees comprise the commercial dimension, while members and authorities comprise the social/political dimension of

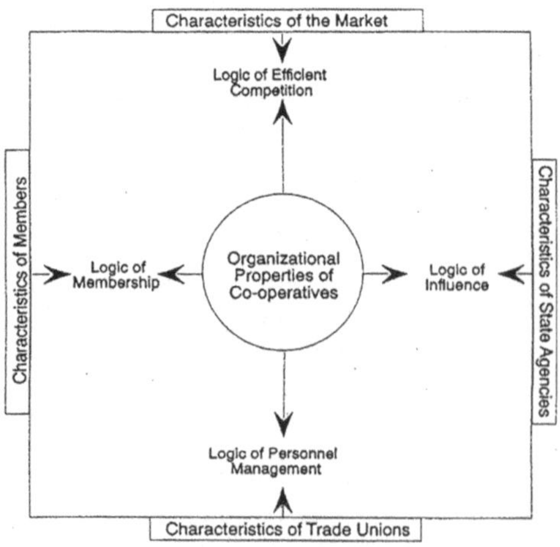

Figure 10.1 The Competing Logics of Cooperative Associative Action.

cooperatives. The commercial dimension is an aspect that cooperatives share with other firms in the market while also competing with them. The social/political dimension of cooperatives is something they hold in common with other non-governmental organizations, voluntary associations, third sector organizations and it is related to their purpose.

2 *Two Schools: A Democratic and a Business School*

There are two main schools concerning the development and future of cooperatives, and they reflect the dilemma of cooperatives as hybrid organizations. According to the associational or democratic school (see Böök, 1992; Craig, 1993; Pestoff, 1991, 2012 among others), cooperatives are primarily regarded as associations that pursue social goals by economic means. In the business school (see Birchall, 1999; Birchall and Simmons, 2001, 2004; Gijselinckx, 2012, among others), cooperatives are mainly business firms that have some unique social and associational features. The associational school focuses on the role of cooperatives as membership associations in a rapidly changing world, where their members have vastly changing needs and demands. Nonetheless, cooperatives need to strategically balance various stakeholders and goals (Pestoff, 2012). The business school considers cooperatives as a 'member-owned business' that need to modernize and professionalize in order to meet the growing competition from private firms, particularly in the retail trade (Birchall, 2012).

However, organizational democracy and business efficiency need to be balanced in a fashion that amplifies the commitment of cooperatives to articulate an integrated vision on ecological, economic and social issues that responds to current challenges in a fashion that reaffirms their cooperative identity. Moreover, in order to build a cohesive cooperative culture, it is necessary for mature cooperatives to refer to and discuss their historical roots in a way that makes their legitimacy more obvious, especially for newer and younger members. This invites them to think about the purpose of a cooperative in its local environment and its role as a key element for future developments. Thus, the need to strengthen organizational effectiveness requires an awareness of the cooperative identity, as well as its ability to act like a democratic organization of users, consumers and/or patients (Pestoff, 1991, 2012; Böök, 1992; Craig, 1993; Pestoff et al., 2015). What do the staff, patients and volunteers at these three hospital groups consider the most important social values and the hospital's mission?

C The Staff Perspective on the Hospital's Social Values and Mission

Hospitals need to balance a variety of goals – medical, financial, political, social and cultural. How are these goals reflected in the perspective of its key stakeholders (e.g. the staff, patients and volunteers) at Japanese hospitals? First, we will attempt to establish each stakeholder's baseline position in terms of its social values, employing somewhat similar questions, and then we will compare and contrast the social values each stakeholder associates with their hospital today. For the staff, a baseline position will be determined by considering two questions related to what was important for them when they first started their employment at the hospital and the balance between them. We will determine a baseline for the patients by asking them why they chose their hospital, while volunteers were asked why they volunteered at the hospital.

1 *Important Values at the Beginning*

The staff was asked what was important for their choice of employer by using two questions – one represents instrumental values and the other shows social values. 'Providing stable work' is considered an instrumental value, while a 'commitment to community activity' is related to expressive or social values. Table 10.1 only includes the proportion of positive alternatives (i.e. 'important' and 'somewhat important' answers), and then it considers the balance between them.

In general, the staff at all three hospital groups agree about the relative importance of these values for choosing their current job. Having stable work clearly outweighs social issues, and this gets much more support from all of them, ranging from 78.5% to 90%. However, the staff at public hospitals attribute somewhat more importance to job security than the staff at *Koseiren* hospitals and Medical Co-ops. Commitment to community activities gets much less support in general. It received support from two-fifths of the Medical Co-ops staff, and one-third of staff at *Koseiren* and public hospitals. Thus, all three staff groups clearly attributed greater importance to instrumental than social values. However, the Medical Co-ops staff was more supportive of social values than the other two staff groups. The balance between them or the relative weight attributed to these two values reflects the difference in favor of instrumental values. It is much

Table 10.1 Importance in Choosing Your Present Job

*Importance at the Beginning**	*Med Co-ops*	Koseiren	*Public*	*Dif. (h-l)***
a) Provides stable work	78.5	84.9	90.0	11.5/P
b) Commitment to community activities	42.1	32.9	33.2	9.2
c) Balance between a and b (a – b)	36.4	52.0	56.8	20.4

*Indicates the proportion of positive answers, 'important' and 'somewhat important', to these aspects of their job initially; and

**Difference between high and low.

greater in public hospitals than in the Medical Co-ops - 56.8% points difference in the former as compared to 36.2% points difference in the latter, while *Koseiren* falls in between them with 52.0% points difference. This indicates that the Medical Co-op staff initially was somewhat more community-oriented than the staff at the other two hospital groups.

2 *Social Dimensions of Co-op and Public Healthcare*

Neither the public hospitals nor agricultural and consumer co-op healthcare provides medical services for purely economic or financial reasons; rather, they exist to promote the citizens' and their members' interests by supplying good quality healthcare, while also pursuing other social values. What social values do these three hospital groups pursue by providing healthcare? Three questions in the Staff Study address the values that they feel are promoted by Japanese healthcare providers. The first is a general question about the staff's perception of their hospital's social mission (i.e. does it make a contribution to society beyond providing healthcare?). The second question addresses the hospitals' social values and mission, while the third question asks about the nature of the most important issues/challenges facing their hospital and shows how they attempt to balance those values.

Beginning with the first question, the staff was asked about their general evaluation of their hospital's social contribution above and beyond the medical services it provides. The staff at both the cooperative hospital groups appears to be more positive about their hospital's social contribution to society than the staff at public hospitals. Approximately two out of five staff members at the Medical Co-ops (41.7%) and *Koseiren* (37.4%) responded positively to this question, while less than one-third did so at the public hospitals (29.6%). The staff at public hospitals appear to have a somewhat narrower view of their hospital's contribution to society, and their primary focus is on providing healthcare and not engaging in community activities.

Table 10.2 introduces the staff perspective on the social values or mission of their hospital. Similar to most other multiple response questions in this chapter, respondents could choose up to three items from a list of ten alternatives that is found in Table 10.A in the appendix. Note that, however, the table below shows the percent of responses for a given item or category, which tends to underestimate the true support for it. Indicating the percent of respondents who support a given item easily results in figures above 100%, which can be confusing. They are multiple-choice questions, and the average number of items selected by the hospital groups was 2.45, so there are nearly two and a half times as many responses as respondents. Table 10.B in the appendix indicates the number of responses, respondents and responses per respondent by the staff, patients and volunteers to questions about hospital social values.

Table 10.2 Staff Perception of the Hospital Social Values and Mission

Hospital Social Values[x]	*Responses*[y]	*Med Co-ops*	Koseiren	*Public*	*Dif.*[z]
Expressive Values[a]	*6,277*	*51.3*	*31.3*	*26.8*	24.5
Instrumental Values[b]	*5,345*	*23.0*	*42.2*	*39.2*	19.2/K
Do Not Know	1,331	5.5	7.8	15.8	10.3/P
Totals (Average Resp.)	16,036	(2.66)	(2.52)	(2.41)	–
Community-Based Integrated Care	3,083	20.2	18.6	18.2	2.0
Patient Participation in Healthcare	2,994	25.2	14.4	10.9	14.3
Promoted Preventive Medicine	2,495	19.1	14.2	10.0	9.1
Highly Skilled Jobs in Local Area	1,193	1.9	9.5	16.1	14.2/P

x = multiple responses, the staff could name more than one alternative; y = Number of responses; z = Difference between the high and low scores; a *Expressive values* include three items: promotes patient participation, engages in preventive medicine and provides care to the uninsured; **b** *Instrumental values* include six items related to alleviating local shortages of jobs and services: provides services in short supply, creates jobs in the local area, provides highly skilled jobs locally, provides training for women locally, promotes local development and prevents depopulation.

Table 10.2 is divided into two parts. The top part combines nine items into two separate categories – expressive and instrumental values and is indicated in *italics*. The detailed answers were reported in the Staff Study (Pestoff, 2017a). However, combining between three and six items underrepresents the true strength of support even more, compared with individual items at the bottom of the table. The proportion of respondents who support expressive and instrumental values, 'do not know' answers and Community-Based Integrated Care (CIC) add to 100% column-wise, regardless of how many responses they provided. The lower part of the table includes the three items that received the most support from the staff and were ranked in first, second or third place. The same format will be employed in Tables 10.5 and 10.7 for the patients and volunteers.

Beginning at the top of the table, there are some distinct patterns in the data. First, the difference in support received by both these categories is rather large. It ranges from 24.5% for expressive values to 19.2% for instrumental values. Staff at the Medical Co-ops provide much more support for expressive values. In fact, the level of support for expressive values by the Medical Co-op staff is nearly twice that of public hospitals. Second, concerning instrumental values, there is a rather large discrepancy in staff support between *Koseiren* and the Medical Co-ops. The former gives them nearly twice as much support as the latter. Finally, 'do not know' answers were nearly three times as prevalent among the staff at public hospitals

(15.4%) as the Medical Co-ops (5.3%). In order to understand these differences, it helps to take a closer look at the most important individual items or values found in the second half of the table.

Three things will be considered. The rank order of support that each hospital group gives to individual items, the level of support each item receives and the pattern of support at each hospital group compared with the other two hospitals. Beginning with the Medical Co-ops, the staff attributes most support to promoting patient participation, Community-Based Integrated Care (CIC) and promoting preventive medicine – ranking them as the first, second and third most important values. However, they give minimal support to providing highly skilled jobs locally. The staff at *Koseiren* show a somewhat similar pattern of support. They emphasize CIC, patient participation and preventive medicine as the three most important values, plus limited support for creating high skilled jobs locally. Finally, the staff at public hospitals demonstrate a clear preference for values like CIC, access to highly skilled jobs locally and patient participation, but at lower levels than the Medical Co-ops and *Koseiren* hospitals, except for the item related to skilled jobs.

Turning to the level of support for the first three items, the staff at the Medical Co-ops attributes them higher levels of support, and the staff at public hospitals gives them less support, while the staff at *Koseiren* hospitals falls in between the other two hospitals. Support for CIC is very similar among staff at all three hospital groups. It comes either first or second for all of them. Promoting patient participation in healthcare gets nearly twice as much support from staff at the Medical Co-ops (24.7%) as the public hospitals (12.5%). Similarly, promoting preventive medicine gets nearly twice as much support from the Medical Co-op staff (18.8%) as the staff at public hospitals (10.1 %). As noted earlier in Chapter 7, promoting preventive medicine is associated with the health literacy outreach strategy adopted by a healthcare provider. Concerning the fourth item, – promoting high skilled jobs locally – the order of support is reversed. It gets much more support from the staff at public hospitals and *Koseiren* hospitals (15.9% and 9.6%) than the staff at the Medical Co-ops (2.2%). Given the high level of support this item receives from the staff at public hospitals, it probably serves as a reflection of their public, professional orientation.

In summary, these separate patterns of support demonstrate that the staff at Medical Co-ops perceive their mission and social profile as comprised of expressive values based on promoting patient participation and preventive healthcare combined with CIC. The mission of *Koseiren* hospitals is related to instrumental values that emphasize alleviating shortages in rural areas as well as CIC, patient participation and preventive medicine. The mission of public hospitals is related to CIC and promoting professional values like highly skilled jobs locally and patient participation but not preventive medicine. However, despite their differences, the staff at all three of these hospital groups show uniform support for the government's key policy in health and eldercare, CIC. It has been the primary, long-term policy goal for eldercare and healthcare for more than a decade. Reaching either first or second priority among the social values not only underlines the importance the government attaches to it, but also indicates an awareness of the need for and willingness by the staff at all three hospital groups to pursue multiple goals. CIC will be discussed in more detail in Chapter 11.

3 *Need for Balancing Social and Financial Goals*

A third question concerning the hospital social values asks the staff about the most important issues or challenges facing their hospital. They could choose three out of the eight alternatives, and the answers are found in Table 10.3. Once again, the proportion of responses is employed here and this underreports support, as noted earlier in Table 10.2. The figures add column-wise to 100%. The three financial matters that are combined in the top row of the table include maintaining a healthy budget, increasing patient/bed turnover and increasing the financial surplus. Despite their different geographical, institutional and social context, support for items in the first three rows of the table demonstrate that the staff at all three hospital groups maintains a similar stance on the issues or challenges facing their hospitals, and there is a large degree of agreement about the

Table 10.3 Three Most Important Issues Facing Your Hospital

*Three Most Important Issues**	*No. of Responses**	*Med Co-ops*	*Koseiren*	*Public*	*Dif.***
Sound Financial Management[a]	4,923	27.4	29.5	27.6	2.1/K
Providing Good Quality Health/Eldercare in the Local Area	4,493	22.8	27.3	28.8	6.0/P
Promoting Good Working Conditions for the Staff	3,986	21.3	23.6	24.7	3.4/P
Promoting Patient and User Participation in Healthcare	2,242	16.2	11.4	8.8	7.4
Other Issues[b]	1,357	9.8	5.9	7.1	3.9
Do Not Know	444	2.5	2.3	4.7	2.4/P
Totals (*Average*)	17,445	(2.68)	(2.66)	(2.60)	–

*Multiple responses, respondents could choose up to three answers; and
**Difference between high and low; a *Sound financial management* combines the three items: maintaining a healthy budget, increasing patient/bed turnover and increasing the financial surplus; and b Other issues = promoting clear organizational goals and working with municipal and/or national governments.

weight attributed to them. There is a clear emphasis on sound financial management, providing good quality healthcare in the local area and promoting good working conditions for the staff at all three hospital groups. Between 20% and 30% of the staff responses at the hospitals lend support to these alternatives. The differences among hospital groups are not great, but the latter two questions reflect professional values and get somewhat more support from staff at public hospitals. Moreover, the level of support for these three issues suggests that the staff at the three hospital groups have a similar perception of the need to balance these three goals rather than concentrating on a single one.

Finally, support for promoting patient/user participation in healthcare varies between 10% and 15% of the responses. The staff at the Medical Co-ops felt stronger about this issue than the staff at the two other providers, which corresponds with the information in Table 10.2. On the technical side, missing data (MD) was moderate and varied between 6.8% and 7.9%, while 'do not know' answers were more modest and ranged from 2.5% to 3.0%. For more details, please consult Pestoff (2017a).

D The Patient Perspective on the Hospital's Social Contribution and Values

Considering now the social values that patients associate with the hospitals, there are some major differences in the data. Not only is the Patient Study much smaller in terms of the respondents with only 631 completed questionnaires, but they were also collected from a smaller circle of hospitals – two Medical Co-ops and two *Koseiren* hospitals. See Chapter 5 for more details. The comparisons in this and the next section on volunteers will, therefore, be limited to these four cooperative healthcare providers. The following topics will be considered here: patients' reasons for choosing their cooperative healthcare provider, followed by two questions related to the hospital's social values. Beginning with the reason(s) for choosing a hospital, patients could indicate more than one reason. In an effort to simplify the data in this table, the answers were combined into three main alternatives – the reputation of the staff and/or hospital, utility or instrumental reasons and membership. These alternatives are indicated by *italics*. Similar to Table 10.2, the figures here represent the percent of responses, which underestimates patient support for any given reason.

There are two divergent patterns in Table 10.4. As noted earlier in Chapter 7, these alternatives show a clear contrast between patient motives for choosing a hospital. Both groups of patients seem to agree that the staff and hospital reputation is an important factor for choosing a hospital, between one-third and one-fourth of the responses mention this. In addition, Medical Co-op patients appear to be mainly motivated by membership in their health co-op (32.8%), while *Koseiren* patients

Table 10.4 Why did you choose this hospital? (Choose more than one alternative when relevant)

*Reasons for Choosing**	*No. Resp.***	*Med Co-ops*	Koseiren	*Dif.****
Reputation[a]	415	33.7	28.5	5.2
Utility/Instrumental[b]	384	25.6	52.9	27.3/K
Membership[c]	369	32.8	12.2	20.6
Other Reasons	96	7.8	6.4	1.4
Total Responses (*av.*)	1,264	(*2.08*)	(*1.96*)	--

*Multiple responses, patients could name more than one reason;
**Number of responses; and
***Difference between Medical Co-ops and *Koseiren*; **a** combines four items: staff is kind and helpful, recommended by a friend, has a good reputation and the staff is competent; **b** combines three items: ease of access, has special medical services and only one available; and **c** combines two items: member of a co-op and recommended by my local co-op.

Table 10.5 Patient Perception of the Hospital Social Values and Mission

*Hospital Social Values**	*No. Resp.***	*Med Co-ops*	Koseiren	*Dif.****
Expressive Values[a]	*725*	*60.4*	*39.2*	21.1
Instrumental Values[b]	*322*	*21.5*	*40.3*	18.8/K
Do Not Know	63	4.7	5.9	1.2/K
Total Responses (*av.*)	1,286	(2.44)	(2.36)	
Promotes Patient Participation	335	26.7	23.1	3.6
Engages in Preventive Medicine	316	26.6	16.0	10.6
Community-Based Integrated Care	176	13.5	14.7	1.2/K

*Multiple responses; patients could name more than one alternative;
**Number of responses; and
***Difference between Medical Co-ops and *Koseiren*; **a** *Expressive values* include three items: promotes patient participation, engages in preventive medicine and provides care to the uninsured; and **b** *Instrumental values* include six items related to providing services in short supply: creates jobs in the local area, provides highly skilled jobs locally, provides training for women locally, promotes local development and prevents depopulation.

are primarily motivated by utilitarian or instrumental considerations (52.9%). On the technical side, MD was marginal and remained between 2.9% and 0.9%. For more details, please consult Pestoff (2017b).

Table 10.5 introduces the patient perspective on the social values and mission of their hospital. Respondents could choose up to three items from a list of ten alternatives that is found in Table 10.A in the appendix. The table is divided into two parts. The top combines nine of these ten alternatives into two main categories – expressive and instrumental values and is indicated in *italics*. The detailed responses were reported in the Patient Study (Pestoff, 2017b). The second half of the table includes the three items that received the most support from patients – ranked in first, second or third place. Keep in mind that the figures reported here indicate the percent of responses, so the table tends to underestimate support for a given item or category. Consult Table 10.B in the appendix for more details.

Beginning with the top of the table, some clear patterns are found in the data. First, there is a notable difference in support for expressive and instrumental values by patients. Patients at the Medical Co-ops overwhelmingly give their support to expressive values, and they attribute much less weight to instrumental values. Patients at *Koseiren* hospitals place much more emphasis on instrumental values than patients at Medical Co-ops and provide them slightly more support than expressive values. Shifting attention to the bottom part of the table, three things will be considered. The rank order of support that patients at each hospital group give to individual items, differences in the level of support each item receives and the pattern of support for each hospital group. First, patients at both hospital groups have similar rank orders for the first, second and third values they associate with their hospitals. Second, Medical Co-op patients attribute equally strong support to promoting patient participation and engaging in preventive healthcare, while CIC gets notably less support. *Koseiren* patients give high support to patient participation, but they attribute less support to preventive medicine and CIC. However, patients at both hospital groups appear to recognize the importance of governmental policy on CIC, and they attribute it to third place in their ranking of important hospital values. Third, the general patterns found here seem to correspond well with the patterns noted earlier in Table 10.2 for the staff at these two hospital groups. Fourth, differences between hospitals in terms of their support for health literacy outreach is reflected in patients' appreciation for preventive medicine. Finally, patients' reasons for choosing a healthcare provider presented in Table 10.4 correspond rather closely with their perception of the hospitals' social values in Table 10.5.

E The Volunteer Perspective on Hospitals' Social Contribution

Turning now to the social values that volunteers associate with the hospitals, once again there are some major differences in the data. Not only is the Volunteer Study much smaller in terms of the respondents with only 236 completed questionnaires, but they were also collected from a smaller circle of hospitals – only two Medical Co-ops and two *Koseiren* hospitals. The comparisons in this section on volunteers will, therefore, be limited to the two cooperative healthcare providers, the Medical Co-ops and *Koseiren* hospitals. First, their reasons for volunteering will be considered, followed by a question related to the hospital social values. Turning to the key question of why they volunteer, they could name one or more of six reasons, which are presented in order of support in Table 10.6.

Table 10.6 Why do you volunteer here? (Choose more than one alternative when relevant)

Reasons for Volunteering[*]	*No. Resp.*[**]	*Med Co-ops*	Koseiren	*Dif.*[***]
To Learn more about Medical Care and a Healthy Lifestyle	117	48.8	35.9	12.9
I Agree with the Purpose of this Hospital	114	50.0	43.8	6.2
Want to be Involved in Improving the Community	100	42.2	42.2	–
To Help People in Need	99	40.1	46.9	6.8/K
Because of Family, Friends and Acquaintances	35	15.7	12.5	3.2
Other, ...[a]	33	14.0	10.9	4.3
Total Responses (*av.*)	488	365 (*2.1*)	123 (*1.9*)	

*Multiple responses; volunteers could name more than one reason;
**Number of responses for a given item; and
***Difference between Medical Co-ops and *Koseiren*; and a includes two items: respondents who claim transportation fees and free lunch among the reasons.

As noted earlier in Chapter 8, volunteers at both hospitals give strong support to four main motives for volunteering: 1) Learning more about medical care and a healthy lifestyle, 2) Agreeing with the purpose of the hospital, 3) Wanting to be involved in the local community and 4) Wanting to help people in need. The relative importance of their motives for volunteering varies between the two hospital groups, but the difference between them is modest except for the first item. The average number of responses by volunteers is nearly equal in both groups, 2.1 for the Medical Co-ops and 1.9 for *Koseiren.*

Table 10.7 introduces the volunteer perspective on the social contribution or mission of their hospital. Respondents could choose up to three items from a list of ten alternatives that is found in Table 10.A in the appendix. Keep in mind that, similar to Tables 10.2 and 10.5, the figures found here report the percent of responses, so the tables tend to underestimate support for a given item or category. Consult Table 10.B in the appendix for more details. The table is divided into two parts. The top part combines nine out of the ten alternatives into two main categories – expressive and instrumental values and is indicated in *italics.* The detailed responses were reported in the Volunteer Study (Pestoff, 2017c). The bottom half of the table includes the three items that received the most support from patients.

Beginning with the top of the table, there is a familiar pattern in the data. First, there is a clear difference of support for expressive and instrumental values by volunteers. Volunteers at the Medical Co-ops overwhelmingly give their support to expressive values but much less support to instrumental values. Volunteers at *Koseiren* hospitals place less emphasis on

Table 10.7 Volunteer Perception of the Hospital Social Values and Mission

*Hospital Social Values:**	*No. Resp.***	*Med Co-ops*	*Koseiren*	*Dif.****
Expressive Values[a]	*304*	*60.6*	*38.1*	22.5
Instrumental Values[b]	*145*	*20.5*	*40.0*	19.5/K
Do Not Know	31	5.0	7.1	2.1
Total Responses (*Average Resps*)	559	(2.53)	(2.5)	–
Promotes Patient Participation	146	28.7	19.4	9.3
Engages in Preventive Medicine	123	24.0	16.8	7.2
Community-Based Integrated Care	79	13.9	14.8	0.9/K

*Multiple responses, volunteer could name more than one alternative;
** Number of responses; and
***Difference between Medical Co-ops and *Koseiren*; a *Expressive values* include three items: promotes patient participation, engages in preventive medicine and provides care to the uninsured; and b *Instrumental values* include six items related to alleviating local shortages: provides services in short supply, creates jobs in the local area, provides high skilled jobs locally, provides training for women locally, promotes local development and prevents depopulation.

expressive values, and they provide nearly twice as much support for instrumental values as the volunteers at Medical Co-ops. Shifting attention to the bottom part of the table, three things will be considered. The rank order of support that volunteers at each hospital group give to individual items, differences in the level of support each item receives and the pattern of support for each hospital group. First, volunteers at both hospital groups have similar rank orders for the first, second and third values that they associate with their hospitals (i.e. patient participation, engaging in preventive medicine and CIC). Second, the Medical Co-op volunteers attribute somewhat similar support to promoting patient participation and engaging in preventive healthcare, while CIC gets notably less support. *Koseiren* volunteers give medium but nearly equal support to patient participation and preventive medicine, while CIC gets slightly less support. In fact, volunteers at both hospital groups give CIC similar support. Like the patients, volunteers at both hospital groups appear to recognize the importance attributed by governmental policy to CIC, and they give it third place in their ranking of important hospital values. Third, volunteers seem to recognize the importance that the Medical Co-ops attribute to preventive medicine and its health literacy outreach efforts. Fourth, the general patterns found here seem to correspond well with the patterns noted earlier in Tables 10.2 and 10.5 for the staff and patients at these two hospital groups.

F Comparing the Staff, Patients and Volunteers' Social Values

The final step compares all three stakeholder groups at the same hospital group with one another in Table 10.8. It underlines the similarities and

Table 10.8 Comparing the Staff, Patient and Volunteer Perceptions of the Hospital Social Values

Med Co-ops/Social Values	*Staff*	*Patients*	*Volunteers*	*Dif.**
Expressive Values	*51.3*	*60.4*	*60.0*	9.1/P
Instrumental Values	*23.0*	*21.5*	*20.5*	2.5
Community Integrated Care	20.2	13.5	13.9	6.7
Average Items	2.66	2.44	2.53	–
Koseiren/*Social Values*	***Staff***	***Patients***	***Volunteers***	***Dif.****
Instrumental Values	*42.2*	*40.3*	*40.0*	2.2
Expressive Values	*31.3*	*39.2*	*38.1*	7.9/P
Community Integrated Care	18.6	14.7	14.8	3.9
Average Items	2.52	2.36	2.50	–

differences among the three key stakeholders and explores what these patterns tell us about the salience of a hospital's social values and mission. The staff's attitudes about social values will provide the starting point for these comparisons. The similarities and differences between their support and that of the patients' and volunteers' help inform us about the strength and coherence of a hospital's social values and the clarity of its mission, as experienced by the patients and volunteers. When all three stakeholder groups show a similar overall balance of values this will confirm the mission of a hospital. By contrast, if they differ notably in their support for a given social value or group of values, these discrepancies will require closer examination and explanation.

Beginning with the Medical Co-ops, there is a clear similarity in the ranking of the two main categories of social values. The staff, patients and volunteers all provide strong support for expressive values, but both patients and volunteers provide more support for them than the staff. They also attribute similar levels of support to instrumental values. As noted earlier, the staff considers CIC as the second most important item, whereas both the patients and volunteers give it a third place in terms of importance. Staff support for CIC is well above that of patients and volunteers. However, in spite of these differences, there is a relatively high degree of correspondence between the values of the three main stakeholders at the Medical Co-ops.

Considering the stakeholders at *Koseiren* hospitals, there is a similar pattern between the staff, patients and volunteers. All three stakeholders rate instrumental values more important than expressive values. In addition, both the patients and volunteers attribute somewhat more weight to expressive values than the staff. The staff at *Koseiren* also gives a bit more support to CIC compared with patients and volunteers. This is, of course, understandable, since the staff is more exposed to and more familiar with the government's policy proposals and directives than the patients or volunteers. However, stronger patient support for patient participation at *Koseiren* hospitals, as noted in Table 10.5, suggests that a more inclusive approach to involving patients might be worth serious consideration, and the benefits of a multi-stakeholder governance system might be worth exploring.

In summary, it is noteworthy that there are some clear similarities among these three key stakeholders regarding the support they give to social values. First, there appears to be little disagreement concerning CIC. While it does get more support from the staff at both the hospital groups than the patients or volunteers, there is, nevertheless, little difference between them concerning its general importance. Moreover, the other two social values demonstrate a high degree of consensus among the respective stakeholders at each hospital group regarding their importance. All three stakeholders at the Medical Co-ops consider patient participation in their healthcare and engaging in preventive medicine much more important than alleviating local shortages in services and jobs, while the opposite pattern is notable for all three stakeholders at *Koseiren* hospitals. This suggests that the social values the staff associates with their hospital group probably serves as a model for patients and volunteers, and these values reflect the hospital's social mission.

G Cooperative Memberships

The staff, patients and volunteers at both the cooperative hospital groups were asked about their membership in different types of cooperatives, as part of the information collected about their social background. A brief comment was provided earlier about the pattern of memberships in the relevant chapters (Chapters 6–8). In each case, there was a very clear difference between the Medical Co-ops and *Koseiren*. It is time to take a closer look at cooperative memberships and compare the pattern found for these three stakeholder groups. Table 10.9 provides a comparison of the staff, patients and volunteers at both cooperative healthcare providers

Table 10.9 Member of a Cooperative?

Hospital gp./co-op memb.	*Health*	*Consumer*	*Agr. Co-op*	*Other-Co-ops*	*MD*
Staff:					
Medical Co-op	92.1	33.3	8.3	0.5	4.8
Koseiren	2.2	18.1	71.9	1.4	20.3
Patients:					
Medical Co-ops	85.5	42.0	15.7	1.0	9.3
Koseiren	3.5	20.2	76.3	6.1	15.8
Volunteers:					
Medical Co-ops	91.3	53.5	19.2	0.6	5.2
Koseiren	1.6	28.1	81.3	–	12.5

in terms of their membership in cooperative organizations. There are three main types of cooperatives that the three stakeholders could belong to, health co-ops, consumer co-ops and agricultural co-ops. The table also includes an 'other co-ops' category and missing data (MD).

There are two clearly divergent patterns of cooperative membership for stakeholders at the Medical Co-ops and *Koseiren* healthcare providers, and these distinct patterns show surprising consistency across all three stakeholders. Starting with the Medical Co-ops, we note that nearly nine out of ten or more staff members, patients and volunteers belong to a local health co-op, and between one-third and half of them also claim membership in a consumer co-op. From less than one in ten to almost one in five also state that they are members of an agricultural co-op. Very few claim membership in other types of co-ops, while between 5% and 10% have MD. The primary form of cooperative membership for Medical Co-op stakeholders is in a local health co-op, and the secondary form is in a consumer co-op. Turning to *Koseiren* stakeholders, between two-thirds and four-fifths claim membership in an agricultural co-op affiliated with JA. Their membership in a consumer co-op ranges from one in five to one in four. The primary form of cooperative membership for *Koseiren* stakeholders is in an agriculture co-op, and their secondary form is in a consumer co-op. Rarely do any of the *Koseiren* stakeholders claim membership in a local health co-op or other cooperative organizations. However, there is much more MD here, ranging from one in eight to one in five respondents.

Neither of these distinct patterns comes as a surprise, and both of these are easy to understand. However, both represent a 'missing dimension' in much of social science research – the institutional structure that facilitates and makes collective action possible. In the context of this study, both these patterns underline the importance of institutional structures for providing cooperative healthcare. Without these structures, providing cooperative healthcare services would be difficult, if not impossible. These institutional structures encompass numerous facets of two separate movements for promoting the collective healthcare interest of their members. They embody the history, local and regional setting, member needs, governance model and social values of these healthcare providers that are manifest in and through the service they provide, their governance model, their work environment and service quality.

H Recommending the Hospital to Friends and Neighbors

Finally, we want to consider the possibility of comparing the view of the staff, patients and volunteers on hospital service quality that was alluded to at the beginning of this chapter. Keep in mind that Chapter 7 showed that between two-thirds and four-fifths of the patients at the Medical Co-ops and *Koseiren* gave broad support to their hospital and staff. What do the different social values and missions mean for the potential

Table 10.10 Recommend the Hospital to Friends and Acquaintances

*Recommend it**	*Medical Co-ops*	Koseiren	*Public*	*Dif.***
Staff	55.0	44.7	41.2	13.8
Patients	73.6	70.1	Na	3.5
Volunteers	76.8	73.0	Na	3.8

*Positive answers, 'agree' and 'agree somewhat'; and
**Difference between high/low scores and Na = not available.

willingness of patients and volunteers to recommend their healthcare provider to friends or acquaintances? Table 10.10 provides a summary of the answers from the staff, patients and volunteers to this question. Only answers from respondents who 'agreed' or 'agreed somewhat' are included.

The difference among the staff at different hospital groups is greater than it is between patients and volunteers. More than half of the staff at the Medical Co-ops is willing to recommend it, while slightly over two out of five would do so at *Koseiren* and public hospitals. However, nearly three quarters of the patients and volunteers are willing to recommend the hospital at both the Medical Co-ops and *Koseiren* hospitals. The reason that both patients and volunteers at the Medical Co-ops and *Koseiren* are more willing to do so by nearly 20% points more than the staff remains unclear. However, the fact that the staff tends to underrate their services compared with their patients and volunteers rather than the opposite is, nevertheless, reassuring. The persons who gain their livelihood from it do not seem to overstate its value. It is also reassuring that the hospitals get such strong support from persons who are not dependent on it for their income. Moreover, another important reflection is that, in spite of their different missions and social values, both cooperative hospital groups get very strong support from their patients and volunteers. The fact that three-quarters of them would recommend it to friends or acquaintances helps to underline that there is no 'one-size-fits-all' solution for accommodating and satisfying the diverse needs of different healthcare stakeholders. It is worth keeping this in mind when comparing different healthcare providers, whether in Japan or elsewhere or planning to restructure healthcare systems after the novel coronavirus, COVID-19 pandemic. Cooperative hospitals could perhaps play an important role, but, if so, what type of cooperatives and whose interest will they promote?

I Summary and Conclusions

It is necessary to keep in mind that reporting the responses for staff, patients and volunteers rather than respondents from multiple response sets tends to underestimate the support for expressive and instrumental values. In conclusion, the following patterns are noteworthy in the data from the staff at these ten hospitals. They provide similar levels of strong support for instrumental reasons for choosing their employer. However, the Medical Co-ops show stronger attachment to social values than the staff at the other two hospital groups. Moreover, the staff present three rather distinct profiles in terms of their hospital's social mission and contribution to the local community. Promoting user and patient participation in healthcare and engaging in preventive medicine distinguish the Medical Co-ops from the other two hospitals. Helping to alleviate local shortages of services and jobs in areas of short supply emphasize the *Koseiren* hospitals' unique role in rural areas of Japan. CIC and providing highly skilled jobs in the local area define the professional orientation of public hospitals. Finally, in spite of these differences, the staff at all three hospital groups maintained a similar balance among the three most important issues or challenges facing their hospitals. Sound financial management, providing good quality healthcare in the local area and promoting good working conditions all received consistent levels of support from the staff of each hospital group.

Considering the patients, some distinctive patterns were found in these tables – in particular, concerning their choice of hospital and the social values or hospital social missions. In addition to hospital reputation, Medical Co-op patients were more influenced by their membership in a local health co-op, while *Koseiren* patients gave utilitarian or instrumental issues greater importance for their choice of hospital. Similarly, they differed clearly in terms of the hospital's social values and mission. Medical Co-op patients emphasize promoting patient participation in healthcare and engaging in preventive medicine, while *Koseiren* patients give more weight to alleviating local shortages. This is similar to the views expressed by the staff of these two cooperative hospitals in terms of the relative saliency of their social values. For the volunteers, we found that they give strong, if not equal, support to the four main reasons for volunteering at both hospital groups. The difference between them is modest for three out of the four motives. Finally, concerning their perception of the hospital's social values and mission, there was stronger support for expressive values by Medical Co-op volunteers and more support for instrumental values by *Koseiren* volunteers. Furthermore, the direct comparisons within each hospital group of the staff, patient and volunteer perspectives on hospital social values and mission illustrated two divergent patterns.

The Medical Co-ops noted the high degree of similarity in the support given to the two overriding social values. They provide much more support to expressive than instrumental values. The difference garnered by the first three individual values related to expressive values is moderate, while support for CIC shows more divergence. One-fifth of the staff responses consider CIC important, while only one-eighth of the patients and volunteers do so. However, both patients and volunteers feel somewhat stronger about patient participation in healthcare and engaging in preventive medicine than the staff does at Medical Co-ops. This suggests that both these two stakeholder groups might like to see even more of it in the daily operations of Medical Co-ops.

Concerning the stakeholders at *Koseiren* hospitals, there were smaller differences among the stakeholders concerning CIC. Nearly one-fifth of the staff responses support it, while only one-eighth of the patient and volunteer responses do. There were only small differences among them concerning the other social values. The staff supports the idea of alleviating local shortages in services and jobs at about the same rate as the patients or volunteers. However, both the patients and volunteers give more support to patient participation in healthcare than the staff. This suggests these two *Koseiren* stakeholder groups would also like to see more of it in the future. Similarly, both volunteers and patients give more support to engaging in preventive medicine than the staff at *Koseiren* hospitals.

In general, we discovered that there is a high degree of consensus among the three main stakeholders concerning their respective hospital's social values. Table 10.10 provided evidence that both of the cooperative healthcare providers have a clear set of social values that amount to a distinct social profile or mission. They may differ strongly from one another on some key issues, but they also combine more than one social value in their mission. Moreover, their missions are able to combine CIC with patient participation and preventive medicine and/or alleviating local shortages in a fashion that underlines the need to balance different social values for the sustainability of the hospitals.

In conclusion, the tables in this chapter provide a rather similar and clear picture concerning the hospitals' social values and mission. Each hospital group has a distinct mission based on a different set of social values. In general, the staff, patients and volunteers share a similar view about what is more and less important for each hospital. This was reflected initially in what was important for the staff when they first started working for their current employer – why patients chose a particular hospital or why they volunteer at a given hospital. It is also seen clearly in the social values that the staff, patients and volunteers associate with their hospital. Medical Co-ops are associated with promoting patient participation in healthcare, engaging in preventive medicine and CIC. *Koseiren* is characterized by helping to alleviate local shortages and CIC, while public hospitals are based on CIC and providing highly skilled jobs in local areas. While these values are also found in the profiles of other hospitals, they do not carry the same weight or are not considered as equally important. Moreover, information about memberships in cooperative organizations for the staff, patients and volunteers demonstrates two distinct patterns. This suggests that membership in cooperative organizations provide the institutional structures that can unite a unique set of social values that both inform their mission and make it possible to realize it.

References

Birchall, J., 1999. What makes people participate in co-operatives? Toward a theoretical model. *J. Rural Cooperation* 27/1, 3–16.

Birchall, J., 2012. A 'member-owned business' approach to the classification of co-operatives and mutuals. In: McDonnell, D., Macknight, E. (eds.), *The Co-operative Model in Practice: International Perspectives*. Co-operative Education Trust Scotland, Glasgow, pp. 67–92.

Birchall, J., Simmons, R., 2001. Member participation in mutuals: A theoretical model. In: Birchall, J., Simmons, R. (eds.), *The New Mutualism in Public Policy*. Routledge, London, pp. 202–225.

Birchall, J., Simmons, R., 2004. What motivates members to participate in co-operative and mutual businesses? A theoretical model and some findings. *Ann. Public Co-operative Econ.* 75/3, 465–495.

Böök, S.-Å., 1992. *Co-operative Values in a Changing World; Report to the ICA Congress*. International Cooperative Alliance, Tokyo, 1992. Geneva.

Craig, J.G., 1993. *The Nature of Co-operation*. Black Rose Books, Montreal, New York & London.

Gijselinckx, C., 2012. Co-operative answers to societal challenges. 9 insights from 2 x 9 cases. In: Brassard, M.-J., Molina, E. (eds.), *The Amazing Power of Cooperatives*. Texts selected from the international call for proposals, International Summit of Co-operatives, Québec, pp. 403–418. Available from: www.sommetinter2012.coop/site/summit-program/scientific-articles-selected.

Marcuse, H., 1964 & 1991. *One Dimensional Man, Studies in Ideology of Advanced Industrial Society*. Routledge Classics, London & New York.

Pestoff, V., 1991. *Between Markets and Politics. Co-operatives in Sweden*. Campus Verlag & Westview Books, Frankfurt & Bolder.

Pestoff, V., 2012. Hybrid tendencies in consumer cooperatives: the case of Sweden. In: McDonnell, D., Macknight, E. (eds.), *The Co-operative Model in Practice: International Perspectives*. Co-operative Education Trust Scotland, Glasgow, pp. 83–98.

Pestoff, V., 2017a. *Staff Study: A Preliminary Overview of the Results from 10 Hospitals*. Ersta Sköndal Bräcke University College & Osaka University, Stockholm & Osaka.

Pestoff, V., 2017b. *Patient Study: A Preliminary Overview of the Questions and Answers*. Ersta Sköndal Bräcke University College & Osaka University, Stockholm & Osaka.

Pestoff, V., 2017c. *Volunteer Study: A Preliminary Overview of the Questions and Answers*. Ersta Sköndal Bräcke University College & Osaka University, Stockholm & Osaka.

Pestoff, V., Kurimoto, A., Gijselinckx, C., Vuotto, M., Hoyt, A., 2015. Consumer and service co-operatives as economic membership associations, Ch. 22. In: Smith, D.H., Grotz, J., Stebbings, R. (eds.), *Palgrave Research Handbook of Volunteering and Nonprofit Associations*. Palgrave, New York & London.

United Nations, 1997. *Co-operative Enterprise in the Health and Social Care Sectors*. United Nations, New York.

Appendix 10

Table 10.A (Question 31) Please circle up to three of the items below which best describe your workplace or hospital

1. Creates jobs in the local area*
2. Promotes patient and user participation in health promotion**
3. Engages in preventive healthcare**
4. Provides health care and elderly care in areas in short supply of these services*
5. Provides training and job opportunities for women in the local area*
6. Provides high skilled jobs (doctors, nurses, etc.) in the local area*
7. Prevents depopulation of the local community*
8. Promotes Community-based Integrated Care (CIC)
9. Promotes local development*
10. Provides health and elderly care to uninsured patients (e.g. Free/low-cost medical service)**
11. Do not know

*Instrumental values and **Expressive values.

Similar questions with similar response items were posed to the patients (Q5) and volunteers (Q14) in the Patient Study and Volunteer Study.

Table 10.B Number of Responses per Respondent in Multiple Response Sets on Hospital Values

*Number of Responses**	*Staff (Q31)*		*Patients (Q5)*		*Volunteers (Q14)*	
	Freq.	%	Freq.	%	Freq.	%
No Responses[a]	175	2.6	42	6.7	6	2.5
1 Response	1,335	19.9	137	21.7	42	17.8
2 Responses	941	14.0	124	19.7	236	15.3
3 Responses	4,273	63.5	300	47.5	148	62.7
4+ Responses[a]	135	1.9	28	4.5	4	1.2
Total Respondents[b]	6,549	100.0	561	100.0	226	100.0
Total Responses (*av.*)[c]	16,036	(2.45)	1,286	(2.29)	559	(2.47)

*Respondents could choose three alternatives; a = not included in the tabulations of respondents or responses; b = total number of respondents who provided from one to three answers; c = the average number of valid responses per respondent is indicated in parentheses.

Question 31 asks the staff about which social values they associate with their hospital. They could choose up to three alternatives. Some staff members failed to answer Question 31, and they are treated as missing data, and others choose four or more items. Both of the groups have been excluded from the calculations in this chapter. The number of staff members who answered and provided valid responses was 6,549 persons from the ten hospitals, and they provided a total of 16,036 valid responses. SPSS tabulations for multiple response sets indicate two different percentages figures. The first is the percent of the total responses, and it adds to 100%. The second is a percent of the cases of respondents saying 'yes' to one or more social value. The latter figure easily exceeds 100%, depending on the number of responses provided by each respondent. If respondents give an average of 2.45 responses in a multiple response set that would add to 245%. The former figure is easier to understand, but it clearly underrepresents support for any given item, probably by nearly two and a half times. The figures in Chapters 10 and 11 for multiple response sets employ the former figure as a percent of total responses, but they clearly underreport the true support for any given item in the tables.

11 Co-production at the Crossroads and Organizational Logics in Japanese Healthcare

This chapter analyzes co-production in terms of four different public administration regimes (PARs) and explores the implications of Community-based Integrated Care (CIC) in Japan. This research suggests a gradual development from traditional public administration to New Public Management, New Public Governance (NPG) and beyond, where NPG might only be a temporary phase of development towards a Communitarian regime. The Japanese policy of CIC attributes a more prominent role to family, friends, neighbors and volunteers as providers of health and eldercare. This seems to foreshadow the development of an aspirational type of co-production, associated with a Communitarian regime, rather than a transformative, participatory type of co-production associated with NPG. Moreover, it compares the perspective of managers and non-managers, as well as various professional groups concerning the social values that they associate with their hospital and the most important issues facing it. The data provides sparse evidence of conflicting logics at play between managers and non-managers. However, it does find some evidence of dissonance between and among the professional logics at Japanese hospitals.

A Co-production at the Crossroads

Citizens and professionals are the main actors in the classical definition of co-production proposed by Ostrom and her colleagues in the early 1970s (Parks et al., 1981; Ostrom, 1996). Today, co-production appears to be at the crossroads between different public administration regimes, each with a different idea about the role of users and professionals in promoting service quality. Thus, co-production may mean something quite different in different public administration regimes that can facilitate or set limits for citizen participation in public services and healthcare. Below, we introduce the concept of public administration regimes and briefly present four of them – traditional public administration, New Public Management (NPM), New Public Governance (NPG) and a Communitarian regime.

From a historical perspective, we will begin with traditional public administration that dominated during most of the 20th Century; followed by NPM starting in the 1980s; and a newer paradigm, NPG, at the turn of the century based on ideas of network governance. We conclude this brief overview by introducing a potential new regime found in ideas of spontaneous community and voluntarism – a Communitarian regime. While these four regimes differ in some important aspects, they also share some common features. Although each of them may be linked to a particular ideology or historical period; they can also be conceived as 'layered realities' that coexist with one another (Hartley, 2005; Osborne, 2010). Thus, more than one regime may be found in any given society at any given time, and operating in different service sectors. One public administration regime may dominate in one public service sector, while another may do so in another. Moreover, they can shift over time through the spread and ascent of a new public administration regime.

Figure 11.1 briefly summarizes some of the main differences between public administration regimes but does not attempt to cover all aspects, as this would take us far beyond the scope and purpose of this chapter. At this point, we will briefly consider the theoretical roots, value base and some key concepts of each administrative regime. These elements comprise crucial aspects of public administration regimes. Two variables are employed to analyze the relations between and among public administration regimes: 1) the degree of citizen activity in providing public services and 2) the institutional arrangement or degree of public responsibility for providing public services. The first variable is rather straightforward and ranges from low to high. The second is more complex but reflects the degree of public versus private responsibility for providing services to citizens. Healthcare or childcare can illustrate this. Is it considered a universal service provided to everyone in a given territory? Does it mainly rely on individual initiative, where access to service often depends on controlling various private assets? In the former case, there is a collective responsibility for providing a service with certain limits or restrictions based on eligibility, while the responsibility is primarily individual in the latter case. This variable ranges from individual to collective.

Both a Communitarian regime and NPG require a high degree of citizen participation in the provision of social services, but they are found at the opposite ends of a continuum ranging from individual to collective service provision. Similarly, neither traditional public administration nor NPM allows much room for citizens to participate actively in service design and delivery, and they also reflect different degrees of individual and collective responsibility for the provision of public services.

1 Traditional Public Administration

Traditional public administration has its theoretical roots in sociology, political science and public policy. It is based on a hierarchical model of command and control, stemming from ideas of Max Weber, with clear lines of vertical authority and responsibility. His ideas were later developed and expanded during most of the 20th Century (Ostrom and

Ostrom, 1971). The value base of traditional public administration is found in public sector ethos or serving the public and its key concept is public goods that are provided by public or civil servants who place a heavy emphasis on professional policy implementation and bureaucratic norms of equal treatment for all citizens.

2 *New Public Management*

Its theoretical roots were found in growing criticism in the 1980s of the inefficiencies of traditional public administration that were articulated in 'public choice' theory and management studies. It promoted ideas of the marketization and commercialization of public services in order to rectify these shortcomings and improve their efficiency and productivity. Managerialism also plays a big role in this PAR. Its value base stems from industry, and it promotes a manufacturing logic that emphasizes service inputs and outputs rather than focusing on outcomes (Osborne et al., 2013). Its key concepts are 'freedom of choice' for consumers and competition between providers in order to promote service quality.

A wave of NPM inspired public administration reform in the 1990s redefined the public as customers of governments rather than promoting citizen participation; this wave focused on improving governmental performance principally by subjecting governments to more market competition (Thomas, 2013: 788). However, introducing competitive market elements and quasi-market reforms appeared primarily to replace one form of bureaucracy with another in both healthcare and social care. Power was transferred from health professionals to managers (Fotaki

Figure 11.1 Public Administration Regimes: Values.

and Boyd, 2005: 238). However, increased reliance on market mechanisms in Sweden and the U.K. occurred with a quiet acceptance of growing regional and geographic inequalities that led to the erosion of the universal character of the welfare state (ibid.: 240).

3 New Public Governance

The theoretical roots of NPG stem from sociology and network theory, and its value base is considered 'participatory democracy' by some (Pestoff, 2009) and 'neo-corporatist' by others (Osborne, 2010). NPG is based on a service logic of production that focuses on service processes and outcomes, where public value is a key concept. It governs through networks and partnerships, where the third sector and social enterprises can play an important role in providing public services and citizens become active co-producers of them. Traditionally, the role of citizens was confined to elections and policymaking, but now, citizen participation shifted to policy implementation and public administration by involving citizens in deciding how policies, once adopted, would be put into practice (Thomas, 2013: 787).

This new school in public administration is based on the premise that the government cannot serve as the sole provider of public services. Instead, the provision and broader pursuit of public ends occur through networks of private and nonprofit entities, members of the public and governments. NPG has become the dominant model of public sector management in the post-NPM era (Alford and Hughes, 2008: 137). Moreover, the discussion of governance revived interest in co-production that occurs when governments partner with nongovernmental entities. It occurs both with individuals and with groups (Thomas, 2013: 788).

4 Communitarian Regime

The following is an early approximation at best, although more clues are gleaned from Brudney and England (1983), Horne and Shirley (2009) and Bovaird and Löffler (2012). Several examples help illustrate the development of Communitarian regimes. After 2010, the Coalition Government in Great Britain introduced a program called Big Society to promote community empowerment by reorganizing public services and facilitating social action (Slocock, 2015; Hudson, 2011). Its value base came from volunteering, philanthropy and charity and is accompanied by big budget cuts for public services while encouraging families, communities and the third sector to fill the vacuum. Similar policies have surfaced elsewhere: in Japan, in the government's policy on health and eldercare known as 'CIC' (Tsutsui, 2013; Agenosono et al., 2014; Tabata, 2014), the NGOizaton in Thailand (Ungsuchaval, 2016) and in Europe, including Denmark (Andersen et al., 2019; Fehsenfeld, 2019) and the Netherlands

(Nederhand and van Meerkerk, 2018), under the label of 'co-production and/or co-creation'. These diverse policy expressions are gathered herein under the heading of a 'Communitarian type of regime'. The government retains responsibility for service delivery, while citizens become 'enforced' co-producers (Fotaki, 2011), since they are now primarily responsible for implementing public services.

Two recent studies of strategic documents in Danish municipalities shows that they regard civil society and volunteering as integral parts of a new kind of public-civil partnerships. Andersen et al. (2019) note that the nine municipalities in their study emphasize the value of active citizenship and invite civil society to become partners in collaborative efforts to improve welfare services while seeking to 'revitalize' civil society through top-down measures with the aim of 'responsibilizing' citizens and civil society (ibid.). Danish municipalities stress the virtues of communities and the value of relations between citizens in local communities as essential for achieving welfare and good quality of life for all citizens. However, they argue that these values can no longer be solely or mainly 'delivered' by professional welfare workers, so they need to facilitate and strengthen opportunities for all those who want to engage and contribute.

Thus, collaboration with civil society becomes the new ideal relation between Danish municipalities and civil society that can create synergy and new, sustainable welfare solutions. At the same time, a strong emphasis is placed on individual citizens and the importance of citizens' active contribution to the welfare society is stressed. One municipality stated that '... individual citizens must take greater responsibility for her/his own life and that of others' (ibid., 6). Therefore, many Danish municipalities regard themselves as facilitators of individual citizens exploiting their own abilities and resources with the aim of helping citizens to 'fare well' by drawing on their relations and networks (ibid., 6).

Similarly, Fehsenfeld's study of five Danish municipalities noted that they want to change the impression that the public sector comprises 'the system' that provides services to passive citizens (2019). Rather, they see an opportunity to shift the power relations, where civil society participates in the provision of welfare services. This requires both citizens and public servants to acquire new roles, where the municipal staff becomes consultants to facilitate the development of welfare services, while the role of citizens is primarily to take greater personal responsibility for providing services. However, this may require giving them a bit more say-so in the design of these services (ibid.).

B The Role of the Principal Actors in Determining Service Quality

Citizens/users and the professional staff are the two principal actors in classical definitions of co-production, although we discussed different perspectives on co-production in Chapters 4 and 7. We will, therefore, briefly contrast the role of each of them in the four public administration regimes.

1 The Role of Citizens and Users in Service Quality

The role of users in the provision of publicly financed services is central to this analysis. The users of public services are either beneficiaries, consumers, active co-producers or 'enforced' service providers. An important attribute of these different roles is related to the two dimensions of our analysis – specifically, the level of activity by service users and the degree of individual or collective action necessary to avail themselves of such services.

Traditional public administration tends to be perceived as paternalistic by many, since it is achieved through the 'professional gift' model of service provision. In this case, citizens are considered the beneficiaries of public services, clearly with a passive role as recipients of services, but without any meaningful exit or voice options available to them. Their main recourse or influence is found in the electoral system that, at best, can provide an indirect, intermittent representation of their interest depending on current issues and the outcome of an election.

New Public Management often attempts to achieve its goals by using a 'carrot and stick' approach to incentives both for providers and users of services, which can either discourage or reward different kinds of behavior. In this case, citizens are considered customers with certain limited choice, but little, if any, voice and no representation. They can choose between preexisting packages or 'offers', but they have very little influence on the content or the features of such packages. Service quality is guaranteed through a competition where consumer choice determines the best quality.

New Public Governance is based on ideas of establishing a partnership between citizens and the government – where citizens are considered co-producers of public services. This not only gives them choice and voice in service provision, but, in some cases, even representation that allows them greater direct influence than either traditional public administration or NPM (Vamstad, 2007; Pestoff, 2009). At this point, service quality is determined primarily by user participation which allows service users to observe service delivery on a weekly or daily basis. This, in turn, promotes a dialog and mutual exchange between the professional providers and service users on things like service quality (Vidal, 2013).

In a Communitarian regime, the role of service users is to provide many services by and for themselves with little or no public support and sometimes alongside, but often instead of the professionals. Citizens are held responsible for providing many of their own services, and users – or their loved ones and neighbors – become service providers, while professionals are transformed into 'back-up' agents who only intervene

Figure 11.2 The Role of Service Users and Professionals.

when the service provided by family, friends and/or volunteers proves insufficient. Determination of service quality becomes more patchwork, since access depends on the availability, willingness and capacity of service providers, which can vary considerably.

2 *The Role of Professionals and Service Quality*

Traditional public administration relies heavily, if not exclusively, on training and professionalism to guarantee service quality (Vamstad, 2012). In a hierarchical command and control system, professionals guarantee service quality through their training. Thus, they alone can decide and prescribe appropriate measures based on their professional knowledge, experience and insights. Collaboration, negotiations and competition are not often taken into account in professional decisions.

New Public Management, by contrast, places heavy emphasis on competition and consumer choice, leaving it to the market to provide a guarantee of service quality rather than the activities or training of professional service providers or negotiations. NPM assumes that better quality providers will attract more customers than inferior products or services. Professionals, regardless of whether public, private or non-profit, will, therefore, focus on competition. Thus, it emphasizes quite different competencies and promotes a mindset based on competitive behavior rather than command and control or collaboration.

New Public Governance emphasizes collaboration and negotiation between partners, regardless of whether public, private or nonprofit.

User participation and mutual dialog between service users and the staff replaces professionalism or competition as the main guarantee of service quality (Vidal, 2013).

Finally, the perspective of a Communitarian regime on service quality remains largely undeveloped in this respect, but professionals are expected to complement users in their service provision by steering them to available resources in the community or to voluntary organizations. However, the consequence of this for service quality or availability for different groups of users remains to be seen.

In summary, we can note that the role of service users and professional service providers shows clear contrasts in these PARs, especially concerning service quality. This analysis demonstrates that co-production appears very much at the crossroads today, with starkly different roles for the key actors – the users and professionals – and, therefore, it can potentially develop in rather different directions. Thus, each direction not only implies different values, but also different roles for professionals and users/citizens. The way in which co-production develops depends, therefore, on the interplay of forces at the micro and macro levels of society that favor the development of one particular PAR rather than the other.

Finally, there is some evidence to suggest a gradual development from traditional public administration to NPM, NPG and beyond. It implies that NPG might only be a temporary phase of development or stopover point on the way towards a more Communitarian type of regime. This is seen in calls for a more prominent, if not dominant, role for family, friends, neighbors and volunteers as providers of health and eldercare. However, a policy that encourages citizens to be more responsible for themselves and others or requiring them to become co-producers adopts a limited view that pursues an aspirational, rather than a transformative, participatory type of co-production that is sometimes associated with NPG. Several recent Danish, Dutch and U.K. studies (Andersen et al., 2019; Fehsenfeld, 2019; Lassen, 2019) suggest that a Communitarian regime is closely allied with aspirational co-production. 'Responsibilized' citizens are offered few alternatives and they are granted little influence on the design and/or provision of services. Let us look, therefore, a bit closer at how CIC is manifested in Japan to understand the role that it plays in Japanese healthcare.

C Community-Based Integrated Care in Japan

Japan has an ambitious policy for elder and healthcare called CIC. It is defined as 'a system in the community which provides appropriate living arrangements and appropriate health, safety and peace in everyday life' (Tustsui, 2013). According to the government's Research Committee on CIC, the ideal size of each community is defined as an appropriate range of a 30-minute walk, which represents a school district or 20,000 inhabitants. In theory, CIC represents a natural evolution of attempts to integrate acute medical care and long-term eldercare. Prior to the 1990s, in Phase 1, eldercare was based on the family, but it faced growing problems which were in part due to increased female participation in the labor market. Phase 2 initiated the Long-Term Care Insurance (LTCI) in 2000, but it only lasted until 2005. It was designed to provide care from society and to reduce social or non-medical hospitalization for elder persons. However, with sky-rocketing costs for the LTCI, Phase 3 which was initiated in 2006 shifted responsibility back to the community to provide care based on the idea of mutual help within local communities (ibid.).

CIC is based on the assumption of a home setting where people can live long and safely regardless of their income. However, this is made difficult by the lack of affordable housing in parts of the country (ibid.). In addition, it also expects community volunteers to play a crucial role in providing daily life support for the frail and elderly. These community volunteers will work under the supervision of nurses employed by local CIC or health centers. The centers should include nurses, social workers and care managers. The centers have three roles: to implement various preventive care services; to provide outreach and counseling services through various community networks for the elderly in need of care; to be in charge of continuous and comprehensive care management support supervised by care managers (ibid.). Networks of informal caregivers may be feasible in better-off neighborhoods, but, in most areas, it will be necessary for the government to play a more active role to create a viable framework to organize such networks and promote organizations in charge of coordinating community activities. While social welfare councils exist in most municipalities, their resources vary greatly (ibid.).

However, it seems that the government institutions are still too weak to put their recommendations into practice – in particular, where vibrant community networks are lacking. A 2014 survey of residents in Adachi City, part of Greater Tokyo, documents three trends in major urban areas that have clear implications for possibilities to successfully implement CIC. It shows a dramatic increase of single-person households that reflect a growing reduction of family support, a weakening of relations between neighbors and the financial crisis putting stress on the sustainability of CIC (Agenosono et al., 2014). This suggests that less well-off communities may not always be able to shoulder these new responsibilities. As noted previously in Chapter 10, the staff at all three hospital groups rank CIC as second in importance in terms of the hospital's social values and mission, although they show different levels of support for such policies.

Avelino and Wittmayer (2016) argue that, in the past decades, Western societies have been characterized by a welfare state that has increasingly outsourced services to the market, resulting in a wide variety of 'public-private partnerships' (PPPs) and widespread 'neo-liberal' discourses applied to all dimensions of life and society (ibid.: 640). However, today, they observe a new surge of 'community-based' initiatives, where the state increasingly calls on 'the community' to take over public services. This is especially clear with reforms such as 'Big Society' in the U.K. or 'co-creation' in Denmark, where governments are attempting to reorganize their responsibilities and tasks vis-à-vis their citizens. This raises questions about how, where and when the community is supposed to take over tasks that have been performed by the market or state for decades (ibid.: 640). However, it remains unclear how the resource-limited third sector could possibly intervene and provide services without new resources when both the state and market have failed for so many decades.

Moreover, one of the earliest major attempts in recent times to deinstitutionalize public service provision and transfer it (back?) to the community was the reform of psychiatric care 50 years ago. It was initiated by President Kennedy, but it stalled soon after his assassination and the war in Vietnam. Nonetheless, closing mental institutions was aggressively pursued by then-Governor Reagan of California and later by President Reagan in the 1980s. It resulted in closing large state-run psychiatric hospitals in the U.S. and shifting patients to community hospitals. However, few if any new funds were made available at the community level. Instead of transferring responsibility to the local community, ironically, it resulted in the local jails and streets becoming the de facto alternatives all across the U.S. (Montross, 2020) and elsewhere. This was a major contribution to the mass homelessness that currently blights so many U.S. cities today and led to the dramatic increase in incarceration (ibid.).

D Organizational Logics and Social Values, by Management and Occupation

Institutional logics are defined as 'the belief systems and associated practices that predominate an organizational field' (Scott et al., 2000). They affect decision-making by steering the attention of decision-makers to certain issues, values and practices consistent with a given logic and deflect their attention from other issues (Vickers et al., 2017). The academic discussion of institutional logics primarily focuses on macro-level institutions like the market, state, civil society, etc. (McMullin, 2020). However, some authors suggest that they are also manifest at the micro-level, in organizations like hospitals (Cucciniello and Nasi, 2014; Van de Broek et al., 2014). The rigidities of professional boundaries and hierarchical cultures within the public sector have tended to prioritize the views of senior clinicians and healthcare managers, without allowing an active role for service users and citizens (Vickers et al., 2017: 11).

Healthcare, in most parts of the world, is a field that is moderately centralized yet highly fragmented, so it is quite likely to experience more than one kind of logic. Moreover, the rapid diffusion of NPM throughout OECD countries in the 1990s contributed to the spread of market mechanisms in many areas of public services, and healthcare was no exception. However, hospitals have multiple occupations, and they also need to balance their professional and business goals in order to be perceived as legitimate (Cucciniello and Nasi, 2014; Van de Broek et al., 2014).

Two European studies explored the adoption and implementation of innovations in healthcare where multiple logics were at play. The first was in Holland (Van de Broek et al., 2014), and the second in Italy and Spain (Cucciniello and Nasi, 2014). Both studies argued that the staff who implements a decision may promote or subvert the intentions of those who adopted it. For example, in healthcare, the decision-makers are board members, the director and senior managers, and they often adhere to a business-like logic. The users according to this approach are primarily nurses who practice a professional or caring logic. Accordingly, in highly complex organizations, like hospitals, it is important to recognize the contribution of various stakeholders to an organization's output and outcome and the fact that their logics may come into conflict. However, there is some ambivalence about whether the focus should be on institutional, professional or organizational logics or perhaps a combination of them.

Chapter 10 compared and contrasted the staff, patients and volunteers in terms of hospital social profiles. The materials presented there demonstrated that each hospital group had a rather coherent social profile – both in terms of the level and pattern of support by key stakeholders for the hospital's unique social values. On the other hand, how coherent are the staff in their own understanding of the hospital's social values? Are there any noteworthy expressions of divergent or conflicting social values that are similar to those noted for Europe, between managers and non-managers, or perhaps among various professional groups, like doctors, nurses, etc.? If so, it might be more a question of divergent organizational or professional logics. If a hospital's social values or social profile is taken as its organizational logic, then professional logics would be the values supported by a given professional group, and differences between them can be seen as an expression of that. Subsequently, it becomes an empirical question of how coherent a hospital's organizational profile is. Are there major differences between managers and non-managers or among different professional groups?

This section explores the possibility of divergent or perhaps conflicting organizational logics between managers and non-managers, or conflicting professional logics among different occupational groups at Japanese hospitals. First, it considers who the managers are in terms of their occupation and gender. Then, it explores the values that hospital managers and non-managers associate with their place of employment in a fashion similar to data presented in Chapter 10. After, it discusses the balance between expressive and instrumental values for managers and non-managers as well as different occupation categories. It also expands our understanding of those healthcare providers by exploring the potential for conflicting organizational logics between managers and non-managers or among various occupational groups.

1 *Who Are the Managers?*

Who are the managers, or who has managerial responsibilities and who does not in this study? First, we will consider this by relating managerial responsibilities to the main occupational categories employed in this study and later to gender. According to our classification, managers are staff who are associated with one of the three following criteria: They are persons who stated that they have a management position, they are a board member or 'staff with a title', which has special significance in Japan. Non-managers are persons who stated that they did not hold a managerial position. The distribution of managerial responsibilities by occupation is noted in Table 11.1.

On average, about one in five employees have managerial responsibility. Doctors are clearly overrepresented among the managers at all of the three hospital groups. More than three-fifths of them are managers at the Medical Co-ops, nearly half at *Koseiren* and two-fifths at public hospitals. For most other occupations, between one-eighth to one-fifth claim to be managers, but one-fourth of the administrators at the Medical Co-ops, and one-fourth of the staff with 'other medical

Table 11.1 Managers and Non-Managers, by Occupation and Hospital Group

Occupation	*Medical Co-ops**		*Koseiren**		*Public**	
*Manager/Not***	*Man*	*Non-Man*	*Man*	*Non-Man*	*Man*	*Non-Man*
Doctor	62.7	37.3	46.1	53.9	42.2	57.8
Nurse	19.3	80.7	13.5	86.5	19.0	81.0
Care Worker	14.6	85.4	5.9	94.1	Na	Na
Oth. Med. Spec.	15.4	84.6	25.1	74.9	23.9	76.1
Administration	26.7	73.3	17.4	82.6	13.6	86.4
Oth. Support Staff	9.4	90.6	5.1	94.9	3.1	96.9
Total Average	18.9	81.1	17.3	82.7	19.9	80.1

*Adds row-wise to 100% for each hospital group; and

**Staff who indicate that they are a manager, board member or are 'staff with a title'; other staff are considered as non-managers.

Table 11.2 Gender of the Managers and Non-Managers, by Hospital Group

Gender*	*Medical Co-ops**		*Koseiren**		*Public**	
	Man	*Non-Man*	*Man*	*Non-Man*	*Man*	*Non-Man*
Male	33.0	67.0	33.2	66.8	38.3	61.7
Female	15.2	84.8	12.3	87.7	16.1	83.9
Total Average	18.9	81.1	17.3	82.7	19.9	80.1

* Adds row-wise to 100% for each hospital group.

specialties' are managers at the *Koseiren* and public hospitals. Next, we will consider the gender divide at these hospital groups in terms of holding managerial responsibilities (Table 11.2).

Over three-fourths of the staff at these ten hospitals are women, but how many of them are managers? One-third of the male staff have managerial responsibilities at the Medical Co-ops and *Koseiren* hospitals, while closer to two out of five men are managers at public hospitals. A woman's chance of becoming a manager is less than half as that of male staff. Anywhere from less than one in five to one in eight female staff (16.1%-12.3%) have managerial responsibilities at any of the three hospital groups. However, given their predominance in the staff, women nevertheless comprise the majority of staff with management positions (53.2%-65.7%) at all three hospital groups. Accordingly, in the following discussion of the staff's perception of hospital social values and mission or important issues they face, there is a relative over-representation of men in management positions, but women comprise the majority of managers.

2 *Management and Hospital Social Values by Hospital Group*

Table 11.3 compares the social values of managers and non-managers in order to explore evidence of a potential conflict of organizational logics in our data. The table reports responses, and, as noted earlier for Table 10.2, this procedure underestimates support for any given alternative by more than twofold. Beginning with the top part of the table, there are some clear patterns in the data. First, there is little discrepancy between these two groups in terms of their support for expressive values. Managers give somewhat more support to them than non-managers in all three hospital groups. However, there are clear differences among the hospitals. On the other hand, both managers and non-managers at the Medical Co-ops give expressive values much more support than they do at *Koseiren* and public hospitals. Second, both managers and non-managers at *Koseiren* and public hospitals attribute instrumental values much stronger support than expressive values as well as much more support than at Medical Co-ops. Moreover, managers provide more

Table 11.3 Social Value Preference of the Managers and Non-Managers, by Hospital Group*

Hospital Social Values*	*Medical Co-ops* *Man*	*Non-Man*	*Koseiren* *Man*	*Non-Man*	*Public* *Man*	*Non-Man*
*Expressive Values***	*56.7*	*49.9*	*32.7*	*30.9*	*31.1*	*25.5*
*Instrumental Values*****	*19.7*	*23.8*	*45.7*	*41.6*	*41.8*	*38.6*
Do Not Know	2.1	6.3	3.3	8.8	7.4	17.9
Average Number of Responses	2.88	2.62	2.72	2.48	2.45	2.12
Promotes Com. Integr. Care	21.6	20.0	18.3	18.7	19.7	18.0
Promotes Patient Participation	26.1	24.9	14.0	14.3	14.2	12.1
Promotes Preventive Healthcare	21.3	18.5	16.8	13.6	11.4	9.4
Provides Highly Skilled Jobs	1.4	2.0	12.4	8.9	20.3	15.0

*Multiple responses, respondents could choose three alternatives,

**Expressive values include three items: promotes patient participation, promotes preventive healthcare and provides healthcare for the uninsured and

***Instrumental values combine six items related to alleviating local shortages: creates jobs in the local area, provides health and eldercare in areas of short supply, provides highly skilled jobs, provides highly skilled jobs locally, provides jobs and training for women locally, promotes local development and helps prevent local depopulation.

support for instrumental values rather than non-managers at *Koseiren* and public hospitals, but non-managers at Medical Co-ops give instrumental values slightly more support than the managers.

Drawing attention to the individual items in the bottom half of the table, the following patterns are notable in the data. First, CIC gets relatively even support from managers and non-managers at all three hospital groups; however, it gets slightly more support at Medical Co-ops. Both managers and non-managers at all three hospital groups rank it first or second among the top three social values. Second, promoting patient participation gets significantly more support from managers and non-managers at Medical Co-ops, and it receives less but relatively even support from both managers and non-managers at the other two hospitals. Third, engaging in preventive healthcare acquires more support from both managers and non-managers at Medical Co-ops, but the difference with the other two hospital groups is less than for patient participation. Fourth, there is a clear difference between managers and non-managers concerning support for providing highly skilled jobs locally. This is a non-issue for the staff at Medical Co-ops, but it is somewhat more salient for the staff at *Koseiren* and significantly important for the staff at public hospitals. It is more important for managers than non-managers at both of the latter two hospitals. In fact, it is the most important single issue for managers and the second most important for non-managers at public hospitals. The weight they attribute to it seems to reflect professional values rather than expressive or instrumental values.

Fifth, there is also a clear pattern found in the rate of 'do not know' answers. They are lowest for the Medical Co-op staff and highest for the public hospital staff, while the *Koseiren* staff comes in between. Managers use this option much less frequently than non-managers at all three hospital groups. Moreover, when taken together, the comparison of the preferences of managers and non-managers does not lend much credence to the existence of major differences in organizational logics. Rather, they reflect the value profiles noted earlier in Chapter 10. Finally, given the similarity in the level of support for CIC between managers and non-managers at all three hospital groups, there is mounting evidence of the growing dominance of a Communitarian PAR in the healthcare sector of Japan.

3 Occupation and Social Values by Hospital Group

The earlier discussion about the hospitals' social values and mission showed a clear pattern for each hospital group. The Medical Co-op's profile emphasized expressive values, the *Koseiren* profile focused on instrumental values, while the public hospital staff underlined their professional status and values. Table 11.4 includes the two aggregate categories – expressive and instrumental values – for doctors, nurses, care workers and administrators, as well as managers and non-managers at the three hospital groups. This allows us to explore evidence of potential conflicting professional logics in our data.

Beginning with the top part of the table for the four occupational categories, there are some clear patterns in the data. The occupations will be discussed pairwise to simplify the presentation, starting with doctors and nurses. First, there is a notable difference in support for expressive values by doctors and nurses at these hospitals. Doctors and nurses at the Medical Co-ops provide much more support for expressive values than they do at *Koseiren* and public hospitals. The level of support for expressive values at Medical Co-ops is more than twice than that of public hospitals, but there is little difference between doctors and nurses concerning expressive values. Second, concerning instrumental values, doctors and nurses at the Medical Co-ops give them much less support than their colleagues at *Koseiren* hospitals and public hospitals. There is a rather large discrepancy between doctors and nurses in their support for instrumental values at *Koseiren* and public hospitals. Doctors give them nearly twice as much support as nurses. This might be interpreted as one sign of professional logics.

Table 11.4 Instrumental and Expressive Values, by Occupation or Manager and Hospital Group*

	Med. Co-ops		Koseiren		Public	
Occupation	Instr.***	Expr.**	Instr.	Expr.	Instr.	Expr.
Doctor	23.0	54.7	53.5	32.5	55.7	25.9
Nurse	21.2	53.3	37.2	32.2	34.6	29.0
Care Worker	26.8	43.7	36.6	28.1	na	na
Admin.	20.5	56.7	47.1	32.7	41.1	21.1
Dif. Staff (h-l)	*6.3*	*13.0*	*16.9*	*4.6*	*21.1*	*7.9*
Manager	21.4	55.3	46.0	32.9	41.7	31.2
Non-Man.	24.9	49.3	41.8	31.1	38.8	25.8
Dif. Man/Non	*-3.5*	*6.0*	*4.2*	*1.8*	*2.9*	*5.7*

*Multiple responses, respondents could choose three alternatives,
**Expressive values include three items: promotes patient participation, promotes preventive healthcare and provides healthcare for the uninsured and
***Instrumental values combine six items related to alleviating local shortages: creates jobs in the local area, provides health and eldercare in areas of short supply, provides highly skilled jobs, provides highly skilled jobs locally, provides jobs and training for women locally, promotes local development and helps prevent local depopulation.

When comparing support by care workers and administrators for expressive and instrumental values, it should be kept in mind that care workers are not employed by the public hospitals, so they are only found in the Medical Co-ops and *Koseiren* hospitals. Care workers show less support for expressive values than their colleagues at the Medical Co-ops but slightly more for instrumental values, making the balance between the two values less favorable for expressive values. Care workers at *Koseiren* hospitals show similar support for instrumental values compared with nurses but slightly less for expressive values than most of their colleagues there. Administrative staff at both hospital groups demonstrate a similar pattern of support for expressive and instrumental values compared with their colleagues in different occupations.

There were some stark differences among occupational groups, noted at the end of Chapter 6, concerning their work environment and whether they were considered Low or High Strain (see Table 6.E). Therefore, these findings come as no surprise. In particular, nurses and care workers experienced an adverse work life situation compared to doctors and probably administrators too. Therefore, the fact that there are lower levels of support for expressive values by care workers at the Medical Co-ops, and lower levels of support for instrumental values by nurses, care workers at *Koseiren* and nurses at public hospitals suggests that different types of professional logics are at play. This is clearly reflected in the balance between expressive and instrumental values. It is much smaller for disadvantaged groups compared to advantaged groups. Therefore, it seems reasonable that they reflect differences in the daily work life of those professional groups. Groups that are disadvantaged in their work life situation will not provide as much support for the social values championed by better-off groups. Thus, these differences provide evidence of the existence of professional logics in Japanese hospitals.

Finally, comparisons of support by managers and non-managers for expressive and instrumental values provide a clear picture. First, differences between managers and non-managers for both types of values are rather small for the staff at all three hospital groups. Second, differences among the hospitals are all that more distinct. Both managers and non-managers at the Medical Co-ops attribute much more weight to expressive than instrumental values. The opposite holds true for managers and non-managers at *Koseiren* and public hospitals; they give somewhat more weight to instrumental than expressive values.

Summarizing these comparisons, there is scant evidence to indicate the existence of sharp or clear differences between managers and non-managers that would lend credence to an argument for conflicting organizational logics at these three hospital groups. The differences noted here simply do not rise to that level. However, there is evidence of conflicting professional logics at work among different occupational categories at Japanese hospitals. This provides an additional reason to consider human resource policies that would promote improvements in the situation for groups experiencing an adverse work life situation. This is also reflected in the balance between expressive and instrumental values. It is much smaller for disadvantaged groups compared with advantaged groups. Efforts to alleviate the cause of such differences would result in a more coherent social profile for each hospital group where no profession(s) felt left out of the benefits enjoyed by their colleagues.

E Management and Important Issues Facing the Hospitals

In Chapter 10, the staff was asked to evaluate the issues that they considered the most important for their hospital's future. This will now be considered from the perspective of the managers and non-managers. They could choose up to three alternatives, and the figures in Table 11.5 represent the proportion of responses from managers and non-managers which underestimates the support for any given issue. The response rate only varied slightly from an average of 2.91 answers to 2.56 responses. 'Do not know' answers were slightly more prevalent among non-managers than managers at all three hospital groups. Note that three economic issues have been combined into a new alternative, *Sound financial management*.

Similar to Table 10.3, three main categories of responses are found in the data – sound financial management, providing good quality healthcare and good working conditions, along with two smaller items – promoting patient participation and an 'other issues' category. Both the

Table 11.5 Perspective of Managers and Non-Managers about Important Issues Facing their Hospital

Issues	Man/Non-Man	Medical Co-ops	Koseiren	Public
Sound Financial Management[a]	Manager	*33.0*	*31.6*	*32.4*
	Non-Manager	*26.1*	*29.0*	*26.3*
	Difference[b]	*6.9*	*2.6*	*6.1*
Good Quality Healthcare	Manager	22.1	29.2	29.3
	Non-Manager	23.0	26.9	28.6
	Difference[b]	*-0.9*	*2.3*	*0.7*
Good Working Conditions	Manager	18.4	19.4	24.6
	Non-Manager	22.0	24.6	24.8
	Difference[b]	*-3.6*	*-5.2*	*0.2*
Promote Patient Participation	Manager	15.6	10.8	5.7
	Non-Manager	16.3	11.5	9.7
	Difference[b]	*-0.7*	*-0.7*	*-3.0*
Other Issues[c]	Manager	10.5	8.2	7.5
	Non-Manager	9.6	5.3	6.9
	Difference[b]	*0.9*	*2.9*	*0.6*
Do Not Know	Manager/Non-Man	0.4/3.0	0.8/2.5	0.5/3.6
No. of Responses[d]	Manager/Non-Man	2.91/2.63	2.81/2.63	2.83/2.56

a This alternative combines three items: maintain a healthy budget, increase the financial surplus and increase bed/patient turnover;
b Difference = manager – non-manager;
c other issues combines two items: promotes clear organizational goals and works with municipal and national governments and
d respondents could choose three alternatives.

managers and non-managers in all three hospital groups have similar rankings in terms of what is most and least important, while the level of support for individual issues only varies slightly or somewhat. Starting with the differences between managers and non-managers, we can note that it is clearest in terms of sound financial management but rather modest for the two other important issues facing the hospitals. One-third of the responses from managers attribute importance to sound financial management, and one-fourth or more of them do so for the non-managers. The differences between managers and non-managers are more modest for the two other issues, providing good quality healthcare and obtaining good working conditions. However, non-managers feel slightly stronger about promoting patient participation than managers at all three hospital groups.

Drawing attention to the differences between the hospital groups, we note the following pattern. There is much less difference among hospital groups concerning the important issues they face than for social values. However, Medical Co-ops emphasize patient participation somewhat more than the other two hospitals, and both *Koseiren* and public hospitals underscore providing good quality healthcare, while public hospitals also push more for good (or better?) working conditions. At the same time, both managers and non-managers at all three hospital groups appear crucially aware of the importance of sound financial management in order to have the resources necessary to achieve their other goals. The marginal differences found here between managers and non-managers do not add weight to ideas about different or conflicting organizational logic.

F Conclusions

This chapter compared the attitudes of managers and non-managers in terms of the potential impact of conflicting institutional logics. Conflicting institutional logics were considered important for adopting innovations in research on hospital staff in European countries like the Netherlands, Italy and Spain. However, the data from this study of Co-production and Japanese Healthcare does not lend support to a similar perspective at the micro or organizational level. Rather, it noted a preference for expressive over instrumental values at Medical Co-ops, and it was clearer among managers. By contrast, both managers and non-managers at *Koseiren* and public hospitals showed a preference for instrumental values. Support for CIC was stronger among managers than non-managers at all three hospital groups. Finally, there was clear evidence that managers at all three hospital groups placed greater emphasis on maintaining sound financial management of their hospital as the most important issue they faced in the future.

Moreover, when considered together, these comparisons of the attitudes and preferences of managers and non-managers provide sparse evidence of conflicting organizational logics. Nonetheless, comparisons of different professional groups do suggest that the impact of professional logics reflects differing work life situations. However, the prominence attributed to CIC in the hospital's social profile suggests the growing dominance of a Communitarian Public Administration Regime in Japanese healthcare. As noted earlier, there was some evidence in the data and elsewhere to suggest a gradual development from traditional public administration to NPM, NPG and beyond. This evidence implies that NPG might only be a temporary phase of development on the way towards a more Communitarian type of regime. The Japanese policy of CIC relies on a stronger and more prominent role for family, friends, neighbors and volunteers as important providers of health and eldercare. However, a policy emphasis that encourages citizens to be more responsible for themselves and others or requires them to become 'enforced co-producers', seems to foreshadow the development of an aspirational type of co-production rather than the transformative, participatory type normally associated with NPG. Moreover and as noted in recent Danish studies, the basic tenets of a Communitarian regime are closely allied with aspirational co-production, since it 'responsibilizes' citizens who are offered few alternatives and they have little influence on the design and/or provision of services.

How will these three hospital groups, with all their differences in work environment, governance models and social values, cope with the possibilities of and adapt to the constraints posed by Community-based Integrated Care? Only future studies of co-production and Japanese healthcare will be able to provide an answer to that important and challenging question.

References

Alford, J., Hughes, O., 2008. Public value pragmatism as the next phase of public management. *Am. Review of Pub. Admin.* https://doi.org/10.1177/0275074008314203.

Agenosono, Y., Kamazawa, S., Hori, T., 2014. Japan's next care system: How do communities participate. London: *3rd Internat. Conf. on Evidence-based Policy in Long-term Care.*

Andersen, L.L., Espersen, H.H., Torzen, A., 2019. *Civil society and civil society organizations in changing times: Needs, infrastructure and strategic position.* Conference paper, Copenhagen.

Avelino, F., Wittmayer, J., 2016. Shifting power relations in sustainability transitions: A multi-actor perspective. *J. Environ. Policy Plan. 18/5*, 628–649.

Bovaird, T., Löffler, E., 2012. From Engagement to Co-production: How users and communities contribute to public services; Ch. 2. In: Pestoff, V., Brandsen, T., Vereschuere, B. (eds.), *New Public Governance, the Third Sector and Co-Production.* Routledge, London & New York.

Brudney, J., England, R., 1983. Towards a definition of the coproduction concept. *Public. Adm. Rev. 43*, 59–65.

Cucciniello, M., Nasi, G., 2014. Evaluation of the impacts of innovation in the healthcare sector. A comparative analysis. *Public. Manag. Rev. 16/1*, 90–116.

Fehsenfeld, M., 2019. *Politisering af frivillighed i samspellet mellem den offentligt og den firvillige sektor: 'Vi ska tänke gadekäret ind'/Politicizing volunteering in the collaboration between the voluntary and public sectors; ResearchGate.* SDU, Odense.

Fotaki, M., Boyd, A., 2005. *From plan to market: A comparison of health and old age care policies in the UK and Sweden. Public Money & Management* 237–243.

Fotaki, M., 2011. Towards developing new partnerships in public services: Users as consumers, citizens and/or co-producers driving improvements in health and social care in the UK and Sweden. *Public. Adm. 89/3*, 933–995.

Hartley, J., 2005. *Innovation in governance and public services: Past and present. Public Money & Management*, 27–34.

Horne, M., Shirley, T., 2009. *Co-production in Public Services: A New Partnership with Citizens. Cabinet Office, the Strategy Unit.* HM Government, London.

Hudson, B., 2011. Big society: A concept in pursuit of a definition. *J. Integr. Care 19/8*, 17–24.

Lassen, A.J., 2019. *Agencements of reanimation. Anthropology Aging 40/2*, ISSN 2374-2267 (online).

McMullin, C., 2020. Co-production of Public Services: Institutional Barriers to the Involvement of Citizens in Policy Implementation. In: Sullivan, H., Dickinson, H., Henderson, H. (eds.), *The Palgrave Handbook of the Public Servant.* Palgrave Macmillan, Cham.

Montross, C., 2020. *Waiting for an Eco. The Madness of American Incarceration.* Penguin Press, New York.

Nederhand, J., van Meerkerk, I., 2018, *Activating citizens in Dutch care reforms: Framing new co-production roles and competences for citizens and professionals. Policy & Politics.*

Osborne, S.P., 2010. The (New) Public Governance: A suitable case for treatment? Osborne, S.P. (ed.), *The New Public Governance? Emerging Perspectives on the Theory and Practice of Public Governance.* Routledge, London & New York.

Osborne, S.P., Radnor, Z., Nasi, G., 2013. A new theory for public service management? Towards a (public) service dominant approach. *Am. Rev. Public. Adm. Rev. 43/2*, 135–158.

Ostrom, E., 1996. Crossing the Great Divide: Coproduction, Synergy, and Development. *World Dev. 24/6*, 1073–1087.

Ostrom, E., Ostrom, V., 1971. *Public Choice: A Different Approach to the Study of Public Administration. Public Admin. Review* (March/April) 203–216.

Parks, R. B., P.C. Baker, L. Kiser, R. Oakerson, E. Ostrom, V. Ostrom, S.L. Perry, M.B. Vandivort, G.P. Whitaker, (eds.), 1981. Consumers as Co-Producers of Public Services: Some Economic and Institutional Considerations. *Policy Stud. J.* 9, 1001–1011.

Pestoff, V., 2009. Towards a Paradigm of democratic governance: Citizen participation and co-production of personal social services in Sweden. *Ann. Public. Cooperative Economy v. 80/2*, 197–224.

Scott, W.R., Reuf, M., Mendel, M., Caronna, G., 2000. *Institutional Change and Healthcare Organization: From Professional Dominance to Managed Care.* Univ. of Chicago Press, Chicago, IL.

Slocock, S., 2015. Whose society? *The Final Big Society Audit.* Civil Change, London.

Tabata, K., 2014. *Health and Welfare Policy in Japan. Toward the Establishment of "Integrated Community Care System".* Buenos Aires: Paper presented at the CIREC 30th Congress.

Thomas, J.C., 2013. Citizens, customers, partners: Rethinking the place of the public in public management. *Public. Adm. Rev.* 73, 786–796.

Tsutsui, T. 2013. *Implementation process and challenges for the community-based integrated care system in Japan. Int J. Integrated Care.*

Ungsuchaval, T., 2016. *NGOization of Civil Society as Unintended Consequence? Premises on the Thai Health Promotion Foundation and its Pressures toward NGOs in Thailand.* ISTR Conference, Stockholm.

Vamstad, J., 2007. *Governing Welfare. The Third Sector and Challenges to the Swedish Welfare State*. Mid-Sweden University Doctoral Thesis 37, Östersund.

Vamstad, J., 2012. Co-production and Service Quality: A new perspective for the Swedish welfare state; Ch. 16. In: Pestoff, V., Brandsen, T., Verschuere, B. (eds.), *New Public Governance, the Third Sector and Co-Production*. Routledge, London & New York.

Van de Broek, J., Boselie, P., Paauwe, J., 2014. Multiple institutional logics in health care. *Public. Manag. Rev. 16/1*, 1–12.

Vickers, I., Lyon, F., Sepulveda, L., McMullin, C., 2017. *Public Service innovation and multiple institutional logics: The case of hybrid social enterprise providers of health and wellbeing. J. Res. Policy*, (open access). doi: 10/1016/j.respol.2017.08.003.

Vidal, I., 2013. Governance of Social Enterprises as Producers of Public Services, Ch. 10. In: Valkama, P., Bailey, S., Anttiroiko, A.-V. (eds.), *Organisational Innovation in Public Services. Forms and Governance*. Palgrave, New York & London.

Part III

Summary and Conclusions

12 Lessons Learned and Implications for Research on Co-production and Healthcare

The final chapter provides a summary of the main findings of this volume considers the implications for further research on co-production and healthcare. Co-production is a complex and multifaceted phenomenon, particularly in healthcare. It was argued that there are two distinct kinds of co-production: aspirational and transformative. The former focuses on individual interactions between patients and professional healthcare providers, and it promotes incremental change. The latter demonstrates a more collective and transformative approach to patient participation. Contrasting them involves more than just comparing the attitudes and activities of the three main stakeholders – the staff, patients and volunteers. It also encompasses issues related to enriching the work environment of the staff and increasing their work satisfaction; facilitating a multi-stakeholder dialog; encouraging greater patient participation and influence; institutionalizing democratic, inclusive governance models; highlighting community-oriented social values and promoting affordable and acceptable service quality. However, both the aspirational and transformative approaches have their advantages, and, hopefully, they can learn from each other. Finally, this chapter also addresses some important issues for future research on co-production and healthcare in Japan and elsewhere. It asks how these three hospital groups – with all their differences – will cope with the possibilities of and adapt to the constraints posed by Community-Based Integrated Care (CIC). It also asks if the COVID-19 pandemic has changed the course of development for co-production and healthcare. Will citizens/users and front-line staff receive greater recognition in future research on healthcare management and perhaps augment the dominant economic models of control?

A Lessons Learned

Chapter 2 considered the potential contribution of the third sector and cooperative organizations for enriching the work environment, promoting and empowering patients and enhancing public goal achievement. Both consumer and worker cooperatives as well as nonprofit organizations can make unique contributions to renewing the public sector and enriching public services. Consumer co-ops can contribute to empowering the clients and consumers of such services, whereas worker co-ops can contribute to enriching and renewing the work life of the providers of these services. Other types of nonprofit organizations can augment the effectiveness of public services in achieving public goals. It also compared the potential advantages and disadvantages of each of the three types of NPOs to enhance public services. Thus, rather than simply privatizing public services, there are clear theoretical arguments for "cooperatizing" them and/or involving non-profit organizations in the provision of social services and healthcare.

In **Chapter 3,** Nobel Laureate Kenneth Arrow (1963) argued that market failure in healthcare leads to societal efforts to fill the gap, and he saw nonprofit healthcare in the U.S.A. as an illustration of this. Based on semi-structured interviews, five nonprofit healthcare providers in Japan were compared in terms of their relationship with the government and the ability to provide a democratic alternative. This overview concluded that Arrow's assumptions about the medical industry in the U.S.A. appeared to hold true in Japan at the beginning of the 21st Century. However, it showed that society could either act to fill this gap on the behest of the government and public authorities or through citizens' initiatives to engage civil society in healthcare provision. Arrow also noted the asymmetric information relations between users and professionals in the healthcare sector. This study found a unique example of an organization attempting to change this. Health co-ops actively engage their members in maintaining their own health, thus turning them into co-producers of healthcare. This embodies the potential for better quality services at a lower cost.

Chapter 4 discussed ideas about co-production in public services and healthcare. In recent decades, co-production has become one of the cornerstones of public policy reform across the globe. With the explosion of interest in understanding and facilitating citizen/user participation in the provision of public services, co-production now encompasses a variety of different phenomena, contexts and levels, and it is studied by a variety of disciplines that employ a variety of approaches. Co-production in public services and patient participation in healthcare have different origins, focus and definitions. This overview reveals that there is a myriad of terms, concepts, definitions and perspectives of this phenomenon. There is no single dominant approach but, rather, a number of clusters that suggest the existence of different schools of co-production in public services in general and most likely in healthcare too. This underlines the ambiguity of co-production as a concept, but it also means that there is no right or wrong approach to studying co-production or putting it into practice. Rather, these diverse perspectives often reflect the underlying cultural, social and political values of researchers and practitioners.

However, it is also indicative of the paradox of co-production. It can either refer to individual and aspirational values in relation to patient participation or to collective co-production with a more transformative capacity. Much of the literature on patient participation in healthcare is aspirational. It focuses on individual patients and describes the relationship between clinicians and patients as a meeting of two experts, each with their respective knowledge and skills. This challenges the traditional relationship between them, and it requires patients to become experts in their own circumstances and, therefore, capable of making decisions and having control as responsible citizens. This places heavy emphasis on the ability and agency of individual patients but also seems to ignore the shortcomings of many patients in this respect and, therefore, the importance of social support for facilitating both their agency and ability. When co-production is transformative, there is a relocation of power with the development of new joint mechanisms where professionals and patients collaborate in the planning, delivery and management of healthcare.

Chapter 5 provided a technical overview of this project on Co-production and Japanese Healthcare. This research project relied on several data sources to address a variety of questions. First, the Organization Study was comprised of interviews conducted in 2013 with the CEOs and board members of the eight cooperative hospitals. Second, the Staff Study was based on questionnaires developed to explore the relation between work environment and service quality at these eight cooperative hospitals in 2016 plus two public hospitals in Osaka in 2017. This resulted in 6,859 respondents from these ten hospitals. Third, the Patient Study and Volunteer Study collected questionnaire data in 2017 at four of the cooperative hospitals. The Patient Study involved 631 respondents and the Volunteer Study resulted in 236 respondents. However, this empirical study, like many others in the social sciences, was subject to certain limitations that are considered briefly.

Chapter 6 discussed the demand/control model of work environment and introduced the Staff Study. The Demand/Control model is comprised of four work life categories: Low Strain, Passive, Active and High Strain. The Staff Study provided information about the work environment, work satisfaction and service quality in Japanese healthcare. It confirmed, among other things, that more satisfied staff provide better service quality than less satisfied staff. There were three main takeaways from the analysis of the Staff Study. First, the Demand and Control model is a robust theoretical model, but it provides little practical guidance about how enlightened HR experts could proactively expand Low Strain and/or Active jobs to all or most employees. The information gained by specifying the hospital groups points to some notable disparities between the Low and High Strain categories among different groups of hospital employees. In particular, nurses and care workers clearly experience an adverse situation in their daily work life.

Second, confronting the theoretical model with data confirmed that hospital staff with the highest evaluation of their work environment and work satisfaction also rated their service quality higher. This also held true for the three hospital groups, although the differences between them were not as distinct as those at the theoretical level. Third, direct comparisons between the hospitals in terms of work satisfaction and service quality might be somewhat misleading, since they operate in a different setting and context. This is particularly true in rural areas where there are seldom any alternative healthcare providers.

Chapter 7 discussed co-production and healthcare and introduced the Patient Study. Both the Medical Co-ops and *Koseiren* embrace health literacy outreach, but the Patient Study suggests that being a patient in a Medical Co-op, nevertheless, does not mean the same thing as being a patient at a *Koseiren* hospital. Patients at the Medical Co-ops are more than just patients, they are also members of a healthcare co-op. Membership provides the social glue that enables and facilitates their working together for a common goal – the health and well-being of all members. The Medical Co-ops promote the active participation by patients in a variety of ways, and they have institutions that facilitate and foster their inclusion in the internal workings of the healthcare provider. Thus, membership in a health co-op provides a key to facilitating and fostering active patient co-production at the Medical Co-ops.

Thus, the Patient Study confirms that there are two kinds of co-production in Japanese healthcare: aspirational and transformative. Aspirational co-production is limited to describing and recognizing the potential benefits of co-production, paying lip service to it and accepting the marginal or ad hoc contributions of citizens to health services. Transformative co-production, on the other hand, includes encouraging co-production by actively facilitating, fostering and institutionalizing it.

However, these two different approaches to co-production not only express two different patterns of patient involvement in the provision of healthcare, but they also represent the differing needs of their patients. In rural areas, utilitarian or instrumental needs to alleviate local shortages in healthcare services and create qualified jobs locally are understandably much greater. Therefore, members of agricultural co-ops express a similar high level of satisfaction with the traditional healthcare services provided by *Koseiren* in rural areas, while Medical Co-op patients do the same with health co-op services in urban areas. Nevertheless, the latter have some possibility of challenging traditional relationships of power, control and expertise in healthcare, rendering it the joint product of the activities of both patients and professional healthcare providers.

Chapter 8 considered the role of volunteers in co-production and introduced the Volunteer Study. It problematized both the tasks and actors involved in co-production processes in healthcare. Tasks can either be core, essential or complementary, and these can be performed by professionals, patients or volunteers. Core tasks are reserved for the staff with professional training. The tasks studied in the Volunteer Study include both the essential and complementary types. Most of the complementary tasks require little or no special training or competencies to perform. Having volunteers perform such tasks is routine and not unusual. However, several of the other activities seem essential and closer to features related to membership in a health co-op than complementary healthcare tasks.

Finally, it noted that more than nine out of ten Medical Co-op volunteers claim that they are members of a healthcare co-op, whereas more than four out of five of *Koseiren* volunteers state that their principal cooperative affiliation was with an agricultural federation of Japanese Agriculture (JA). By establishing an ancillary organization, the health co-ops can mobilize community stakeholders and benefit from the resources they bring with them, as well as allowing them to engage members in the management of their own and others well-being.

Chapter 9 contrasted three models of healthcare governance in relation to external efficiency in service provision in Japanese healthcare. It argued that governance models can help explain some of the most notable differences in work environment, work satisfaction and service quality as well as patient participation. These three governance models embody different levels of staff autonomy and patient inclusion in decision-making. The first is a hierarchical command and control model that allows for little autonomy or discretion to either the staff or clients. Traditional public services embody the hierarchical model. The second is a model that involves more autonomy and inclusion than the first model, but the leaders make decisions on their behalf of the group they serve. This stewardship model is based on a 70-year public private partnership (PPP) in Japan that provides healthcare to large groups residing well beyond the reach of the public healthcare services. The third is a more horizontal, multi-stakeholder model that attributes greater autonomy to both the staff and their clients to resolve some key issues about service provision and quality together themselves. It embodies a bottom-up democratic model of governance that has existed and evolved in Japan for nearly 80 years.

Governance models demonstrated significant interaction effects with the work life situation of the hospital staff. The data showed that the democratic multi-stakeholder model promoted greater control and influence than either the stewardship or command and control model. It also demonstrated that the staff at a democratic multi-stakeholder model had more frequent and inclusive discussions about hospital affairs with key stakeholders than the staff at the other two hospital groups. It follows from this configuration that a governance model can make an important impact on a hospital's work environment and service quality that contributes to the external efficiency of healthcare providers. Thus, governance models, rather than ownership per se, appear to require closer attention in research on work environment and service quality in healthcare and other publicly financed services.

Chapter 10 discussed and compared the social values and missions of Japanese hospitals from the perspective of the staff, patients and volunteers. The staff presented three distinct profiles in terms of their hospital's social mission and contribution to the local community. Nevertheless, in spite of their different social values, the staff at all three hospital groups maintained a similar perspective on the three most important issues or challenges facing their hospitals. Sound financial management, providing good quality healthcare in the local area and promoting good working conditions for the staff received similar levels of support from the staff of each hospital group.

Each hospital group has a distinct mission based on a different set of social values. In general, the staff, patients and volunteers provide a similar story about what is most important and least important for each hospital. Medical Co-ops are associated with promoting patient participation in healthcare, engaging in preventive medicine, facilitating Community-Based Integrated Care (CIC) and providing care to uninsured. *Koseiren* is characterized by helping to alleviate local shortages and supporting CIC, whereas public hospitals are based on supporting CIC and providing highly skilled jobs in local areas. These values are found in the profiles of the other hospitals, but they do not carry the same weight nor are they considered equally important. Moreover, information about membership in cooperative organizations from the staff, patients and volunteers shows that it provides the institutional structures that can unite a unique set of social values that both inform their mission and make it possible to realize it.

Chapter 11 discussed co-production in terms of four different public administration regimes (PARs) and explored the implications of CIC in Japan. It compared the perspective of managers and non-managers, as well as various occupational groups concerning the social values they associate with their hospital and important issues facing it. This data explored documentation of conflicting logics at play between managers and non-managers but only provided sparse evidence of this. There was little difference between managers and non-managers or the hospital groups in terms of their stance on the most important issues they face. Nonetheless, it did find evidence of dissonance in the professional logics at Japanese hospitals.

However, this research suggests a gradual development from traditional public administration to New Public Management (NPM), New Public Governance (NPG) and beyond, where NPG might only be a temporary phase of development on the path towards a Communitarian type of regime. The Japanese policy of CIC attributes a stronger and more prominent role to family, friends, neighbors and volunteers as important providers of health and eldercare. A policy that encourages citizens to take more responsibility for themselves and others or requires them to become 'enforced co-producers'. This seems to foreshadow the development of an aspirational type of co-production that is associated with a Communitarian regime rather than the transformative, participatory type that is potentially associated with NPG.

Finally, some brief reflections based on this research seem appropriate about steps to improve the situation for staff and patients at Japanese hospitals and to augment control of their everyday interactions follow. First, public hospitals need to seriously consider possibilities for adopting a more employee-oriented HR model that allows the staff more control of their daily tasks. In particular, nurses are in dire need of improving their work environment to reduce the stress that they experience and increase their work satisfaction. Second, *Koseiren* hospitals should explore and develop a governance model that promotes greater staff and patient insight and influence. Third, the Medical Co-ops need to adjust the balance between the demands of NPM and Communitarian regimes with their own hospital values. Moreover, all healthcare providers should consider policies that more actively and systematically promote health literacy outreach efforts.

B Contrasting Aspirational and Transformative Co-production

The chapters in this volume focus on different topics and involve different stakeholders co-producing Japanese healthcare. In an effort to bring together these findings, Table 12.1 contrasts the characteristics of two different systems or models for citizen participation in the provision of public services and healthcare in the 21st Century, in a fashion that highlights the main findings of this project on Co-production and Japanese Healthcare. These two systems are labeled Aspirational and Transformative systems, after the findings of Chapter 7. They differ in numerous respects, as seen in greater detail in the pages that precede this final chapter. Their main characteristics are contrasted in Table 12.1. Some of the discrepancies identified herein tend to exaggerate their differences for the sake of the argument and clarity. However, they share some attributes, so it is often more a question of degree than kind. Nevertheless, when taken together, they help distinguish two widely diverse approaches to citizen participation in public service delivery and healthcare. These characteristics range from the origin or start of a hospital – the principal actors providing healthcare services, the type of PAR in which they thrive, to the school of co-production and type of tasks performed by citizens/users.

The origin of aspirational healthcare providers differs historically from transformative healthcare providers. *Koseiren* hospitals trace their origin back to the end of World War II, when the post-war government proposed a PPP between the agricultural cooperative movement, Japanese Agriculture (JA) and the government. It was designed to

Table 12.1 Contrasting Two Systems for Promoting Citizen Participation in Japanese Healthcare

Features/Systems:	*Aspirational*	*Transformative*
Origin or Start	PPP/PSP	Self-org. to meet underserved needs among local residents
Type of Public Administration Regime	New Public Management (NPM) and/or Communitarian	New Public Governance (NPG)
Main Characteristics	Well-meaning, but ignores structural barriers and organizational culture	Stubbornly optimistic in pursuing participatory democracy
Primary Focus	Individuals	Collective and structural
Principal Actors	Public bodies, firms and/ or civil society organizations	Nonprofit organizations, co-ops and social enterprises
Time Frame	Short-term and ad hoc	Long-term, structural changes
Value Orientation	Instrumental values	Expressive values
Service Provision	Standardized	Standardized and flexible
Political System Focus	Input side	Output plus input side
Work Environment	Business administration	Participatory administration
Governance Models	Stewardship and/or command and control	Democratic and inclusive
Health Literacy	Individual agency	Active outreach
Type of tasks performed by citizens	Complementary	Essential and complementary
School of Co-production	Service management, value chain or co-creation	Output side of the political system and co-production

provide social services and healthcare in rural areas where the government could not reach and, therefore, did not provide an adequate level of service or healthcare. *Koseiren* was established as an affiliate of JA to provide these services. By contrast, several of the local Medical Co-ops in this study and elsewhere in Japan trace their origin to a catastrophic event or local shortages that reflected the unmet healthcare needs of local residents who are often in urban live or suburban areas.

The type of PAR where aspirational systems more readily develop are NPM and a Communitarian Regime, whereas transformative systems thrive better in a NPG regime. The primary focus of an aspirational system is to promote the needs of individual clients or patients, whereas the focus of a transformative system is on resolving collective needs and eliminating structural hurdles and barriers to citizen access to and participation in healthcare. The main characteristic of an aspirational system is well-meaning, but it ignores the importance of structural barriers and organizational culture as hurdles to citizen participation, whereas transformative systems are stubbornly optimistic about pursuing participatory democracy.

The principal actors in an aspirational system are public bodies, for-profit firms, nonprofit organizations and civil society organizations, whereas they are more likely to be democratically controlled social enterprises, co-operatives and nonprofit organizations in a transformative system. The time frame for an aspirational system is short-term, often in relation to the economic or election cycle, whereas a transformative system pursues long-term solutions that seek structural changes. The value orientation of an aspirational system is primarily instrumental and pragmatic, whereas a transformative system promotes both instrumental and expressive values – such as patient participation, preventive medicine, etc. The service provision of an aspirational system is standardized, whereas a transformative system combines both flexible and standardized service provision. The political focus of an aspirational system favors the input side of the political system with strong emphasis on voting, demonstrating, petitioning, etc., whereas the political orientation of a transformative system is on the output side, by involving citizens in the daily tasks of implementing reforms once they are decided and codified.

The work environment regime of an aspirational system reflects a typical business administration approach; whereas a transformative system emphasizes participatory administration and encompasses both the staff and clients or citizens/users as partners in service provision. The appropriate governance model for an aspirational system is either a stewardship or 'command and control' model, whereas the governance model for transformative systems is both inclusive and democratic. The focus on health literacy in an aspirational system is on individual agency, whereas a transformative system emphasizes active organizational outreach. The type of tasks performed by citizens/users in an aspirational system are limited to complementary tasks, whereas they also include essential tasks in a transformative system. Finally, the school of co-production that best corresponds with the characteristics of an aspirational system is a value chain or co-creation approach, whereas it corresponds with a traditional input/output model of public administration in a transformative system.

Considered together, the chapters in this volume compare and contrast two widely different approaches to co-production – specifically, aspirational and transformative co-production. The former focuses on individual interactions between patients and professional healthcare providers, and it promotes incremental change. The latter demonstrates a more collective and transformative approach to patient participation in healthcare.

However, both the aspirational and transformative approaches have their advantages, and, hopefully, they can learn from each other.

C Implications for Future Research

The final paragraphs of this volume will consider some important issues for future research on co-production and healthcare in Japan and elsewhere. They include: the advantages of the comparative method for studying co-production; the place for various schools of co-production; an individual or collective focus of research on co-production; the development of four PARs; the third sector, co-production and participative governance; CIC and what that means for the future of co-production and healthcare. Six issues are discussed in the following paragraphs.

First, the comparative method is a key methodological tool in political science, and there are two basic strategies or approaches for comparing countries, institutions or organizations. Either one can choose relatively similar countries or institutions and look for differences between them, or one can choose rather different countries or institutions and look for similarities between them. Comparing political parties and parliaments in the Nordic countries with one another is an example of the former strategy that focuses on differences. Comparing the political parties and parliaments of Sweden and Japan is an example of the latter strategy that would try to explain any potential similarities between them. Organizations operating in the same field or sector in a country are assumed to be more similar than organizations found in diverse fields, sectors or countries. An earlier study of alternative providers of childcare in Sweden, as alluded to in Chapter 2, compared parent co-ops, worker co-ops and nonprofit providers of childcare with one another and with public childcare services. In spite of operating within the same field, this study found major differences between and among these providers in terms of work environment, parent participation and goal fulfillment. Similarly, this study of Co-production and Japanese Healthcare compares three different service providers in the same field and country – specifically, Medical Co-ops, *Koseiren* and public healthcare services in Japan. In spite of operating in the same field, we found some major differences among them in terms of work environment, staff satisfaction, service quality, governance models and social values. In both cases, we compared similar organizations operating in the same field and country but, nevertheless, found major differences.

Lifting the focus to the general pattern of alternative provision of childcare in Sweden in the early 1990s and healthcare provision in Japan in the late 2010s illustrates the advantage of a strategy of comparing widely different countries, institutions and organizations while searching for similarities. These two cases represent very different services, size of organizations and cultural settings yet there are, nevertheless, some notable similarities between them. In spite of the temporal, size, service-specific and cultural differences between these two services and their settings, third sectoral organizations, cooperatives and social enterprises appear to produce quite similar results in terms of being able to enrich the work environment for the staff, facilitate the participation of clients in service provision and enhance public goal fulfillment. In addition, they promote new forms of democracy and participatory governance of public services. Hopefully, the phenomena of co-operative and third sector provision of publicly financed services and healthcare will gain more attention among social scientists – particularly, in multidisciplinary projects that focus on co-production, work environment, governance, service quality and/or social values, etc.

Second, scholars from different academic backgrounds have different perspectives on a variety of social science phenomenon – including childcare or healthcare – and it is natural for them to view it from the perspective of their own discipline. This is especially true for newer topics like co-production, and it is highly relevant for complex and multifaceted phenomenon that invite multidisciplinary approaches. Ostrom argued in her seminal article on 'Crossing the Great Divide' that co-production was very relevant both for the study of politics and economics (1996). However, she lamented that scholars from those disciplines rarely have a dialog about it, resulting in a situation where each discipline employs its own perspectives and tools to study and explain this new phenomenon.

The rapidly growing interest in co-production is attracting interest from a variety of fields of study, so it is logical to find a growing number of approaches to or perspectives on this phenomenon. It is reasonable to assume with the rapid growth of a new field that eventually, there will be different schools of study, as seen with co-production. The existence of at least three or perhaps four schools of co-production was recently discussed, plus a mixed one that combines several different approaches. They include a public administration/political science school that is framed on Easton's input/output model; a value chain school that is grounded in business administration; a co-creation school that is based on a service marketing/management approach; a potentially emerging voluntary or third sector school and a group of scholars who combine the perspective of two or more of these schools. It is important to recognize each of them for what they can contribute to the study of this new phenomenon and acknowledge their strengths and weaknesses while remembering that there is no single unified approach or understanding of this multifaceted phenomenon. Thus, there is a need to understand these different perspectives and adapt research on co-production and healthcare to recognize and embrace them and their unique contribution to the study of co-production.

Third, much of the discourse surrounding co-production and most of the examples of it focus on individual acts rather than collective action in co-production. This is perhaps a logical result of the methodological individualism employed by economists and other scholars who dominated much of the early efforts to recognize, delimit and define this new phenomenon in public service provision. It is based on the principle that subjective individual motivations explain social phenomena rather than class or group dynamics. In neoclassic economics, human behavior is explained in terms of rational choices, as constrained by prices and incomes, where an individual's preferences are taken as given. With the dominance of economic thought, particularly during the spread of NPM, it comes as no surprise that most academics and politicians promote individual rather than collective solutions to a variety of challenging issues. The focus of the pioneers of co-production was on individual contributions to the provision of public services. Although they recognized that groups of citizens and their organized efforts could make a contribution, organized groups were nevertheless systematically excluded from their study.

Ironically, the prime example of citizen participation in providing local safety and security was a citizen group known as 'neighborhood watch'. Clearly, this type of group is not a random or happenstance collection of people who might share a common interest of enhancing their safety and protection together with the police, regardless of where they live. Rather, in addition to their common interest in neighborhood safety, this is a group of citizens who live in close proximity with each other, in a more or less well-defined geographical area and where people have a sense of community and share social capital. Most importantly, they belong to an organization with certain rules and regular meetings, etc. It represents their common interest in safety and protection and that they are willing to work together with one another and the police to augment this. Unfortunately, methodological individualism overlooks or fails to recognize the contribution of this type of collective action phenomena.

In her Nobel speech, Ostrom acknowledged this when she stated that 'social scientists need to recognize that individual behavior is strongly affected by the context in which interactions take place rather than being simply a result of individual differences' (2009: 430–31). She emphasized the implications of this clearer in her closing passage in Stockholm:

> *Designing institutions to forge or nudge entirely self-interested individuals to achieve better outcomes has been a major policy prescription for more than half a century, yet it has failed miserably... When the world we are trying to explain and improve is not well described by a simple model, we must continue to improve our frameworks and theories to be able to understand complexity and not simply reject it (2009:436).*

An academic toolbox grounded on methodological individualism proved inadequate for studying and understanding collective co-production. Fortunately, the comparative method of political science appears more promising. It facilitated the identification of two distinct types of co-production in Japanese healthcare. In Chapter 7 discussion on aspirational and transformative co-production, it is maintained that the former described, recognized, paid lip-service to and eventually tolerated individual co-production, whereas the latter encouraged, facilitated, fostered and institutionalized patient participation in healthcare. Data from the Patient Study also showed that patients in the latter form of co-production participated both as individuals and together with each other in collective action. Therefore, aspirational co-production is primarily an individual phenomenon, whereas transformative co-production attempts to combine both individual and collective co-production. Failing to recognize the contribution of both types of activities to co-production in healthcare only provides part of the picture.

Individual co-production builds on existing citizen/provider interactions at the point of service delivery, while collective co-production involves enlarging this interaction to encompass groups of citizens in shaping and administering public financed services. This implies fostering 'horizontal' relationships between active citizens, and it can take a variety of forms. Collective co-production attempts to move public services away from a centralized, standardized and competitive agenda and towards a model of provision that is more localized, flexible and collaborative. It implies a more diverse approach, encompassing a variety of methods and forms that rely on collaboration between local government and local community groups that is supported and facilitated by central government. In healthcare, it requires a collaborative partnership with community groups, including third sector organizations (TSOs), cooperatives and social enterprises that can potentially engage in co-managing and/or co-governing healthcare. Moreover, it also requires that healthcare organizations actively embrace health literacy outreach. Exhibit 12.A in the appendix briefly introduces another model of collective co-production, the Espriu Foundation in Barcelona.

The complexities posed by the interplay of co-production, work environment, service quality, governance models and social values reflect the type of cross-sectoral and multilevel collaboration implied by CIC. However, our initial interviews in 2013 with the CEOs and boards of cooperative hospitals suggested that there was a lack of awareness by the Ministry of Health, Welfare and Labor of the benefits of this type of multilevel and multisectoral collaboration. Involving TSOs, such as health co-ops in the provision of healthcare, can not only augment citizen and patient participation, but it can also make it more sustainable. Engaging proactively with organizations that promote transformative co-production and wholeheartedly support CIC provides the government with a unique opportunity to explore the costs and benefits of collective co-production in a more systematic and focused fashion.

Without mutual collaboration between the government and organizations that are willing and able to promote collective co-production, it is highly unlikely that they will thrive and survive in the post-COVID-19 era.

This would be a lost opportunity for promoting CIC and instituting collective co-production, together with a well-established and highly motivated group of health and eldercare providers. Finally, more research on collective co-production and healthcare will improve our framework and theory of co-production that can not only facilitate our understanding of the complexities of collective co-production, but also guard against rejecting it for a simpler framework limited to individual acts.

Fourth, four distinct public administrations regimes (PARs), discussed in Chapter 11, have bearing on and set constraints for the development of co-production in public services. This is evident from the classic roles attributed to the key stakeholders in co-production relations (i.e. the professionals and citizen/users). Two dimensions help identify and delimit the four PARs and the relationship between PARs: 1) the level of user activity, either active or passive and 2) the degree of societal engagement in the provision of important social services that range from individual to collective. Both traditional public administration and NPM posit clients who are basically passive, whereas both NPG and a Communitarian regime are based on active citizens/users. Similarly, NPM and a Communitarian regime focus on individual services provision, while traditional public administration and NPG promote collective solutions to delivering social services and healthcare. The differences in the role played by citizens/users and professionals are partially reflected in different schools of co-production. Therefore, the public administration/political science school includes both individual and collective citizen/user participation in the design and provision of public services, while the value chain and co-creation schools put more emphasis on individual solutions to citizens' needs.

The literature on institutional, professional and/or organizational logics compared the promotion of NPM objectives with those associated with traditional public administration. In healthcare, managers are assumed to pursue one set of interests, while nurses and other care providers often adhere to another set of values. This contrasts efficiency and economic responsibility with values of caring and good service quality. However, this study focused on professional and organizational types of logics, and it showed that this is not necessarily the case. The Staff Study showed that managers and non-managers were capable of balancing the need to make a surplus or profit with the hospitals' social values. It is not simply a question of either/or, but rather of recognizing that making a surplus is necessary for pursuing and achieving other important social values. The economy is seen as a means to achieving certain ends or social goal, rather than an end in and of itself. On the other hand, this also implies the need for an organization or hospital to balance various goals and not focus on a single one for too long, lest the organization risk changing its character. It would, therefore, be interesting to compare and contrast healthcare providers in different PARs and different countries.

Furthermore, some scholars maintain that public administration has developed from traditional public administration to NPM and currently to NPG. More recently, a fourth PAR was proposed – a Communitarian regime. Many scholars expect that NPG would comprise a more socially oriented regime than NPM. However, growing evidence suggests that NPG might only be a halfway point or temporary stage in the development of a Communitarian regime.

Both the market and state show a propensity to adopt and adapt key academic concepts for their own purposes. The contemporary academic debate surrounding the relations between civil society and the state illustrate three intertwined tendencies concerning public efforts to engage civil society in the co-production of public services. First, it greatly expands the scope of co-production to include new groups and/or reorganize existing phenomenon by involving civil society and citizens in the provision of traditional public services. Second, it shifts responsibility for providing social services from one group or sector of society to another (i.e. from the public sector to civil society, volunteers and private citizens). Third and sometimes inadvertently or perhaps intentionally, it turns an existing concept on its head by reversing established roles, like equating the concept of co-production with co-creation. Despite the 'good' intentions of the government, co-creation may, nevertheless, seem like a Trojan Horse for many citizens. Promises of 'empowerment', 'influence' and 'democracy' can, in reality, become public services that are turned over to civil society and 'responsibilized citizens', without much backup from public sector professionals but further cutbacks in public funding for social services and healthcare. This could be explored by more systematic research on co-production in public service provision and health and eldercare.

Fifth, the academic perspective of TSOs has shifted significantly in recent decades. De Tocqueville considered TSOs as 'schools of democracy' (1835). However, society experienced massive changes that transformed it from rural and agrarian to urban and global during approximately 200 years since then. Putnam argued that TSOs could 'make democracy work' (1993); however, more recently, he lamented that 'checkbook membership' seems to go hand-in-hand with 'bowling alone' (2005). Brandsen et al. warned about the perils of 'engineered' or 'contracted-out' civil democracy (2017). This has important implications for citizen participation and democracy. Accordingly, what kind of democracy do we want to embrace?

Held analyzed and contrasted classical and 20th Century models of democracy (1996). Participatory democracy combines ideas of pluralism and direct democracy (ibid.). However, what can current models of democracy contribute to emerging models in the 21st Century? Easton furthers that quest by distinguishing between the input and output sides of the political system (1965). The input side is related to decision-making, political parties, elections, legislatures, etc., while the output side implements decisions made on the input side and is comprised of public administration and public services, etc. Traditionally, democratic reforms focus on the input side, by mobilizing citizens, making their voice heard, giving them more influence, etc. Ostrom and her colleagues made a radical departure from this when they introduced the concept of co-production to analyze citizen participation in the provision of public services (1996). Such a shift opens entirely new possibilities for democratic innovations in the provision of public services on the output side of public policy-making.

The time is ripe for scholars who are interested in issues related to democracy and public administration to consider other institutions and sites where citizens can learn democratic habits and adopt democratic routines in their daily life. One such institution or site could be membership in social enterprises and social co-ops that provide social services and healthcare. Such organizations have the potential to become a new school of democracy in the 21st Century, when many of the older 'schools' no longer seem to function well. Herein lies one of the main challenges and opportunities posed by co-production that was explored from different perspectives in the chapters of this volume.

Co-production is a central concept in NPG, and it is an essential part of a broader framework to provide a new theory for public service management. Moreover, co-production is central to effective public service delivery, since it helps to achieve societal goals by placing the experience and knowledge of service users at the heart of effective public service design and delivery (Osborne et al., 2012). Ostrom notes that regarding citizens as clients or voters restricts them to playing relatively passive roles (1993). The latter limits them to selecting among political candidates or the former to receiving what others provide for them. This leaves their fate in the hands of others rather than this being something that they can control. Expanding citizen participation in the provision of public services, she argues, can result in a more participatory collaborative governance model (ibid.: 230).

Participatory governance relies on significant user and staff participation and influence in the organization of welfare services. Considered together, the concepts of co-production and participative governance can make a significant contribution to developing a broader framework and provide the base for a new theory that is not only for public service management, but also for participatory democracy and a participatory state. The concepts of co-production and participatory governance share the common vision of a new and more active role for citizens in the provision of welfare services of consequence to them and their loved ones. These ideas can make a major contribution to developing a more democratic framework and more nuanced theories necessary to challenge the dominance of NPM and the growing threat posed by a Communitarian regime and/or the populism facing many advanced democracies today. Rather than concentrating on efficiency and the cost reduction potential of co-production, research should also consider other important societal values like democracy and how to help it survive and thrive in the post-COVID-19 era.

Finally, there are several questions that were not possible to address within the limits of a single study, in spite of its unique data sets that cover the staff, patients and volunteers at ten hospitals and three groups of healthcare providers in Japan. Future research on co-production and healthcare should attempt to combine a variety of methods and stakeholders. It should include text and document studies as well as survey studies that embrace more than one key stakeholder with field studies that employ ethnographic and anthropology methods. This could help resolve some of the limits of the current study. In particular, in depth studies of community or collective co-production could provide a valuable addition to the current study. It is important to document and compare community volunteering, health literacy outreach efforts, health study groups and community social capital. These topics are not readily documented by text documents or survey studies.

How will these three hospital groups – with all their differences in work environment, governance models, service quality and social values – cope with the possibilities of and adapt to the constraints posed by CIC? Will this policy become equated with similar efforts to promote co-creation in Denmark and the Netherlands or 'Big Society' in the United Kingdom? Will this result in both citizens and public servants acquiring new roles? Will this promote a policy where the latter becomes consultants who facilitate the development of public services, while the role of citizens is primarily to take greater personal responsibility for providing these services for themselves, their family and neighbors? Finally, what does the development of public service provision look like in other countries and sectors? Are other countries actively promoting reform policies of health and eldercare that are similar to CIC? If so, how much support do these public sector reforms get from actors in the healthcare sector, the healthcare staff, different types of service providers and the public in general?

Finally, has the COVID-19 pandemic changed the course of development for co-production and healthcare? Will the importance of citizens/users and front-line staff receive equal attention in future research on healthcare management as economic models of control? Only future studies of co-production and citizen participation in healthcare will be able to provide an answer to these important and challenging questions in Japan and elsewhere.

References

Arrow, K., 1963. Uncertainty and the welfare economics of medical care. *Am. Econ. Rev. 53/5*, 941–973.

Brandsen, T., Trommel, W., Verschuere, B., 2017. The state and the reconstruction of civil society. *Int. Rev. Adm. Sci. 83/4*, 676–693.

Castano, J., 1990. The Health Cooperatives in Barcelona, Barcelona: conference paper.

De Tocqueville, A., 1835/40 [2000]. *On Democracy in America/Democracy in America*. Chicago University Press, Chicago.

Easton, D., 1965. *A Systems Analysis of Political Life*. J. Wiley & Sons, New York.

Espriu, J., 1995. *Mrs Life*. The Espriu Foundation, Barcelona. www.fundacionespriu.coop.

Osborne, S.P., Radnor, Z., Nasi, G., 2012. A new theory for public service management? Towards a (public) service dominant approach. *Am. Rev. Public. Adm.* 43/2, 135–158.

Held, D., 1996. *Models of Democracy*. Polity Press, Cambridge.

Ostrom, E., 1993. *A communitarian approach to local governance. Natl Civ. Rev.* 226–233.

OstromE., 1996 [1999]; Crossing the great divide: Co-production, synergy & development. *World Dev.* 24/6, 1073–1087; reprinted in 1999 as Ch. 15, *Polycentric Governance and Development. Readings from the Workshop in Political Theory and Policy Analysis,* McGinnis, Michael D. (ed.), Ann Arbor, MI: Univ. of Michigan Press.

Ostrom, E., 2009. Beyond Markets and States: Polycentric Governance of Complex Economic Systems. *Stockholm: Nobel Prize Lecture on December 8, 2009*, 408–444.

Putnam, R., 1993. *Making Democracy Work. Civic Traditions in Modern Italy*. Princeton University Press, Princeton, NJ.

Putnam, R., 2005. *Bowling Alone. The Collapse and Revival of American Community*. Simon & Schuster, New York.

Appendix 12

Exhibit 12.A Espriu Foundation: Integral Health Cooperatives in Barcelona

In Spain there are several multi-stakeholder cooperatives in different parts of the country. In Barcelona a multi-stakeholder cooperative healthcare organization was started in 1974. By 1990 it had 161,000 members and opened its first hospital (Castano, 1990), with 367 single-bed rooms. Its services cover surgery, intensive care, general medicine, pediatrics, obstetrics, gynecology, psychiatric, etc. According to Catalonian law any cooperatives may include both the employees and clients among the ranks of its members, and give them voting rights, if the statutes permit it (*ibid.*).

The organization of Integral Health Cooperation in Barcelona was started by Dr. Espriu and the Espriu Foundation. It was based on a (con-)federation of four separate cooperatives, one for doctors, another for consumers or health insurance clients, a third for other hospital workers and a fourth, which is a peak organization where the three of them join forces and co-manage their integral health cooperative efforts (Espriu, 1995). The option of creating a multi-stakeholder confederation of separate single-stakeholder cooperatives stemmed from a fear among doctors that the non-doctor members, who would outnumber them, could perhaps gain the same rights, duties and status as the doctors (*ibid.*, p. 231). The doctors' ambition was, nevertheless, to provide 'collective medicine'. In medicine, as in many other professions, there are a minimum of two parties: the patient and the doctor. The patient is the one who pays and suffers because of illness, and it is the doctor who puts his knowledge and reputation into play, for which he gets paid (*ibid.*, 231). In spite of the differences between them, the Espriu Foundation emphasizes the harmony between these two groups. 'To our understanding, this harmony will be impossible if one attempts to include both these collectives in a single cooperative, as well as the other workers who are not doctors. In this way the internal conflicts would be numerous and serious and, furthermore, the advantages proper to second and subsequent level cooperatives would be cast aside' (*ibid.*, 232).

Source: Pestoff, 1998, p. 120.

Index